Jim Christy

JIM CHRISTY
A VAGABOND LIFE

TRAMP
LIT
SERIES

IAN CUTLER

FERAL HOUSE

For
JIM CHRISTY
and
VAGABONDS
EVERYWHERE

CONTENTS

FOREWORD BY LUIS E. NAVIA

T he only way to truly learn from a philosopher is to recall the way he or she lived. Actions are the definitive measure of the effort that has been made. That is, the effort to shed light on the uncertain road ahead, in an earnest attempt to help others make their way through an otherwise dark world.

When I first met Ian Cutler more than a decade ago, our common thread was Diogenes of Sinope, the ancient Greek Cynic who chose to live in a tub and carried a lantern in search of an honest man. We shared an affinity then, as we do now, for the Cynic sensibility and a steadfast belief in its capacity to improve the human condition, today more than ever.

For the Cynics, the daily battle they waged was with the smoky haze known as *typhos*, a madness that permeates human existence, confuses the mind, and withers the soul. Overcoming it requires acknowledging its presence and raging against it, each in our own way, but ultimately, with the end goal of living a life in accordance with nature. Futile as such an endeavor may feel, and seemingly insignificant in a rapidly changing, unnatural landscape, it is the attempt made to attain absolute freedom—the most difficult of feats—that ultimately matters.

Jim Christy understood this. He recognized the cloud for what it is and made a choice: remain chained and forever delayed or go wandering in search of happiness now. So he opted for the latter. Christy felt an urgency to be human, to do better, to embrace the present, that he could not ignore.

What lies ahead is the story of a tramp-writer and modern-day Cynic who has lived his life in pursuit of the unexpected and, along the way, created a body of work on par with the adventure. Christy writes in the same manner that he has lived: compelled by wanderlust, guided by instinct, and ruled by no one. It is art that defies convention by an artist who lacks pretense.

Ian Cutler's biography of Christy is a carefully composed and painstakingly researched celebration of the global rambler's adventures and the legacy of vagabond literature to which he rightfully belongs. Excerpts from Christy's poetry and prose, including unpublished works, bring the chronology to life. The result is an effortless, fascinating read and a stirring homage to tramp-writers. No surprise then that by the end it feels as if we have only just begun.

That, of course, is Cutler's intention. His passion for sharing his subject with a wider audience is palpable. In Christy he has found a vagabond-philosopher, determined to live free in a hostile world, who has spent a lifetime recording the journey. Through Christy's example, we are inspired to look closer at what it means to be human; through his writings, we can experience it first-hand through the eyes of a seasoned tramp.

Luis E. Navia is Professor of Philosophy at New York Institute of Technology. His books include *Socrates: A Life Examined* and *Diogenes of Sinope: The Man in the Tub*.

PROLOGUE

By the time Jim Christy had read Jack Kerouac's 1957 novel *On the Road*, at the age of seventeen—discovering in that defining moment both his tribe and his love of literature—Christy was already an experienced "road kid." He had embarked on several lone adventures including, just prior to his thirteenth birthday, a ten-week tramp from his home in South Philadelphia to the Canadian border and back. Such early impulses were the result of a certain malady common to all tramps-of-choice (as distinct from tramps-of-necessity) the world over, a human condition frequently referred to as wanderlust: an involuntary lure of the alien and the exotic that could be regarded as the reverse of homesickness—Christy was sick at heart to see the world.

On the Road may have been an affirmation to Christy of his own strange and unconventional yearnings, but he did not need a mentor in the art of vagabondage. Christy had always been an individual, refusing to embrace convention for the sake of fitting in, choosing instead the freedom to define his own identity. This individualism was also accompanied by cosmopolitan instincts, a sovereignty of spirit that left Christy feeling alien everywhere but claiming everywhere as his home. But in spite of a flirtation with anarchism in which Christy read widely on the subject, including Emma Goldman's *Living My Life* three times, this rebel against modern life had no interest in changing the world or creating Utopias. His was a private, not a public, protest, an escape from the burden and banality of mainstream society's expectations and obligations.

In this sense, "tramping" or "vagabondage" (from the Latin *vagārī*, to wander), is no more than a personal strategy for survival in a hostile world created by certain other humans. But Christy has always been in good company, attracted to other fugitives and self-exiles from tedious uniformity: hobos, vagabond artists and musicians, conscientious objectors, carnival freaks, rogues, and reprobates from all layers of society. A poem by Christy published in 2013 shows that his own feelings of alienation from the human world had very early beginnings indeed. "Ready or Not" reflects the same sentiments as those of one of Samuel Beckett's fictional tramps in *The Unnamable* when, at the point of leaving his mother's womb he announces, "I am being given, if I may venture the expression, birth into death." Christy's contribution is as follows:

READY OR NOT

No, no! Stop!
Mama, Mama, please don't
Scream. Stop pushing, relax.
Eat ice cream. Nibble a pickle.
Get even fatter. I like it like
That. Like this. My current
Residence; it's perfect. Couldn't
Be beat. Plenty to eat here. Warm.
No worries. No job. No teachers.
No unemployment lines. No
Rejection letters or fist fights
In alleys at the back of bars.
No angry lovers, no bad music.
I've even gotten used to Father's
Weekly thrusts. So, mama, please
Please get up from the Joe Weider
Incline Bench, your birthing chair

Of choice. Birth me not, Mama
Stop that pushing this instant.
No more of that screaming. I wish
To stay right here
In a cozy ball.
Can't you understand that,
Mama?
Shit.
Here we go.
And oh, it's cold.
And our screams are one,
Mama.
(Jim Christy, *This Cockeyed World*)[1]

But Christy's real forebears were those tramp-writers born during the late 1800s who influenced Kerouac in the first place. In this respect, the writing and the life of Jim Christy, born James Christinzio on July 14, 1945, presents us with the conundrum of a Victorian vagabond adventurer born seventy years too late. Christy even missed out on participating in the world described in Kerouac's writings that first identified to the young hobo he was not unique in his unconventional response to the world. And so, within the wider classification of societal misfits, Christy may well be one of the last representatives of that rare and much overlooked tradition, the tramp or vagabond writer.

It is understandable that during the financial crashes and associated depressions of 1873, 1893, and 1930, armies of tramps-of-necessity took to the road out of desperation to find work or simply survive. However, during this same period, a small but significant number of individuals deliberately exiled themselves from mainstream society simply out of a lifestyle choice. At a time when many of us are again questioning whether the acquisition of material possessions give our lives any real meaning, there is much we can learn from the spirit of these tramp-writers about surviving in the world today. One of the underlying questions posed by the life choices of Christy and his predecessors is: What possessed adults and teenagers, many from comfortable, even middle-class, homes, not only to abandon their families and communities for a life on the road in the first place, but also to commit their adventures and philosophy to print? When a friend of Christy's, Daniel Zeleniouk, recently asked him, "Jim, how'd you get interested in books and writing?" he got the now predictable answer, "Well, I didn't read much until I was in my late teens when I picked up a book called *On the Road.*" When pressed on the subject, Christy does recall starting to write a short story about baseball when he was thirteen, but was sixteen before a version of it got published in a weekly newspaper, together with a macabre dog story that he wrote about the same time. A few days later, the following arrived in an email—that's how it goes with Jim Christy:

> I woke today thinking of your question about what started me writing. I guess it was the early traveling, and when I learned that others had written about their travels, I thought I might try my hand at it. Had those first attempts been a whole lot better, they might be considered terrible! I didn't come up with anything decent until I began writing those early political screeds, polemics, and harangues. Most so-called adventure writing has always bored me. Road tales, too. They're too relentless, have too much what I would call, upholstery. Predictable. Read London's The Road, then Kerouac's On the Road. The former isn't even in it. The thing with Kerouac is the spirit and attitude with which he approached his trips. He may not have ventured far and wide but he did it with an adventurous attitude. Which reminds me that my least favourite genre is modern travel writing.[2]

As essential as getting an appetite for writing, Christy's introduction to *On the Road* also turned him into a voracious reader. Not that he didn't already have advanced skills in that department. Christy had, in fact, been a compulsive reader from a young age without, it seems, ever having being taught—even if that reading material was confined to hot-rod magazines. He was later told that at the age of eight (third grade) he was reading at the level of a second-year university student. How he came by this information is more bizarre than the fact itself. One afternoon, aged around nine or ten, he was called to the school office where he was surprised to see his parents. He was informed that he had been "picked," among several other hapless kids from across the city's schools, to participate in a long-term research project at the University of Pennsylvania to identify why some kids are good readers and others not. About ten from each category were picked, and although Christy had no recollection at the time which grouping he was supposed to represent, he surmises with hindsight that it must have been the bright kids. He was matched with a kid from the other group who could not read a line. The pairs were also matched by age, socio-economic, and racial background, but he never got to meet his counterpart or even know their name. Christy was informed it was a big honor to be part of the study and remembers it all being very hush-hush. Over the six or seven years that he continued to be involved, and between his many tramping adventures, Christy spent countless hours in the company of a string of psychiatrists, sociologists, and psychologists:

> ...a bunch of men in lab coats and sports jackets. Some of them scribbled madly, others fixed you with stares. I can remember thinking how ridiculous and obvious were these latter. But the whole deal was that you were supposed to be cut off and on your own, just the kid and the adult.[3]

At the conclusion of the study, aged either eighteen or twenty-one (Christy forgets which), there was supposed to be a big gathering with dinner, a party, and grand speeches. But after putting up with it until he was about fifteen or sixteen, the whole thing became a tedious ordeal and Christy quit, no longer prepared to give up his Saturdays traveling to the university.

But to return to Christy the adult reader, as he discusses above, this newfound love of literature clearly influenced his early polemical writings following his arrival in Canada, not to mention his personal philosophy articulated in his second book *Beyond the Spectacle* (1973). *Spectacle* will be discussed further in the epilogue of this book. But in an essay Christy wrote for Canada's *Globe and Mail* in 2002, titled "Looking for literature in all the wrong places," we are provided with a characterization of Christy the "tramp reader," as distinct from the tramp-writer. When Christy's literary friends went traveling, they did so weighed down with enough reading material to last the entire trip. Not so Christy, even though he was never without a volume in his pocket. For the purposes of tramping hobo-style, he says, "it is ... necessary to travel light. Yet it is also necessary for me to have my daily reading fix." Christy maintains that packing enough reading material is not only an encumbrance to tramping, it also means missing out on the "thrill of the search." "I have never started out on any trip with more than two books," yet neither has he ever wanted for reading material. Christy never failed to find all of the reading material he required to feed his appetite in the most remote corners of the world—further fueling the imagination as to how certain English-language books ended up in the places they did in the first place: *Parnassus on Wheels* by Christopher Morley from the shelf of a tailor's shop in Addis Ababa; an Ernest Haycox novel in Belgrade; Flaubert's *Dictionary of Received Wisdom* in Quetzaltenango, Guatemala; the complete works of Alexander Trochi and of Edward Beck in Florence; Hans Zinsser's *Rats, Lice and History* from a pub in Nuuk, Greenland; and from Puerto Escondido in Mexico, Kevin Baker's novel *Dreamland* about the early days of Coney Island, *Suits Me*, the biography of the transgender musician and bandleader Billy Tipton, and Bonnie Bowman's *Skin*. "In Mexican beach towns, the best places to find books, for reasons I can't fathom, are boutiques for women," which included picking up in various such locations all five novels by the Greek-American lounge singer Eddie Constantine. The added benefit of acquiring one's reading material in such an arbitrary manner is discovering reading material that would otherwise have eluded him entirely. "One lives in hope, despite past experience, of great and exotic reading discoveries to come. Maybe a Francis Carco novel in Ho Chi Minh City."[4]

But literature and tramping were not the only influences on Christy's writing. From an early age Christy was mesmerized by the movies and acknowledges that film was an important and certainly earlier influence on his life than books. He remembers his mother taking him to the Italia Theater when they lived on Catherine Street, South Philadelphia, to watch Anna Magnani and Burt Lancaster in *The Rose Tattoo*. Later he would regularly spend all day Saturdays at the Colonial Theater watching film noir and westerns, his favorite genres. But more of movies and Christy's own sometime career in the film industry later.

As for why Christy took to the road in the first place, this is a theme that will be returned to time and again in this book. The theme of wanderlust will also be revisited in the epilogue. But in order to better appreciate the more recent lineage of the tramp-writer, a genus of which Jim Christy is a latter-day representative, it is important to summarize here the life and times of some of these earlier proponents of the art. Indeed, as will be revealed at the end of this prologue, it was while researching these other literary vagabonds for an entirely separate project that the author accidentally stumbled across Jim Christy in the first place.

Though many of these earlier tramp-writers achieved some degree of critical acclaim during the Victorian/Edwardian period in which they were published, today they remain largely forgotten. One of the aims of this book, through the life and adventures of a modern-day vagabond, is to revive an interest not only in the life and writings of Christy himself, but of the other authors who contributed to this much neglected genre. Jim Christy shares most of the traits and characteristics common to the tramp-writers listed below: a thirst for adventure and the exotic; a refusal to identify with any tribe yet feeling at home everywhere (cosmopolitanism); physical strength and endurance, the ability to survive hostile circumstances—including starvation, hard labor, beatings, and jail; intelligence and philosophic wisdom; freedom from the tyranny of possessions; a rejection of man-made borders, laws and customs which are seen as artificial; freedom also from the restrictions and responsibilities imposed by rules, regulations, and responsibility to family and friends; the ability to enjoy relationships without being bound by them; a lifestyle that embraces the seductions of the "natural" world—living in communion with nature; and the ability to live in the present, taking pleasures now, not deferring them for later—whether for a pension or the promise of heaven. These characteristics can be traced all the way back to the philosophy of the ancient Greek Cynics,[5] of which Christy must also be counted a modern-day representative. For some of the tramp-writers discussed below, we can further add a taste for alcohol, experience as a sailor, frequent visits to jail on vagrancy and other trumped-up charges, and prowess in the pugilistic arts—the latter applying to Flynt, Black, Everson, Davies, Kennedy, Horn, Tully, and Phelan, as well as Christy himself, and also others not discussed here such as Al Kaufman and Louis L'Amour.

The principal characteristic to remember here is that these tramp-writers were, first and foremost, *individuals,* even if they shared a similar lifestyle and philosophy of the world. The writing and ideas of those listed in the mini-biographies that follow (presented in order of birth) will be more fully discussed in the epilogue of this book, alongside a review of Jim Christy's own philosophy.

London-born **Morley Roberts (1857–1942)** was one of the most prolific tramp-writers with over eighty published novels, plays, essays, biography, and verse to his credit. Yet apart from Roberts' biography of his close friend and fellow novelist George Gissing—thinly disguised as fiction in the *The Private Life of Henry Maitland*—Roberts' work is sadly even more obscure today than Gissing's. Like most of the other tramp-writers discussed here, Roberts experienced feelings of wanderlust from an early age, yet it was not until eighteen that he dropped out of the university to enroll as a steerage passenger on a sailing ship bound for Melbourne. After three years tramping Australia, followed by a short spell as a civil servant at the War Office in London, Roberts bought himself a passage to America, initially heading for Texas, then working his way to Chicago on a cattle train. After returning to Texas (from where he adopted the hobo moniker Texas Charlie), Roberts set off for Iowa, St. Paul, and then north across the Canadian border to Winnipeg, tramping west through the Rockies on foot to Vancouver. From there he walked most of the way back across the American border to Washington, then on to San Francisco arriving penniless in 1885. After further tramping adventures including Spain, Portugal, and the South African veldt, Roberts would embark on a round-the-world trip that included a sojourn at Robert Louis Stevenson's Pacific island home of Opolu, spending several hours with that writer. Stevenson died later the same year.

Bart Kennedy (1861–1930) published twenty-one books and a weekly magazine, *Bart's Broadsheet*. Born in Leeds of Irish parents, Kennedy lived and worked in Manchester factories from the age of six and did not take up tramping until the age of twenty. He arrived in Liverpool with one shilling and worked his passage to America, arriving in Philadelphia without a penny in his pocket. Kennedy describes tramping the streets in a state of elation at the prospect of having a whole new world before him. After walking to Baltimore, surviving on his skills as a boxer en route, Kennedy signed on to work as an oyster dredger for fifteen dollars a month. His tramping career may well have ended here, being washed overboard from a steamer in a hurricane and having his yawl surrounded by ice in the Chesapeake Bay. But Kennedy would survive to have many other adventures, including drilling and dynamiting in mines, being jailed for vagrancy in New Orleans, a failed suicide attempt alone in the Rocky Mountains, hand-to-hand combat with hostile Native Americans, touring the U.S. Pacific coastline as a bass singer in an opera company, and a memorable tramp through Spain. The *New York Times* obituary of Kennedy describes him as "the tramp novelist ... pioneer of the staccato method of short story writing," and *The Times* [UK] obituary describes his writing as "written with vigour, but in a curious jerky style."

The adventures of **Alfred Aloysius Smith (1861–1931)**, aliases Trader Horn and Zambezi Jack, began when he was expelled from school at the age of sixteen for being an "untamed and troublesome boy." Horn's behavior was a result of that same sickness of the heart to see the world described above. And so, after turning seventeen, Horn signed an apprenticeship with the Liverpool firm Hatton and Cookson to work for that company in equatorial West Africa's ivory and rubber trade, taking free board and passage on the SS *Angola*. The fantastic adventures that followed, including his search for the white goddess and battles with river pirates, are the subject of Horn's first book *Trader Horn: A Young Man's Outstanding Adventures in Equatorial Africa* (1927). Further adventures included a spell in Buffalo Bill's Wild West Show and time as a hobo in the U.S., as well as participating in piracy off the East African coast. The first of Horn's trilogies was co-written with the help of South African writer Ethelreda Lewis, whom he met in his late sixties peddling kitchenwares at the writer's home. Their ensuing friendship saved him from starving to death in a Johannesburg dosshouse. A Hollywood movie and celebrity followed, so no need to recount Horn's adventures further. What Christy shares with Horn, less apparent with some of the other tramp-writers, is his appetite for the more exotic adventures recounted in Chapter 7, such as "In Search of the Golden Madonna," "A Month in a Cartagena Dungeon," and "On the Caddy Trail."

Josiah Flynt (1869–1907) published fourteen books and essays in a short life ended prematurely by his addiction to alcohol and narcotics. Fatherless from a young age, Flynt was brought up by his mother in Evanston, Illinois. A closeness to his mother throughout his life mitigated the worst excesses of tramping, and was responsible for Flynt graduating from the University of Berlin. His first tramping expedition and earliest time in jail occurred at the age of five, the first of many such adventures that even whippings from his father and pleas from his mother failed to prevent. Flynt's writings are some of the most frequently quoted first-hand accounts of hobo life and culture, some of which influenced the more celebrated tramp-writer, Jack London. Flynt made the following distinction between the vagrant and the "wanderlust vagabond": "He is free from the majority of passions common among vagrants, yet he is the most earnest vagrant of all. To reform him it is necessary to kill his personality, to take away his main ambition. And this is a task almost superhuman."[6] Flynt has been described as a gifted actor, as comfortable and at ease with the tramping and criminal classes as he was with philosophers, politicians, and others notable in public life. Among those Flynt spent time with on his travels were Ibsen, George Augustus, Horatio Brown, Tolstoy (as a guest at his farm), and the Apache chief Geronimo. A friend and fellow writer of Flynt's, Emily Burbank, provides a description of Flynt that applies equally to the other tramp-writers discussed here: "it must be remembered that Flynt was the tramp writing, not the literary man tramping."

As well as his hobo credentials, **Jack Black (1871–1932)** was also a professional criminal, or "yegg," a term applied to the generally more feared outlaw hobos—as opposed to those who survived simply by begging and casual labor. Black's principal criminal activities involved burglaries, armed hold-ups, and safe-cracking, but like Flynt and London, Black was also addicted at various times to narcotics—in his case combined with the thrill of gambling. Born near Vancouver, British Columbia, but raised in Missouri, Black's adventures and philosophy are contained in a single volume, *You Can't Win* (1926), published six years before his death. Black's autobiography is also the subject of a 2016 movie of the same name, starring, co-produced, and co-written by Michael Pitt. As with Flynt and London, Black's writing had a major influence on the Beat movement and its writers, particularly William Burroughs, who in his first book, *Junkie* (1953), reflected much of the style and subject matter of *You Can't Win*. As with Jim Phelan's (see below) writings on penology, *You Can't Win* is also an important social history on many aspects of criminality and prison life during the particular period covered. One important distinction is that Phelan spent thirteen continuous years behind bars for a murder he did not commit; Black on the other hand was the habitual criminal, constantly in and out of jail, with a total incarceration time of about fifteen years including several prison breakouts. Black was a reformed character by the time he wrote his book and part of his motivation for writing it was to dissuade would-be criminals from a life of crime, at the same time pointing out the inability of the courts and judiciary to deliver justice. During his writing period Black was also involved in journalism, writing essays, and participating in lecture tours. It is thought that he drowned himself in 1932 after telling friends that if life got too much for him he would row out into New York Harbor and drop overboard with weights tied to his feet. In his darker moments Black described this state of mind as being "ready for the river."

William Henry Davies (1871–1940), distant cousin of the English stage actor Sir Henry Irving (1838–1905), preferred to be known as a poet, the most memorable fragment of his poems being the opening two lines of "Leisure": *"What is this life if, full of care / We have no time to stand and stare..."* But it is for his prose memoirs of twelve years tramping in the Americas and Britain, recorded in *The Autobiography of a Super-Tramp* (1908), that he is best known. Davies was a complex character, neither entirely at one with other tramps, being too bookish, nor comfortable in the literary world of London, having arrived in that company as something of a social oddity. Not to mention the fact that he only had one foot; he lost the other after a failed attempt to jump a train in Renfrew, Canada, on his way to join the Klondike gold rush. Davies credited his taste for alcohol with being raised in a pub in Newport, South Wales, and given porter to drink at bedtime, "in lieu of cocoa or tea, as is the custom in more domestic houses." Davies' adventures are rich and entertaining, alternating between paid work, begging, and tramping. Like many of the other tramp-writers discussed here, including Christy himself, Davies recalls near-death experiences, such as the time he lay semi-conscious with malarial fever in a Mississippi swamp, surrounded by wild dogs and vultures waiting their chance to make a meal of him. As with Christy also, Davies frequently had to resort to his skills as a boxer to protect himself from being robbed or otherwise abused.

Leon Ray Livingston (1872–1944), unlike most of the other tramp-writers listed here who celebrated their anonymity and life in the margins of society with no thought of competing against fellow vagabonds for publicity, seems to have openly courted celebrity. He unashamedly promoted himself as is evident from the covers of his twelve self-published books, where he introduced himself as "America's Most Famous Tramp who traveled 500,000 miles on $7.61" (from which he adopted the moniker "A-No.1") and crowned himself "King of the Hoboes." Yet Livingston's achievements as a child tramp from the age of eleven were second to none. Born into a "well-to-do" family in San Francisco, to a French father and German mother, Livingston claims that by the age of eight he could speak both these languages fluently, to which he later added Spanish. At the age of eleven he was sent home for bad behavior with a note from his teacher requiring his father's signature, but Livingston ran away rather than face disgrace. So started another hobo career. He took a river steamboat from San Francisco Harbor to Sacramento then walked to a water stop along a railway track where he rode a freight to Truckee, eventually expelled from the train by a brakeman at Winnemucca in the Nevada desert. From there he beat his way to Chicago while hidden among sheep in a stock car, then struck out for New Orleans. From there he took a job as a cabin boy on board a British schooner plying trade among the ports of Central America. He jumped ship in Belize, and from there to Guatemala, onwards to Mexico and home. But only ninety-seven miles from his destination, and still only twelve years old, Livingston paired up with another hobo and continued his tramping adventures.

Livingston's second tramp to Latin America was an extraordinary affair. First he beat it by rail to San Luis Potosí in central Mexico from where he set off for the port of Vera Cruz. There he secured passage as a cabin boy on a German schooner bound for Venezuela, to the port of La Guaira and then on to Maracaibo where he jumped ship to continue his journey to Brazil and the fabled diamond mines. In Maracaibo he met Tom Hanrahan, a boy of his own age from Pennsylvania. By now, well schooled in the art of begging, Livingston soon collected the equivalent of $48. The pair set out together, assisted by the purchase of two donkeys, for Bogotá in Colombia and then onward to Quito in Ecuador. After crossing through the snow and ice of Andean mountain peaks they eventually reached the navigable source of the Amazon tributary, the Rio Napo. Here, having carried them for 1,250 miles, the burros were exchanged for a large ironwood canoe to continue the next 5,000 miles of their tramp by river. After three months they reached the Marañón river in Peru from where they would enter the Madeira River, and then the Amazon proper. But on the night of July 1, 1887, while camping on a slight rise on the confluence of the Amazon with the Rio Negro, tragedy struck. Tom was bitten by a deadly snake and died after ten minutes of convulsions. It took Livingstone a further two months to reach the safety of a mission settlement, and a further nine months recovering in hospital from malaria and starvation before he was well enough to continue his many further adventures. He was still only fifteen years old when Tom died, and eighteen before he returned to America via London after signing on as a crew member on a cattle boat out of Buenos Aires.

Like Flynt, Livingston, London, Tully, Phelan, and of course Christy, **Jack Everson (1873–1945)** was a child tramp. Aged eleven, and after a particularly vicious beating from his father, Everson resolved to leave home. He jumped a train heading for New York with an older boy. By the age of fourteen, Everson had served his second jail sentence, this time for possession of a stolen Colt .45 revolver which he agreed to peddle for a tramp who failed to tell him the gun had been stolen. At the age of sixteen Everson boarded a ship to work his passage to Australia via Honolulu. He was to serve many other jail sentences including time on a chain gang. His tramping exploits were interspersed with periods of employment including stints as a gold prospector and snake-oil salesman. Everson's tramping adventures are chronicled in a single volume, *The Autobiography of a Tramp*, written during the last year of his life, aged seventy-two, and not published until 1992 by his then eighty-six-year-old son. Everson's adventures should stand alongside the finest writings of the period, both for the richness of the narrative and the sensitivity of the telling. Yet this writer is little known and his work is out of print. Like many other tramps turned writers, Everson's early childhood was comfortable and middle-class. His mother, Rebecca (Carrie) Jane Billings Everson, was the pioneer inventor of the oil flotation separation process in the mining industry.

Jack London (1876–1916) is one of the better known tramp-writers, not least because of his prolific output including 120 short stories, twenty-six full-length prose works, twenty-two essays, forty-five poems, and six plays. His daughter Joan claims that London's writing spawned more than forty movies in different languages. London started his "career" as a fourteen-year-old oyster pirate in and around San Francisco Bay, out-sailing and outsmarting many experienced adults plying the same trade. London did not take to the road and beat trains until he was sixteen under the predictable moniker of Sailor Kid. His hobo initiation, jumping a train with a group of other road kids, ended tragically when one of the gang fell under the train wheels, amputating both his legs. A prolific rambler in these early years, London's adventures included joining Kelly's Army, the 1894 march of hobos and unemployed from California to Washington, DC. After the already celebrated Leon Ray Livingstone placed an ad in the "Help Wanted" column of the *Sunday World Magazine* stating "Wanted—travelmate by hobo contemplating roughing trip to California," he received a reply from an eighteen-year-old Jack London. His book *Coast to Coast with Jack London* chronicles their adventures from the East Coast to San Francisco, by which time both were severely ill with malaria. After London's year-long trip to the Klondike in search of gold at the age of twenty-one, and a round-the-world sailing trip that had to be abandoned in Tahiti after he contracted a tropical disease, the rest of his short life was devoted mainly to writing and drinking—the demons of the latter being the subject of his book *John Barleycorn*. London's first autobiography, *The Road*, is one of the most frequently quoted works of tramp literature, inspiring other tramp narratives, not least Jack Kerouac's *On the Road*. *The Road* itself was inspired by the earlier writings of Josiah Flynt (seven years older than London) whom London acknowledges in his dedication for the book. Both Flynt and London had a lifetime struggle with drugs and alcohol resulting in their premature deaths—London at forty and Flynt at thirty-eight.

Edinburgh-born **Stephen Graham (1884–1975)** was a journalist, essayist, novelist, and tramp, a profession which he describes as follows: "He is the walking hermit, the world-forsaker, but he is above all things a rebel and a prophet, and he stands in very distinct relation to the life of his time."[7] Graham's adventures and observations are documented in over fifty books and essays, many no longer in print. Graham spoke fluent Russian and many of his books concern his experiences of that pre-revolutionary state, as did his work as a freelance correspondent for *The Times*, *Harpers*, and the *New Yorker*. Based on Graham's writings, one can only wonder just what a different place Russia was only one hundred years ago. Yet Graham also hiked thousands of miles across America on foot, including large stretches of the Canadian border where he tramped with American poet Vachel Lindsay. As well as covering vast stretches of the American wilderness, Graham also roamed the streets of New York, Chicago, and other cities not to mention padding the roads of Great Britain and large tracts of continental Europe. Yet, as with most of the other tramps discussed here, Graham expressed the extreme feelings of restlessness that are the hallmark of those bitten by the wanderlust: "It is true the wanderer often feels bored, even in beautiful places. ... I get tired of this world and want another. That is a common feeling, if not often analysed."[8]

Following the death of his mother at the age of six, **Jim Tully (1886–1947)** was left by his father in an orphanage for the next six years of his life. The institution was run along prison lines, with strict rules and beatings for infringements. What Tully got from his incarceration was ready access to classical literature and a passion for reading and writing. After eventually being rescued from the orphanage by his older brother, he was then sent to work on an isolated farm with an illiterate farmer. There Tully slaved for two winters in sub-zero conditions in threadbare clothing before finally running away, still aged only thirteen. He eventually returned to his hometown of St. Marys where he lived with his older sister and found work in the furnaces of a local chain factory before finally succumbing to his latent wanderlust. There are many parallels between Tully and Jim Christy apart from their obvious tramping, frequent arrests for vagrancy, and writing. These include, as children learning about sex for free from "professionals" in the art, professional boxing, working as a tree surgeon, and a sometime career in the movies. But the most interesting comparisons are to be made with their time spent in carnivals and with carnival performers, in Tully's case chronicled in his book *Circus Parade* (1927). Tully's first role in the carnival was unique. He was employed by Amy "the Beautiful Fat Girl" to crawl under a heavy glass stage on which the five-hundred-pound Amy danced, and shine different colored lights up through the glass to illuminate the angelic dancer—at the same time praying that the glass would not break. Tully's road kid adventures are graphic, such as nearly losing a foot on his first train ride, escaping from the blind baggage of another train handcuffed to another hobo after kicking a railroad detective from the train, and a nightmare train journey as Tully, burning with fever and his throat aching with thirst, risked riding lying flat on the roof of a cattle car in order to reach Chicago and medical help. Then there was a twenty-one-hour trip spent clinging to the Fast Flyer Virginia roaring through the tunnels of the Blue Ridge Mountains. Such adventures are best read in full in Tully's second book, *Beggars of Life* (1924), in which a young James Cagney later played Tully in the stage version. A successful writer with sixteen books to his credit, it was Tully's writing that brought him to the notice of first his lifelong friend H.L. Mencken, and later the screen tramp Charlie Chaplin, whom he worked for as ghostwriter and publicist for many years before they finally had a falling out. Tully's outspokenness and his hostile and ridiculing reviews of the movie industry and its stars—including openly criticizing Chaplin for casting the sixteen-year-old schoolgirl Lillita McMurray in the lead female role for *The Gold Rush* and getting her pregnant—would earn him a reputation as "the most feared and hated man in Hollywood."[9]

Dublin-born **Jim Phelan (1895–1966)** published twenty-five books and collaborated on others. He also wrote poetry, song lyrics, plays, film scores, and, in the last years of his life, narrated a TV documentary for BBC Wales on gypsies. Phelan embarked on his first tramping adventure at the age of four, using his natural gift in chicanery to make the one-hundred-mile trip to Tipperary. When in danger, he wrote, it is the tramp's natural impulse to "turn around and head for the horizon." At the age of seven, fearing a beating from his father, Phelan headed off to the canal basin and hid himself under a tarpaulin covering a barge—his first sailor tramp. By the age of thirteen he managed to sail as far as Glasgow where he joined a gang of slum kids and "learnt to speak Scotch." Phelan was an infant prodigy, already at school by the age of twenty-one months (with a photo and school certificate to prove it) and reading better than most adults by the age of three. But to the disappointment of his parents and teachers his destiny did not lie in academia. Phelan's tramping career in Ireland, the UK, America, and France, was brought to an abrupt end when at the age of thirty-nine he was accused as an accessory to a fatal shooting—linked to his Irish Republican associations—and sentenced to hang. Coincidentally, the trial judge was the Right Honourable Sir George Arthur Harwin Branson, PC, grandfather of business tycoon Sir Richard Branson. On the eve of his execution his sentence was commuted to life imprisonment, and the thirteen years that Phelan would serve in six different prisons provided the apprenticeship for his career as a writer of unique works on tramping and penology, as well as his fiction and essays. After his discharge from prison, Phelan continued tramping right up until his death at the age of seventy-one.

And it was Jim Phelan who led me to Jim Christy in the first place, by way of his widow Kathleen Phelan, one of the few women tramp-writers I have encountered in my research and more of whom later. It is not as though Christy is a household name. Regrettably, although he has an impressive list of published books (thirty-one to date), plus plays, art exhibitions, travel, and adventure, even in his adopted home of Canada, Christy remains as obscure as many of those tramp-writers born a century earlier.

This raises a phenomenon, alluded to earlier, about people who have no interest in the vacuity of celebrity—those whose energy is focused on discovering the world at eye level and beneath their feet rather than star-gazing—and who may even deliberately exile themselves from mainstream society to find solace in the margins of civilization: the odd, the abject, the quirky, and the downright weird. Such people are in turn often rejected by mainstream society as weird themselves, an animate threat to everything that makes life safe and predictable. For Christy, this included his father's disappointment that he dodged the Vietnam draft instead of doing the patriotic thing, and also refusing to follow the family tradition of becoming a gangster. Add to this the handicap that books by tramp-writers defy easy categorization, even though Christy's work has been compared to the "hard-boiled" genre credited to the earlier tramp-writer Jim Tully. The tramp-writer's disregard of literary convention poses a challenge for publishers and booksellers alike: how to market their work and where to display them on the shelves—as though those should be the primary criteria for great literature!

In Christy's case, I am not writing about a long-dead author, though his work remains as obscure as the Victorian writers listed above. This brings me back to the reason for writing this book: to slowly but surely shine a light on writers who deserve to be better known. And the reason they are not better known is that—as the tramps they are—their writing simply reflects the world they inhabit and the way they see it, a long and noble tradition that has been replaced in modern times by the plot-driven narrative. But real literature defies the artificial genres that feed the appetites of the current reading public who have to be told what to read by reviewers and book clubs. The life we live between being born and dying isn't a plot-driven narrative with a beginning, middle, and an end, even though this volume *does* attempt to present Christy's life in some semblance of a chronological order. Vagabond literature reflects life as it is, which for the most part is just the present passing—much like the view out of a moving, open boxcar door. But I continue to digress. How did I stumble across this modern-day literary vagabond in the first place?

As previously mentioned, I was introduced to Christy by one of the Victorian-born tramp-writers I referred to earlier. Well, not in person of course. During my research into Jim Phelan, Phelan's grandson, Les Singleton, sent me a chronicle written by Christy of his own connection to Phelan, together with Christy's contact details. Christy had met Phelan's third wife, Kathleen Newton (whom Phelan had tramped with for the last twenty years of his life) on a boat from Spain to Morocco, nearly five years after Jim Phelan's death in 1966. Kathleen had made a previous such trip shortly after her husband's death, tramping and hitchhiking alone from Britain, through France and Spain to Morocco, then onwards through Algeria, Tunisia, Libya, Egypt, by boat to Turkey, and onwards again to Iran, Afghanistan, Pakistan, India, and Tibet. By the time Kathleen met Christy she was a fluent Arabic speaker. Christy spent several weeks tramping in Morocco in Kathleen's company, the full story of which is related in Chapter 5.

At the time I started writing to Christy, it was my belief that he was the last person to have reported any sighting of Kathleen, nearly five years after Phelan's death. Jim Phelan's first wife, Dora Mary Brien, had died in 1924 from septicemia following a minor injury only a year after Phelan had been jailed as an accessory to murder. Phelan married his second wife, Jill Constance Hayes, a political activist who had visited him while in prison toward the end of his thirteen-year incarceration. On September 8, 1940, Jill was severely injured in the German bombardment of London and died sometime afterwards in a nursing home. The story of how Jim Phelan met his third wife is told in Chapter 5 of this book.

In any case, after writing a piece about Christy's meeting with Kathleen Phelan, five separate individuals left messages for me to say that they knew of Kathleen more recently—including Phelan and Jill's son Seumas. In fact, Kathleen had only just died, on November 26, 2014, the day before her ninety-seventh birthday, in the caravan where she was living in Cirencester—only one hour's drive from where I live in Cardiff. The following obituary appeared in *The Times*: "PHELAN Kathleen Tramp and Vagabond died peacefully in her sleep, in her caravan ... once met never forgotten."

Imagine my feelings of deprivation, particularly as Kathleen was the first woman tramp whose story I have attempted to write. The owner of the caravan site had tried to contact me some time ago, when Kathleen was still alive. The wretched contact form on the website was not working. I could have met Kathleen and talked with her face to face. But no good harboring regrets; there must be hundreds of people who did meet and enjoy Kathleen's company during her lifetime, including of course Christy himself. How Christy ends up on a boat to Morocco, and how he fulfills his ambition of becoming a writer, is one of the many stories that now follow.

VAGABONDS, MOBSTERS, GUNSLINGERS, AND FREAKS

J im Christy was born in Richmond, Virginia on July 14 (Bastille Day), 1945. His father, Angelo Christinzio (born in Philadelphia just after his parents arrived in America from Molise in Italy), met his wife, Kathleen Dolby, a native Virginian and part Rappahannock Indian, while Angelo was stationed there during World War II. Christy describes his father as, "an Italian street guy who couldn't be separated from those streets." Those streets were the tough Italian neighborhood of South Philadelphia, chronicled in Christy's fifth book *Streethearts* (1981) and also featured in the Sylvester Stallone *Rocky* films. Christy would appear as an extra in *Rocky IV* at the age of forty-nine, but more of boxing and Stallone later.

After his discharge from the army, when Christy was little over a year old, Angelo Christinzio returned to the streets of South Philadelphia where he lived with his wife and new son in a narrow rented row house at Fifth and Reese Streets. The family later moved to 714 Catherine Street where Christy attended a nursery school at the Settlement House next door, then kindergarten to second grade at a local Campbell School. Across the street from their new home, the Fleischer Art Academy at 719 Catherine Street ran free art classes for the poor. Christy had early aspirations of becoming an artist and wanted to attend classes at the Fleischer, "but my mother wouldn't let me because people seeing me would know we were poor! Honest? Of course, they were poor, too." Neither could Christy expect support for his artistic ambitions from his father. Angelo Christinzio had inherited a job from *his* father in the Democratic political machine, controlled at the time by what was popularly referred to as the Mafia. Philadelphia Godfather, Angelo "The Gentle Don" Bruno, was Christy's actual godfather.

As though connections to Philadelphia's crime family were not provenance enough for the fledgling vagabond, Christy's cultural heritage on his mother's side (described in the chapter titled "It Ain't O.K." from *Between the Meridians*, 1999) was even more notorious. Christy is great-nephew of Billy Clanton who, along with Tom and Frank McLaury, was shot and killed by Wyatt Earp, two of his brothers, and Doc Holliday, in the one-sided "Gunfight at the OK Corral." Billy was only nineteen when he died, and although unarmed at the scene, Christy's other great-uncle, Ike Clanton, escaped with his life only to be shot in the back six years later by a lawman straight out of a mail-order private detective course, "wearing the tin badge that came with the course for twenty-five cents extra." The Clantons, their older brother Phineas, and the McLaury brothers were part of a loosely knit gang of over two hundred known as the "Cowboys," so called because they rustled cattle across the border in Mexico to sell back in the U.S. The Hollywood myth of the legendary shootout created by Earp himself contrasts widely from accounts documented more recently by historians. But Wyatt Earp and Christy's own research into the tale will be returned to in Chapter 7, together with an account of the manner in which Christy, at the age of thirty-six, first learned of his relationship to the Clantons. For now, we return to the streets of South Philadelphia and the local street-market where Christy grew up. The following extended passage from *Streethearts* gives a vivid description of the sights and smells of his childhood, as well as providing a rich social history of a community long since disappeared:

> The Market started at Christian and went south past Montrose
> Street which had always been the centre of the Italian
> community.... It was there in the cafés surrounded by pushcarts
> with goats bleating on the street, that the first criminal
> organisation had been born. ... The Market continued over
> Washington Avenue and down as far as Wharton. On a Saturday
> morning it was a teeming casbah like in the movies, only more

strange, because there were no Arabs or Orientals but thousands
of Italian ladies haggling with butchers and fruit sellers. ...If you
looked all the way down Ninth Street you saw the green awnings
rising and falling in the breeze, the tin roofs buckling and sagging
as if it were an uneasy sea ... Above these roofs the buildings were
brick, the second and third floors used for storage or apartments
and kids and women leaned out over the sills and looked down
on the street. ... Black marble surrounded windows with yellow
Hermes olive oil tins stacked around the perimeter. Inside
some of these stores were barrels of olive oil under hanging wheels
of provolone and romano. Wooden bins with spices, the smell
of oregano and fennel mixing with the cheese. Sausage, salami,
pastrami, prosciutto. And from down a tiny street like Hall Street,
garlic and tomato paste smell of someone's Saturday dinner.
...I walk along. Wilted leaves of escarole lie in the gutters. A man
in a filthy apron is hosing blood and chicken feathers from the
sidewalk. Near the side door of the produce mart a middle-aged
man is lifting baskets of bell peppers, Italian tomatoes, fresh Jersey
corn, clumps of bitter Romaine and exotic purple egg plant onto
a wagon, while an old man stands by and watches, idly patting
the old horse on the nose. ...The old nag drops a golden plop of
steaming shit onto the asphalt and it becomes part of the smell
of the street.[10]

Christy daily witnessed the underworld life of the adults in his community.
His father, a local ward politician, together with other cronies, would fix it
for Italian folk in trouble in return for favors come election day: "a guy shoots
another guy who was hassling his wife, another guy's son just out of the army
needs a job...."

All the dealings in the back rooms of those Italian social clubs were
done openly and under the full protection of the powers that be,
for they were those powers. There was none of the muttering, the
glances at the door, the leaning over the table and the clandestine
whispering that went on in the kitchen in back of Aldo's [Joe's]
luncheonette.[11]

Crooked as many of the dealings may have been, they also served an important social function. There is a fascinating description of Italian funerals in *Streethearts*, and Christy explains that no small amount of Democratic Party funds went toward paying for the funerals of those families who were too poor to pay themselves, not to mention also slipping the widow "a clean white envelope of five ten-dollar bills to tide her over the next few weeks." Strangers appeared at doorways and everyone looked at them wondering who they could be. The word was then spread that they were the well-off cousins from out of state. In reality they were guys in rented suits from other neighborhoods hired by the bereaved to attend the wake. They arrived in brand new "borrowed cars" with New York license plates and acted rich.

> And always there were the professional mourners. Italian women who walked dry-eyed into the parlour or the funeral home, took seats at the front and began to wail. ...They would stare ahead stoney-faced in their wailing; then leave to go home to boil the noodles....[12]

As well as the dubious activities carried out in the kitchen of his uncle Joe Verrechio's luncheonette on Fifth and Catherine Street, Christy was witness to similar business conducted in Pat and Ange's Taproom at Passyunk Avenue and Christian Street run by two other uncles. One of these, Christy's favorite uncle, Angelo "Jumbo" D'Antonio, kept a revolver in a cigar box next to the cash register. Christy describes this uncle as "so big and tough looking, yet he could completely disarm you with his gentle manner and quiet voice." But on one particular afternoon, the gun proved useless. Christy describes his uncles' bar as having swinging doors like those in Western saloons, "dark like a saloon should be," with a heavy scarred mahogany bar and wide plank floors covered with sawdust. The room had two curtained windows that let in a warm glow of sunlight. Off the taproom was another larger room with thirty or forty tables and a stage supporting an ancient upright piano.[13]

On the day in question, Christy's uncles were at the bar and Christy was playing in the sawdust on the barroom floor. He described witnessing his first killing as though it was choreographed in slow motion. The two shuttered doors of the bar swung open and into the taproom stepped a guy in a suit and hat. Uncle Rio looked up. The rest of the scene is described in Christy's own words:

The man calmly, almost in a whisper, spoke a single word, 'Reuben.' He unbuttoned his suit jacket and reached inside with his right hand.

I looked at the men along the bar. Two pairs of men moved left and right leaving only the one in the middle, Reuben. Sheepie.

Sheepie turned and slid off his stool, his arms spread at his sides like those of Jesus in the paintings of him beckoning the lambs and the little children.

From under the man's left arm came the blunt, shiny gun. The men all stared at the gunman's hand.

Sheepie took a step forward. A short lick of flame burst from the revolver. Then, as Sheepie reached for his chest, came the sound of a muffled BLAMM! Sheepie bent like he was going to pick up a coin from the sawdust, and when he was in a crouch he turned slowly and fell over on his back.

[...]

I watched as the blood spread and consumed his starched and snow white shirt. Then everybody moved like a photograph come to life. Rio grabbed the gun from the cigar box next to the cash register and rushed out of the bar.[14]

We hear no more of this event except that Rio's gun failed to fire. Christy keeps copies of old newspaper clippings of South Philadelphia that further illustrate the hazardous nature of life on those streets. These reports include one from the *Philadelphia Daily News* dated January 12, 1982, about the murder of the aforementioned Angelo D'Antonio who, with his brother, had continued to run the same tavern where the unfortunate Sheepie had been gunned down all those years earlier, and long after the neighborhood had become predominantly Afro-American. A masked gunman walked into the bar and demanded the contents of the cash register, shooting D'Antonio in the process. When a friend recently asked Christy what he thought would have become of him if he'd stayed in South Philadelphia, he replied, "I'd either be rich or dead."

In spite of growing up steeped in the rich culture of those South Philadelphia streets, and although as streetwise and able as any of the other Italian kids, and more able than many, Christy always felt different: outside and above of the narrow, day-to-day concerns of his "own people" and had cosmopolitan leanings from an early age. Far too curious and adventurous to stick to his own neighborhood, at the age of seven he risked his skin walking alone into an African-American precinct and proving that Italian kids were just as tough on the football field as the black kids who were ready to show him how they treated intruders. For his trouble, Christy got invited to play regular matches with them and spent time at the home of his friend Dwight Edwards, whose older brother Tommy Edwards recorded the 1958 number-one hit "It's All in the Game."[15] It was, and still is, in Christy's nature to be a free spirit, refusing to subscribe to any particular tribe yet entirely comfortable with any tribe he chooses to identify with. Aged only eight, he had already identified with black music. Left alone one day in an antique shop while his father was doing a deal in the back room, Christy went directly to a pile of 45s and bought one at random by Doc Starnes and his Nite Riders. The tracks were "Six Button Benny" (a style of overcoat) and "Don't Hang Up the Phone," a genre Christy recalled as "sort of black doo wop." This event would lead on to a discovery and lifelong appreciation of jazz which, unlike the rock 'n roll favored by his white contemporaries, Christy describes as "the real music of the outsider, the outlaw, the rebel." Christy went on to spend a lifetime in jazz clubs around the world and met many of the jazz greats of at least three generations.

Taking pleasure in challenging the cultural norms of his day, at the age of twelve his way of dressing was so individual that it defied any recognizable classification. As one schoolmate observed, "Christinzio, you dress like a nigger," while downtown, "The wops on the corners laughed at me. Called me a hillbilly. Screw them."[16] Difference sometimes made him the cool dude, at other times a suspicious character, yet as well as finding himself in the company of minor and major celebrities, from an early age Christy often also sought out and befriended the underdog, the cripple, the tramp, and the circus freak. He describes "weird folks and oddities" as being a normal part of his childhood, and so encountering them when he hit the road or traveled with carnivals seemed nothing out of the ordinary. "They just seemed natural to my environment and so I took them for granted later and throughout my life." Christy describes several such characters from his own extended family, starting with an Italian barber who had what seemed like little more than half a leg, to which was attached a huge well-polished black ankle boot.

> This barber had a buxom, bleached blond wife. My father's mother
> and his sister, were big gun carrying women who took numbers
> (illegal lottery). That sister, my aunt Lena, and her husband Joe,

had a child that they kept in a locked room. To the kid I was, he seemed like a monster. There was an iron-grill doorway. He could only grunt. Ran around in there all day like a highly energized gorilla. They called him 'Boom-Boom.' There was a deaf and dumb couple, aunt and uncle. My uncles Angelo and Pasquale owned a tavern where, at age ten, I saw a guy, a crook, of course, shot and killed in front of me. There was an old piano in the back-room and sawdust on the floor. My first girlfriend had a brother who had suffered some brain injury at birth and I have vivid memories of him laying in this sort of elongated baby's crib. I would have been nine, ten, eleven, and he would have been sixteen or seventeen. He had limited movement. It was a horrible sight. A skeleton head with thin skin stretched over it. Then I'd go to the southland and everyone there was straight out of an Erskine Caldwell novel.[17]

An example of such a trip south is described in *Streethearts* when, at ten years old, with his mother and brother, they made a trip to visit his mother's family in Virginia while Christy's father was clearing up some "business" at home. Christy befriended a kid with polio and their adventures, as is Christy's first acquaintance with hobos and his first taste of tramping, are described in *Streethearts*.[18] In spite of the polio kid's disability, he was resourceful and intrepid enough to introduce Christy to his second sexual adventure with two sharecropper's daughters in a corn shed; his first had been at the age of seven with his cousin "Candy" in the space between the washing machine and refrigerator in the family apartment—unconsummated due to the premature arrival of his mother. In any case, on the occasions that his Virginian friend was not around, Christy would wander the countryside with his possessions wrapped in a bandana. He had already become familiar with the tramps and hobos who constantly arrived at his grandmother's house for something to eat, she being one of those kindly souls who never refused those in need:

> I had seen men come around to the back porch, knock on the
> screen door and humbly offer to do a job of work in return for a
> sandwich or a slice of lemon meringue pie that was cooling on
> the kitchen windowsill. My grandmother always obliged them. ...
> The men always looked mysterious to me, they had weatherbeaten
> faces and slotted eyes.

One man sat on the back porch at the huge round table and my grandmother set a meal before him and he said, 'Thank you ma'am, I have my own utensils.'[19]

From the side pocket of the hobo's jacket he removed a red railroad bandana which he carefully unknotted. The inside of the bandana revealed a plug of chewing tobacco, a watch without the wrist band, and a fountain pen. The man tapped the green pen and said to Christy, "Always write a postcard home when you're on the move, boy." The boy nodded politely in response and replied, "Yes sir," wondering why the tramp had offered him this advice. Was he going somewhere? Who knew? Maybe he was someday.[20] The young Christy thrilled to hear these wandering vagabonds tell their stories. He wanted to see all the places they talked about, not knowing that one day he would, and not just on the American continent but across the globe. But that particular summer, Christy started imitating these tramps by setting forth with his own bandana full of the necessities of life:

> In the afternoon, before turning back, I'd lie down under a tree and spread out my bandana, eat the corn bread and cold chicken, sip water and wipe my lips like any respectable tramp.
>
> When I had finished the food, I slid further down between the thick roots of the tree and stared up at the top leaves, at the blue sky peeking through. One by one I considered all the great and exciting things I could do in life. If I couldn't choose between them all, it didn't matter, I would certainly do them all.[21]

All too soon Christy's summer vacation was ended and he returned to a new home and a new neighborhood at 831 Ritner Street, twenty blocks south of his previous home. There Christy would have to earn recognition from a new gang who watched him closely that first day as his mother insisted on dragging him by the hand to the store. He knew he would have to fight his way into the gang to gain acceptance, now made harder by the "momma's boy rap" he had acquired as a result of his mother's custodial care. But gain it he did, taking his place in the pecking order of what would become a great new bunch of friends, unlike, he says, the ones who lived on Catherine Street.[22] Closest of these were Joey Segal, Bobby Degregorio, Ralphie Fortunato, and Eddie Schwartz, "the toughest guy in the neighbourhood." Here Christy attended the Francis Scott Key Elementary School, and in a passage from his unpublished work *Brookdale*, Christy provides an unflattering description of the teachers he encountered there:

> ...it was as if the school-board sent out hunting parties at night to roam the darkened streets and odiferous alleys, to drag back these creatures. Seemed like every male teacher had a club foot, a hump at the back of his neck under the suit coat or a raging skin disease in birthday cake colours. Every woman teacher, except Miss Barca, had to have been closing in on seventy, at the very least, and sporting warts, wens and whiskers, suffered elephantiasis or had Olive Oyl sticks for legs. Each one came armed, a yard stick for long range attacks and for close up work, chopping up knuckles particularly, a metal-edged ruler.[23]

Here Christy met and hung out with his first girlfriend, Loretta DeGregorio, a rare phenomenon in that neighborhood, coming as she did from a Protestant family. Loretta's father was a cop and they lived next to a barber shop at the corner of Ritner and Darien Streets. The barber, Christy recalls, had a son two years older than himself who, rumor had it, was missing a testicle, resulting in the unfortunate tag of "the one-ball barber's son." Christy recalls going with Loretta to Oregon Avenue to ride horses around a small fenced lot. After Loretta, he went out with a girl named Christine Giordano whose sister, Christy says, was big on American Bandstand. It wasn't long before the ten-year-old Christy started establishing his own business interests and marking out his own territory. First carrying groceries for local housewives, then setting up shop in the back of a bar to run a loan shark operation. First he figured out who had money and who needed it, and when he had mentally filed this information, he set out to circulate money from the former to the latter. He would often double his return on lending quarters, even dollars. "If I discovered a kid needed money, I would offer it to him at my rate and he would pay up. If he grew reluctant to pay off I would have to lean on him."[24]

When the inevitable happened and one kid refused to pay up, calling Christy's bluff and threatening his dominion, Christy had to take action to protect his reputation. He picked a time and a place that would guarantee an audience: the kid's classroom just before the next lesson. "I believe you owe me three dollars and fifty cents." "You're nuts. I don't know what you're talking about. Get outta here." Christy made a motion as if to turn away, then spun back, grabbed the other guy by the collar, and pulled him down from the sill hitting the desk opposite. He placed one leg in back of the other boy's, reached around and grabbed him by the chin, slamming him back and then hitting him as hard as he could in the stomach. As his victim lay face down on the floor, Christy pressed one foot between his shoulder blades and told his friend Ignace to go through his pockets. The whole time the rest of the class was screaming and hollering.[25]

The next morning on his street corner patch, Christy's friend came running up to warn him that the older brother of the kid he had taken the money from was on his way with two other thirteen-year-old kids with the intention of doing Christy harm. Christy enlisted the help of two other ten-year-old friends who, in spite of the odds stacked against them, were determined to stick by their friend, but more importantly, were of extremely courageous disposition:

> ...they hove into view, coming from Wolf Street down Mildred towards us, walking right in the middle of the street like three gunfighters. The guy in the centre was nearly six feet tall. On his left was Tone's brother who wasn't much shorter and was carrying a chain. The third kid wasn't very tall but he made up for it in width. I thought we could be in some trouble here.[26]

But the audacity of the younger kids won out. Bernie, the largest of the three ten-year-olds, broke the tall guy's shins with a baseball bat, while little Ignace split the stocky kid's skull with a knuckle duster. Christy, having ducked at the right moment, had already disabled Tone's brother whose chain wrapped itself around a lamppost instead of its intended target. Two of Christy's assailants were hospitalized with their injuries, which enhanced Christy's reputation on the street and opened the way to expand his operation. But Christy was not violent by nature, and certainly not the brutal type he would later encounter in the mob—either because they became immune to human emotion entirely or simply got off on sadistic power. No, Christy's strategy of putting the other guy out of action before he did harm to you was born from shrewd observation of the Machiavellian school. He understood that those who failed to acknowledge the violence around them would wind up a victim of it, either by being physically hurt or worse, or scuttling around furtively in constant fear:

You had to walk out of the front door every morning and stride down the street and be cool and ready for anything. Not to do this was to go peeking and hiding, ducking and dodging through life, to shrivel up inside…. That was no way to live, in fact, it was a bit like dying, bit by bit, day after day.[27]

That was how Christy had it figured out. It wasn't about getting off on violence. It was an everyday fact of life on those South Philadelphia streets. Driven by his outrage of seeing helpless kids beaten up or frightened out of their lunch money, Christy decided to become a vigilante, a latter-day Zorro without the mask, and formed his own protection racket named "The Robin Hood Protection Service," from which he drew the triple benefit of protecting the persecuted, enhancing his personal reputation, and making some cash on the side. "It was different from the usual operation, since it was run by a guy who took in stray dogs."[28]

As well as being a street-fighter, from the age of ten Christy also got involved in amateur boxing, fighting for two years in the Police Athletic League.[29] He describes South Philadelphia as being immersed in boxing, and how males from the age of ten to fifty would greet each other on street corners by "putting up their dukes, giving a little head bob, and slipping an imaginary punch." It was just the natural and friendly thing to do. Christy quotes Tex Cobb, who went fifteen rounds with Larry Holmes, as saying that "in South Philadelphia, even the winos throw jabs."[30] "Everybody had an uncle or father who fought." Three of Christy's own uncles had been fighters and he even remembers his own father fighting regular bouts with his friend Billy Winston. Christy's father wrote to Christy about Winston in a letter while the latter was writing *Streethearts*: "a good looking coloured boy … anywhere there was enough space to set up a ring or mark off a sixteen-to-twenty-foot square." Christy would often hang out in his Uncle Joe and Aunt Lena's luncheonette where one of the regulars was Joe "The Iron Man" Grim (Saverio Giannone), so-called because of his ability to take punishment without being knocked out. Christy relates an anecdote about his father's uncle, the lightweight Andy Juliano: "Three years before he died at age eighty-eight, Uncle Andy was in his yellow Corvair convertible at a traffic light on Moyamensing Avenue when two hoods jumped him. He laid both of them out with a tyre iron."[31]

But because boxing was part of Christy's everyday life, it did not feature in his childhood fantasies or those of his friends. Instead they dreamed of major-league baseball stardom: "They occupied a region apart from the world of ordinary men, far beyond fathers and uncles, and this was the sphere to which we aspired." But even playing baseball involved fighting. The nearest baseball field was at Third and Oregon Avenues, six blocks away. It not only involved walking through other gangs' territory but passing through two distinct black neighborhoods. "The kids would be waiting for us with fists, rocks, chains, and brass knuckles," but having reached the pitch, Christy had to fight again to stay and play against other groups of kids rivaling for the same opportunity.[32]

Christy had all the makings of a top-notch gangster had he chosen that line of work. But by the age of eleven he was already getting tired of the gang culture, and had enough sense to realize that such a life could only end in personal grief. In an ugly battle between black and white gangs at the school, one of Christy's friends lost a lung from a sharpened nail fired from a zip gun (a block of wood with a groove from which a nail is fired with a heavy-duty rubber band held back by a trigger). The black kid who fired the missile was found stabbed to death in an alley some days later.[33]

> I knew damn well where it was going to end. It was going to end with me missing a lung like Johnny Santori or, worse, face down in an alley like Bad Thomas and, if not, I would be doing it to someone else and paying for it in joints with names like Rahway and Dannemora. It was all there, in the cards in my hand.[34]

At the age of eleven, not only did Christy have the sense to realize that the life of a hoodlum was a mug's game, more remarkably, and here is the emerging philosophy of the tramp and cynic, he also knew that to go "straight"—in the sense of settling down to the daily grind of a mundane job to support a wife and kids—was in some ways an even worse fate than that of a mobster. The life of a respectable, or even disreputable, vagabond adventurer was of much greater appeal to the young itinerant, and to this end he now set his sights on the more exotic surroundings of downtown Philadelphia's nightlife. His new scam, carefully researched so as not to muscle in on anyone else's territory, was as a shoeshine boy at the entrance to the Trocadero Burlesque Palace (today's Trocadero Theater in Chinatown) on the corner of Arch Street and North 10th Street. Christy had befriended a stripper, "Liberty Bell," in the tavern across the road, who had in turn made it good for him with the Trocadero's manager:

From inside [the Trocadero] appeared a short, squat Italian, in a stained tuxedo that looked like he had rented it for his brother's wedding ten years ago and never taken it back. From the side of his mouth that didn't have the cigar, he growled for the men to pay up or move along. I thought he was going to chase me too, but he barked, 'At's awright kid, I been expectin ta see ya. You da frienda Miss Bell's, ain't ya?'[35]

Christy had positioned his homemade shoeshine box so that his customers would have a partial view of the Trocadero's stage from the sidewalk through the theatre doors, a tantalizing enough reason to stop for a shine—often not even bothering to check the result before dropping a quarter in the box. The shoeshine box Christy stashed in the tavern across the road with his friend the barman so as not to arouse suspicion by carrying the box around his own neighborhood. On the Friday and Saturday nights that he worked, he told his parents that he was simply staying over at a friend's. Christy was made welcome in the girls' dressing room and Liberty started getting him to walk her home for her own protection—not that she couldn't take care of herself. As soon as they were out on the street, men started falling out to catch sight of Liberty. "Cars screech to a halt, horns honk, guys whistle, women look in awe all because she has somehow managed to contain her 48-23-38 body in a long pink skirt, very tight fire engine red sweater that matches her lips, and pink stiletto high heels." Christy asked if this happened every time she walked down the street and got the answer, "What do you think? That's why I asked you to walk me home." Liberty calculated that if she had Christy in tow she'd get less hassle because the men would figure that she had her kid with her.

> She seemed to be tottering on those heels and her breasts were so outrageous that I kept thinking she was going to pitch forward. I took a few quick steps to get in front of her.
> 'Where are you going?'
> 'I'm gonna catch you when you topple over.'
> 'Wise ass. Get over here.'[36]

But life was soon to change catastrophically for the young entrepreneur. One night when Christy was sneaking home from his duties downtown, he came across three big-shot mobsters in his parents' kitchen, one of whom he recognized as a former date of Liberty Bell. Christy stopped and listened to the rest of the conversation hiding behind the trashcans in the yard—simultaneously thinking about all those movies where the person in his position bumps into a trashcan sending the lid clattering across the pavement and getting hit in a hail of bullets. His father was clearly being extorted into doing something he did not much like the sound of:

> 'I can't. I just can't. I gotta wife and two kids.'
>
> 'Angelo, we all got a wife and kids. ...'
>
> 'But my wife doesn't understand any of this. And my boys are only twelve and five for chrissakes.'
>
> 'Ange, your poor little twelve year old, huh? He hangs around the Trocadero Burlesque with the broads anna bums, what're you tellin me?'
>
> 'Whats'at?'
>
> 'Your kid, inna dressing room witha broads.'
>
> 'My kid?'
>
> 'The same.'
>
> 'How do you know that?'
>
> 'I seen him in there. They give him wine in the bar acrossa street.'
>
> 'God, what've I done wrong?'
>
> 'Kids today, Ange.'[37]

And from *Brookdale*:

> So these here are the options, Chris. One, you do it and you prosper. Two, you don't want to do it, well, then you got to get out of the picture. You understand that, of course. Number three, and I know you well enough to know you wouldn't even consider this particular option on account of you know the consequences, but you'll pardon me but I got to mention it on account of you-know-who told me to mention it. So that option is you try to have it both ways or you make some noise to Dilworth about, and well we're big boys and we know where that leads, as I said.[38]

Christy never did find out what it was that his father had been asked to do for the mob that so tormented him. But he acknowledges that it wasn't true that the mob would obliterate you and your entire family if you didn't do their bidding. Instead, Christy's father was told it was all right, he was making a big mistake but no hard feelings, and he should come around the house for dinner sometime—even though he'd been given orders to get out of town. All Christy knew about what occurred that night is what he recalls of the conversation repeated above, the rest was speculation. In the event, it must have been something devastating as, before the meeting was over, Christy could hear his father sobbing. That Christy's nighttime adventures had been exposed was no longer his main concern; in fact his father never mentioned it further, maybe was even secretly proud of his son's spirited resourcefulness.

In any event, a week later the deed must have been done because Christy's father led the boy, eyes shut tight, around a street corner and proudly revealed, "a big beautiful new Buick all wet from rain and gleaming under the misty street lamps. Glistening dark blue with shiny chrome." But it was not the new car that would change Christy's life; the rest of the payoff for whatever his father had been asked to perform for the mob was a change of home and a change of name, and only two days to say his goodbyes. The family was to relocate from the familiar streets of South Philadelphia, to suburbs way out west of the city.

As devastated as the menfolk of the family might have been at the prospect of moving to middle-class suburbia, for Christy's Virginia-raised mother, this was a dream come true: getting away from what she regarded as the slums of South Philadelphia to her own house in the leafy suburbs with a yard, grass around it, and even a garage. But Christy's reaction was pure panic. He could not believe what was happening and stared out of the window at the familiar red brick tenements with the cars squeezed up on the curb, the telephone poles drooping their wires, the trash cans spilling their disgusting contents onto the sidewalks, and the neon glowing in the bars. "The fights, the hanging out, the singing on the corner, the jive, and the bullshit. Downtown, tenderloin, honky-tonks, Dolores and her long legs, Liberty strutting down Tenth Street, cabs honking ... The tears welled up in my eyes. The lump was there in my throat."

'Aren't you thrilled?' ... 'Thrilled my ass. I ain't goin.'
My mother smiled and took my arm. I looked at her sitting

there happy as could be. I could see it in her eyes, they were glittering, as bright as the new Buick.

'Of course you're going, young man.' She shook my arm playfully and drawled, 'Oh, you'll just love it. We bought the most beautiful house on a corner with a nice yard for you to play in. A yard with a nice lawn and trees. The neighbors are friendly and they're a better class of people. You'll have the time of your life.'
'I bet. Yeah, and I bet it has a garage too!'
'It does. How do you know?'
'Jesus Christ!'[39]

Now as every dyed-in-the-wool, self-respecting vagabond knows—even at the tender age of twelve—the life now described by Christy's mother is not designed to fill one with exultation. The notion of a "garage" had been a standing joke among Christy's friends ever since one of them had admitted that he did not know what a garage was, and was astonished at the idea that people actually kept their cars in little houses in their gardens. The following reaction from Christy, when his mother described the place they were going to live, is hardly surprising: "Brookdale! Yeah, right. Lawns and kids who wear white socks. Jumping over the brooks and capering across the goddamn dales. What is going on?" Christy looked at his father but couldn't read him. "There was nothing on his face. He wasn't happy; he wasn't unhappy. He was blank."[40]

On his last day in South Philadelphia, while the movers were packing the van, Christy went downtown to say his goodbyes to his new friends. But it would be a day to remember for more reasons than the impending move to the suburbs. Dolores with the long legs had always had a soft spot for the shoeshine boy, and between the matinee performances that Saturday afternoon, with the dressing room door firmly closed, Christy would finally complete his apprenticeship in the art of lovemaking, and from a virtuoso of the profession.

When it was over, Dolores lit a cigarette and smoked and didn't say anything. She seemed to be watching the smoke drift to the ceiling of the dressing room so I watched it too. When she was finished she ground the cigarette out in the ashtray on her stomach and sighed.

'Well I guess you better be going. You'll miss the big move. Poor kid.'

'Yeah.' I got up off the floor, gathered my clothes and dressed.

'Bye, doll,' she said.

I looked back at her. She was naked except for the ankle bracelet on the leg that was raised, the heel of her foot resting on the wooden chair by the makeup table. Her triangle of hair was thick and dark and I knew how wet it was. I wondered how long it would be before I saw one of those again.

'See you, Dolores.' She just looked in my eyes and blew smoke rings to the ceiling.[41]

Christy caught the trolley down to Eighth and Wolfe and walked the block to the place on Ritner Street where the moving van had just pulled away. His father was packing their final belongings into the big shiny new Buick and his mother, fists planted on her hips, declared, "And where have you been, Mr. Big Shot with your nigger clothes and greasy hair?" Christy was sorely tempted to respond: "Well, Mom, I've been at the Trocadero Burlesque where I was taken advantage of by a stripper in her dressing room who was, I don't know, ten or maybe even twenty years older than me." But he just said, "I've just been around saying my goodbyes." And so, after a quick half wave, half salute to his girl Loretta and friends who were watching the drama from Dumbrowski's luncheonette across the street, off they set for "Brookdale."* It seemed a million miles away to Christy, but it only took an hour and a half to get there. It was November 10th, 1957. Christy was twelve years old.

*A note on Brookdale: In his published works, Christy has used the fictitious name Brookdale to refer to the suburban town of Springfield (Delaware County) on the west side of Philadelphia. His reason for refusing to name the actual town in his writing was conveyed in an email dated July 25, 2016: "A very sensitive topic because I hated the place, hated every minute of it, and all the people too. I went into a shell so as to avoid all of my creepy classmates. I can't convey the depths of my hatred for that place." But Christy is now ready to exorcise some of his old ghosts and we are told that the location of his new home was 57 North Brookside Road, Springfield, on the corner with Congress Avenue.

1   Jim Christy, *This Cockeyed World* (Toronto: Guernica Editions, 2013), p. 24

2   Jim Christy, email to the author, February 19, 2017

3   Jim Christy, email to the author, April 9, 2017

4   Jim Christy, "Looking for literature in all the wrong places," (Toronto) *Globe and Mail*, 2002

5   See Ian Cutler, *Cynicism from Diogenes to Dilbert* (Jefferson, NC: McFarland & Co., 2005)

6   Josiah Flynt, "How Men Become Tramps," *The Century*, volume 50, issue 6, Oct. 1895, p. 945

7   Stephen Graham, *A Tramp's Sketches* (London: Macmillan & Co., 1913), p. 329

8   Ibid., p. 40

9   Paul J. Bauer & Mark Dawidziak, *Jim Tully: American Writer, Irish Rover, Hollywood Brawler* (Kent, OH: The Kent State University Press, 2011), p. 169

10   Jim Christy, *Streethearts* (Toronto: Simon & Pierre, 1981), pp. 49-50

11   Ibid., p. 61

12   Ibid., p. 60

13   Ibid., p. 62

14   Ibid., p. 63

15   Ibid., pp. 20-21

16   Ibid., p. 176

17   Jim Christy, email to the author, August 22, 2014

18   *Streethearts*, op cit., pp. 67-81

19   Ibid., p. 68

20   Ibid., p. 69

21   Ibid., p. 71

22   Ibid., p. 73

23   Jim Christy, *Brookdale* (unpublished manuscript)

24   *Streethearts*, op cit., p. 103

25   Ibid., p. 105

26   Ibid., p. 107

27   Ibid., p. 108

28   Ibid., p. 109

29   Jim Christy, *Flesh and Blood* (Vancouver: Douglas & McIntyre, 1990), pp. 13-15

30 Ibid., pp. 17-19

31 Ibid., p. 18

32 Ibid., pp. 19-20

33 *Streethearts*, op cit., p. 111

34 Ibid., pp. 139-140

35 Ibid., p. 146

36 Ibid., p. 160

37 Ibid., p. 186

38 *Brookdale*, op cit.

39 *Streethearts*, op cit., p. 190

40 Ibid., p. 109

41 *Brookdale*, op cit.

2

ESCAPE FROM SUBURBIA

O n the family's arrival in Springfield, the sights that met Christy's eyes were even worse than he had imagined. "The men were mowing tiny lawns, the women were wheeling station wagons back and forth to shopping centres, and the kids really did have crewcuts." As soon as they pulled up in front of their new house, Christy saw what would be his new "gang" down the street, riding around on their English bicycles or just standing around in white socks and loafers, tossing footballs in the air and staring at him. His parents had hardly started unloading the car before his mother started pressuring Christy to go and introduce himself to his new "playmates": "You're in a different kind of neighbourhood now, a nice neighbourhood. And you will have to learn to act differently, young man." "I don't want to act no different." Christy's mother pressed her fingernails into his forearm, smiling all the while but saying through clenched teeth, "Don't argue with me in front of all these people. March right over there. You have to start off on the right foot." Deliberately stepping out with his left foot, Christy reluctantly crossed the road.

He could not have known then that by crossing that road he was beginning a six-year prison sentence relieved only by periods of absconding from home and school with all of the additional castigation brought down on him by these misdemeanors. But this is how Christy describes that first encounter from an extended passage from *Brookdale:*

As it was, however, the journey began with that single step. At first, they seemed fascinated by my shoes but slowly their collective gaze rose up my black high-rise slacks with the pink piping along the leg seams, over the black satin shirt, and fastened on my hair. Twice as long as all of theirs put together, my hair was pompadoured in front and combed back on the sides with Vitalis. They looked at one another and back at me.

'You always dress like that?' one of them asked.
'Like what?' I replied.
They ignored that and the crewcut in the middle said, "I guess you don't play football."
'Oh? Why do you guess that?'
Sidestepping it, he said, 'You want to play a game now?'
'Sure, what are the rules?'
'Touch. No rushing the passer.'
'What's touch?'
'Touch. Touch football. You never heard of touch football?'

The guy with the ball—he had on a Penn State sweatshirt—muttered 'Maybe he never heard of *football.*'

[....]

The reason I had never played touch football, I said, was because we had only played tackle football. There were two kinds, I explained, ordinary tackle football and what we had called 'rough tackle' which meant, basically, that there were always big pileups when a ball carrier went down. 'Yeah,' says I. 'Rough tackle was cool. You'd have this big mound of guys pile on and try to make the guy at the bottom yell out.'

'Where did you do this, at the park?'

'The park? There weren't any parks close by. We played it on the streets.'

'The streets? Get out!'

'No, man, it's the truth.'

'Horseshit!' pronounced the guy with the English bike.

And it was not a good natured "horseshit" as if I had been goofing around and said something in the order of, 'Well I get the ball in the end zone, dodge the first eight guys, leap over another one and streak one hundred and eight yards and right on the one-yard line have to twist away from a guy, step on top of him and somersault over the last guy and land in the end zone as the buzzer sounds and we win the game by a single point.'

Nope it was a mean "horseshit" and they laughed too, a mean laugh. Now this was something new, this attitude. Myself, I was always ready to believe most anything anyone told me. Within reason, of course, and playing tackle football on the street was not only within reason but a daily activity from October through March. See, I figured, if somebody was jiving it would show itself sooner or later. In the old neighbourhood, if a guy came up with a story that on the surface seemed kind of wild, we might laugh but not *at* the guy. If we perhaps doubted what he was running down, we'd maybe kid him along but never commit ourselves to totally disbelieving because that way we left ourselves open to looking—if he turned out to be dealing the legitimate goods— worse than *he* would have looked if it was exposed that he had been jiving.

So here I was, age twelve, having just that very morning lost my virginity and these guys couldn't conceive of the fact that there were kids somewhere in the world who played tackle football on the street. If they couldn't handle that, they certainly wouldn't have ears for other things, like about the Troc and the girls or Leon's, this bar near the theatre where I was a mascot and knew characters like Baseball George or Virginia Ding Dong Belle; sure, and I could just imagine telling them about my little loan-sharking business or the zip gun murder of the black kid Bad Thomas.[1]

For sure this was one neighbourhood Christy would not have to fight his way into, but on returning to the house he was berated again by his mother, "I was so embarrassed watching you play with those nice boys. The way your hair flopped in your face. You look like some juvenile delinquent. ... You just think you're so smart but don't you make fun of those kids because you're going to get a flat top, too. ...a real flat top! And I'm going with you to the barbershop and make sure you get it cut short." From that moment, Christy started planning his escape. His forays into real tramping and vagabondage would soon follow.

One can only imagine Christy's devastation at having to leave behind the streets of South Philadelphia, the place he had grown up and established his reputation as a resourceful and popular vagabond, for the tedious vacuity of suburbia. It was around Christmas of 1956 when his father had got into the deal with the mob which resulted in being given a new identity and the new home in Springfield. In his unpublished work *Shift and Glitter*,[2] Christy reflects on his lost life. He had been intensely happy on the streets of South Philadelphia. On weekends he had been free from early morning until late in the evening.

> The streets were a rich universe, especially when I started
> working, at age seven, and later, made forays to downtown, to
> shine shoes out front of the Trocadero Burlesque parlour. ...
> Brookdale was no dreary subdivision, either, but more like a dreary
> small town. The other kids bored me to tears with their flattop
> haircuts and regimented games. I began to run away as soon as
> I could manage it, the first time, as soon as school was out, an
> agonizing seven months after we moved in. I hit the road at the
> beginning of July, a week or so before my twelfth birthday.[3]

Christy had to enroll for the remainder of that school year at Scenic Hills Elementary School before going on to Springfield High School in September. Scenic Hills School had been built seven years before Christy arrived in Springfield, and here he describes the physical building in *Brookdale*:

> ...it sat very modernisticly on its hill; one story, sprawling, tan brick
> and glass, looking like a place where they sent wealthy alcoholics
> to dry out, and the view might really have been scenic, oh, perhaps
> two-hundred and fifty years before when no Cape Cods and split

levels marred the hills and vales which were then covered with trees that hid a few longhouses or whatever those long gone Lenapes had lived in.[4]

And from an email:

My very first day going to Scenic Hills they sent a girl to the office to escort me to the "homeroom," her name was Jackie Ferrante. I thought it was a big deal meeting her because her father was a star of the Philadelphia Eagles professional football team, so I says to her 'You must be from South Philadelphia, too.' She replied that thankfully they had gotten out of there when she was very young, because had she lived there past the age of eight all sorts of horrible character traits would have developed.[5]

But things got even worse for Christy that same morning when a voice behind him in the corridor shouted "Hey, you!" Christy describes the incident in *Brookdale*:

I knew perfectly well without looking who the "you" was but I found the tone objectionable. I continued walking. 'You in the black shirt! Halt this minute.'

Curious as to who was being so rude while imitating a guy in an old English movie, I glanced over my shoulder at a tall, heavyset kid that I recognized from class. I stopped and waited for him.

'Hey, how ya doin?'

He answered with a question. 'You are from South Philadelphia, are you not?'

He was nearly six feet tall, this kid, and must have weighed a good fifty pounds more than I did. He had strange black eyebrows and a blond crewcut. His brown eyes seemed to float behind thick glasses.

'Yeah, you got it. That's where I'm from. What about it?'

'Why don't you go back to where you came from?'

'Listen, fatso. I'd go back if I could, don't worry.'

Given his size, I thought I might be at a definite disadvantage if push came to you-know-what, so, wishing to avoid trouble, I turned, like peace-loving Gary Cooper, only shorter, to be on my way.

'My mother says only trash comes from South Philadelphia.'

There was no hesitation among the impulses this time; they had a rocket ride along the nerve route to the finish line. In other words, I stopped on a dime, pushed off my right foot, pivoted, and brought my right fist up on an arc that ended flush on his nose. A perfect punch and, big as he was, it knocked him off his feet and on his prat.

His glasses dangled from his ear and he looked up at me with a stunned expression, as if to say, 'What happened?'

He put a paw up to his nose and winced. He next looked disbelievingly at the blood on his fingers. I stood, waiting for his next move, that turned out to be rather comical. Rather, it was hilarious. The overgrown goof scuttled away on his ass and didn't stop doing so until he had put another ten feet between us. Then he got up and ran.[6]

On his lunch break Christy's mother had asked him how his first morning in school had gone. Three minutes after the one o'clock bell to return to school, he heard a disembodied voice from a PA system asking him to report to the principal's office. There stood the principal, the kid who Christy had punched holding a Kleenex over his nose, and the kid's mother, 'whose eyes were shooting daggers at me.' The head teacher was clearly intimidated by the wild, gesticulating woman in his presence. It turned out that her precious boy had been a big deal on national television game shows that brought prestige to Springfield, and although Christy suspected that the head believed his story, "justice" had to be seen to be done to dissipate the irate mother's demands for vengeance:

> 'This ...this hoodlum....' She gave me a look designed to wither.
> '...savagely attacked my Walter without provocation. He undoubtedly heard about Walter's success and hoped he was carrying money. You know how his kind thinks. When Walter stood up for himself, the hoodlum assaulted him viciously. ... Thank heavens my Walter was able to get away from him.' 'Yeah,' I said to myself, 'by doing a hell of a good imitation of a terrified crab.'[7]

Christy protested and even suggested that Walter be asked to give his own account of events, but the mother was having none of it. The upshot was that Christy was suspended from school for the rest of the week, during which time his own mother's wrath knew no bounds: "This boy was in a world of trouble. This boy was kept in the house for an entire week, except to be marched half a mile to the barbershop, to get the idiot crewcut. Back home, I wasn't even allowed into the yard for exercise that even convicts got."[8]

Christy took some small degree of comfort from the fact that he had set an all-time Scenic Heights record: "Shortest time enrolled in school before suspension: three hours, forty-six minutes." As an afterword, Christy recalls bumping into Walter on a streetcar in Philadelphia years later but Walter never brought the incident up. Christy describes how the very fact of being different was the cause of all his troubles. "There was a hideous obsession with the rest of them about fitting in. The staff, teachers and coaches went along with that. It was the kind of place where if they had shown *Rebel Without a Cause*, the kids would have booed James Dean."[9]

Now one would have thought that a James Dean character such as Christy would have attracted attention from some of his female classmates, even if he alienated himself from the boys. Not a bit of it; Springfield was an unforgivingly conservative town to its very core and his female classmates were budding "Stepford Wives" with no interest in a foreigner from South Philadelphia. In the passage from *Brookdale* that follows, Christy relates a very bizarre and abusive practice at the school that involved the pupils maintaining notebooks in which one imagines they were supposed to "assess" each other's attributes. The result was a particularly malevolent form of bullying that one cannot imagine schoolteachers condoning today—although, hurtful as it must have been, to the battle-hardened Christy it provided no more than idle amusement at his own expense.

> There were these horrible black and white-speckled notebooks that were passed around in the classroom, making their malicious ways up and down the rows. They were sort of assessment records of and by one's fellows. Each kid had a page. Each kid got to rate the other kids. You put down your comments, drew a line under them, and added your number. At the back of the book was an alphabetical listing of students showing each individual's number. You were thus able to ascertain who was saying these things about you.

In addition to the student pages, there were other ones with headings like "Biggest Creep" and "Flattest Girl."

I took a masochistic delight in looking up my page, although not every day. At least, they thought *something* about me, enough that their comments had to carry over onto another page. I was the only student honoured with two pages.

[...]

At Scenic Heights some kids only had a few measly comments under their names. These were your average kids whom no one hated and for whom no one had any particular affection. They weren't ugly or pretty, were neither brains or what were called fairies. No letters on their sweaters. They went about their business so matter-of-factly that twenty years later when you came across their photographs in the yearbook, you'd say, 'Who's that guy? I don't remember him at all.'

Not me. No sirree Bob. Coming upon my countenance, they'd chortle, 'Christ! That creep! Uggghhh!'

What they said back then in those black and white-speckled notebooks was a lot worse. It ranged from 'World's Biggest Jerk' to 'Worst Looking Kid in School' through 'How far did you have to chase him for those clothes?' to the more inventive response to the question: 'Would you go out with him?'—the answer being, I swear to God, 'Sure if I was a blind nigger with polio.'[10]

Christy only ever had one date, Linda Johnston, a girl whose looks and personality he describes as intimidating the other boys—but not Christy, who invited her to the high school prom. He describes it as a chaste date with one goodnight kiss, and that the girl eventually went on to become a Rockette in Manhattan's Radio City Music Hall. Christy describes one other girl he was sweet on during his high school days, Patti Simpson, who confessed to Christy later that she liked him too, but that she could not go out with him while they were in school for fear of ruining her reputation. Patti contacted Christy sometime after they graduated to ask if he would escort her to a wedding in Philadelphia. He did, after which Christy took her out for supper to Cous,[11] a mob-owned restaurant in South Philadelphia—paltry recompense for the misery of his high school days. Apart from one girl that Christy used to see from the neighboring town of Media, the only real lovemaking Christy enjoyed during his schooldays in Springfield was with older women who hit on him, such as a math teacher with polio hired by his parents for extra tuition in algebra and, aged sixteen, a customer on his rounds as a van driver. Christy later reflected on his relationship with his classmates, noting that to be accepted, to be one of them, you had to act in a boorish manner: make fun of other students who had some flaw, guffaw if a girl fell, dropped her books, and showed her underwear, that kind of thing. Christy had no time for such juvenile behavior:

> To me these guys, and the girls, were just immature. If they had been immature and pleasant, that would have been just fine. I was willing to make allowances. At first they thought I was backward because I wasn't like they were. They assumed I didn't know how to be like them, like I studied it but was too dumb or un-savvy to get it right. Later, when they got hip to the fact that I didn't want to be like them, well, that just made it worse.[12]

Christy's mother was delighted with the move from South Philadelphia to the white suburbs. She was a proud Virginian and liked to let on to folk that she was descended from the FFV (First Families of Virginia), even claiming that Springfield was a few steps down the social ladder from her Virginian home. But from her arrival in Springfield she became a changed woman:

> ...her jaw didn't unclench for weeks nor her eyes cease to blaze. It scared me to see the—what?—hatred in them. The house was occupied by an unseen presence, like fetid swamp air from a horror movie. It got into everything, it was there creeping between the carpet and the floorboards, wiggling through the string beans in their compartment of the Swanson TV Dinner trays; it was there when you turned on the lamp, it contorted Ed Sullivan's features on Sunday night, and Topo Gigio's, too.[13]

In contrast, Christy describes his father as a broken man who never really recovered being wrenched away from his streets, his relatives, and his work with the Philadelphia "family." "Ever since the big shot with the silver hair paid a visit to our Ritner Street kitchen, pops was a changed fellow, sort of like he had gone away." We know of Christy's relationship with his mother—she was fairly tyrannical toward all the menfolk in her family—but the following unpublished piece by Christy, *Rolling Hill Road*, provides a rare insight into Christy's relationship with his father:

I walked to the top of Rolling Hill Road to look down at the town I despised. It didn't look any better from up there. I'd crossed Indian Lane in my climb and remembered asking my father if there'd actually been Indians around here. He said there had been but they'd had to be destroyed to make way for civilization. I surveyed civilization below, the cul-de-sacs and the crescents, the split levels and colonials, the inter-urban trolley line that carried unhappy looking commuters into Philadelphia and back. I looked down and back and forth. Sometimes I was there just past dawn, other times far into the night. The little trolley traveled through that progress, that civilization with its auto-upholstery shops, carpet cleaning concerns, and a Bob's Big Boy where you could get a hamburger sort of like the one in the chubby fingered hand of "Bob" himself bulging out of his convertible.

‘So how were the Indians destroyed?' I asked. ‘In battles with the Cavalry?'

‘No. We gave them blankets infected with smallpox and sometimes we invited them in for a pow wow, and then we opened fire.'

‘That wasn't fair.'

‘Yeah? Well think of how many lives that saved. If it had been a regular fight, lots of our people would have been killed. They were savages anyway. We built this country.'

He was overlooking the existence of my half-Indian grandmother, not his mother. She was Rappahannock, from southern Virginia, same tribe as Pocahontas. I mentioned her, saying maybe she'd scalp him in the night but not me since I had a little of that blood in my veins. He waved me off, with that dismissive peasant Italian gesture that was so familiar.

‘Where are all the Indians these days?'

‘On Reservations out west.'

'Sort of like the Italians born and raised in South Philadelphia who were put in concentration camps in the good old U.S.A.'

That got him angry, and he told me I was a wiseass little punk too smart for my own good. I was fourteen years old and miserable. I had already run away from home three times in the last year or so and was ready to do it again.[14]

The most notable of these adventures had happened over a year previously, soon after commencement of the school holidays in July, 1958. Christy had enacted his pledge to run away from Springfield and embark on his most audacious adventure to date. His parents were due to depart for Virginia on holiday and Christy persuaded them to let him stay behind in Springfield with his one and only school friend, Robert Garzarelli,[15] making up an elaborate excuse about how a trip to Virginia would interfere with his baseball career. Robby had had to ask his mother to phone Christy's mother to verify the story. Mrs. Garzarelli had some kind of mental illness and used to sit in front of the TV all day watching the pictures with the sound off, while her three kids were in the background all tuned in to different radio stations:

'Hey, Ma. Ma!' Robby screamed at her. 'Jim's gonna run away from home so you got to call his mother and pretend he'll be staying with us for three weeks.' ... Mrs. Garzarelli went to the phone and spoke with my mother like both of them were normal.[16]

The plan was that both boys would head out hitchhiking and bumming rides on trains together, but by the time they got to the outskirts of Wilmington, seventeen miles away, Robby backed out, leaving Christy to continue on alone.

I got as far west as Chillicothe, Ohio and for a reason I no longer remember, turned north. It didn't matter where I went, it was all an adventure. In Reading,

Pennsylvania, I had slept in the bins out back of Hess Brothers' Department Store and was awakened by the screams of the guy who opened the lids to dump cardboard in those same bins. Wasn't expecting to see a twelve year old in there.

I hitched rides and even rode a freight train once. All the drivers were friendly. I always had a story for them, usually that I was going to my grandmother's house or to see the baseball game at such-and-such a town, which I had read up on in the paper of the town I had started from that morning. At night, I usually slept in fields or the roadside woods. I still had shoeshine money but wouldn't have risked getting a hotel room. Anyway, it was more fun sleeping under the stars.[17]

From there he traveled to New York and six weeks after absconding found himself at the American end of the Niagara Falls bridge. He was trying to figure out how to get into Canada without papers when a character he describes as looking like a rugged version of Ronald Colman came striding toward the American side of the bridge tapping a cane before him. "He was wearing a short leather jacket and an ascot in August and the toe of one of his army boots was wrapped with electrician's tape."[18] The passage that follows is from another of Christy's unpublished works, *Reet, Petite, and Gone*.

> He stopped suddenly, gave the sidewalk a peremptory poke with the tip of his lacquered black cane and fixed me with an imperious gaze.... He was haughty as could be, this fellow I had been laughing at as he came stepping along from the Canada side as if heading a military parade. ... His hair was wavy and steel grey. He had a pencil line moustache.
>
> [...]
>
> He couldn't have heard me laughing, what with Niagara Falls roaring like that, and the whole time I had been digging him, he was staring straight ahead. Yet, notice me he did, and stopped and I stopped. I was silent for half a minute and perhaps a bit intimidated, he being—to my mind—an obvious nut and maybe a trifle dangerous, and me being twelve years old.[19] But as soon as he spoke the tension broke. He didn't say, 'What the hell you laughing at, kid?' But, rather, 'May I enquire as to the subject of your mirth?' And me being a smart alec, answered, 'You just did.' [20]

As would happen many times during his wanderings—those situations where one instantly recognizes a kindred spirit—an immediate bond of comradeship struck up between the child and the adult vagabond. Furthermore, each had been equally amused by the demeanor of the other. The aging tramp informed Christy that he was just returning from Toronto where he had visited a former servant from his motherland. And in turn, Christy told the elderly hobo that he had run away from home:

> From day one I wanted no part of it, and nothing happened to change my mind. I bided my time until the summer when school let out and my parents went away for a couple of weeks, down to Virginia where my mother came from, and let me stay at a friend's house. Immediately, I flew the coop.
>
> 'And here I am,' I told the Count. 'I mean, I mean, after all that stuff in Philadelphia, that kind of action, get my meaning, I just can't make it in goddamned Brookdale.'
>
> [...]
>
> My folks were due home a week ago but they probably cut their holiday short when they couldn't reach me by telephone at my pal's home. By now the cops were looking for me, "all-points bulletins" had gone out like in the movies. I tried to feel guilty for hurting them but reasoned that I couldn't feel any worse than I had being there in Brookdale.[21]

Instead of showing concern for Christy's plight, or suggesting strategies to reunite the young runaway with his family, his new acquaintance treated Christy as a fellow gentleman of the road. Christy, clearly confused by all this talk of a country estate and servants running around, assuming also that the old man's accent was Canadian, ventured,

> 'And all this was over there in the motherland, in Canada?'
>
> 'Goodness gracious, no. This was in Mother Russia.'
>
> 'Russia! Holy shit!' thought I. They had come into my kindergarten class and taken away the teacher because she knew about Russia and here was I standing on a bridge talking to a guy from there.[22]

This is how Christy met the aging Russian Count Navrotolov, or Navratilini (Christy can only accurately recall the "Nav" part of the name). Most of the Count's family, including his mother and father, had been slain in the 1917 revolution fighting against the Bolsheviks. He also became separated from his sister, whom he never saw again. After having to abandon his university education, the Count had subsequently served as a soldier for three or four countries, as well as the French Foreign Legion.

The friendship between the Count and the former servant of his family estate requires some explanation. On first encountering Kalju again in the West, the Count had had to consider whether the former serf had, on the side of the Bolsheviks, been involved in the looting and burning of his former employer's home, even in murdering the Count's father and mother. But such doubts were soon cast aside on hearing Kalju's own tale. The Count learned that the proletariat utopia had been supplanted some years later with a new form of tyranny. Kalju was sent to work on a potato farm but the leaders of the revolution, in their wisdom, decided that peasants should work in factories and factory workers move to farms. And so Kalju was relocated to work in a ball bearing factory in the Ukraine. As the Count recalls:

> It was nothing more than slavery. A brutal joke perpetrated on the
> poor people by their saviours. And where did Stalin get the idea for
> this slave system? ... From the factories of capitalist America![23]

Kalju managed to escape to the Baltic but was conscripted by the Nazis until the Russians reinvaded occupied Estonia in 1944. After the war he was kept at an internment camp in England, then worked in the South Wales coal mines, before eventually making it to the Canadian Northwest Territories. The Count had first bumped into Kalju on a street in London, England, before renewing their relationship again in Canada. By now, they both shared a common bond as Soviet exiles, although for very different reasons: "The nobleman and the serf. Living testimony to the propaganda of the revolution. It did indeed render us equals." At the time of Christy's meeting with the Count, Kalju was living in a boarding house in an immigrant area of Toronto, surviving on odd jobs and spending his earnings in a drinking club frequented by other economic and political fugitives from Russian expansionism:

> They drink. They quarrel. They drink some more and fight the old
> battles. Each becomes bellicose when the memories take hold.

And each stumbles home like Silenus. They are all united, however, in their utter hatred of the Soviets.[24]

Below is another story the Count related to Christy, in this case concerning the Count's sexual exploits in Siberia, one that also removed the road kid's last, lingering doubt about his new companion's sexual proclivities:

'I had an eye for the ladies. Even in those Arctic climes. I still do.'
That I was extremely glad to hear. What with him being a Russian and the stuff my mother had told me about certain grown men where little boys were concerned.

'An eye, if not a terrible lot of opportunities. One evening at a small settlement on the steppes, a young Eskimo girl entered my hut, approaching me with one upraised and clenched fist. I reckoned she was about to have a punch at me. But, no; she threw at me the contents of her hand. And what do you suppose her fist had enclosed?'
'Search me.'
'Curious choice of words. Lice. She threw at me a handful of lice.'
'Lice? No kidding? Geeze, you must have really offended this Eskimo, huh?'
'I had offended her not. The opposite, in fact, as it turned out. This, you see, was and perhaps still is, the way the young ladies make known their desires. One throws love at the object of one's affection. My lice are your lice, sort of thing.'[25]

The Count would make a lasting impression on Christy, not least persuading him to take up reading literature. In any case, the two struck up an immediate friendship and the Count suggested that as "there was no sense standing there betwixt and between ... I might accompany him on a walk if I saw fit. So off we went." It took the pair a week to walk the sixty miles to Albion, as the Count had to make the rounds of every trash bin along the route; for which reason, as Christy would discover later, the Count had earned the moniker Count Garbáge:

We tramped and we talked, our gait broken only when the Count paused to scrounge. Spark plugs, toggle switches, chrome backed

side view mirrors, mechanical pencils without lead, rubber
soldiers, and hunks of metal twisted into intriguing shapes by the
passing traffic, all of these engaged his wonder.[26]

Christy soon joined in on the scavenging and one day came across a novel
about sailing ships with the cover and half the pages missing. He offered it to
the Count all the same, from which innocent exchange came a very profound
statement: "You probably won't want it on account of it ends on page 73 in the
middle of a sentence." "Doesn't matter in the least. The book is like life itself."[27]

And so on they trudged and rummaged, all the while bearing insults of
"dirty hobos" from kids roaring past and throwing beer cans at them through
car windows. But the Count seemed oblivious to such taunts, as though
being pelted with beer cans "was the most natural thing in the world.... To
all obscenities, he was deaf." Some nights the pair slept rough, but on others
they would seek hospitality. One night they came across one of those long
stainless steel diners resembling a Pullman coach:

> The windows needed washing and the paint was chipped and
> faded on the cement steps out front. A woman, maybe fifty years
> old with plenty of make-up and bleached blond hair, sat at the
> counter drinking coffee.[28]

After having soup with a bread roll, the Count announced to Christy that
he had arranged for them to sleep the night at the diner, Christy in one of the
booths while the Count disappeared out back with their hostess to her trailer.
After the adults had retired, the young hobo made the most of his situation,
helping himself to a White Owl cigar and half a bottle of wine that had been
left out. After putting five nickels in the jukebox, he then settled into the corner
booth with his smoke and a tea cup from which to drink the wine.

One night, after sleeping out rough, a simple bit of foraging by the Count
was to have a lasting effect on Christy. That afternoon, the Count picked up
a letter from the sidewalk written by a girl who had gone away to college
and was writing home to her friend. The young and old hobos discussed the
letter from every possible angle, creating different possible narratives about
the two friends:

These are the true literature, these letters I find lying about.
Yes, my great regret is that I have not been able to maintain a
collection over the years. Being peripatetic, you see.... Perhaps I
might have printed them in one volume someday. I have found
them everywhere. Particular favourites I carry about on my
person for weeks, months, years, in some cases, tucked away in
my billfold. Joyful, commonplace, unnerving, pretentious, tragic,
excruciatingly boring, and comic. Again, like life itself, and that
is the point and why I pick them up. I would call my book Pages
From the Sidewalks of Life. What do you think of that?[29]

And so it was on an instinct thirteen years later that Christy stooped down
to pick up a letter from the sidewalk of a Vancouver street, a dinner invitation
from the lieutenant-governor of the city. He has picked up hundreds of such
letters and fragments of letters over the years. "I don't pick up laundry lists
or shopping lists or advertisements, just correspondence between actual
human beings." Letters picked up from where they were dropped, found
their way to him via someone's possessions, the wind, a garbage collection,
et cetera. Some letters were found in places bearing no connection to either
the sender or the recipient. Each letter tells part of a story about the lives of
random people unknown to their new reader. Nevertheless, now and again,
Christy would select a letter or two to ponder over and wonder about the
lives of those involved.

But, unlike the Count, who had discarded or abandoned hundreds of these
letters over the years, Christy kept hundreds in three thick folders on his desk.
He continues to reflect on the stories and fates of the letters' characters, and
has even contemplated writing a full volume himself, also titled *Pages from the
Sidewalks of Life*. For the time being, a few of these fascinating epistles can be
read in the chapter by that name in *Between the Meridians*.[30] Christy laments
that, with the advent of electronic text of various forms, "most people don't
write letters anymore." And furthermore, "When are they even on the street?"

But back to the story of the Count. Christy continued to travel with him to
Albion, where they stayed at the house of a Russian friend of the Count's, Alexi
Koschev, who traded in books from a very hot house where the air "came at
you like walls closing in, laden with the odour of fish, cigarettes and unwashed
body." Christy, while grateful for a place to stay the night, was relieved for
the opportunity to get some fresh air when Alexi asked if he would pop to

the store to get some pretzels—specifying Bavarian pretzels—to go with the vodka he was in the process of pouring out. But Christy nearly got busted as a runaway when a cop apprehended him for stealing the pretzels. When the storekeeper confirmed that the pretzels had been paid for, the cop, irate at not having made an arrest, looked around for another excuse to persecute Christy:

> He got hopeful again when he discovered where I was headed.
> 'That Commie, huh?'
> I told him I was in the company of my uncle.
>
> 'Is he a Commie too?'
> 'No, the both of them, they hate the Commies.'
> 'Oh, yeah? We'll see about that.'
>
> Into the backseat of the cruiser I went. ... He battered the door with his stick and Koschev opened up.... 'Where's my uncle?' ... The count appeared and picked up immediately.
>
> 'Ah! My little nephew returned from the store and—allo!—an officer with him! Can I be of some assistance, sir?'
> 'Yeah, this here punk with you?'
> 'My nephew is with me. What seems to be the problem?' ... The Count was a good six inches shorter than the cop but managed to look down on him.
> 'Plenty suspicious characters around.'
> 'Yes, you are certainly right about that.'[31]

Even though Christy had escaped the clutches of the law once again, he got the feeling that the cops were closing in on him. "They had stopped me plenty of times in the last few weeks." Furthermore, school would be starting in a week's time and, because the truant officers would be making their rounds again, "it wouldn't do to be walking down the road in the middle of the day." The Count had told Christy that he was on his way to work for another Russian aristocrat. She had offered him the position as "groundskeeper of her run-down property ... a polite way of offering the Count a home, if he wanted one." And so Christy, having to make alternative plans, decided to pick up with his old pal Baseball George in Leon's bar, opposite the Trocadero in downtown

Philadelphia, and tour the country with him to watch the ball games. The Count approved of the plan, never at any time encouraging Christy to return home or to school.

Alexi was to drive the Count to his new home, and reluctantly agreed to drop Christy off at the turn-off for the Philadelphia road. Before they parted, the Count gave Christy a large package wrapped in brown paper. After waving the Count off, Christy unwrapped the package to reveal a photograph of the Count as a dashing young officer, dressed in French Foreign Legion uniform bedecked with medals, and with "a familiar twinkle in his eye." Christy later framed the photograph and proudly displayed it in whatever apartment he happened to be residing in, until eventually someone stole it. Christy ends the piece in *Between the Meridians* by saying that he hoped it would one day be thrown away, adding, "Perhaps someday it will turn up, there on the sidewalk."

But what of Christy's plan to go on the road with Baseball George? On arriving in downtown Philadelphia and Leon's bar, he was met with the sad news that George had collapsed and died in the middle of a baseball game in Wrigley Field Stadium, Chicago. A good ending for George but Christy's plans were now scuppered. That night he slept on a bench in Independence Mall only to be awakened early by the stabbing finger of a uniformed police officer, thrusting a photograph of the fugitive, complete with description, in Christy's face:

> 'You know,' he said, studying the photograph, 'you look better since your hair grew out.'
> 'Yeah, tell that to my mother.'
> 'You tell her. We're gonna see her soon. I'm afraid it's all over, kid.'
> 'Don't bet on it.'
> He laughed, 'Let's go.'[32]

In spite of the punishments Christy brought down on himself for running away from home and school, the wanderlust was to prove too powerful a pull to resist. The following spring, Christy ran away again after reading a Sunday magazine supplement about the Beat Generation. He had been idly flipping through the pages of the magazine and was about to get on with the chores his mother had set him when his attention was caught by some colored photographs of "very curious people arranged in sundry positions on old furniture under paintings that were huge explosions of colour."

And the people: guys with beards or hoodlum types dressed like lumberjacks, girls in men's white shirts with nothing on below except black leotards. I read the captions and discovered the girls were called chicks, the men cats, and together they were known as beatniks. They lived in pads, these "hirsute habitués of the demimonde," whatever the hell that meant.[33]

The article went on to describe a lifestyle that rejected "the American Way of Life," substituting in its place a rootless, peripatetic lifestyle fueled by wine, marijuana, folk music, jazz and "free sex." But what particularly caught Christy's eye was that although the movement reportedly emerged in San Francisco's North Beach and New York's Greenwich Village, a new group had recently taken hold in Philadelphia. Sure enough, there was photo of a couple of these beatniks sitting on the edge of a fountain with the caption, "Right: Cat and chick strike 'cool' pose in Rittenhouse Square." At which point Christy was jerked from the fascinating prospect of becoming a beatnik by his mother's voice telling him to change his clothes and attend to his chores in the yard, but not before picking up some items from the store.

On his way out through the door with money for the groceries, Christy grabbed his six-year-old brother by the hand and shouted back at his mother that he was taking David with him. After getting the purchases, Christy shoved the bag into David's hands, told him to go straight home and give the stuff to his mother, and then set off to the local interurban station to wait for the next trolley into Philadelphia.

After walking around Rittenhouse Square for a while looking for beatnik types, Christy spotted a likely candidate: "he was wearing a red and white striped t-shirt, scarf knotted at the neck, jeans, sandals without socks, and he was carrying a book." The guy had a thick mop of orange hair and as he sat on the edge of the fountain and opened his book, Christy approached him. "Hey, man, there a coffee shop around here?" An extended version of the conversation that followed can be read in the final chapter of Christy's *Travelin Light*, but after the beatnik's initial indifference to being accosted by the thirteen-year-old, by the time Christy had related the story of his recent tramp with the Count, it was the beatnik who was in awe of him. After their conversation, Barney, the redhead, took the junior hobo along to introduce him to his companions. First they went to a place called the Palette on Locust Street where a guy sat tuning his guitar under a spotlight and "variations of the people in the magazine article sat at tables trying to look exceedingly bored." Barney started introducing Christy around the place eliciting some nods, much indifference, and—forgetting her cool—a chirpy "Hiya!" from a girl with raccoon-shadowed eyes who promptly shut up when her male partner glared at her.

It was not long though before the aura of cool started to wane a bit for the streetwise Christy. Barney told him that the carrot cake in the place was excellent. "Carrot cake? You kidding me, Barn? They make cake out of carrots? C'mon." But Barney insisted so Christy used some of the change he'd kept from his mother's groceries to participate in this new culinary experience, and all the while the guy under the spotlight was still tuning his guitar.

> A year and a half before I was running a numbers racket and pulling jobs and now I was eating carrot cake. What would my old pals Louis Scarface and Nicky Blue think if they saw me? Well they weren't going to see me because they were not about to come into a place like this unless it was on business, business of a larcenous nature.[34]

Christy's attention was then distracted by "a six foot blonde wearing a black t-shirt, jodhpurs and riding boots ... as if she had just come from the sporting goods department of Lit Brothers." As she came "shuddering" toward their table, Christy muttered out of the corner of his mouth to Barney, "I don't believe it." Barney responded, "Jim, I want you to meet Jennifer, my girl." To which Jennifer replied, "Let's leave this place Barney, it's so ersatz." "Right," says Barney, "We'll cut over to the Cave." On their way over to the Cave, a cellar coffee bar appropriately sited for Philadelphia's underground inhabitants, Jennifer engaged Christy in conversation about her studies in German Literature at Bryn Mawr where she was reading Schlegel. Christy told her that he knew lots of Schlegels—there being a sizeable Jewish as well as Italian community in South Philadelphia:

> Used to have a pal named Knocky Schlegel, had a big scar across his right eye. Still has it, I'm sure. Coloured kid sliced him right down the face with a blade only, luckily, Knocky had his eye closed real tight, so his eye is okay but the scar looks weird because it goes right to the edge of the eye top and bottom, kind of like a road to the river when the bridge has been washed out.[35]

Two different universes of discourse had collided, with Jennifer ignoring Christy's description of Knocky Schlegel to counter that the only Schlegels she was interested in were Karl Wilhelm, his brother August Wilhelm the critic, and their uncle, the famous dramatist Johann Elias. Christy couldn't care less but he politely replied, "Some family." Not a good move, because Jennifer then treated him to a detailed description of the entire extended Schlegel family, before launching into a history of the Romantics.

Barney tried to salvage the situation by saying to Jennifer, "Uh Jen, Jim here is only thirteen." To which she responded, "Oh, he certainly doesn't act thirteen," and continued with the philosophy lecture that would have gone on unabated but for their timely arrival at The Cave. After the place closed down the trio took a moonlit walk across the Chestnut Street Bridge to the pad in Powelton Village that Barney and Jennifer shared with another couple, Marty and Gwen, on the third floor of the decayed grandeur of a huge nineteenth-century townhouse. In the morning Christy made a deal with Marty and Gwen that he could crash on their sofa in return for washing the dishes and keeping the place clean.

Christy stayed with the beatniks for six weeks. In order to occupy himself during the day—these beats held down jobs and studies—and to avoid downtown for fear of being picked up by the cops for truancy, Christy's daily routine involved cutting over to the black neighborhoods in West Philadelphia and walking along Market Street in the shadow of the El tracks, reading the *Daily News* over a coffee and sinker in the Horn & Hardart, checking out the contents of the pawn shops, then in the afternoons going to the movies "with the juicers and the ladies killing time till Bingo started." Later he would return to the coffee shops where he would meet up with Barney and Jennifer and hang out with other beatniks who by now had adopted him as a junior member of their tribe, often inviting him to sit at their tables to listen to his jive.

All good things eventually come to an end, though not in the climactic series of events that now followed. First Christy got high on marijuana and made a hallucinatory trip across the Chestnut Street Bridge, the edges of which Christy was hanging onto for dear life since by that time it had become a swaying rope bridge bucking and dipping into the water. The following morning Christy was full of the joys of beatdom, life was good, and was about to get better. He and Gwen were alone in the apartment and over coffee she started telling Christy how bored she was with her life, worse still she was only having sex with Marty twice a week—so much for the "free sex" part of the beatnik life. Gwen said to Christy that, "advanced" as he might be, he could not understand what a deprivation this was: "I mean, being a virgin, twice a week may sound great to you but let me tell you, it isn't." Christy put Gwen straight that he wasn't a virgin but that twice a week still sounded pretty good. Gwen asked Christy if he had enjoyed making love and got the reply, "Yeah, I liked it. And I fully intend to try it again someday if the opportunity ever presents itself." Well, Gwen did not need any more encouragement than that and the pair spent the rest of the day in bed together. Sitting in The Cave later, Barney told Christy that he could no longer crash at Gwen and Marty's. Free love was clearly not on Marty's manifesto, because on being told by Gwen how she'd spent the day, the two had an almighty fight and Barney came over to warn Christy not to return to the pad. But it was not Christy's lovemaking that ended his stay with his newfound friends. A moment later, the door of The Cave burst open and six cops, four in uniform, two plain-clothed, burst in.

> They moved through the narrow room upending tables, tossing chairs, pulling paintings from the walls, scattering beatniks like ten pins. For a moment I sat stunned, watching them; then I got caught up in the action. I caught an open hander and hit the deck. A table fell on top of me.

From his vantage point under the table Christy watched the rest of the action. The singer's guitar was wrenched from his arms and stomped on, the owner was knocked to the floor unconscious after trying to protect his espresso machine—which was pushed to the floor and smashed—and all those in the coffee bar, Christy included, were summarily arrested and carted off to jail where they spent several days while the cops tried to pin various charges on them. Christy himself was interrogated about whether he smoked marijuana, was a communist, a pinko, and, when they discovered his age, whether he could help them pin a morals charge on the older beatniks. Not because Christy had been taken advantage of by a twenty-three-year-old female—with little persuasion by the former; no, their sole interest was adding charges of homosexuality to the list of un-American activities, wanting to know whether Christy had been taken advantage of by any of the men. The outcome of the arrests was even more bizarre than the bust itself. Christy had been puzzling where he had seen the lead cop before. "He went about six foot six, 250 and had a mug that looked like he had hidden in a cave during the evolution."

The cops had invited the press to the police station to write up a piece about how they were "ridding the city of brotherly-you-know-what of communist-inspired atheism and perversion. Can't have all those ne'er-do-wells flaunting their disrespect for this country, and here in the very cradle of its liberty." But a rogue journalist covering the beatnik bust called into question the actions of Inspector Frank Rizzo who led the raid, referring to his reputation as a "cowboy" and his nickname on the inside as the Cisco Kid. The reporter gave two versions of how the inspector came by his moniker. One that he carried a pearl-handled revolver, the other that several years earlier a kid had given him the name after watching Rizzo running down a bad guy.

It then dawned on Christy where he had come across the inspector, then a sergeant, before. He was that kid! Some six years back, Christy had been on Christian Street in South Philadelphia between Fourth and Fifth when a guy tried to hold up a corner store. As the cops went into the front door, the thief flew out the back and down an alley with the cops in hot pursuit. In spite of the weight he carried, the neanderthal Rizzo managed to keep pace with the fleeing fugitive while his less fit colleagues were bending over gasping for breath. Christy, who witnessed the whole scene, said to the other cops. "Da Cisco Kid'll get him, don't worry." The other cops burst out laughing. "At's pretty good. Da Cisco Kid. Pretty funny. Just da name for da Sarge." After collaring the crook and pushing him into the cruiser, his colleagues laid into him mercilessly. "Yo Ceesco! Nice work, Ceesco." They told Rizzo what Christy had said, adding, "Wait'll we get it around da precinct. Da Cisco Kid!" Christy's last sight of Rizzo was the cop cocking his thumb at him through the open cruiser window and giving him a wink as they drove off.

It was reading the coverage of the incident and remembering the wink that jogged Christy's memory and made him wonder if there was a spark of humanity hidden away somewhere inside the brutish cop. So Christy plucked up the courage to have a word with the inspector in private and reminded the astounded cop of the incident and how he had come by his nickname. After recounting the good old days in South Philadelphia, the inspector returned half an hour later with a deal:

> I would be let out in the custody of my parents but I'd have to
> tell the papers, particularly that prick from the *Bulletin*, that the
> Inspector didn't get his nickname because he was a pearl-handled
> revolver-carrying cowboy but because of a cute bit of Norman

Rockwell Americana. 'And what about my friends?' 'I'll let them
faggots out too.'[36]

Christy's beatnik party had ended and he was confronted with the unwel-
come sight of his parents, "in the midst of wife beaters, child molesters, hookers,
grifters and grafters ... my old man obdurate and glowering, my mother with
quivering jaw muscles and eyes crackling with fury." And so it was from a
clutch of beatniks and reporters with notebooks and cameras, that Christy
was led "walking right out of jail and back to 'prison.' "

As for the Cisco Kid, Francis Lazarro "Frank" Rizzo went on to serve as
Philadelphia's police commissioner from 1968 to 1971, becoming mayor in
1972 on the ticket, according to Christy, "I'm gonna make Attila the Hun look
like a faggot."

Between these vagrant interludes away from school and his parents,
Christy did try hard to attend to his studies and get through high school, the
quicker to fulfill his traveling ambitions. Oddly, it never occurred to him at
the time that he could have just quit school in exchange for the permanent life
of a vagabond. So he stayed in school for as long as he could bear, and before
the impulse to decamp became irresistible once more. It has already been
mentioned that in addition to being afflicted by the wanderlust, Christy was
also captivated by society's oddballs and exiles, those authentic characters
who embraced their difference and to hell with the rest of society's narrow-
minded conventions and prejudices. On more than one occasion, both before
and during high school, Christy sought to satisfy his yearning for the strange
and exotic in the company of carnival "freaks" and "roughies," no doubt
stimulating his interest by reading *Amusement Business*, the weekly magazine
of the fairground, carnival and theme park trade.[37] More of Christy's carnival
adventures later, but it is worth noting here the respect and high regard Christy
had for carnival performers, and the disgust he felt toward those redneck
bigots who had morbid curiosity at best, at worst caused actual bodily harm,
or even murdered, those they described as "freaks of nature."

One particular sideshow performer who made a lasting impression on
Christy was Frances O'Connor. She had been born without arms and made her
livelihood appearing in carnivals demonstrating her skills at eating, drinking,
and smoking, using her feet. Christy was not to meet O'Connor for another year,
at the age of sixteen, and would meet her again at the age of eighteen when
making a trip down south with his parents. They had stopped at a Howard

Johnson's restaurant in Alexandria, Virginia, when O'Connor came in with some other circus folk. Again, it was the morbid curiosity that the performer attracted (including from his own folks) that roused Christy to anger:

> My main memory ... was not the view of her thighs and white panties that this afforded [O'Connor eating and drinking with her feet], but the stares of the other diners. The dumb and rude looks she got which shocked me and, later, when I worked in carnivals, I saw these people again, rubes staring at the freaks.[38]

O'Connor starred in the 1932 horror movie *Freaks*, directed by Tod Browning. The success of Browning's first film *Dracula* (1931) ensured his success in the movie industry, and hence freedom to produce *Freaks*. Like Christy, Browning also ran away to join the circus at sixteen, a clear influence on *Freaks*. But the original version of the movie was banned due to controversy over certain scenes and the use of its cast members. And although it had been Browning's intention to portray the carnival performers in a positive light, the reception of the final movie wrecked Browning's film career.

Christy's description of carnival life in "Alligator Man" from his book *Jackpots*[39] evokes similar scenes to those in Jim Tully's *Circus Parade* (1927), when local residents armed with tire irons, baseball bats, et cetera, descended on the carnival to wreak fear and havoc among the troupe. Their particular targets were the freaks of nature who provoke fear and loathing among certain sections of the provincially minded. According to Tully, it was not unusual for circus folk to lose their lives at the hands of local thugs, and having no family of their own, would receive all due rights and ceremony within their circus community. Unlike the rednecks described above, Christy had nothing but admiration and respect for carnival performers and wanted a part of the life. He spotted an advertisement for a roughie in *Amusement Business* for a show he calculated he could join at their tear-down in Kokomo, Indiana, but not before spending twenty-four hours in Canton County Jail, Ohio, for hitchhiking on the interstate and refusing to pay the fine.

The story of how Christy got arrested for jaywalking is one of his most absurd tales and is the subject of his poem "Suspicious Behaviour." After getting a lift from a "skinny black trucker" driving a Peterbilt semi-trailer, the driver asked Christy to take the wheel from the passenger side. Assuming that the driver needed to make some adjustments to his seat or reach for a thermos,

Christy took the wheel and focused his attention on the truck's hood and the six-lane highway rushing toward him. When the driver took the wheel again with one hand, Christy's attention shifted to the driver's work pants, now halfway to his knees exposing his "pale blue satin johnsons with lace trim" shrouding his prize possession at which he was now flailing away with his left hand accompanied by wild utterances of pleasure.

Christy forced his view back across the Peterbilt's hood at the highway stretching before him and then the view out of the right side window, not a convincing distraction given the driver's outbursts of ecstasy causing the truck to start lurching dangerously down the interstate. At this point in the poem Christy embellishes the absurdity of the situation with a spoof parody of a conversation between a helicopter traffic reporter and the station's anchorman coming over the airways through the Peterbilt's radio:

'Now, over to Jim in the Whirlybird
With the WXOX traffic report.'
'Thank you, Bob. Traffic's moving smoothly
On I-77, along the Canton-Akron corridor, except,
That is, for one old Peterbilt conventional.'
'What seems to be the problem. Jim?'
'Well, Bob, it appears the driver is abusing himself....'
'Abusing himself? You mean ....?'
'That's exactly what I mean, Bob. Right there
In front of God and six lanes of rush hour traffic
And he's not alone.'
'You mean, there're two self-abusers?'
'No, the passenger's pretending not to notice as the truck
Begins to lurch and jolt, like, you'll
Pardon the expression, a kangaroo....'
'A kangaroo, Jim?'
'That's right, Bob. A kangaroo trying to get
To the outhouse with a broken leg.'
'Very metaphorical or picturesque, or whatever
The hell it is Jim.'
'Thanks again, Bob. Now let me just add
That this kind of activity is definitely a traffic hazard,
You have to do something like that, pull over.

Pull over at a rest stop.'
'Jim, you mean, pull over if you have to pull it out,
Sort of thing.' 'Yes, thanks for the slogan, Bob. Folks,
Think of your fellow drivers or your passenger,
For heaven's sake.'[40]

Paralleling the finale of the driver's own performance, the truck bucked to a halt, stalling in the curb lane, and Christy got down from the cab to the driver's parting words—the latter wiping his hand on his heavy-duty green work pants—"That was some ride, say what, Whitey?" But it was not the driver who drew the attention of a highway patrol cruiser arriving that moment at the scene. As the truck lurched away up the highway, the officer, gun drawn, approached Christy. "Don't you know there's a law against hitchhiking on the interstate? You look suspicious boy. I'm going to have to take you in." If Christy had had any thoughts about explaining to the officer how he came to be standing on the interstate, he clearly thought the better of it and faced whatever was to follow his short but eventful ride.

After this abusive encounter with an altogether different kind of freak, and still aged only fifteen, Christy did make it to the carnival in time to help with the final tear-down and loading up for the next show. So it was that Christy found himself pulling up tent pegs in Dubuque, Iowa, with his new friend, Leland the Alligator Boy, when local rednecks decided to attack the carnival:

Most of the carnies engaged directly in the battle, others saw
to getting the freaks into trailers and trucks because they were
the operation's most valuable assets. The yokels no doubt told
themselves that they'd be striking a blow for America if they put
the boots to a pinhead. Only Jenny the fat lady got into any kind
of hand to hand combat but the dwarf, Big Marty, used his cut
down bow and arrow from a perch on the roof of a Mack cab and
protected by the rise of the trailer. The arrows were metal-tipped
and effective.[41]

The fight lasted about twenty minutes while the police just stood on the sidelines and watched. When the last remaining tent was set alight they stepped in to protect not the carnival property, but a nearby shopping center and truck park. Christy spent the rest of the night with Leland going over the events of that evening and drinking cheap brandy. After a month with the carnival, Christy left them at Denver with the intention of beating a train to San Francisco and there acquiring passage on a ship to Hawaii, but this trip would have to wait for a further five years.

In May of 1960, Christy surprised his mother (never having attended a school outing before) by pleading with her to allow him to go on a school trip to the Naval Academy in Annapolis, Maryland. But Christy's enthusiasm for joining the trip was not because he had any interest in becoming a naval cadet; Annapolis was the home of WEXI, "the radio station that I listened to at night in my room while supposedly doing my homework."[42] So keen was Christy to get to Annapolis that he even agreed to get his hair cut and wear the obligatory checked sports jacket and tie:

> It took only a couple of hours to get to Annapolis and, not
> surprisingly, I had a seat to myself. Staring out the window I tried
> to ignore the antics of my class mates who bopped each other on
> the head, let go the usual sounds of flatulence and made fun out
> loud of those below them in the hierarchy. And none was lower in
> the hierarchy than me.[43]

Christy had always felt exiled from mainstream society, even though he was, of course, a self-imposed exile. He had nothing but contempt for the vacuity of the human herd represented here by his classmates, who in turn, because of their stupidity, looked down on Christy. But he knew things, and imagined other things, that their tiny world of banality could never contemplate. The events that took place on this 1960 trip illustrate just the kind of outcast Christy was. His thirst for adventure always outweighed pragmatic considerations, in this case the trouble that would be brought down on his head for transgressing societal rules. For those with the wanderlust running through their veins, life is too short and mundane for happiness to be postponed. There is a sense of urgency, coupled with childish innocence to grab the moment when it presents itself. For tramps and Cynics alike, heaven can be acquired here on Earth, even if its pleasures are few and fleeting in an otherwise disappointing and disagreeable world. And so, while trudging in file through the streets of Annapolis with his classmates, all the time looking for signs of his favorite black recording artists, Christy eventually spotted a poster stapled to a telegraph pole advertising a live concert, including Bobby

Bland and Screamin' Jay Hawkins, to perform in town that very night. The bus was to leave for Springfield at five and the show started at eight, and Christy knew that if he disappeared from the crowd and stayed over, it would cause trouble, a lot of trouble. The dance probably wouldn't be over until midnight and with only six dollars in his pocket he'd also have to find a place to stay until morning. He had already calculated on the standard three-day suspension that would follow.

> Then there was the hassle on the home front. My mother would go on the rampage, suspend all privileges—such as they were—double the chores and, worst of all, keep referring to the incident for months. All that versus the chance to see Jay Hawkins, Bobby Blue Bland and the Ebonites, whoever they were. I considered both sides of the issue and made my decision. It took a New York minute.[44]

It is worth noting here a similar New York minute described by tramp-writer Josiah Flynt (1869–1907) in his autobiography *My Life*, published the year after his premature death brought on by alcoholism and cocaine addiction at the age of thirty-eight. A direct legacy of vagabond literature can be traced from Flynt, through Jack London, to Jack Kerouac, and from there to Jim Christy, each writer in turn being influenced by the former; except that, thankfully, the legacy of premature deaths from alcoholism ended with Kerouac. Here is the line in which Flynt describes his own decision to turn full-time hobo—having already had several tramping adventures and spells in jail between the ages of five and seventeen: "There was no long consideration of the matter, I merely quit on the spot; and when I knew that I had quit, that I was determined to live on what was mine or on nothing, the rest of the Road experience was a comparatively easy task."[45]

But to return to the concert, Screamin' Jay Hawkins' famous theatrics, such as appearing from inside a coffin on stage, are described in the first chapter of *Between the Meridians* titled "Spell on Me," a reference to Hawkins' hit, "I Put a Spell on You." The most painful part of the whole affair was not the fallout that would follow Christy's return home, it was having to attend the gig dressed like "the apex of Junior Jaycee fashion." But attend the show he did, and later walked around the dark Annapolis streets too excited to sleep, until finally crashing in a room at a black boarding house:

In the morning, after a breakfast of eggs, grits, side bacon, and
cornbread, everything sprinkled liberally with Louisiana hot sauce,
I hit the road, goosing the ghost towards home and another kind of
pandemonium that awaited me there.[46]

And it would be a full three weeks before Christy did arrive home, suffering
suspension from school and the wrath of his mother for his trouble. After this
episode of absconding, Christy became aware that for every unauthorized day
he spent out of school, three points were being deducted from each of his school
grades. He figured that if he carried on tramping, he would never graduate
and be free to follow his dreams. For this reason, Christy tried to confine his
wanderings to the weekends or vacation times when school was closed. Even
so, he was still getting into big trouble at home and suffering right up until
graduation. Then there was a three-month interlude in a place that no longer
exists and which Christy won't name, but he liked it better than he did high
school. This is how he describes it in *The Long Slow Death of Jack Kerouac*:

> I was a month from my seventeenth birthday, it was June, 1962, and I
> was no angel. I'd just been freed from custody after being wrongfully
> charged in an episode involving a car, another guy, his knife, and his
> girlfriend. Although my innocence was eventually established, it was
> obvious even to me that the path I was on led to more trouble and
> more after that. I would probably have some fun along the way, but I
> could already see the shadow of the Big House.[47]

Christy relates only one anecdote from his time in "the big house," as he
refers to it with a certain irony. He had previously been acquainted with this
Italian kid whom he met up with again in the big house. He describes Golf
Ball as having those 1960s teen idol looks of the Fabian variety that had girls
swooning at him, the more so because he drove around in a '54 Mercury two-
door hardtop. Christy describes how the kid secreted golf balls in the ashtray,
between the seats, and other convenient places in his car. When he took a
girl for a ride in his car and started petting, he would get himself aroused by
pushing a golf ball into her vagina. Presumably word got around via the young
women of the neighborhood amongst much sniggering. Hence the moniker.
But on meeting up again, Christy could not resist asking him why the golf
balls, particularly when the kid had everything else going for him. The kid's

response was that Christy must be some kind of idiot not to appreciate the finer arts of lovemaking. To add to the absurdity of the tale, Golf Ball had a friend he hung out with who had chronic acne boils evenly distributed on his face making his head resemble a golf ball, and so presumably deriving double the grief as a result. End of sporting digression.

If Christy had been wrongfully arrested on this occasion, he was, as he admits, no angel. Neither did his sojourn in the big house turn him into a reformed character. His love of cars did not stop at fixing them; he had been stealing cars since the age of fourteen. "Not for larcenous reasons, not to vandalise them, and not for the hell of it. I just loved cars, and couldn't wait two years to get my own driver's licence. I'd take them from parking lots, drive around, and return them later to another section of the same lot."[48] If Christy should get any credit here, it's not that he didn't trash the cars—the consequences would have been the same regardless of his motive or modus operandi—but that he was able to indulge his obsession without getting caught. Christy eventually obtained his driver's license on his sixteenth birthday, in July, 1961.

But to return to 1962, following his release from the big house, Christy got his old job back at the Bazaar of All Nations in neighboring Clifton Heights, making and selling caramel popcorn. And it was through a chance purchase at a bookstore in the Bazaar that Christy would discover his love of literature, at the same time validating his idiosyncratic persona. Christy had always been aware of his outcast status. Not fitting in with any tribe, the distinctions of which were "exactly defined and cruel," he acknowledges that he "was the guy least likely to have a date" back in Springfield, being neither "a brain, an athlete, a greaser, a straight-arrow, nor what was called a fairy."

As part of a three-for-a-quarter deal in the bookstore, Christy picked up a bio on Babe Ruth from the sports section for his brother, and two volumes at random from the section in the bookstore labeled "SSSEX!" Up until that time, Christy's reading had been confined to hot-rod magazines. But, heeding the Count's parting words to him to take up reading, Christy returned to the popcorn booth to start his education. After discarding the Babe Ruth bio, and getting bored with a book about a young kid's rise to pop stardom, complete with an illustration on the back cover of scantily clad bimbos posing on the ladder of his success, Christy became mesmerized with the third book which he described as "...characters careening across country in automobiles in search of kicks."[49] The book that had been carelessly tossed in the section marked "sex" for being unclassifiable was Jack Kerouac's On the Road.

In *On the Road*—its characters and its author—Christy at last found his tribe, his family, even if a common feature of that family was to be exiled from mainstream society, and sometimes from each other. Of course (at least for those who were straight or bisexual), they also shared some of the same preoccupations as the average American male: bars, fast cars, and the inside of bras. But they also represented everything that your average all-American hero, patriot and good ol' boy was not, with the kind of unconventional behavior, dress, and hairstyle that marked one out as "un-American"—a rather paradoxical designation considering that this was a nation built on cultural diversity and the pioneering spirit.

Of course, Christy had fully identified with Kerouac long before he'd ever heard of him: "I was prepared for *On the Road*. The experiences related therein were not entirely alien to me." But discovering Kerouac was the first time that Christy became aware of anyone else who shared his unorthodox obsessions: wanderlust, beating trains, unscheduled road trips, an affinity with the mad, the bad, and the outright weird, and a love of jazz—in those days, synonymous with being a communist. For the first time he realized that his interests and enthusiasms were not pathological as he'd been led to believe. They were, in fact, inclinations worthy of celebration in a book, "a book that was not merely anecdotal, a book I must have realised intuitively was important literature." But back to that singular moment sitting in the popcorn booth, being mesmerized for the first time by the written word was an experience that would later fuel his desire to become a writer himself:

> The back cover of the third book had a tiny photo of the author in the bottom left hand corner. He was a rugged-looking guy who needed a shave. ... I started reading. I was hooked from the first line. And that first line, the first page, even the way the page looked, has remained burned in my mind, just as the characters burned like roman candles. ... Immediately, I began to live with the characters in *On the Road*. I didn't read the book so much as experience it. Probably for the first time since childhood games, I was so thoroughly absorbed that I had not thought of myself or for myself. The odd time a customer called, I filled the order as if in a trance."[50]

At the time, Christy had no idea that the book had already earned an infamy nationwide and had the same effect on others that it was now having on him. He has spoken with others since who, on reading the book, immediately quit their jobs, their school, and set out for adventure. A significant section of a whole generation put aside their previous way of thinking about the world and opened up to listening to new music and reading new books. But for Christy, "the most important, and most overlooked, of the gifts in that book, and all others written by Kerouac, is the gift of compassion."[51] More on Christy's discovery of literature in Chapter 4.

One particular event that took place in October, 1963, is included here for no other reason than it provides a unique insight into a less flattering side of Lyndon B. Johnson who was at the time vice president, and his own take on Jack Kerouac. A friend of Christy's had been dating a girl whose father was a close friend and aide of LBJ, and Christy's friend had fixed them up with a weekend date with this girl and her friend in Washington. That evening they went to LBJ's house to check out if his youngest daughter, Luci Baines, wanted to hang out with them. She declined, but as they were leaving the house one of the other girls asked Lucy, "What's your father doing tonight?" To which she replied, "Oh, probably the usual." As they drove away, Christy asked what the usual was: "Many times ol' Lyndon has a few too many," said Cathy. "And some of those times he comes by my house or Charlene's. Wants to see our fathers who are usually asleep by then like most people."[52]

The foursome went to some clubs but only the girls could buy alcohol as a local law only permitted women to be served at eighteen and men not until they were twenty-one. The story on returning to Cathy's home is told by Christy in *Shift and Glitter*:

> The basement had been decorated to resemble a tavern with a mahogany bar, a pool table, leather chairs. We were down there playing records, drinking and dancing. Long about two in the morning, there was the sound of heavy footsteps from outside, by the window five or so feet off the ground. 'What the hell's that?' 'It's probably Lyndon,' one of the girls said. And there came the Vice President of the United States, rear-end first into the rec room.
>
> It didn't bother him seeing Jamie and me there. He smiled a big loose smile and asked for a shot of bourbon. Jamie normally outgoing and a bit of a braggart was awed and he shrunk back. Cathy and Charlene treated the Vice President like the wayward uncle. I made him a drink and handed it to him. He thanked me, glanced at the table and suggested a game of pool. I am one of the

worst pool players of all time, but Lyndon Johnson wasn't any better. 'Not my game,' he drawled.

He held his empty glass out to one of the girls, I held my own out. They treated me with new respect, seeing that Lyndon had taken to me. Later, they said that he usually ignored strangers.

After we'd had a couple bourbons together, he said, 'How come you don't ask me a bunch of political questions and that kind of thing?'

'Aw, you probably get enough of them all day, Mr. Johnson.'

'You damn right about that. Ask me some other kind of question. And call me Lyndon.'

I had just a year or so earlier discovered the novel 'On the Road,' the writer Jack Kerouac, the beat generation and a whole new wide world. I was profoundly influenced by all that, and, having had the right amount to drink, I asked, 'What do you think of Jack Kerouac, Mr., um, Lyndon?'

He straightened up, having been leaning over the table, fixed his eyes on me, he was about six feet one, but he seemed like a giant; he had that weirdest of traits, charisma. I had no idea what he might say but what he said was, 'Son, I went on the road when I was a boy. Bunch of us piled into an old Chevy and drove to California. Had us more fun than a barrel of monkeys. None of these middle-class people I have to deal with all day every day ever did anything like that.'

He told stories about that trip and other trips when he drove all over Texas garnering votes and making promises, told about the weird characters of the backcountry. Eventually, the girls telephoned someone to drive him home. 'You get so-and-so to come fetch the vice president.'

The day after Christy graduated from high school in 1963 and turned his back on Springfield for the last time, he headed down to Virginia in his newly acquired '51 Chevy on a deal that didn't work out, ended up living with his aunt in Petersburg, and got himself a job at an Amoco petrol station outside the Fort Lee Army Base.[53] It was while working at the gas station that Christy started hearing reports about the Vietnam War, now into its second year, that would later influence his decision to avoid being drafted there himself. He got into conversations with soldiers who had already served a term in Vietnam and was shocked by the stories they had to tell. "One guy would break down in tears because they used to take Vietnamese up into the helicopters for questioning, then throw them out." A few weeks later Christy bought himself a 1949 Hudson, not inadvertently the same model as the one driven by Kerouac's friend and traveling companion, Neal Cassady, on one of their iconic road trips. Later that same year, after sparring in a gym to earn some money, Christy was encouraged by a trainer to take a couple of professional fights. He won both but decided there were less risky ways of making money. Then in the fall of that year, hungry for a taste of the lifestyle he had discovered in the writings of Kerouac and clearly not put off by his early flirtation with the beats in Philadelphia, Christy decided to enroll in university:

> College would, I thought, consist of professors with enthusiasms to pass on and students eager to absorb it all; there would be all-night discussions about Camus and Sartre, and wild wine and marijuana parties with beatnik coeds. There was none of that. The courses were dull and easy and the students invariably buttoned down. I was so bored I stopped attending classes to work full-time in the college shipping and receiving department. My chores didn't take more than a couple of hours each shift, the rest of the time I spent hidden away at the back of the warehouse, sprawled on crates, reading. I liked the job mainly because it enabled me to get in a minimum of hours of paid reading but also because the head of the department was a dead ringer for Henry Miller. I called him "Henry." He never asked me why I did this and he probably didn't give a shit. His name was Louie.
>
> One Sunday morning, my nemesis, the dean of men as well as the football coach, Dr. Glenn Killinger, who had been on Walter Camp's very first collegiate All-America football team, burst into my room at my off-campus residence and caught me in bed with a female. This was what he called The Final Straw. I mean coming after all my other major infractions like not wearing my freshman beanie, not showing patriotic zeal when they gathered students together to salute the flag, for being caught reading suspect material.[54]

On another occasion, Killinger saw Christy strolling through the quad reading—sin of sins—a copy of the *City Lights Annual*. The result was a two-hour lecture on the virtues of being pro-American and the evils of communism while standing to attention in Killinger's office. And so it was in January of 1964, only three months after enrollment, that Christy was expelled from the university. He purchased an old '54 Ford, hurriedly threw some possessions on the backseat and, for reasons he no longer remembers, headed for Memphis, Tennessee. After a couple of aborted jobs including another spell with a carnival, Christy returned to downtown Philadelphia where he got himself a job with the Philadelphia Electric Company. It would be Christy's longest paid job, lasting a full year until he quit in January, 1965:

> Everyone assured me that my future was secured. I showed
> promise, they declared, working as a glorified messenger boy
> on the executive floor, running errands for the President, the
> Chairman of the Board, and the two Senior Vice Presidents. ...the
> work was easy and often even fun. Occasionally, I would while
> away an afternoon buying theatre tickets for one of the bosses or
> picking up a gift for his wife or delivering a message to someone
> at the Union Club on Broad Street. The doorman of that august
> establishment would nod and call me "Sir."[55]

Sometimes Christy would accompany a chauffeur to the airport to meet VIPs. On one occasion it was the actress Jean Simmons who was the celebrity guest at a promotion at Wanamaker's department store. Christy had to ride with her in the backseat of the car, act as her bodyguard at the store, and show her to the hotel afterwards:

> When we got to her door, and I was saying good-bye, she invited
> me in for a drink and I learned the truth of the expression "weak
> in the knees." She was by far the most beautiful human being I had
> ever seen.[56]

But most of Christy's work involved photocopying and fetching coffee rather than minding celebrities. Even so, he was popular and well treated. Having a regular job, though, did not stop Christy from indulging in vaga-bondage. He would embark on a Friday evening after work and return on

Sunday evening, even early on Monday morning before work. He calculated a 250-mile limit for a two-day round trip, either hitchhiking or by bus if he had the funds. "Wheeling, West Virginia, is the town that was on the edge of my trip perimeter. ... I did this for years: Pittsburgh, Baltimore, D.C., Richmond (265 miles), even Boston but that was pushing it."[57] On one of these forays Christy admits to having made it as far as Piqua, Ohio, around six hundred miles from Philadelphia.

During whatever spare time Christy had left, he used it to indulge his new found love of books, even attending night classes in ancient Greek literature. He tells in *Shift and Glitter* how one evening, a copy of *Ulysses* in his hand, he boarded the executive elevator to go home and the chairman of the board stepped in behind him: "He smiled at me when he saw the book and began to recite Homer in the ancient Greek. After that elevator ride, whenever I saw him, we'd talk about Homer or Euripides." But Christy was not destined for a life in an office: "I lasted a year and gave my notice. They were disappointed. Told me to think it over, that I was about to make a very big mistake."

Such a mistake is a concept only understood by those who view life from the security of the predictable and the mundane. For Christy, "fortune" was to be found in the unforeseeable adventures that only befall those who cast themselves to the mercy of happenstance. What Christy could not have anticipated was the extent of the turmoil in America throughout 1965 that would in turn directly influence his own adventures.

---

1   *Brookdale*, op cit.

2   The title *Shift and Glitter* was taken from a letter from Thomas Wolfe to his mother: "For we have outlived the shift and glitter of so many passing fancies."

3   Jim Christy, *Shift and Glitter* (unpublished manuscript)

4   *Brookdale*, op cit.

5   Jim Christy, email to the author, July 28, 2016

6   *Brookdale*, op cit.

7   Ibid.

8   Ibid.

9   Ibid.

10   Ibid.

11   Christy relates a story connected to Cous that it was in this restaurant that mob capo Chickie Narducci was put through a meat grinder after his murder and was served up as meatballs.

12   *Brookdale*, op cit.

13   Ibid.

14   Jim Christy, *Rolling Hill Road* (unpublished manuscript)

15   Robert Garzarelli's younger sister, Elaine Garzarelli, would become one of Wall Street's top financial analysts and start her own company, Garzarelli Capital, Inc.

16   *Brookdale*, op cit.

17   Ibid.

18   Ibid.

19   In *Between the Meridians*, Christy gives his age as thirteen on his tramp to Niagara because a prospective publisher told him that no one would believe that he had made this journey aged twelve. For the record, Christy was a week or so short of his thirteenth birthday when he made that trip.

20   Jim Christy, *Reet, Petite and Gone* (unpublished manuscript)

21   Ibid.

22   Ibid.

23   Ibid.

24   Ibid.

25   Ibid.

26   Ibid.

27   Jim Christy, *Between the Meridians* (Victoria, B.C.: Ekstasis Editions, 1999), p. 75

28   *Reet, Petite and Gone*, op cit.

29   *Between the Meridians*, op cit., p. 77

30   Ibid., pp. 70-83

31   *Reet, Petite and Gone*, op cit.

32   Ibid.

33   Jim Christy, *Travelin Light* (Toronto: Simon & Pierre, 1982), pp. 136-137

34   Ibid., p. 142

35   Ibid., p. 143-144

36   Ibid., p. 164

37   *Amusement Business* only ceased publication in 2006.

38   *Shift and Glitter*, op cit.

39   Jim Christy, *Jackpots* (Victoria, B.C.: Ekstasis Editions, 2012), pp. 45-50

40   *Marimba Forever* (Toronto: Guernica Editions, 2010), pp. 100-101

41   *Jackpots*, op cit., p. 48-49

42   *Between the Meridians*, op cit., p. 14

43   Ibid., p. 15

44   Ibid., p. 18

45   Josiah Flynt, *My Life* (New York: The Outing Publishing Company, 1908), p. 99

46   *Between the Meridians*, op cit., p. 23

47   Jim Christy, *The Long Slow Death of Jack Kerouac* (Toronto: ECW, 1998), pp. 33-34

48   Ibid., p. 37

49   Ibid., p. 34-35

50   Ibid., p. 84

51   Ibid., p. 36

52   *Shift and Glitter*, op cit.

53   *Flesh and Blood*, op cit., p. 40

54   *Shift and Glitter*, op cit.

55   Ibid.

56   Ibid.

57   Jim Christy, email to the author, November 28, 2014

3

1965

T he year of 1965 was a momentous year, not just for Christy, but for America as a whole. The following list of events (in chronological order) demonstrates just what a crazy year it was:

- Lyndon B. Johnson sworn in as president for second term, announces his "Great Society"
- Malcolm X assassinated
- State Troopers clash with civil rights protesters in Selma, Alabama
- First American troops arrive in Vietnam
- Martin Luther King, Jr. leads second attempt to march from Selma to Montgomery
- Police clash with 600 members of the Student Nonviolent Coordinating Committee in Montgomery
- 1,600 civil rights marchers descend on Montgomery Court House
- Voting Rights Bill lodged with Congress
- Third march from Selma to Montgomery attracts 25,000 people. Led by Martin Luther King, Jr.
- Around 270 people killed in series of 50 tornadoes in 6 Midwestern states

- U.S. troops sent to Dominican Republic to prevent a "communist takeover"
- First public burning of Vietnam War draft cards
- U.S. troops in Vietnam increased from 75,000 to 125,000, and number drafted increases from 17,000 per month to 35,000
- Voting Rights Act of 1965 signed into law
- Watts Race Riots, 34 killed and 1,032 injured over the week of rioting
- Hurricane Betsy kills 76 in New Orleans
- First draft card burner arrested under a new law
- 100,000 involved in antiwar demonstrations in 80 cities across America

Christy was directly involved with, or influenced by, some of these events, spawning a whirlwind of adventures on and off the road. It was also a year in which Christy met people who would change his life, and experienced events that would affect his view of the world. Indeed, so much happened in this one year that it is not always possible, even for Christy, to maintain an accurate chronology of events. But then neither is it entirely necessary for an appreciation of the tale that now unfolds. However, with Christy's help, here is an attempt to present the events of 1965 in the order they happened.

After seeing in the New Year with a girl named Carolyn Treece whom he'd met the night before, and staying with her at her parents' house for three days—they having spent the festivities elsewhere—Christy headed off to Florida to enjoy some winter sunshine. And it was in Florida that Christy first met Val Santee (not his real name) at a bus stop during the first week of January in 1965, both headed for Miami. This is how he describes his first impression of Santee in *Shift and Glitter*:

> I first noticed Val Santee because he reminded me of a guy I had gone to high school with or, rather, he reminded me of the other guy's cowboy cousin. He was a rougher version, dressed like a ranch hand who'd left his boots in the bunk house and put on brogans for his trip to the tropics. I went back to sleep and didn't think of the guy again until we nodded recognition at the rest stop.

When they got back on the bus, it was Santee who approached Christy first, walking to the back of the bus and asking, "if he might take the seat across the aisle, very awkward and polite." Although Christy says he didn't look like the reading type, he inquired about the book Christy was reading. The two immediately hit it off, discovering that they had much in common including a shared feeling of alienation from mainstream society. "The point, as far as Val Santee and I were concerned, is that we were the only ones anywhere near our age that we knew or had even heard of, who thought any way at all as we did." This is the story that Santee related to Christy.

Santee was only sixteen when he'd been expelled from school, had been married for over a year, and was the father of one child with another on the way. He'd found a job in a local grocery store but the manager had fired him after asking if he was "the notorious high school commie." Not yet seventeen, out of work, and with an infant son and heavily pregnant wife to support, Santee had robbed a gas station, and after being caught had been given the usual choice in those days of jail or the army. He chose the army, but not being able to adjust to the discipline, he was forever getting into trouble.

> The first time he went to the stockade was when he would not obey
> an order to fish a cigarette butt out of a latrine urinal. The order
> giver, one of those crewcuts, was not satisfied with his explanation
> that it wasn't his cigarette butt. The sergeant's response to that was
> to order him to pick it out with his teeth. Thirty days.[1]

After his release, Santee went AWOL, got captured, and so began a cycle of misdemeanors and punishments until he was given orders to ship out to Korea. "I told them, I wouldn't report for duty, and if they shipped me out by force, I'd go over to the North Koreans." Eventually the army tired of the determined rebel and gave him a general discharge. But there were still no jobs in his hometown, so he took work away and sent money home. From the strain of his responsibilities, loneliness, and being hungry for travel and adventure, Santee finally abandoned his family and set out for Cuba, via Miami where he picked up with Christy.

> Val later told me that he was amazed when I neither criticized
> his politics and view of the world nor made moral judgements
> about his abandoning wife and kids. After that night, dug down
> in the sand, talking, the rhythm of the waves, the stars in the
> black sky, we became the closest of friends. We discovered,
> furthermore, that although our political perspectives were

different, we both wanted to see a radical transformation of government and society.

We had so much in common and were different in so many ways. He brooded, disappeared into some dark place, came out of it and was ebullient, wanting to rush around and have adventures. ... Val would disappear, sometimes for days at a time but he always returned with allusions to certain "friends" he had. Friends I never met. He would be evasive, like he was doing some hush-hush underground work. I do know for a fact that he spent time at the Fair Play for Cuba Committee.[2]

Christy stayed in Miami until the end of the winter, getting the odd job when he was broke, such as sparring with professional boxers, washing dishes in a seafood restaurant, and three weeks in a Miami hotel doing pretty much everything expected of him, which included keeping the female guests entertained. The job advertisement specified, "Must be in good physical shape, clean and presentable."

Eventually the pair decided to hitchhike back up north and were offered a lift by a nineteen-year-old "hillbilly greaser" named Pete, and his pregnant fourteen-year-old wife Marie. Pete was driving a '49 Studebaker with rusting wheel wells and bald tires. "It spewed blue-grey smoke from the exhaust pipe and stopped with a screech of metal on metal." The couple did not have a cent between them, everything having been blown by Pete on the car, which, in the short time that Val and Christy spent with them, required significant amounts of money in gas, oil, and tires just to keep it on the road. Val and Christy marveled at how easily Pete and Marie managed to acquire everything for their needs. Their scam involved finding a church or a minister's house and informing the minister that they were hardworking Christians trying to get home, and that they needed gas, oil, a gasket, et cetera, and of course food. The minister would furnish them with a note to give to the local gas station attendant, and their needs would be met. Christy describes their modus operandi when it was his turn to work the scam:

I remember walking with Marie up to the door of a minister's house, Pete's wedding ring on my hand, in some little Florida town, her keeping her distance until we rang the bell. When the door opened she was stuck to my side, and sticking her belly toward the minister. She looked about to cry. I told the guy that we were trying to get back to North Carolina and my wife was pregnant. We had jobs and family up there, were legally married and hardworking Methodists (naturally, the denomination changed to fit the parson or the church). I was surprised when the guy had his wife make us sandwiches, and gave us some money out of his pocket. I thanked him profusely, and when we were back in the car Marie made fun of the guy for being a sucker and mocked me for being so polite to him.

Our biggest score led to our arrest. It was Sunday in Hobe Sound. While the car was up on the lift getting new tires, a lube and a gasket for the oil pan, we repaired to a restaurant on the main drag. The staff, knowing we were charity cases, gave us lousy service, slamming down our plates, spilling our coffee, talking about us amongst themselves and to the other customers. Maybe it was out of general hostility or perhaps because we each grabbed a cigar upon leaving, that someone called the cops. The guy was waiting for us as we pulled away from the service station. A tall trooper with a John B. Stetson hat and mirrored shades. He chewed his gum slowly, lips covering his teeth.[3]

The trooper was not happy with the car's papers and when he asked them if they'd ever been arrested previously, they all lied except Pete, who stupidly admitted to spending a year in the reformatory in Petersburg, Virginia, for auto theft. Being a Sunday, the four vagabonds had to spend a night in the cells before they could be brought before the judge the following morning. Fortunately for them, the judge appraised the situation for what it was:

He realized that Pete wasn't the smartest hillbilly to come out of the holler and that the process of registering a motor vehicle properly was a mite beyond his capacities. And he even smiled when I said, 'Judge, you've seen the thing. If we were going to steal a car, I'm sure you don't really think we'd steal something like that?'

He did a pretty good job, for the trooper's sake, of covering up his smile. The trooper went from beside himself with joy at busting an auto theft ring to fit to be tied when our sorry-ass crew walked out of the hoosegow as free citizens.[4]

1965

The next night, after spending an hour by the roadside fixing the exhaust pipe, the four spent a night at a tramp hostel by a lake, way off the main road. Christy's description of the place and its inhabitants is absurdly comical. By this time the Studebaker was on its last legs and because it could not make highway speed, they were forced to crawl along side roads, eventually leaving Pete and Marie at a service station in Jessup, Georgia. They walked out of town, got a lift in an old Dodge with a farmer, then another from some members of Little Richard's band in a gleaming yellow Pontiac Bonneville convertible. The trip continued in the same fortuitous fashion, introducing all kinds of odd characters and situations, but the following account after alighting from the Bonneville emphasizes just how primitive the South still remained even post the Civil Rights Act of 1964:

> They let us off somewhere in South Carolina and we went immediately to a gas station to piss. There was a "White Men" and a "White Women" washroom. On the side of the building was scrawled the word "colored" above an arrow that pointed to the rear. The "colored" washroom was a hole in the dirt surrounded by a few planks and branches stuck into the ground.
>
> Val, despite my warning, stormed into the office to protest this injustice. The man calmly reached into his desk drawer, pulled out the first .357 Magnum I'd ever seen, showed us each the barrel of it, then levelled it at Val, saying, 'Niggers piss different from me, and I got this here for anyone who says they piss the same as me.'[5]

Christy had to persuade his friend not to take the matter further as, even if they didn't wind up shot, he reasoned they'd likely get jailed for disturbing the peace on the basis that all the other whites in town were likely to be of the same persuasion. Shortly after this Val took off again, and when Christy realized that he wasn't coming back, he decided to pay another visit to Carolyn Treece, the girl he'd met on New Year's Eve.

> She was glad to see me. 'I hope you've gotten that kind of thing out of your system,' Carolyn said when she answered my knocking on her door. By which she meant my wanderlust. I didn't tell her I'd only begun.[6]

And so it was that after playing house for three days and uncomfortable at being in her parents' house, Christy headed off for Selma, Alabama. After taking a train to Memphis, and being aware of the treatment that could be expected for Northern rabble-rousers with long hair arriving in Selma, Christy, savvy as ever, visited a local barbershop:

> I came out of there resembling your average redneck, shaved
> up the sides, a little pompadour; an idiot in other words (few of
> your genuine rednecks had crewcuts). I caught the night bus to
> Selma, and practiced my southern accent on some of my fellow
> passengers. Hell it wasn't difficult to slip into. I'd made my first
> sounds south of the Mason-Dixon, and grown up listening to my
> mother's way-down-home drawl. Nobody questioned me, said,
> 'You sound funny, boy. Where you from?' ... Selma resembled the
> set of a movie about fascism come to America. A Dixie police
> state. The bus station at seven in the morning bristled with
> hatred. None of it directed at me. I saw other guys from up north,
> stupid enough to have hit town with their longer-than-average
> curly locks, collegiate sideburns, and broadcloth striped shirts,
> with corduroys.... Out on the streets, there seemed to be plenty
> of citizens interested in baseball, at least they carried Louisville
> Sluggers, and walked around as if heading for batting practice."[7]

After hanging around for a bit watching Martin Luther King—in the company of a young Jesse Jackson—trying to make speeches and being thwarted, Christy wandered around trying to pick up information from police and local rednecks that might be of use to the demonstrators, before heading back into town where he spent "a lonely night in a hotel room that smelled of chewing tobacco and reminded me of the one Robert Mitchum had at the beginning of *Cape Fear*."

> The next day not long after noon, a massed force of police and
> firemen attacked those of us who had congregated in the town
> square in an impromptu protest. There had been confrontations
> all night and throughout the early morning hours. Most of these,
> it is beyond any doubt, were instigated by police. The blacks were
> still, by what seemed to me almost otherworldly self-control,

maintaining a non-violent front. I suppose the police and firemen and their vicious cohorts were eager to wreak some mayhem and spill some blood. ... They had billy clubs, baseball bats, lengths of chain, iron bars and worse than any and all of these: fire hoses. ... The pressure was enough to kill half a dozen of those unfortunate enough to take the full force of the blasts to their stomachs or heads. I saw a geyser of blood erupt from the mouth of one man my age, and at the same time, saw the back of his pants turn dark with blood, blood flowed from his eyes and ears too. Another kid, hit in the back was hurtled ten feet through the air and against the broad trunk of a sycamore tree. I managed to keep in back of the guys holding the hoses by circling the opposite of the way they moved. But I was knocked down in the melee and trampled. Someone stepped on my head, I stood up and was hit across the lower back by a baseball bat.[8]

For his trouble, Christy spent the night crushed into a cell, black and white together, witnessing the brutalities of the police:

Two cops were pulling on the arms of an immense black lady, which caused her to topple forward down the two narrow steps at the back of the wagon. When she hit the ground that was all the cops and their accomplices needed. They went to work on her with their clubs and bats, not sparing any part of her body. I'm sure they smashed her skull in. They must have. She was never seen inside the jail, no ambulance came. The last I saw of her, some men had her by the ankles and were attempting to drag her off.[9]

When those inside the cell started voicing their outrage at what they had witnessed, the police started smashing at the hands that were gripping the bars:

All night, people moaned and cried. Some with smashed knuckles, broken fingers, and broken hands, others from sheer hopelessness and despair. Blacks and white crying together, and keeping each other upright. We had succeeded in integrating the Selma cell blocks.[10]

After returning to Philadelphia, Christy spent the next few days at the public library reading philosophy, "which I still was young enough to believe held some answers." He then got some work posing nude for life drawing classes, before being invited back by one of the students to her apartment where he spent the following month. After tiring of that liaison and becoming restless, Christy again visited Carolyn Treece, who by now had a new boyfriend. He was reporting to the army in two days and offered Christy the use of a cabin he had in the woods. After moving into the cabin, Christy got himself a job as a trainee butcher. "I had my own chopping block, was learning a trade; again a good future was laid out before me but again I wanted no part of it."

After quitting his budding career as a butcher, Christy headed west for Wheeling, West Virginia, "anxious to, right away, put a few hundred miles between myself and my old life." After spending a night in Wheeling—one of his first tramping destinations at the age of twelve—Christy hitchhiked onwards to Du Quoin in southern Illinois, arriving there late at night and sleeping in the back of a closed-down service station.

> The next morning Val Santee and one of his brothers came and found me drinking coffee over a campfire with an old tramp. He'd been dossed down less than a hundred yards from where I'd slept on the ground. He told me he walked all over the United States, Canada and Mexico, and made sure to read the local newspapers wherever he was. 'Just find a newspaper in a trash barrel, sit down somewhere and study the place I'm at.'[11]

Val was with his twin brothers, Louis and Lewis, though Christy admits that he never had the slightest notion which was which. One of them suggested they "go and see Fats." Fats turned out to be the real Minnesota Fats (Rudolph Wanderone, played by Jackie Gleason in *The Hustler*, alongside Paul Newman). Christy had not realized that there was a real Minnesota Fats, and they headed out to a local roadhouse to watch him play pool, listen to his yarns, and discover that his real hustle was at cards.

> So there I was with my great buddy Val Santee driving through the southern Illinois scrubland to his hometown of West Frankfort that had already taken on a mythic quality in my mind. When we were on our own, the first thing Val did was bring me to see the

Chicago-St. Louis bus come in. There was the man with the rifle, keeping blacks from getting off. 'No niggers allowed within the city limits!' he announced to one man who didn't know enough not to try and alight.

'Man, I need a drink of water.'
'You can't get you no water in West Frankfort, boy.'

I refrained from reminding Val of the day in South Carolina when he called me down for not arguing with the gun-toting service station owner.

Val's father looked like a movie Indian. It took a few days for him to warm up to me though. Seems he thought I might be a homosexual who'd taken a fancy to his son. The old man, Val Sr. grew up in the hills to the south. His grandmother had been part of the Trail of Tears march of Cherokees from North Carolina to Oklahoma. When she got sick on the trail, she just lay there as the rest kept trudging west.[12]

And so as well as having shared interests and outlooks on the world, Santee and Christy both also shared the legacy of having Native American blood in their veins. Christy recalls how he would sit up late into the nights with old man Santee listening to his stories. The area where the Santees lived was coal mining country and the old man told Christy about the area's historical labor disputes. He told Christy he had to shoot a guy once during an attempt by the mine owners to break a strike at Orient No. 5 mine, the same mine where several miners later lost their lives on August 15, 1968. Following the shooting, old man Santee fled to Quebec, later returning to Pennsylvania under the pseudonym Frenchy and sporting a particular style of moustache to complete the masquerade. Later the old man became a Church of God minister via a correspondence course and went around preaching at homes for the elderly and tiny backwoods churches. He actually took Christy along with him to a Sunday service at an old folks' home where Christy got drawn into taking part in an unplanned charade. The Reverend Santee topped off his sermon by requesting Christy to come up to the "altar" and tell the assembled congregation how he had been a serious sinner (at least that part was based in fact), and that he'd found Christy in a bad part of Chicago lying in the gutter swilling wine. And so Christy embraced the theater but got his own back on the old man by questioning what the reverend was doing in that bad part of town with all its brothels in the first place. After completing his confession to the assembled old folks, an old man came up to Christy and asked if him if they had met at the Battle of the Bulge, the last major German offensive of World War II in 1944. Christy would have been in utero at the time.

Val and Christy spent the next two weeks floating down the Little Wabash, Wabash, Ohio, and Missouri rivers in a seventeen-foot-long freighter canoe, until they hit the confluence with the Mississippi where "floating" was no longer possible. They slept mainly on the river banks, but one day they spotted a lineman's hut and were contemplating sleeping in it when the owner happened by and gave them permission to use it. The owner was the actress Jocelyn Brando, Marlon's older sister. When the river tramp was done, Val phoned another of his brothers, Earl, who'd served time for armed robbery, to drive the pair back to West Frankfort. From there Christy continued on alone, Val making excuses about not being able to go along that Christy suspected was to do with him missing his wife and hoping she would take him back. In a few weeks, Christy would himself be married.

On his arrival in Kansas City, Christy got a job in a café for a week before moving on again. As he ran over to a Cadillac that had just pulled over to give him a lift, another car pulled right up to him. Christy apologized saying that he had already been offered a lift in the first car, and on asking the driver if he knew the guys in the second car, he got the reply, "Yeah, they're my bodyguards." After being dropped off, Christy was offered a construction job that lasted ten days, and with the job over and money in his pocket, he got back on the highway. Within an hour, he spied the speck of a small car making its way toward him across the prairie from the direction of Fort Smith Air Force Base.

> I studied it for something to do. As it got closer the speck turned into a Triumph roadster, British racing green in colour. There was a young woman driving. She reached the intersection, started to pull onto the highway, saw me, and backed up. 'You want a ride?' ... She was wearing sunglasses and had dark thick curly hair; her features were strong, distinct, or so it seemed from what I could see of her face, the bottom of the sunglasses seeming to perch on high cheekbones. The fingers on the leather-encased steering wheel were long and slender, the nails

long ovals covered with a clear gloss. All that I noticed as I climbed in.[13]

The woman asked Christy where he was headed and he said California. When she pulled up to the intersection where she was turning south and Christy reached to open the car door, she asked him if he'd ever been to Mexico, that she had a small house on the border, and would he like to be shown around. Well, not having anything particular planned, why would any young vagabond refuse such an offer? The two had not been able to engage in conversation due to the noise of the wind in the open-top car, but on arrival at their first break at a truck stop, they introduced themselves to each other. Linda was aged twenty-six, Christy a month short of his twentieth birthday. They got further acquainted at the next stop where they shared a motel room.

> There was sadness at the edge of everything she said or did. I was aware for the first time in my life, of being with a woman and not a girl, I really do mean 'being with' rather than having sex with.[14]

Linda's story was that she had been visiting her boyfriend who was an officer at the Air Force base. They had grown up together in a small Texas town and got engaged to be married, even though, as she admitted, she never loved him and would never love him. She had never had any say about her life, everything being decided for her between his parents and her mother. Linda's father, who was divorced from her mother, had advised her to run away, but she had nowhere to run away to:

> 'It's like I'm playing a part in a play that somebody wrote for me. I never said anything because somehow I wasn't entirely aware of what was going on. Maybe it's the same way for him but I don't care about that. For the first time, I want to put my own happiness first.' ... It took us three or four more days to get to Brownsville on the Rio Grande, at the far southeastern edge of the state. We'd take side roads and have picnics, make love in fields in the sunshine, in fields at night. At the very beginning, I assumed I was a diversion, something to take her mind off her problems with her boyfriend and to fill the last days of her vacation from work.[15]

After showing Christy her "cute pale-yellow house," the pair strolled over the International Bridge and into the Mexican town of Matamoros. The bridge transported Christy into another world, one that seemed to exist on a different, altogether more interesting plane, with more color and noise and the best food Christy had ever tasted. Linda got a kick out of observing Christy's exhilaration at the discovery of his new surroundings. "We roamed around crowded streets, ate tacos and chimichangas, drank Bohemia beer and shots of mescal. ... A teenaged guy asked us if we wanted to get married. Before I could figure that out—was it a euphemism for someplace to go for sex? ... I heard Linda say, 'Yes. Yes. We do.' "[16]

And that is how in May of 1965, Christy was led down some alleys, into a pink-colored house on the other side of a cement wall, and married by an overweight priest who bore a resemblance to Anthony Quinn. Twenty minutes later they were husband and wife, but not before a reception in their honor attended by relatives of the priest and his wife, and anyone else who happened to be passing. "Everyone treated us wonderfully. Somehow we got back to Brownsville and I woke up several hours later, for the first time in the bedroom of the yellow house."

Christy was passionately in love with his new wife, and she with him. When she had to be at work by nine, Christy wandered around town, frequently stopping at a coffee shop across the street from where Linda worked, staring across at the second-floor window of her office, "Thinking she was somewhere just beyond the glass through which I couldn't see." But Matamoros had its own allure, and Christy soon became such a frequent visitor that the border guards at both ends of the bridge would just give him a nod or a wave when he passed.

One day, in a cantina in Matamoros, Christy encountered the brother of the priest who had married him. Raoul was a local gangster and invited Christy to visit his establishment, "a very tastefully appointed brothel." Before long, Christy was displaying the entrepreneurial skills he had learned as a kid in Philadelphia. He would pick up a carload of rich college kids in Brownsville, drive them to Raoul's establishment across the border in a '47 Dodge sedan provided by Raoul, and be given a share of the takings: "It's twenty bucks for the usual but twenty-five for gringos. For every gringo you deliver, you make five dollars." We are not told what the women made.

Whatever Christy got up to in the day, he was always back by 5:30 to pick Linda up from work. Sometimes Christy would cook, sometimes they would eat out at a restaurant or barbecue place on the beach. But this idyllic life was shortly to come to a sorry end. Linda's mother was scandalized when she heard that her daughter was sharing her house with a young drifter, even questioning the legitimacy of the marriage.

> 'Linda, what have you turned into? You act like a whore picking up trash from along the road. ... How could you do this! What about Harley? You were engaged to him. A fine man, Harley. ... You've gone and ruined your life. For what? Tell me what? For that? That piece of trash? He's hardly more than a juvenile delinquent. It makes me want to throw up to think of you giving yourself to him.' ... Linda was distraught and that night cried herself to sleep in my arms.[17]

A couple of days later, Christy was accosted in the street by Linda's thirty-year-old brother, who warned Christy to stay away from his sister and then got physical with him. The outcome was that Christy laid the guy out. Then a younger, tougher brother was dispatched with similar results. The sight of her second brother on the ground with a broken nose and split eyebrow, covered in blood, made Linda start reappraising her loyalties. The couple made a visit to Linda's father, who was completely accepting of his new son-in-law. He warned Linda that she would end up miserable for the rest of her life if she followed her mother's and brothers' wishes, but that was to underestimate the power wielded by Linda's mother. Having failed to rid herself of her unwanted son-in-law by dispatching her sons, the mother turned up at the couple's home where Christy was standing by their cement-block garage. On approaching him she drew a handgun and let off a couple of rounds. Christy instinctively turned his body sideways and to the left as the shots rang out, but although he avoided the bullets he was badly injured by the flying debris from the cinderblock-and-concrete wall. Christy refused to go to the hospital to avoid having to explain the cause of his injuries but Linda managed to remove most of the particles from his back with tweezers. Christy carries the scars of the shooting to this day.

Christy realized after this event that things had changed. Linda cried a lot and became sad and withdrawn. She did not want to get married to the air force officer, did not want to live the kind of life that her mother had carved out for her, but she also found it impossible to go against her. Then one night she asked Christy to go with her to the beach, and after having dinner on a blanket on the sands, Linda started crying as they walked along the beach. Christy said "Okay, let me have it."

> Linda said that she had to go against her father's advice, had to go against her own wishes and her instincts, and bow to her mother's pressure as well as the imprecations of her intended. He was going to forgive her, and have a lawyer annul our marriage if, in fact, it even existed in the eyes of Texas.[18]

As absurd as the circumstances of Christy's wedding may at first appear, he had developed a deep bond with Linda and would never forget her. Their marriage was never formally dissolved, but in 1972 Brownsville police contacted Christy in Toronto to inform him that his wife had been found beaten to death in Matamoros, the Mexican town they had regularly frequented just across the border from Brownsville. And so it was that Christy became widowed from the wife he still loved but had not seen for seven years.

Returning to 1965, the day after the pair were forced to separate, a dejected Christy was boarding a bus without the slightest idea where he was heading, randomly buying a ticket to Beaumont, Texas. And it was in Beaumont that another important event was about to unfold in Christy's life. It was late afternoon on a Friday in the summer of 1965 when Christy, just turned twenty, stepped down from the bus in downtown Beaumont. Through the bustle of people rushing home from work, Christy glanced up and across the hood of a truck:

> ...what I noticed was a man in a Hawaiian shirt, long grey blond hair nearly to his shoulders, who was leaning against a brick wall smoking a black stogie. His chino pants were baggy, shoes of woven strands of soft leather.[19]

> ...this man had the most incredible face I'd ever seen. It was as if a sculptor had been commissioned to make the head of a Hollywood leading man but said to hell with it, and sabotaged his creation, going surrealist on his simple, straight-forward head. ... He had a cloth bag much like mine, the kind that used to be called a gym bag. Between the straps was a rolled blanket. He set

the bag down by the curb, lit the stogie, and looked right over at
me as if he knew I was watching him. 'His face,' as Melville said of
Queequeg, 'was a crucifixion to behold.' The man levelled his gaze
on me and waited for whatever I had in mind.[20]

As we are informed in these two separate accounts, this was the manner
in which Christy first met Floyd Wallace, his soon-to-be hobo mentor. Floyd's
moniker was the Greeley Kid, so named after the Colorado town where he'd
been raised. The older vagabond had just stepped off a sailboat at Port Arthur,
after shipping out of Liverpool, over to South America, up the Atlantic coast
through the Caribbean to Tampa, New Orleans, and then across the gulf to
Port Arthur. Although arriving with a friend he'd met in New Orleans, with
the intention of hanging out around the waterfront, Floyd had come up to
Beaumont to visit the widow of a close friend whom he'd just been informed
had died of a heart attack.

After striking up an instant friendship, Christy and Wallace took up
rooms in the boarding house run by the widow of Wallace's friend; he in turn
introduced them to someone who needed help on a construction job. As it
turned out, Wallace had friends just about wherever he went, and when two
weeks later the work was over, the pair lit out from Beaumont together in
the caboose of a freight train headed north, courtesy of railroad employees
who knew him well:

> The trainmen not only treated Floyd with the utmost respect, but
> they seemed to defer to him as well. ... We had enough money to fly
> out of there first-class but that would have violated the principle
> of the enterprise, and we never would have met those great
> trainmen.[21]

After switching trains in Dallas and Oklahoma City, the pair arrived in Tulsa
where they visited another friend of Wallace, Sam Spry. Christy does not hide
his fascination when Spry answers the door, minus his legs and suspended
by his arms from brass rails: "I couldn't help be reminded of an orangutan
but in place of jungle lianas, elevated rails led through the living room to the
kitchen with tracks branching off to bedroom and bathroom." When Spry
asked Christy, "What the hell are you looking at? ... Something peculiar about
me?" Christy with his usual forthrightness declared, "Damn right there is ...

you're not what usually opens the door," instantly endearing the young to the old vagabond, who burst out laughing.

Over twelve hours around the kitchen table, and some serious drinking, the two older hobos reminisced over their early tramping experiences and of two years fighting in the Spanish Civil War; naturally, because of their socialist and Wobbly leanings, on the Republican side:

> Their conversation ranged over jobs of work and old radical heroes, time on picket lines, battles with yard bulls, scissorbills, cops and management thugs. They freely divested themselves of political opinions ... weren't guys who'd put off having a good time until after the revolution. Their reminiscences, therefore, included bust-ups and jackpots and uproarious nights with often a good deal of female companionship. Not that either of them bragged or even became graphic; no, it was all said in a sort of joyful reference.

These were guys who had lived. They'd grabbed life, embraced it, wrung its neck, kissed and fondled it, kicked it in the keister and held on tight. They'd taken some shots in return but didn't seem to hold any grudges.[22]

Christy lists some of these Spanish Civil War adventures in *Between the Meridians*. He then asked Floyd the obvious question as they eventually departed Sam's bungalow, "I guess he stepped on a mine or something like that, huh? Over in Spain." But Floyd replied that Sam Spry had not lost his legs in that or any other war zone. Paradoxically for a hobo, hundreds of whom lost limbs beating trains illegally, it was during a brief spell working for a railroad company that Sam lost his legs. Due to the carelessness of a fellow railroad employee while Sam was attending to the coupling between two boxcars, the train backed up prematurely: "Sam tried to leap free but he leaped too late." And from *Shift and Glitter*:

> No. Old Sam made it through the whole sorry mess without so much as a scratch. People used to want to stand or maybe I should say kneel next to him during battles for good luck. He comes back to Oklahoma and makes the mistake of begging for his old brakeman's job back. I say, begging because he had a reputation as being a Red. Hell, anyone of us who were over there was called

a Red. Well, sir, they give him the job back and he's not there two weeks before he gets knocked down and a freight car rolls over him, severs his legs."

After Tulsa, the pair headed for Denver where Floyd made some phone calls to find out that the woman he was looking for was singing at a roadhouse out of town. Having realized that Christy was in a bad way after having to leave Linda behind in Brownsville, Wallace sought to distract his new friend with some female companionship. After sprucing themselves up in the shower of a local YMCA, the pair headed out to a country-and-western venue where Wallace's friend Mae was performing. A friend of Mae's was making quite a hit on the dance floor, but in spite of the attention the younger woman was getting it was Christy who left the place in her company under the hostile stares from local cowboys.

The pair hung around the area for a few days, went to hear Mae sing again, and then took off for a picnic high up in the foothills of the Rockies. Floyd decided he wanted to pay a visit to his hometown of Greeley, so Christy thumbed a ride to Colorado Springs and holed up in a cheap hotel for a few days and wandered around. Later, the pair met up again in Denver from where they headed out east to Omaha on a freight train and then up to Sioux City with little trouble. From Sioux City the pair beat it in a Great Northern boxcar for the town of Britt in northern Iowa. The annual National Hobo Convention that originated in Chicago in the late 1890s was permanently relocated to Britt in 1900. In August, 1965, when Christy first visited Britt with Floyd Wallace, there were still some genuine hobos to be found among the tourists and the curious drawn to visit:

> When we dropped down [from the train] by an abandoned water tower, I was fancying myself quite the hobo but that delusion lasted about five minutes. There were men in Britt that year that had been riding side-door pullmans for over fifty years. In the days when they'd started out, many of the old-timers they encountered were the original American hoboes, men who'd had no place to return to after the Civil War and just kept moving. There was an actual election of a hobo king, and a parade and street-fair as well as a variety show at the high school auditorium but mostly the convention consisted, as it always had, of hoboes sitting around fires swapping yarns.[23]

In his story "End of the Road,"[24] Christy describes returning to Britt years later, only to discover that it had become a tourist sideshow organized by the local Chamber of Commerce, with few real hobos remaining, and those who did attend getting moved on by the police as soon as the tourists and their money had left. The Britt Hobo Convention continues to this day, with hobo "craft," music, et cetera, for sale all the year round in the Britt Hobo Museum on the purchase of a three-dollar admission fee. The museum was opened in the former Chief Theater in 1980, a sad commercial parody of a once proud and long since vanished hobo institution. But we are still back in 1965, and after spending a few days meeting some of the real old-timers in Britt, Christy and Floyd set off for Kansas City where they had arranged to meet up with some of the other hobos:

> There was a camp between an embankment and some spur lines in K.C. Again Floyd knew a dozen people there and one of them was an old man called Pop Stewart. There was a crowd of 'bos around him, his own retinue; he was a little fellow with long white hair and a white beard. When he saw Floyd, he recapitulated what him and the others were discussing. 'To be brief, Greeley. To be brief, I have the rheumatism pretty bad and I'm afraid I can't be hotfooting it around the country no more. So I'm gonna have to buy me an automobile.'[25]

Pop had to explain that he was not planning to actually drive the car. No. With the help of the assembled hobos, Christy included, he went to a local used car lot, bought a 1930s four-door Nash sedan for seventy-five dollars, had it pushed back across the highway, and let it roll down the hill, declaring, "Where it stops is where I'll make my home."

> When it stopped, and Pop was convinced it wasn't going to start up again, he began to clean the thing with a whiskbroom. He opened the winged hood and the trunk lid and all the doors, and tried the windows. He spread his bedroll in the backseat and stored some gear in the trunk.
> After dinner, a side of pork roasted on wood scrounged from around the camp, with carrots and potatoes simmered in a drum with onions, I went into town and got arrested. By the time, I got

back three days later, Pop had fixed himself a cute little retirement home. He'd washed the Nash, and made a fence around it with branches and different lengths of metal pipe and a couple of golf clubs. He'd made shelves in the trunk and arranged knickknacks on the dashboard.[26]

Eventually, having had his fill of the road stories of others, Christy wanted to experience some excitement of his own—as though he had not already had more than most people. He decided to first make a pilgrimage to Twelfth Street and Vine, famous in the song "Kansas City," and with a particular significance for Christy, being based as it was on sections of the Charlie Parker composition, "Parker's Mood." But Christy's arrival at Twelfth and Vine did not live up to anticipation:

> There was nothing but run down wooden buildings, stores
> with signs that hung by broken chains over the pavement and
> dilapidated houses on weed lots. I was standing there like an idiot
> in a trance, when the cruiser pulled over and two guys got out, one
> black, one white, and shouted at me. They asked me what I was
> doing there and I made the mistake of telling them the truth. What
> I got for my honesty was handcuffed, taken to jail and booked for
> disturbing the peace.[27]

And here, from *Shift and Glitter*, Christy relates a story from one of the other inmates, for no other reason than the absurdly comedic image it creates—although clearly not for the victim. In the next cell to Christy's was a Mexican on a rape charge:

> He was fixated on 1947 Buick convertibles, and not just any kind,
> but pale yellow ones. I mean, he was sexually fixated on them.
> He told me that when he was ten years old he had seen a colour
> photograph of a white woman sitting on the left front fender of a
> yellow '47 Buick convertible, and had an orgasm.
>
> 'Jesus, Cheem. I saw the picture and immediately I embarrass
> myself. I swear to you I never touched myself. I didn't have time to
> do that. One look and BAM!'

Ever after that he had been aroused by pictures of the same kind of vehicle, even without a girl on the fender. He collected magazine photos of them and had a few years earlier bought a book about Buicks with colour photographs. ... He otherwise led a normal even happy life ... and a girlfriend who'd promised to marry him. ... Just a few weeks earlier, he'd been walking home from work, taking his usual route, and there in the parking lot he always crossed was the car of his dreams. He'd never seen a real one.

Unfortunately, just as he turned out of the alley and saw the car, he also saw the woman.

'Cheem, she was *veinte, treinta* feet from the car and I was getting stiff and I spoke the words in my head, "No, lady, no. Don't let that be your car." '

But it was her car and she was a rich woman. The Mexican was passing by just a few feet from the car when the woman opened the door and got behind the wheel, the skirt rising up her stocking legs.

'I try to close my eyes but I cannot!'

He pushed her down onto the seat and had his way with her.

'I swear to you by my mother that I could not have done otherwise. I had no control of myself. I rape her. It is terrible. But I never hit her or hurt her except to push her over. It was over in two, three seconds.'

Christy had been sentenced to one week, but on the third day Floyd Wallace, in the company of a six-foot-six Indian by the name of Flow Bear (Christy notes being relieved the name was not spelled "Flaubert"), who "looked like the man you'd pick to play the baddest Indian in the movie." Floyd had gone looking for Christy and when he found out where he was, the hobos stumped up the bail money. That night Christy, Floyd, and Flow Bear crossed the Missouri River to attend a party of whites and Indians at a Kansas farmhouse. The next day was the last time Christy would ever see Floyd, and the first time that he became fully aware of the significance of the draft:

The day before, Floyd had told me he was headed up to Canada, and that day was the first time Canada or the idea of Canada, ever entered my head in any personal way.

'You want to travel up there with me?'

'Naw. I mean I'd like to but I have to get to California. It seems like I've been trying to get there forever.'

'Okay, but you go to Canada now, you'll beat the rush.'

'What're you talking about?'

'This war in Vietnam; they're going to start drafting guys like you. And, believe it or not, Canada will let guys in who don't want to go into the U.S. Army and they won't send them back.'

'You're kidding.'

'No, I'm not. I've been reading about it. You believe in what's going on over there in that faraway country?'

'No, I do not.'

'Well not believing in it, are you going to take part in the War? Go into the Army?'

'I'm not going into the Army. I know that.'

'How you going to avoid it?'

'Now that I don't know.'[28]

And so, for the first time since Linda had rerouted his trip to California on the Oklahoma highway, Christy set out once more for the Golden State, heading south to avoid Denver and then crossing over into New Mexico and Santa Fe, hitching west on Route 66, before arriving one night in riot-scarred south-central Los Angeles. The following day Christy hopped a freight to San Francisco, and immediately on his arrival met up with a woman named Emerald with Indian heritage (Asian, not Native American). She claimed to be able to "see things" in people's eyes: "Something like lust but not really lust. That and something more, something complete." Well, whatever it was that Emerald saw in Christy's eyes, they spent eight days together enjoying the sights of San Francisco and enjoying each other.

The highlight of this particular excursion was a visit to the City Lights bookstore and publisher, seller of many of Christy's literary heroes. Then a visit to Emerald's Uncle Singh's establishment, the Mars Hotel at Fourth and Howard, featured on the opening page of Kerouac's *Big Sur* as the "skid row hotel" where Kerouac arranges to meet his friend for a secret return to San Francisco before spending some quiet time in his friend's cabin in the woods. Instead, Kerouac makes a public and noisy drunken entrance to that city where his friend finds him lying on the floor of his room at the Mars among empty bottles and leaves him to complete whatever debauchery he'd started. Presumably because of the iconic image of the hotel already made famous by Kerouac, the Mars features in the 1972 David Bowie video for "Jean Genie," as well as the 1974 Grateful Dead album cover of *From the Mars Hotel*. At any rate, Uncle Singh obligingly let Christy tear out the page from the registration ledger dated 1960, where Jack Kerouac had signed himself into the Mars: "To me it was like coming upon a holy relic."

Then one day Emerald told Christy that she had to go to Fresno for a couple of days. The police apparently used Emerald from time to time for her psychic powers: "I used to find puppies and toys for the other kids when I was little. A couple of years ago I found a little boy who had been missing for three years. He was in a house with a family of hillbillies in Bakersfield." An eight-year-old Filipino girl had gone missing from her neighborhood and police and neighbors had asked Emerald for help. Christy never saw her again despite hanging around San Francisco for several weeks more.

After meeting a guy at City Lights bookstore who was looking to share his two-bedroom apartment, Christy got himself a couple of jobs. First as a Wells Fargo messenger boy—without the pony—then making sandwiches in a tavern: "I wore a white smock and apron and chef's hat, and had my own station, surrounded by hams and roasts of beef."

While still in San Francisco, around August of 1965, Christy got the urge to make a sea voyage, only to realize that getting onboard an oceangoing vessel was not a straightforward affair. Apart from the chainlink fences and security guards, there were impediments to getting legitimate work on board because of unionized labor. But with the help of "a fella who knew a fella," Christy managed to ship out on a non-union sugar boat with a non-union crew for Honolulu:

> It was probably a wreck, a mess, a bucket of bolts and a tub of rust
> but I didn't notice any of that or not much of it because it was a
> ship, my first ship. ... I worked in the galley and I put in my time
> slopping grey paint over the old hulk, painting over the rust. I liked
> the effect of the grey over bubbles and pits. There were no fights,
> nobody with a wooden leg or a parrot, no Queequeg, and the Chief
> Steward didn't try to bugger me. I didn't earn any money, either, at
> least not on board. The deal was that you worked your passage.[29]

1965

The ship docked after five nights at sea and Christy did manage to earn some money with the unloading, enough to hit the bars of Honolulu, swap yarns with some old sea dogs, and get wasted. He also hitched up with an old school friend from Springfield who, after graduation, had moved to Hawaii with her parents. Jane drove Christy around the sights of Honolulu in her '53 Dodge convertible. The full story of Christy's Honolulu adventure, and an unexpected consequence, can be read in "Sugar Boat." (*Jackpots*, 2012)

Soon after his return to San Francisco, Christy attended his first anti-Vietnam War demonstration in which several hundred protesters attempted to stop the trains transporting soldiers to the docks to board ships bound for Vietnam. But the demo was a flop, as most of the demonstrators were unwilling to face down a small group of Hells Angels guarding the track and throwing the usual, "pinko, homo, commie" taunts at the demonstrators:

> There were probably some pacifists among the protestors, too. But not that many. Most of them were simply afraid. If not physical cowards—which is nothing to be contemptuous of—they were certainly moral cowards, unwilling to embody or inhabit what they insisted were their beliefs. After that I was ready to head east. I was fed up with these people, a type that I hadn't encountered before. They may have resembled beatniks but they were soft and bland, and knew nothing of the world.[30]

Christy contrasts these "suburban college kids and professors who ruffled their hair for a weekend in town," with the more streetwise beats he had spent time with while still in high school and also the last of the real beatniks he had encountered in New York's Greenwich Village. Bored with the whole thing, Christy resolved to tramp back to Philadelphia, but was by this time experiencing some dread at the thought of being drafted and sent to Vietnam, well aware that he was registered 1-A with the draft board. On arriving one night, freezing cold and hungry, in a desolate Truckee, and finding nowhere open for food or warmth, Christy headed toward a light in a coach in the train yards and pounded with the side of his hand, his knuckles being numb with cold:

> The door opened with a blast of oily warmth and I was looking at a stout old-timer in overalls and a matching cap.
>   'Excuse me, but would you let me come in for a minute? Just

long enough to get warm and then I'll be on my way.'

The railroader eyed me up and down and removed the corncob pipe, the yellow plastic stem all wet and chewed up.

'Yeah, it's cold out there. Got company rules though.' ...

'Thanks, sir,' I said stepping over the threshold. 'You're not the shack are you?'

There was that laugh again. 'No. I'm not the shack and I'm not a sir, either.'

'What?' I thought maybe he was telling me not to be so formal.

'I mean I'm a she and not a he.'[31]

This is how Christy became acquainted with Frank,[32] the railroad lady who had spent her working life as a man. This was now Frank's permanent home, all fitted out with a cot to sleep in, "a lantern hanging from the ceiling, a pair of seats from a passenger car, a station master's roll-top desk, a footlocker, green shades on the windows, railroad magazines stacked by the desk, cupboards and shelves stocked with tools and gear. Nothing to indicate the inhabitant was a woman."[33]

Frances Marie (now Frank) had come from New Mexico aged fourteen years when her parents' ranch went bust. Her mother took Frank to California to stay with an older sister. "Big old country-girl me, gallumphing in there carrying our two suitcases, my little old mother by my side. I felt like Frankenstein's monster." Frances Marie told Christy that she went with her mother to San Bernardino, got a job, and even a couple of dates with men, "They sure must have been hard up." After graduating high school, and a brief obsession with waitresses in uniform, she decided life would be easier as a man. So Frances Marie cut her hair, wore men's clothing, and became Frank. What's more Frank worked as a man, and took on all the railroad jobs open to men, including the tough work of stoking engine boilers. She told Christy a story of how one day she had been drinking alone in an unfamiliar bar, and realized she was being discussed by a group of men. One finally announced in a loud voice, "Let's go over there and damn well find out."

We wrecked that place and I took my lumps but they never settled the question. Yeah, that was the last of the real old days. Sort of the final puff of smoke. I kept booming till 1959 and

joined up steady with the Northern Pacific here. Just when
morals started getting looser, the union rules got tighter and
made the booming life [itinerant railroad work] history. I'm the
yard watchman here now.[34]

Christy crashed the night in Frank's caboose and was woken to coffee and
a five-dollar bill wrapped in a note for the waitress of a local diner, whereupon he could breakfast before setting out for Reno. On his arrival in Reno,
Christy got himself a job as a line rider, delighted at getting the real thing on
horseback rather than its modern equivalent of fixing fences from the back
of a motorcycle. But this idyllic existence was not to last, as when the work
finished Christy was once again at the mercy of local vagrancy laws. Christy
describes how at the time, if you wanted to guarantee a bed for the night,
you needed to sign in at the local mission hostels before noon. And being a
big gambling town, there was as much call on the missions from "tapped-out
gamblers" as there was from penniless drifters. And so one night, unable to
get a bed in a hostel, Christy took a rest in the Reno bus station waiting room
to plan his next move. After dozing off he got nudged in the side by a fellow
vagrant warning him not to close his eyes if he wanted to avoid getting thrown
in jail for vagrancy. He recognized the other guy's accent as also being from
Philadelphia and they fell into swapping stories. Tony Amsterdam (Dutch) was
a mobster from South Philadelphia who had driven down to Reno in a Cadillac,
lost everything at the tables including his car, and was now waiting for money
to get wired through to the Western Union office next door. Before leaving
to pick up his money and head home, Dutch gave Christy his card and urged
him to look him up when he was next in Philadelphia. More of Dutch later.

I was terribly sleepy. There were two choices: I could go outside
and be nabbed right away or stay where I was and probably fall
asleep and be nabbed on the next sweep. And that second thing is
what happened.

The guy whacked me on the shins with the stick, and led me to
jail. I got in about three hours sleep before they woke me to give me
bologna chunks, a slice of white bread and weak coffee with sugar. I
went before the judge and got thirty days on The Ranch; from what
I could gather, some sort of work place out in the desert.[35]

When Christy protested the harshness of the sentence, just for dozing off in a bus station, the judge warned him to shut it or get another thirty days. The Ranch was so crowded that Christy had to spend the next six days in the city jail, not an entirely futile time as the sheriff's wife prepared his meals and the sheriff's daughter brought them to him. She was kind to Christy, chatted to him, and brought him some used paperback books to read which he paid for. The only other diversion at the jail was the view from Christy's cell window of the Truckee River, in particular a guy who turned up at the river each day in a bathing suit and flippers, apparently in search of gold rings. After the six days Christy was shipped out to The Ranch, which resembled an old army base that had been converted to a prison camp. The boredom of the city jail was now replaced with having to be on red alert just to protect oneself from the guards and other prisoners:

> ...murderers, rapists, armed robbers, smash and grabbers, harmless nuts, drunks and vagrants—were all thrown together, divided only by race ... whites, blacks, and Hispanics, and the only solidarity was amongst the blacks. The Puerto Ricans hated the Mexicans, and the Mexicans hated the Central Americans and Colombians, and the Colombians hated everyone. One would have thought the Latins might have banded against the common enemy, the blacks, who hated them almost as much as they hated the whites. Ninety percent of the whites were stone redneck racist trash but when confronted by a black guy in for killing the white landlord who overcharged him for rent and always tried to cop a feel off his girlfriend, it did no good to declare you'd been busted in Selma, Alabama, or to state any other bona fides. You had to come out swinging or, rather, come in to camp swinging. First guy who promoted you, you had to attack; try reasoning, and you were due for misery.[36]

And Christy did have to come into camp swinging. A tall skinny black guy hit on him straight away, told Christy that he would be "reaming" him by nightfall. When Christy looked straight past him, he added that he was glad Christy was scared because "white meat's better when it's scared." Whereupon Christy laid him out on the ground for the advantage of the assembled crowd, busting his jaw into the bargain. For the benefit of the other blacks, he made it clear that the whites were not his people either. Christy describes the subtle nuances of speech and gesture that allowed others to know where you were coming from. Even though it was next to impossible to breach racial lines for real friendship in such a place (Christy did succeed in befriending a Mexican gang boss before his time was up), it was possible to earn a kind of silent respect that kept you out of the worst kind of trouble. The work gangs were tough, but Christy also managed to talk one of the guards into letting him switch duties from handling the rolls of barbed wire to digging post holes, harder work but at least it was solitary.

Christy was let out after nine days (plus the six he did in the city jail) and used the money he'd been given for fencing to buy a bus ticket for Cheyenne. By the time he arrived he was broke again and forced against his better judgement to steal a loaf of bread, then set off tramping east in the cold October weather, freezing at nights: Lincoln, Omaha, Des Moines, to Davenport where he got busted again for vagrancy. This time, however, the desk sergeant was friendly and let Christy off early on the promise that he would do some work in the sergeant's mother's yard, "putting the garden to bed for the winter." With the money Christy had been given by the desk sergeant for this work, Christy bought a bus ticket to Chicago, not prepared to spend November nights out on the road. From there, on to Philadelphia, "and four nights later, I was sleeping with Carolyn Treece in her parents' king-sized bed."

Christy also moved back into Carolyn's ex-boyfriend's still unoccupied cabin on Cobb's Creek. There he fought the notion that he had wasted the last year bumming around the country for no good reason. One day Christy stopped at his parents' place in Springfield to collect mail and his old troubles resumed:

> 'Where did you get that car?' My mother demanded to know. I was driving Carolyn's Caddy and I told them the truth, 'It belonged to my girl friend.' 'Is she your age?' 'Yes.' 'Well she must be a whore to have enough money for a car like that.' And so it went: I looked like a bum, I was wasting my life, my head was still filled with anti-American ideas, I was going to wind up a bum in the park. That last was one of my father's favourite lines. I wanted to tell him that was one goal I'd already achieved. I got out of there as soon as I grabbed the mail and what clothes remained in my old chest of drawers in the room I had shared with my brother.[37]

Christy had become aware that full-time students were exempt from the draft board and managed to re-register at West Chester College for his second term—regardless of having taken a year out hoboing, getting married, and doing time. He told them that he had matured since Dean Killinger had caught him in bed with the girl in his off-campus residence. His next visit was to the draft board to get his student deferment.

Christy had another brief flirtation with politics—or rather anti-politics. Driving near Springfield, Christy picked up a black hitchhiker named Delmore Scudder. They immediately fell into a discussion about anarchism, a subject of which Christy had previous experience, having hung around Philadelphia with Bruce and Ruth Elwell—American branch of Situationist International—the previous year. Anarchism was a passion of Scudder's, who was something of a disciple of the writer and anarchist philosopher Paul Goodman. At the time Scudder was involved in establishing a social revolutionary group linked to Pennsylvania's Swarthmore College and its program of mentoring select groups of students in the liberal arts.

On entering Scudder's apartment in Chester, surrounded by dozens of jazz records, the two fell into discussing the relative merits of Yusef Lateef, Rahsaan Roland Kirk, Stanley Turrentine, and other virtuosos of the art—Scudder astounded that a white guy would have such an in-depth knowledge of the subject. Christy stayed at Scudder's apartment for a time. It was in an exclusively black neighborhood and Christy recalls giving rides to the local kids around the streets, many of whom had never been in a car. As a result he become very popular with the parents; as he observed later, not something that would be possible today.

But to return to the politics, Scudder had invited Paul Goodman to be the first of a series of key speakers he had organized at the Chester Quaker Meeting Hall. Surprisingly, Goodman condescended to turn up but the event was a disaster. Goodman, the worse for drink, started publicly humiliating Scudder, and patronizing his local audience. Things deteriorated even further when they all went back to a house someone had donated for the guests to sleep that night. Goodman devoted his time not to anarchism but to hustling young men and scorning the females. That night Goodman could be heard prowling the hallways knocking on the doors of young guys, begging them to let him in. Christy recalls Scudder's devastation at Goodman turning out to be a tawdry sexual predator rather than the revolutionary hero he had revered. Delmore's society folded soon after this event, confirming Christy's cynicism that the celebrities of the anarchist world were pretty much as self-serving as any other brand of politician.

A short time after this incident, Val Santee showed up at the cabin on Cobb's Creek. It being too small for the both of them, they drove to Chester and crashed for some nights at Delmore Scudder's place, before renting an apartment in the small town of Interboro between Chester and Springfield, near Philadelphia's International Airport. There they both got a job with the Horn & Hardart restaurant chain, Christy on the grill out front and Val in the restaurant. But, as Christy points out, this wasn't your regular grill. Horn & Hardart was run on factory lines with customers collecting their meals from rows of coin-operated, slot-machined, glass hatches very much as one collects mail from a post office box.

A week or so after moving into their apartment, there was a heated exchange with the landlord, a youngish ex-marine who lived downstairs with his wife and daughter. On hearing the sounds of Bob Dylan, jazz, and other subversive music through the floorboards, he concluded that the pair must be communists and threw them out. Val did another one of his disappearing acts and Christy started getting moved around the various central Philadelphia Horn & Hardart chains. But we have now left 1965 behind and are about to enter another unexpected twist in Christy's adventures.

---

1   *Shift and Glitter*, op cit.
2   Ibid.
3   Ibid.
4   Ibid.
5   Ibid.
6   Ibid.
7   Ibid.
8   Ibid.
9   Ibid.
10   Ibid.

11   Ibid.

12   Ibid.

13   Ibid.

14   Ibid.

15   Ibid.

16   Ibid.

17   Ibid.

18   Ibid.

19   *Between the Meridians*, op cit., p. 237

20   *Shift and Glitter*, op cit.

21   *Between the Meridians*, op cit., p. 238

22   Ibid. pp. 242-243

23   *Shift and Glitter*, op cit.

24   *Between the Meridians*, op cit., pp. 54-60

25   *Shift and Glitter*, op cit.

26   Ibid.

27   Ibid.

28   Ibid.

29   *Jackpots*, op cit., pp. 149-151

30   *Shift and Glitter*, op cit.

31   *Travelin Light*, op cit., pp. 67-68

32   Ibid., pp. 67-85 and *Shift and Glitter*, op cit.

33   *Shift and Glitter*, op cit.

34   Ibid.

35   Ibid.

36   Ibid.

37   Ibid.

4

FROM GANGSTER TO DRAFT DODGER VIA SUMMER OF LOVE

I t was while working one night at the Horn & Hardart grill that Christy met up again with Tony Amsterdam (Dutch) from the Reno bus station. Christy looked up from the grill and saw a guy, with two dark-looking Sicilians in suits, staring at him. The main guy had a napkin tucked into his collar and was eating away at a slice of pie. When he'd finished eating, he walked down to the counter and said, "Remember me?" Tony Amsterdam then nodded to the other two to step outside and invited Christy to sit with him at a nearby table:

> You're wasting your life, kid. I want you to come work for me,
> Jimmy. You said you were out tramping around because you
> wanted to learn about life and I told you, you ought to know a lot
> about life on account of where you come from. But there is a lot
> more to learn and if you come to work for me you'll learn it. Not
> only that but I'll give you more money every week than you make
> here in a month, and you only got to work a few hours.[1]

When Christy asked what the job was, Tony said, "You'll do a little pick-up, a little delivery." He gave Christy his card and told him to report to his office on Friday morning. There Christy learned he would be involved with the numbers racket. The first thing Tony Amsterdam insisted was that Christy buy himself an outfit fit for his new job:

> '...today, you go over to Jacob Reed's, get a suit, couple of pair
> of nice slacks, and a sport jacket. Nothing makes you look like
> a Protestant. ... And then on your way to City Hall, go see my
> paisano, Pasqual Amano on Passyunk, near Broad. Got a shoe store
> there, get a nice pair of kicks, Filippo Verdis, something like that.
> That's all on me. But I expect you to get some more vines when
> you start making some money.'
> 'I will, thank you. What am I going to City Hall for?'
> 'Get your permit.'
> 'Permit for what?'
> 'You're going to be carrying around sums of money and you got
> to protect yourself. I got you a pistol here.'[2]

The following week Christy did the rounds with the guy he was replacing—resentful but wary that Christy was clearly in favor with the boss, and more significantly, that Angelo Bruno himself was Christy's godfather. He could not resist commenting though on the fact that Christy was only part Italian, and then didn't look like he had much Italian in him at all, and that he could never be a "made man," something that bothered Christy little.

Christy's patch ranged from the southern part of the downtown area further south into the residential neighborhoods. He had to meet with storeowners and other guys who'd wait to meet him in bars. They were the "runners" who recorded the numbers and took the money. "The payoff numbers were based on the results on the tote board at Liberty Bell Park, north of the city where harness races were held. For instance, if the total money bet at the track of an evening was $87,655; the weekly number in the illegal lottery was 655."[3]

In the territory adjacent to Christy's, his counterpart there made regular stops at the luncheonette owned by his aunt Lena and her husband Joe. Christy's aunt took the numbers in a passageway between the store area and a back room. And so Aunt Lena was surprised the first time Christy turned up at the luncheonette with the other pick-up man. And maybe secretly pleased also that her nephew had given up the life of a vagabond to earn an "honest" living. At any rate, every Friday afternoon, Christy did his rounds with the nine millimeter in a lightweight holster attached to his belt at the back of his waistband. The job was finished in three and a half hours maximum for which Christy was paid seven hundred dollars a week, "more," he says, "than my father made." So much money in fact that he was not always sure what to do with it. Being able to walk into a bookstore and buy a new hardcover book probably gave him more satisfaction than blowing it on cars and clothes.

Christy also enrolled for his second year at West Chester College in order to keep out of the clutches of the draft board—if not the clutches of the very conservatively dressed Cheryl who worked at the draft board and had a voracious sexual appetite. Cheryl was a mechanical lover and the only variety to their lovemaking was the immediate location of their meetings, including on one occasion the draft board office floor after closing.

After a couple of months of running the numbers, Tony Amsterdam promoted Christy (referred to by his co-workers as Christinzio) to his loan sharking operation and raised his salary to a thousand dollars a week. This involved going around with a couple of goons to clients that Tony had loaned money to at exorbitant rates, but only when they had exhausted all other means of acquiring the money. He even had Christy sit in on some of his interviews with clients to learn the business. "You're smart, kid. I want you to understand as much about all this as possible. Maybe I'll put you through law school."

Most of Tony's clients paid up, but his real money was made from those who couldn't or wouldn't make their payments. And that is where Christy, "along with the goons, Michael and Donato" came in. "They were big and dangerous and probably not as dumb as they made out," although Christy had to later revise that assessment. "Tony carefully explained their duties and they were intent on doing what Tony told them. They weren't built to improvise."[4]

Christy was given an attaché case with the lists of recalcitrant borrowers, together with dossiers on the history of their transactions. Those who were late on a payment for the first time were just warned about the economic consequences of not being on time:

> I expanded on that message, varied it, improvised, adjusted the
> language to suit the borrower who was usually extremely nervous
> and out of sorts. I didn't have to say anything to frighten them
> or threaten them, the presence of Michael and Donato took care

of that. It wasn't just that they were big and rough; they had the blank look of impersonal killers who would do anything or not do anything and not give a shit either way.[5]

The borrowers who were continually missing payments but who did eventually pay up "required harsh words and some mild physical reminders of what might be in store." Others got beyond ever being able to pay the money back, "...which is how Tony came to own parts of houses and businesses all over Philadelphia and the Jersey Shore." The third category of borrower acted as though nothing was amiss and warnings were there to be ignored. These were given special attention by Michael and Donato short of killing the client. "The dead don't pay vig, as Tony was fond of stating." But Christy was nobody else's man and an event finally happened that made him reappraise his situation:

> The final incident in my big-time criminal career happened when we called on a dentist at his office on Broad Street, half a dozen blocks south of City Hall.
>
> This man represented the fourth type of borrower [in the account in *Shift and Glitter* Christy adds that he was the only person in this category]. The first time I went to his place with the goons, he treated us like neighborhood kids he'd caught ringing his doorbell and running away. The second time, he pretended not to know what we were talking about and to be thoroughly outraged at being visited by thugs.
>
> We went to see him one more time. Tony had called all three of us into his office and warned that the dentist was in serious trouble. In fact, Tony said, he didn't have any advice on how to handle him, but that it was likely we would have to handle him. 'I've about given up on that bastard, if you get my meaning.'[6]

What happened in the dentist's surgery is described in several pages of *Jackpots* in graphic detail. But it is the effect on the budding mobster that is the real story here. Just as Christy was starting to earn some real respect both from his boss and his comrades in arms, he acknowledges a feeling of disgust at what he had become a part of. More than the actual violence itself, he felt sickened at knowing that he had unquestioningly gone along with the performance, all the while feeling disgusted by the dentist during the preamble to the beating, and justifying to himself that the guy was only getting what he had coming to him. He had become absorbed in the whole affair without being properly conscious of his own part in it:

> Where was all of this leading? How long would it be before someone got killed on my watch, and that would make me the killer, as much as Michael and Donato?
>
> How much, I thought for the hundredth time, only now more urgently, did those other ideas I espoused, ones about peace and justice and building a better world, how much did they really matter to me?
>
> Who was I? What would become of me? What did I want to be? Was I going to align myself with the Walt Whitmans and Henry Millers, the Jack Kerouacs and Emma Goldmans, or the Michaels and Donatos, the Tony Amsterdams and Angelo Brunos? I had been strutting through a gangster dream. ... I was determined to bring to an end that gangster dream.[7]

After tossing his gun into a trash can, Christy spent the next couple of nights fretting about the consequences of his decision. He knew too much about the operation, including names and addresses, and was tortured by images of the goons coming after him on Tony's orders when he did not show up the following Friday. Instead he took the bull by the horns, phoned Tony, and told him everything that was on his mind, "leaving out the part about Henry Miller and Emma Goldman." Tony's first reaction was, "Why'd you throw the gun away?" followed by, "Forget it. We got enough guns around here to go fight the gooks in Asia." Then he invited Christy to meet him for dinner at Di Capeli's on Rittenhouse Square to talk things over. Christy's mind was churning with all of the possibilities, convincing himself that what Tony really had planned was to have him taken out over his ravioli, or finish the dinner and then offer him a ride home. Christy imagined himself smiling with a false sense of security as he got into the Buick with Michael and Donato waiting in the front seat. "Yeah, I was going for a ride, all right."[8] But Tony Amsterdam was charming, "...in the self-conscious way of a hood trying to be charming," and Christy enjoyed a delicious meal accompanied by no small amount of praise:

We need a guy like you. You tell me you got these other things on your mind. But that doesn't necessarily make for any conflict. I mean, you will be a part of everything but a little cut-off from it too because on the one hand, you're only half-Italian, and then because your mind is a little cut off from it. This thing, being in it and apart from it, it's perfect for us. A guy like you is hard to find. In fact, we never found such a guy yet. You know what's going on but you got brains. I mean you got the balls as well as the brains, and the street thing too. Oh, sure we could go down to Morris Street, Montrose, walk up and down and pick us a dozen kids with brains, groom them, but they won't have what you got. I'll make you rich, kid.[9]

But Tony's pleas were to no avail and out on the street Tony was shaking his head at Christy's big mistake. Christy, still only twenty years old, walked away from his career as a gangster—but not from gangsters altogether. With enough money to pay for the operation, Christy's first stop was at a private clinic to get himself a needed hernia repair. There, an older patient sharing the room with him eventually introduced himself as Myron Falcone. When Christy raised his eyebrows Falcone explained—Jewish mother, Italian father. Unlike Christy, he had made his career with the mob; like Christy he had accepted that he would never be a made man, and for the same reason. Myron also had a lot of inside knowledge of the fight game and, in between Carolyn's unrelenting demands on Christy in spite of his post-operative debility ("That's some hot dame, kid," as Myron observed, although Christy kept his thoughts about Myron's wife Rita to himself), the two whiled away the hours swapping notes both about the Philadelphia mob and about boxing: "Myron Falcone who was the first person to tell me how they fixed the Liston-Clay fight ... [later] corroborated by others in the fight game." After their recuperation, Myron made Christy the offer of driving him and his wife down to a place they had in Florida:

'I got a '65 Cadillac,' Myron said. 'A white one with white wall tires. Four door. You drive. We sit in back. I spring for all your meals and motel rooms, give you money for you to catch the train back, and a few bucks besides.'

What was college, educationally speaking, compared to driving a big-time gangster and his gun moll wife to Florida in a year-old Cadillac, and getting paid for it?

'Yes, I'll do it.'[10]

After dropping Myron and Rita off in Hollywood, Florida, now with money in his pocket, Christy headed down to Miami Beach to visit some of the sites he had haunted the year before—only to be disappointed at how everything had changed. But, as they often do, new situations take over from old memories, and in the most unexpected way. Christy was sitting on Lincoln Drive, "eating a media noche sandwich in the middle of the afternoon and reading the *Miami Herald*," when an article hidden away on the back page caught his eye. It was a story about Christy's childhood screen hero, the Western star Lash Larue. Christy recalled Larue as standing out from all the other Saturday afternoon idols like Tarzan, Roy Rogers, or Gene Autry, whose portrayals in contrast Christy found unbelievable:

> Lash was different. He was vined down all in black and had that whip. But more than the whip, he had The Look. The black eyes clamped on you under thick brows. Lash knew the score. He always seemed to need a shave. We saw his movies at the Colonial Theatre.[11]

Christy had a fascination with movies all his life, ever since his mother and he, aged four at the time, were escorted from a theater in Hopewell, Virginia, because the child avenger created a ruckus in the auditorium after Roy Rogers was jailed unjustly. By the time Christy enrolled in university, in order to satisfy his insatiable appetite for unconventional as well as classic movies, he revived a defunct foreign film society, procured the movies, wrote the brochures, and operated the projector, in order that he could watch movies that would otherwise be unavailable to him: *Battleship Potemkin*, Carl Dreyer's *Joan of Arc* starring that other vagabond writer Antonin Artaud, *La Strada*, *Alexander Nevsky*, *Seven Samurai*, *The Red Shoes*, and the like.

Christy's later work in movies and television is recounted at the end of Chapter 6, but to return to Lash Larue, the headline that caught Christy's eye and disbelief on this occasion was "Former Children's Cowboy Star Lash Larue Arrested for Vagrancy." Larue had fallen on hard times and had been working in carnivals. Christy describes the photograph of his former hero after his arrest as "Just a ride boy or roughie. One night he got drunk and the cops vagged him." And so Christy headed for the Miami City Jail to visit Lash. There they spent four hours in the day room chatting together about carnival life and movie stars until a woman showed up to collect him. Christy describes her as a nice-looking woman who reminded him of a younger, slimmer version of Rita. She was a performer in the kootch show attached to the carnival and had taken up a collection among the other performers for Lash's bail. The three of them left the jail together and on rounding the corner Lash invited Christy to join them for a drink, but he declined. They shook hands and Christy watched them heading off together toward a bar doorway lit up by a tilting neon martini glass hanging over the sidewalk, complete with pink glowing swizzle stick and a pink olive. The girl had her arm around Lash, his shirt flapping in the breeze, as they vanished into the dark doorway of the joint.

Some weeks later, after resuming his studies at West Chester, Christy was on a bus with a girlfriend from the same college, Ellen Sinclair. They were returning from her parents' house to spend the weekend at Christy's place. Ellen pulled out some papers she was carrying in her bag and when Christy asked what they were, she replied, "Some guy's writing." By the time they had arrived in West Chester, Christy was so entranced in what he was reading that he did not respond to being shaken by Ellen who thought he'd fallen asleep. Christy's discovery of Charlie Leeds and his writing is described in *Beyond the Spectacle* ("The Legendary Charlie Leeds"), *Travelin Light* ("To Hell with this Cockeyed World"), and also in *Shift and Glitter*:

> There was no one on the bus, even the driver had gotten off. But I hadn't been dreaming, I'd been reading.
>
>   'Who is this guy?'
>
>   'A friend of my sister's in Atlantic City. A musician called Charlie.'
>
>   'Jesus. You have a change of clothes in your bag, don't you?'
>
>   'Yeah, why?'
>
>   'We're going on a little trip.'
>
>   'Where to?'
>
>   'Atlantic City.'[12]

After they had checked in with Nancy, they started hitting the bars and clubs of Atlantic City looking for Charlie Leeds, who it seemed everyone—by this time including Christy—regarded as some kind of legendary character.

It turned out that Charlie was an extremely difficult guy to locate, and even if one could locate him, there'd be no guarantee that he'd be coherent.

> Atlantic City wasn't much in those days, like a flashy old dame way past her prime in rundown shoes and a ratty fox stole, half the sequins gone from her dress; you could still enjoy her if you closed your eyes and thought of the way things used to be.[13]

They had no luck that night, but around noon the next day, the door to Nancy's apartment was opened, "and in walked a guy in a belted benny carrying an attaché case."

> He looked like a racetrack tout with his pencil-line moustache and shifty eyes; he wore seersucker slacks and white tennis shoes and on his large head was a cloth cap like drivers of Triumphs and Morgans wore. He merely muttered as Nanette (Nancy) tried to introduce us, and kept walking back to the kitchen. That was Charlie Leeds. Peeking around the archway, I saw him take some papers out of the attaché case, toss them on the table, and sit down. ... He looked wary as I sat down at the table and excused myself for interrupting him. He mumbled, looked at me waiting for whatever it was I would say. I told him I'd read some of his stuff. 'Oh, man,' he said, it sounded like a spoken groan. 'They're not much. Just my personal things.'[14]

Charlie had played bass as a band member with some of the greats, including Al Cohn, Charlie Parker, Woody Herman, and Buddy Rich, and was still, by the time Christy met him, in demand as a session musician. But it was his writing that really impressed Christy. As he now told Charlie: "The capital letters, spacing between words and phrases, all that, it's like, well, I may be nuts, but it's like reading a musical score." Christy's assessment of Charlie's writing marked the beginning of a close friendship between these two unorthodox characters. "Wow. Nobody's ever picked up on that before. They just think I'm trying to be eccentric. That's pretty groovy, you digging that." The musicality, particularly the spaces between the notes, is what Christy had picked up on, and what Charlie himself had set out to capture in his writing. None of Charlie's work had been published, and he wouldn't have known how to go about getting it published anyway. He could never complete anything but wrote numerous versions of the same piece. Christy agreed to take all his writing away and read through it, on the basis that he would type it up in exchange for lessons on the bass from Charlie. They would meet up in two weeks' time. After chatting for an hour or so, Charlie took his leave to meet up with a cocktail waitress in some club:

> 'And that,' Nanette (Nancy) said, after the door had closed, 'was Charles Thornton Leeds, self-admitted dope fiend and general all-around fuck-up. Not to mention, the only genius I've ever met. ... I don't know what you said to him,' Nanette said to me, 'But I've never seen him have a conversation with anyone that lasted that long.' ... Well, I never got a music lesson and never did type more than a couple of pages of his stuff but we became fast friends.[15]

Christy met up with Charlie Leeds a couple of times in Atlantic City, and also saw him perform. On one of those occasions he sang. He sounded like Chet Baker and Christy wondered if he was imitating Chet. Christy was told later by a couple of well-known musicians who knew both Charlie and Chet that it had been the other way around, which can be verified by a Victory Record of Charlie singing with Buddy Rich that predates any record of Chet Baker's. Christy has never been able to locate that disc.

There are lots of fascinating stories and anecdotes in Christy's writing concerning Charlie Leeds. One of these concerns Charlie's obsession with roses (and the recipients of his roses) that he fabricated in a workshop at his mother's house with the aid of a variety of tools and a soldering gun from scraps of fabric, chunks of lead, wire, and other metal and plastic bits and pieces.

Back in West Chester in August of 1966, and ten days before classes were to resume after the summer break, Christy got news that Charlie Leeds had—with persuasion from the authorities—signed himself into the Federal Narcotics Hospital in Lexington, Kentucky, for a detox: "a place that deserves its own volume in the history of jazz." Christy jumped a freight train to Lexington to visit his friend, but on arrival was informed that hospital visiting hours were already over. Christy made his way over to the university campus where he got harassed by a carload of crewcut yobs shouting the usual "pinko, homo" taunts reserved for anyone without the obligatory shaved head—insignia of the good ol' redneck bigot. Enraged at their insults being ignored, they nudged Christy with the car bumper before piling out of the car and attacking him. When the campus police arrived to break up the fracas, it was the "pinko homo" they turned over to the custody of the Lexington city police. The police bought the story that Christy had attacked the "gridiron heroes" for no reason and threw him in jail for disturbing the peace. When Christy finally made it to the Federal Narcotics Hospital, the first thing he noticed were the surrounding fields:

> ...where roamed weird cows with misshapen udders and twin tails; there was even a two-headed calf. The hospital ran an experimental agriculture farm as, I suppose, a sort of sideline that made one wonder what they did to the junkies. ... Charlie looked healthy, for Charlie. He told me about the other times he'd been there for the cure. Four or five times dating back to 1949. He didn't mind being in Lexington. They always had a good band. Whenever Charlie was off the streets and in an institution, he played alto saxophone rather than the bass. He never played the sax on the outside, but he'd been institutionalized so many times, he was very good on it. 'Oh, man. I want to play it in clubs but I'm just not good enough to play jazz.'[16]

Sometime prior to visiting Charlie in Lexington, Christy had received a letter from the warden of the State Penitentiary at Menard, southern Illinois, to inform him that prisoner 33464 (Val Santee) had requested he be allowed to correspond with Christy, but that he must first write to show his agreement. The warden gave no information about why Val was in prison, and it wasn't until Christy received his first letter from Val that he discovered Val had been given a forty-year sentence for first-degree murder—the crime itself was never disputed. Val gave Christy instructions to contact his first and second wives, and a friend, and told him also that his family had been informed that Christy, and no one else, should receive Val's personal effects. Val Santee's stoicism shines through in that letter:

> My outlook on life and everything in general will no doubt undergo quite a bit of changing. At the present time I am still in a sort of fog bank. My folks are looking into the possibility of a new hearing for me. Who knows what the future holds! Now Jim, do not despair and grieve, for you must go on and 'do it all' for two of us now.

Do you mind? I think not. Smell every flower twice; laugh extra
hearty! Live for both of us.[17]

And so, at the end of June, 1966, after his visit to Charlie and leaving
Lexington, Christy headed off for Menard State Prison on the banks of the
Mississippi. On his arrival, Christy was told that his visiting rights had been
removed, having been judged a "bad influence" on his friend: "The things
you write about in your letters can only fill the prisoner's mind with notions
that are not conducive to his integrating himself into the community." But,
even though it would be his last, the visit went ahead anyway. Christy was
appalled at just what kind of community his nineteen-year-old friend would be
integrated into. There are graphic accounts in *Shift and Glitter* of Val's fellow
cellmates on death row and Christy's fears for his friend's safety at the hands of
trustees who had nothing to lose by doing what they wished with their fellow
inmates. All the way back to West Chester, Christy was preoccupied with Val
stuck on the row with those people, and not eligible for parole for another
decade. He doubted that Val could survive such an ordeal and wondered if
he'd ever see his friend again.

But back to Charlie Leeds. The account of Charlie in *Beyond the Spectacle*
ends in 1968 with a brief exchange of words between the two friends on
the boardwalk in Atlantic City, just after Charlie had been charged with a
drug-related offense and given a thirteen-year sentence. Leeds had been in
prisons and mental hospitals over forty times, always connected in some
way with drugs. The chronicle in *Beyond the Spectacle* ends with Charlie
shoving a package containing a couple of hundred pages of his writing into
Christy's hands: "he ran off down the boardwalk and I never saw him again."
Charlie was to report the next day to begin serving his prison sentence for
the drugstore caper.

The story of how Charlie came to be arrested in 1968 is told in *Travelin
Light*, and reads like a parody of the slapstick screen adventures of his name-
sake. Just one of the tragicomic escapades that punctuated Charlie Leeds'
life involved him entering a drugstore to get some prescription drugs. When
the pharmacist kept him waiting too long, Charlie had lain down in a laundry
basket in the stockroom, pulled some clothing over his eyes, and fallen asleep.
When he woke up, he was covered in more uniforms that had been tossed on
top of him by employees going off duty, oblivious of the new occupant of the
laundry basket. By now the place was locked and empty. Before figuring how

he would get out of the place without setting off the alarm, and wary of doing so, Charlie thought he may as well pick up his prescription anyway:

> There he was, a forty-four year old man, crawling on his belly across the polished linoleum floor of a drugstore headed for the shelf where they kept the paregoric. ... He stopped first when he came to the cough medicine ... snatched a bottle, and took a drink. Just before he got to the paregoric he paused to reach up and feel around in the cash register drawer. The alarm went off. Charlie ran to the back door and couldn't get it open. He jumped into the laundry hamper and burrowed down deep. A few minutes later the cops arrived, flashed their lights around ... but not in the hamper. They mumbled about some kind of mistake and left.[18]

Charlie got the paregoric, but not before helping himself to a quart of almost-melted ice cream from the fridge and scooping it into his mouth with his fingers, then, as he reached above the four-foot alarm trigger "for a handful of Christmas trees [Tuinals]," it went off for a second time, as he must have known it would. Once again he dived into the laundry hamper but this time the cops discovered him on account of the trail of melted ice cream that led to his hiding place—"Bing Cherry," as he recalled to Christy later.

But Christy *did* meet Charlie Leeds again after writing his *Beyond the Spectacle* account. And, with Christy's help, Charlie's writing was published by Prism International Press and November House in 1970 under the title (inspired by Chaplin's 1914 movie) *Tillie's Punctured Romance & The Love Song of Rotten John Calabrese plus selected short subjects.* The book received favorable reviews and spawned two stage plays: *Tillie's Punctured Romance* (circa 1979, Toronto), and *Beat for Sparrows* (co-written by Leeds' niece Karen Schuler) which premiered in Los Angeles in 2001. Al Pacino's agent had approached Christy about an interview with Pacino, with a view to the actor playing Charlie Leeds in *Beat for Sparrows,* but it never materialized.

A woman named Martha, to whom Christy had shown Charlie's work, started a correspondence with Charlie in prison, and on his parole the pair got married. Christy describes a trip Charlie made to visit him in Toronto where Charlie stocked up on drugs, legal in Canada but banned in the U.S. This was a happy but short-lived period for Charlie, who was re-arrested for breaching his parole and returned to prison. Christy describes how Charlie never really recovered from his re-arrest, even though he was released six months later. The following year he was back in another drug rehab facility, and by 1974 Martha had left him and Charlie had experienced his first heart attack:

> He had started to drink. It was a necessity. He got beat on the dope deals and he had to have something. The girls took him for bread. Everything was coming apart. One of the last times I saw him, he had just gotten out of the hospital two days before. He had been pronounced dead. His heart had stopped. He said, 'Man, I was lying on the table and it was beautiful, I had this dream about you and Lana Turner and the twelve apostles....'[19]

Christy received a telegram that Charlie was desperate to see him. On his arrival, he found Charlie "drunk, sick and raving." Christy immediately ran into the usual institutional red tape: it was against hospital rules to admit someone more than twice a year and Charlie had been admitted on twelve occasions which prompted the following retort from Christy: "Then, what's one more time? ... Should I take him back to the Boardwalk, lay him down there, near the Diving Horse? Let him expire right there with your name pinned to his chest?"[20] The hospital did admit Charlie, and the last image Christy had of him was disappearing in a wheelchair through the lobby's swinging doors, all the while engaging the nurse with his banter. Christy's epitaph to Charlie Leeds in *Travelin Light* reads, "I loved him and he died ... And you can play that on your mother-fuckin' piano sometime." (see note on Charlie Leeds' ancestry[21])

But back to our own hero in 1967 and his continued college education. Christy describes it as being even more absurd than before, citing a course he signed up for called Middle Eastern Studies that he walked out of after the first few minutes. The professor teaching the class had declared to his students in the opening session that there was one thing they had to understand from the outset if they hoped to make any sense of the situation in the Middle East. "...all the problems in the region are the fault of the Arabs."[22]

The aspect of college that most infuriated Christy was the petty rules around the dress and behavior of its students. The expulsion of a liberal arts student for having hair down to his collar was the catalyst for Christy's confrontation with the college authorities. After being denied a meeting to protest this treatment of a fellow student, Christy and some others organized a series of protests that attracted local and regional news coverage. Right-wing students organized counter-protests and the college recruited student spies to infiltrate not only the protesters' meetings but other activities also. This included a party of jocks and cheerleaders, twenty of whom, some seniors, were subsequently expelled for consuming alcohol and cross-gender fraternization—and all this off campus. The social and political culture of the time meant that these upstanding and spineless students took their punishment and refused to complain or protest, even when Christy visited their hangout to try to persuade them to challenge the decision:

> I reminded them of all the names they had called us during our rallies and protests, probably the least offensive being 'coward.' But yet here they were, big tough athletes, being thrown out of school yet doing nothing about it. Just bowing to the authorities that have no legal right to censor them or any other students, no matter their politics or the length of their hair, for what they do off campus and, come to that, no reason to censor anyone for what they do on campus as long as it doesn't break any civic laws. I said that I had an idea to get their expulsions rescinded.[23]

While the majority of the jocks remained hostile and suspicious of Christy, others came to see him later to take up his offer of threatening the president and three of the deans with a legal challenge. The outcome being that Christy secured the services of Pennsylvania's ex-governor, George M. Leader, and in a humiliating meeting with President Sykes and the college governors, Leader told Sykes that if he allowed the case to go to court he would become the laughingstock of the entire American higher educational system. Not surprisingly, following the meeting the expelled students were promptly reinstated. For his trouble, the most Christy got was a nod of acknowledgement from one of the jocks, anxious not to be further associated with an obvious political agitator.

Christy was living together with Ellen at the time in a big apartment above a bakery on West Main Street in West Chester. As well as running the foreign-film society at the college, Christy had work driving and managing a mobile library. He was now asked to carry and show movies at locations around the county, as well as stacking the main library shelves. Through Ramona the librarian, Christy was introduced to her brother, the wildlife author, filmmaker, and ex-carnival roughie, Daniel Mannix. Mannix, whom Christy describes as "the first real writer I'd ever met," started accompanying him on some of his film showings and giving talks about his film. Mannix was over six-and-a-half feet tall and seemed to have been everywhere and done everything. Christy's first thought was that he wished he could have introduced Mannix to Floyd Wallace. The pair hit it off from their first meeting and Mannix was keen to go out with Christy in the bookmobile and discuss his movie. When Mannix discovered that Christy had worked in carnivals, he tested him out with questions like: "So in that last ten-in-one where you worked, what was the blow-off?" or "You ever notice how the tip is bigger the farther you get from the East Coast?" Soon the pair were rolling along Chester County back roads talking about "armadillos and iguanas, pinheads and half-n-halfs. Mannix had also written about the orgy of sadism that was the Roman games and about the history of torture. He'd tell about fire-breathers and elastic men, about carnie gaffs, hunting with bows, arrows, and slingshots."[24]

The college administrators finally got even with Christy for embarrassing them by identifying him to police who had uncovered a plot to blow up patriotic monuments around Philadelphia, including the Liberty Bell. Christy suffered beatings and three days in jail before the less dim-witted police officers realized that he couldn't have been involved in a plot organized by black activists, who were hardly likely to "let a white boy into their club."

It is the natural pattern of the vagabond's life to lurch from highs to lows and back again. That is the serendipitous existence experienced by those who refuse to seek out tedious predictability. After the sweet victory over the college governors, then the stitch-up that followed, an unexpected distraction again presented itself to Christy. He had a college friend with whom he had endless debates about music. Gerry Ammons was always trying to seduce Christy with late-sixties psychedelic rock, but the old jazz aficionado was having none of it. Christy's musical tastes have always remained unshaken: R&B, "hard country" music, and always jazz. From a young age he had always listened to serious black or country music stations on the radio while his contemporaries were listening to Top Forty hits. "I wasn't trying to be different, the other just didn't interest me. Later I went to jazz clubs, the ones that would let in an underage white kid, and hid at the back somewhere." Lester Young remains Christy's all-time hero and he describes Oscar Peterson's "Night Train" as his first "grown-up" jazz piece. "I tried it because I was a Sonny Liston fan, and that was the tune he trained by." Christy lists off some of his, not always predictable, all-time favorites such as Louis Armstrong, Big Joe

Turner, Andy Kirk's Clouds of Joy, Jay McShann and of course Charlie Parker, Art Pepper, Joe Albany, Billie Holiday, Peggy Lee, The Orioles, The Ravens, Lonnie Johnson, Hank Williams, Cliff Edwards, some Woody Guthrie, Lefty Frizzell, Gary Stewart, Jimmie Rodgers, George Jones, and Bobby Bare. The list goes on but represents the soundtrack of the thirties to fifties rather than the sixties music of his contemporaries. The debates were good-natured, and when Ammons asked Christy to accompany him to a concert that summer, the offer was politely accepted, even though the name on the bill was a twenty-four-year-old white woman posing, so Christy saw it, as a "ballsy blues mama."

'What's this for?' I asked as he handed me a ticket.

'Concert next Saturday in Philly at the Palestra. I don't have anybody to go with.'

'Who is this person?'

'You're kidding? You don't know who Janis Joplin is?'

'Nope."

'You've never heard of Janis Joplin?'

'Never.'

'That's weird, man. Wow.'[25]

But by the time Christy got to see Joplin perform, and chatted to her later in her dressing room, he had become fascinated both by the singing phenomenon and the woman behind the voice—ignoring, as best he could, the hippie band members and, as he further describes, their overly long guitar solos. Joplin also admitted to being sick of hippies, even if "I am one myself, in spite of myself." This would have been shortly after Joplin's brief relationship with Country Joe McDonald. Christy and Joplin became close friends, arguably because of their self-styled rebel status and—although having accidentally landed in the sixties and (Joplin at least) being defined by that cultural phenomenon—mutual admiration of beat poetry and blues traditions. They kept in touch and spent time together in Philadelphia, New York, and Toronto when Joplin was on tour. As a footnote to the Janis Joplin digression, Christy had, coincidentally, met Joplin's father in Texas a couple years earlier when, in his role as an insurance salesman, he had handled things for the parents of Christy's first wife.

By this time, Christy had all but finished with college and was dividing himself between West Chester and New York. He continued to show films once a week and then headed off to stay with his friends, the aforementioned

Bruce and Ruth Elwell who rented an apartment in an old East Side tenement at 56 Eldridge Street, Manhattan. It is worth noting here an observation that Christy recounts in *Real Gone* (2010) because it gives us a clue to the vagabond's existential nature, a mindset that is a prerequisite for the life of a tramp. The passage below, in which Christy contemplates his immediate surroundings from the Elwells' apartment in 1967, shows that he was as comfortable with his own company as he was with the company of others, and more than able to distract himself in the most banal and abject of circumstances.

> My room was at the back and my window looked down into a vast
> courtyard, as did all the other back windows of the entire block
> of tenements. The open space was filled with concrete rubble,
> bricks, plumbing pipe, and whatever had been thrown out the back
> windows, including kitchen chairs and huge records. I used to sit
> at the window and ponder those records. On what kind of machine
> could they have possibly been played? There were no doors that
> gave onto this courtyard. One day I saw a dead cat sprawled across
> the top of an old-fashioned cabinet radio, and over the course of
> several weeks, I watched as it decomposed and became a skeleton.[26]

But 1967 was the "summer of love" and anyone of a certain age who considered themselves anti-establishment, and was inclined to adventure and kicks, would, as Christy observed, have been foolish not to go to San Francisco.

> Larry Nicodemus and his Italian girlfriend Laura Longo were
> all for it and so was Ed Vogel but he didn't have a girlfriend.
> I suggested he drive up to New York and put an ad in the
> Psychedelicatessen on Tompkins Square. He drove up to the
> apartment and I took him over to [the] place; he pinned his note
> on the bulletin board and when he got back to West Chester,
> there had been three or four calls. 'Chick wanted for trip to San
> Francisco! Must travel light.'[27]

The story from here, covering the rest of 1967 and 1968, is told in *Real Gone*, which opens with Christy taking a road trip with five friends to the Haight-Ashbury district of San Francisco, epicenter of the summer of love. By way of juxtaposing two very different American zeitgeists, the book describes the violence following the murder of Martin Luther King, Jr. in the spring of 1968 when, less than a year on, the peace and love of '67 was followed by bloody insurrection as the army and police turned their aggression inward against its own citizens and parts of the country became a virtual civil war zone. The synopsis on the back cover sums the book up as follows: "the novella records the very moment that an empire reached its peak and started its decline." At the same time that America was fighting this war within its own borders, its aggression was also focused outward. 1968 was the peak year of the Vietnam War. But to return to the "summer of love," although Christy wanted to see the San Francisco phenomenon for himself, he was, as he repeatedly insists, no hippie. As a cynic par excellence, Christy dispels the romantic myth of the sixties and exposes it for the treacherous sham that it really was:

I walked the streets of Haight for the rest of that day and part of the next. By that time, I was bored with the entire scene. It just seemed like a massive convention of conventional suburban kids taking some time out from their schooling and their careers to gather their future nostalgia.

[...]

Of course, there were others who confessed to believing that if you spread what they called "love" around it would come back to you. But there was too much self-consciousness at work ... I didn't feel sorry for them but I did for the innocents, and there were many of these, because they, more often than not, were prey for the opportunists, the rapists, the crooked drug dealers, the guru hustlers, crooks of all sorts.

[...]

What went on in the Haight reminded me of the colonisation of some foreign land, only these Americans didn't come in military garb, the guys in suits in their wake, but they had a prescribed uniform just the same. Just two years earlier, I had walked the same streets with Emerald. It was a Russian neighbourhood then with great corner grocery stores and working men, babushka ladies, good food in cheap restaurants, and apartments to rent for thirty-five dollars a month. The invaders had since discovered the area and transformed everything they found. ... The borscht and pierogi places now served bland barley soup at exorbitant prices. The corner shop that had smelled of pickles and cabbage became a head shop, oppressive with the smell of incense and indistinguishable from the head shop a few doors down. And rents? Well you had to have some money from mommy and daddy.[28]

Not having money from mommy and daddy, Christy and Ellen found a room in the Fillmore District, San Francisco's black neighborhood, where they slept on the couch and floor of a showgirl acquaintance. One of the visitors to the apartment was the comedian Redd Foxx. Christy also had his first casual meeting with Chuck Berry at this time, and would bump into him several times throughout his life. Christy describes it as more a mutual acknowledgement than a friendship, a typical vagabond comradeship—well, in Christy's case at least: "Over the years, I'd see him in various cities, a couple of times we talked, a couple of times we just nodded to each other, like vague acquaintances. Once backstage in Atlantic City, he said, 'Hey man. Haven't seen you for a while.' "[29]

On a difficult return trip from San Francisco (tension had developed between the six friends after Christy punched one of them out) the travelers stopped at a hick diner in western Pennsylvania. They took six stools at the end of the counter but the waitress ignored them and continued chatting to some locals at the other end of the bar, even when they asked for the menu. The group gave up hope of a meal and eventually walked out, with the waitress' dishcloth thrown at their backs:

> When we were on our way, I looked over my shoulders at the diner that seemed to glow in the distance. I hadn't noticed the American flag before on its pole. The flag seemed also to glow, as if from some inner light, of righteousness no doubt.
>
> We got to West Chester around two in the morning. Everyone was sick of everyone else. The summer of love was over.[30]

On Christy's return from his trip to San Francisco, he received his draft papers and was ordered to report for induction into the army at Philadelphia's

Armory Hall. The scene that follows provides a further illustration of Christy's Cynic credentials: contempt and ridicule for authority, matched by a total disregard of the consequences in defying that authority. This particular style of outspokenness and freedom of speech among the ancient Greeks was referred to as *parrhesia*. It applies both to speech and defiant actions, and in the case of the Cynics, "performances," such as Diogenes begging alms of a statue to get practice at being refused. The best-known anecdote of Cynic *parrhesia* is Alexander the Great's reported meeting with Diogenes when the latter was sunning himself in a Corinth park. When Alexander tells Diogenes he will grant him any wish of his choosing, the Cynic replies, "Stand out of my light." This Cynic digression underlines Christy's own brand of *parrhesia* in the Armory Hall parade ground as part of a line-up of 250 naked recruits:

'Step forward to be inducted into the U.S. Army!' barked the guy with the short haircut in the dry-cleaned uniform.

Two hundred and forty-nine young men stepped forward. The sergeant, or whatever he was, strode over to me and, with mock politeness, asked whether I'd failed to hear him.

'I heard you.'
'Well what's the matter? You afraid?'
'Everything's fine and I'm not afraid.'
'Sir. Call me Sir.'
'No. I won't do that.'
He shook his head. 'You don't have your thinking cap on, sonny. You're starting your army career out on the wrong foot. You're going to give in, eventually, and this incident will be on your record. You'll regret it.'
I said nothing.
'Stand at attention!'
I had my weight on one leg.
'No, sir. I'm not in the army and I don't have to do anything you say.'
'When I get you in the back room, you'll do what I say.'

While we were having our conversation, I glanced at the line of young men beyond him, many of whom looked over their shoulders with interest. I could see the fear in some of the faces.

They didn't want any part of the whole deal. ... Three-quarters
of the others are brothers. Why fight for America when you can't
even get served in most restaurants despite some bullshit civil
rights legislation that isn't enforced anyway?[31]

Christy stood his ground and was turned over to other military personnel so
that the sergeant could get on with his inducting. First they tried to humiliate
Christy by ordering him not to put his clothes back on while they interrogated
him. He ignored them and dressed anyway, then refused to move or talk. Then
they tried ignoring him before finally arresting him, whereupon Christy demanded
to speak with a lawyer. To cut a long story short, the lawyer got Christy released
on the basis that the military had failed to take into consideration his enrollment
at a university for a course of study. Having already left West Chester College,
to avoid the draft Christy had to enroll without delay at Cheyney State College
in Chester County, America's oldest university for black students.

I doubt that in my limited time there I saw more than three or four
other white students. People joked about Cheyney, insisting the
academic standards were so low that they would accept anyone who
applied. I had five courses, and before heading to New York I attended
four of them twice, and one three times, it was black history.[32]

But on this occasion, Christy never made it to New York. Instead he
absented himself from college to undertake an assignment in New Orleans
for the Philadelphia-based investigative journalist and civil rights lawyer
Vincent Salandria, who was challenging the Warren Commission findings
on the Kennedy assassination. Salandria was working with Big Jim Garrison,
the New Orleans District Attorney (played by Kevin Costner in the film *JFK*)
who claims he was prevented from uncovering the truth behind the Kennedy
assassination by a federal government conspiracy. In *Real Gone*, Christy claims
that Garrison suspected no less than Christy's old drinking buddy, former vice
president Lyndon B. Johnson, of being responsible for the cover-up.

The more entertaining story is Christy's own. On arrival in New Orleans,
he was sitting in the front seat of the car around the corner from Bourbon
Street with his black friend Johnny Parker. While their third companion went
to a bar to buy cigarettes, a redneck cop accosted the pair:

'Hey boys. Whereyat?'

'Huh?' said Johnny.

'Wassat Niggah?'

Johnny didn't reply.

'How come you two sitting together?'

I told him we were waiting for our friend.

'Thasso? Looks mighty peculiar, white man and coloured man all cozy in the front seat like that. Any good citizen passing by, seeing you, well, they could be excused for thinking you was, you know. Sweethearts.'

'Oh, shit, man,' Johnny exclaimed.

'Hey, niggah. You got you a smart mouth.'

I wondered what was taking Marty so long. After a few more minutes of the cop's angry banter, he had us get out and lean against the car. Then he frisked us, cuffed us and marched us down Bourbon Street and around another corner where a squad car was parked. We were taken to the Parish Jail and arrested for disturbing the peace.[33]

On arrival at the jail, Christy insisted on his statutory phone call and was nearly beaten for his trouble. But when he told the police that he was represented by no lesser lawyer than the district attorney himself, instead of provoking the police to more anger, the fact that two out-of-town kids should ask for the district attorney was a cause for much mirth: "Jim Garrison! Well har har har! Why big Jim deer gone represent you and the nigrah? Tell me that, boy." And when Christy got through and asked for the district attorney they assumed that he was either talking down a dead line or joshing with someone down the phone:

'Whale boy, what big Jim say?'

'Yeah, boy. He coming down to fetch you and the nigrah?'

'He's on his way here right now.'

More laughter.

'Awright then. We take you back to your cell, you can wait for him in comfort.'[34]

Imagine the chastened and embarrassed police, who had laughed at and taunted the pair, prodded them with their nightsticks and pushed them around the jailhouse, when half an hour later in walks Big Jim himself, and demands the police apologize for their behavior to his clients:

> Now it was all, 'We're mighty sorry, Mr. Garrison. All a misunderstanding. Mistaken identity.' ...
>> 'Then you owe these young men an apology.'
>> They had to be encouraged to come around to that. Then one of them looked up at me and said, 'Guess we messed up. I'm sorry.'
>> I nodded. Two more apologised to me.
>> Garrison said, 'You're forgetting Mr. Parker.'
>> Well they didn't like that at all but it was one of the finer moments of my life, listening to them do it, 'We sorry, Mr. Parker.'[35]

The pleasure of that event lasted well beyond the business transaction in New Orleans. All the way back up north in the car was the repeated refrain from Johnny, "We sorry, Mr. Parker! We sorry, Mr. Parker!"

Back in New York, Christy soon became bored senseless with all the politicking by those he describes as joyless, anarchist theoreticians. But at least these revolutionaries took it for granted that there were a bunch of crooks in the White House. This in contrast to those Christy describes as "campus radicals, off-campus radicals, and lefty media darlings who all seemed surprised that their government lied to them, and believed that there could exist a government that didn't lie to them. 'That's what governments do,' I was forever replying. 'That's what governments have to do.'" [36] Regardless of Christy's aversion to politics, he would join the 100,000 others who marched on the Pentagon in Washington on October 21, 1967, an event he later describes in the style of the Cynic diatribe:

> And tragedy it was, because of the great hopes smashed to smithereens, not by cops or "fascist" politicians but the arrogance of opportunists without a shred of conscience. Sure there were black power types, fresh out of prison on armed robbery beefs promoting eighteen year old, bra-less blondes with the hard sell of Oppressed Victim and there were sanctimonious idiots sitting in a circle around the pentagon vowing to make it levitate ... of course

there were thousands of marchers in a floral patterned lockstep....[37]

Christy goes beyond the mere ridiculing of those who believe in "vague notions of 'peace' " and fantasies of toppling government and replacing it with a totally new system. He makes it clear why he thinks the protesters were lamentably naïve—and does not exclude himself from that naïvety:

> My stupidity was not in believing in Revolution but in revolution
> in America. Hell, I had just turned twenty-two and it is the right
> of youth to believe in the idea of revolution, youth demands it
> or should (or did). But I also that day realised for certain and
> unequivocally that the power of the American mass media was too
> vast and overwhelming, that it was destined to level and co-opt
> everything in its path.[38]

On the return trip from Washington to New York, Christy made a brief stopover at Cheyney State College, but not to resume his studies. He was anxious to meet Muhammad Ali, who was at Cheyney State as part of a tour of speeches following having been stripped of his heavyweight title for refusing to participate in the Vietnam War. Christy, the only white student in the gymnasium that day, listened to Ali speak for half an hour before the boxer made his way along the line of waiting students. Christy was getting a few dirty looks from the other students but no one disputed his right to be there. Ali walked along the line of students as one by one the brothers stepped forward to shake his hand. By the time he got within fifty feet of him, Christy could tell the champ was getting bored with the whole thing. "Hey, how you doin, brother. Uh huh. Uh huh. ... Hey, how you doin, brother. Uh huh. Uh huh." When Ali got within two students of Christy he glanced up but hid his reaction to seeing a lone white guy in the line-up. But ever the comedian, Ali could not resist the opportunity that presented itself. Extending both hands toward Christy as though he was keeping a ghost at bay, and to the cheers and applause that broke out from the entire auditorium, Ali grabbed Christy in a bear hug—producing even more roars from the crowd—raised his hand by the wrist, and whispered in Christy's ear, "The fuck you doing here, boy?"[39]

It was Christy's last visit to the university. Having decided to take his chances with the draft board rather than continue as a student, Christy headed once more for the Lower East Side apartment in Eldridge Street. There he went from job to job, all the while avoiding the draft and hanging out with the flotsam and jetsam who passed through the flop on Eldridge Street. This included beats Peter Orlovsky and Kerouac's erstwhile companion Herbert Huncke (credited with coining the term "beat"). Janis Joplin would also look Christy up when she was in New York. But Christy was no celebrity seeker, he just hung around the kind of places where bumping into showbiz and sports folk was inevitable. As with tramp-writer Jim Tully, Christy did not suffer fools gladly, particularly the rich and famous, only making time for those who were worth the trouble: "I've never been a scene-maker or a hail-fellow-well-met type, which is probably why I've made extremely close friends all my life." Celebrity or not, many of these folk were themselves vulnerable, as Joplin's untimely death testifies.

On the fourth of April, 1968, Christy was at a political rally in the Lower East Side when the assassination of Martin Luther King, Jr. was announced. Christy acknowledged experiencing the feeling that a turning point in American history was about to take place. But he could not have foreseen the level of violence that would soon be unleashed on American citizenry:

> I never believed in his cause, never thought non-violence as a
> method for change was anything other than a pipe-dream. But
> alive, preaching non-violence, King served as a beacon and an
> anchor. Gone, all hell was going to break loose.[40]

And it did. Intending to travel to Martin Luther King's funeral with his friend Ted, the pair never made it further than Weldon in North Carolina. That night they were picked up in Weldon by the sheriff for no particular reason and kept in the cells overnight without charge. This made sure they could not make it to the funeral, and the sheriff knew it:

> Way I figure it, if a coupla fellows from up Nawth wanted to get to
> Uhlanna (Atlanta) ... And they was hitchhiking and didn't get killed
> on the way, well, by the time these boys reached Uhlanna, Martin
> Luther Coon's funeral would be over by about ten hours. Y'all
> come again, heah?[41]

As there was now no point in continuing the trip, the pair set off back to New

York. But by now the entire South was under siege and martial law had been declared in several cities, including Baltimore where the pair were dropped off by a friendly college professor. Making it as far as the Greyhound bus station in Baltimore, they then needed to acquire a pass to walk the three blocks to the Trailways depot in order to continue to Pennsylvania. It took them half an hour to walk the three blocks as they had to show their passes to the pairs of police who were stationed every ten yards. As they crossed the street to the third block, a cop holding a German Shepherd yelled at them, "Where the hell you think you're going?" Another cop grabbed their passes and ID, and motioned with his handgun toward a parked car at the curb. "Turn around, hands on the roof, legs apart." As soon as they were in position the cop with the German Shepherd shouted "Get 'em!" and the dog snarled and bared its fangs. Christy had to check the impulse to wheel around, which is just what the cop wanted, an excuse to set the animal on them. Christy listened to the dog snarl and even felt its nose touch his leg. "Not yet!" the cop barked at the dog, and to Christy and his friend, "I just wanted you to know that Rex here follows orders."[42]

The usual long, moronic police interrogation followed along the lines of why weren't they in the army, didn't they love America, would they rather be living in Russia, were they queers, before the situation was saved when a sniper took a pop at the police from a window across the street. In the ensuing pandemonium Christy and Ted made their escape on foot and then bus, only to end up at another roadblock at Wilmington, Delaware. Here they encountered more cruisers and crackling cop radios, "more lawmen defending America with machine guns and automatic pistols." They were told they couldn't go into town and would have to walk around it, and so they did. Yes, the summer of love was definitely over, but before the end of 1968, Christy would cross the border into Canada and would not return to the USA for a further eight years.

It is important to note here that, prior to his decamp to Canada, Christy had gone underground to avoid a treason charge and ten-year prison term for draft dodging—the board now being hot on his heels. By this time, Christy was using three sets of fake ID to avoid his capture: his previous identity as Jim Christinzio; Lee Shannon, the name of Val Santee's favorite brother and fictional pseudonym; and Val's own identity, Val not having much use for it at the time. But in September of 1968, Val Santee was granted a retrial in Franklin County, Illinois, on the basis of civil rights violations, including beatings received while in custody. Christy was invited to be the key witness at the trial, and paid full expenses by the state for his travel. Securing the retrial was to serve another purpose:

> 'Jim, I'm going to ask you a very big favour. You can say no, and
> I won't have any hard feelings. I wouldn't even dream of asking
> except, well, you've been the only real friend I've ever had and we
> think alike about so many things. I can't even ask you without you
> giving me permission to ask.'
>
> 'Go ahead, ask.'
>
> 'If I have to run, I'm going to need a car, maybe a couple of cars,
> you know, stashed here and there. And I was hoping that you ....'[43]

By the next morning the cars were in place. Number one, Christy's green and white 1956 Chevy Bel Air two-door hardtop, the one he had driven out in with his girlfriend to southern Illinois from New York City a couple of weeks earlier, waited out front of a restaurant with keys in the ignition. Several miles out of town was car number two, the 1948 Plymouth four-door sedan that had been sitting around the Santee home for months. The third vehicle, a 1964 Ford two-door sedan that Christy had borrowed from one of Val's brothers, was hidden on a dirt road fifteen miles from the Plymouth. Val had given clear instructions for the positioning of the cars but Christy had given considerable thought to the order in which they were placed: the Chevy would provide a quick getaway, the Plymouth was inconspicuous, if not slow, and the Ford was powerful, dependable, and big enough for Val to sleep in. In a paper bag on the front seat of each car, Christy had placed a jug of water, food, and a thermos of coffee. He wondered if Val would get as far as the first car. He didn't. Every other time that Christy had met with Val in prison or a courtroom, Val was just strolling along in the company of a guard. On this occasion Christy was dismayed to see his friend being led from the jail to the courthouse shuffling along in shackles, chains scraping along the pavement like a scene from a 1930s prison movie.

After the aborted escape from the courthouse, Val's sentence was eventually reduced to one to fifteen years, and he ended up serving eight. The month following the retrial, October, 1968, Christy used his travel expenses from his court appearance to flee across the border to Canada. He did not see Val again until Val visited him in St. Augustine, Florida, ten years later in 1978.

This would be the last time Christy actually met with Val in person. There was a communication with his friend by letter in 2005. Then, after tracking Val down again by email in late 2016 to ask how he felt about being identified by his real name in this book, silence followed the formal request from the author for Val's real identity to be made known—hence the continued use of the pseudonym.

Christy's arrival in Canada in the aforementioned Chevy will be described in the next chapter when, according to Christy, his real tramping began. The stories related so far are only the prelude to the life of this vagabond adventurer who, at the time of his arrival in Canada, was still only twenty-three years old.

1   *Jackpots*, op cit., p. 53

2   Ibid., p. 54

3   Ibid., p. 56

4   Ibid., p. 60

5   Ibid.

6   Ibid., pp. 62-63

7   Ibid., p. 66

8   Ibid., pp. 67-68

9   Ibid., p. 68

10   *Shift and Glitter*, op cit.

11   Ibid.

12   Ibid.

13   Ibid.

14   Ibid.

15   Ibid.

16   Ibid.

17   Ibid.

18   *Travelin Light*, op cit., pp. 29-30

19   Ibid., p. 32

20   Ibid., p. 33

21 Charlie Leeds' great-grandfather, Jeremiah Leeds (born in 1754) was a Quaker and the first permanent settler in what is Atlantic City today. Jeremiah's son and Charlie's grandfather, Chalkey Steelman Leeds, was the first mayor of Atlantic City from 1854 to 1856. Chalkey Leeds was the son from Jeremiah's second marriage to Millicent Steelman, when she was only twenty-four and Jeremiah sixty-two. After Jeremiah's death, Millicent turned their large home into a boarding house known as Aunt Millie's, the first hotel to exist in Atlantic City—to put this in context, by 1918 there were approximately 12,000 hotels in Atlantic City. Chalkey was also married twice and had eleven children. Chalkey Leeds and his brother, Robert B. Leeds, owned the whole of the land upon which Atlantic City was built. Christy picks up the saga as follows:

> "There was and probably still is—although it has closed down—outside the Bally Hotel and Casino—a statue of Charlie's grandfather, the mayor. He was known as Chalkey. There's an ongoing character in the first parts of the TV series *Boardwalk Empire* based on his grandfather, called the Commodore."* (Jim Christy, email to author, January 29, 2015)
>
> *Chalkey Leeds should not to be confused with the character Chalky White in *Boardwalk Empire,* played by black actor Michael K. Williams— who also played Omar Little in *The Wire.*

22 *Shift and Glitter,* op cit.

23 Ibid.

24 Ibid.

25 Ibid.

26 Jim Christy, *Real Gone* (Toronto: Quattro Books, 2010), p. 53

27 *Shift and Glitter,* op cit.

28 *Real Gone,* op cit., pp. 21-23

29 Ibid., p. 25

30 Ibid., p. 27

31 Ibid., pp. 28-30

32 Ibid., p. 32

33 Ibid., pp. 36-37

34 Ibid., p. 37

35 Ibid., p. 38

36 Ibid., p. 41

37 Ibid., p. 42

38 Ibid., p. 43

39 Ibid., p. 47

40 Ibid., p. 63

41 Ibid., p. 75

42 Ibid., p. 83

43 *Shift and Glitter,* op cit.

5

ON BECOMING CANADIAN

T he expenses Christy had been paid by the State of Illinois to attend Val Santee's retrial as a witness funded his travel to Canada in October of 1968 in his 1956 Chevy. Being refused entry into Canada at the Thousand Island border crossing, he drove back to Syracuse, New York, left the Chevrolet in a parking lot, and flew straight back to Montréal where he was admitted and got the necessary visas. Christy then returned to Syracuse, picked up the car and, accompanied by the aforementioned Ellen Sinclair and her sister Margie, arrived in a foreign-feeling Ottawa on a very warm and sunny October Friday afternoon and checked into a motel. "The people didn't look the same as Americans. The architecture, the smells, the rhythms, all seemed different."[1] Christy had already made a scouting expedition to Toronto two months earlier, to be told that the job situation in Toronto was grim and that he would have better luck in Ottawa—"a fib they told so as not to increase their workload."

Christy and Ellen took up rooms on Florence Street in Ottawa but Christy was not fated to settle in that city. He had taken a job selling ads for a new magazine that never existed and so his description was broadcast on the radio, warning potential merchants of the deception. Christy found out too late to collect his earnings that he was the victim of a scam. He'd been making $100 a day which he handed over to the "Editor-in-Chief" to be told that he would get his money once it had cleared through accounting, and only managed to salvage $70 that was thrown at him by a fleeing woman assistant when, on his return to the office, he demanded the $900-plus due to him. Christy had become bored with Ottawa in any case, and so it was that in January of 1969, having already made several trips to Toronto by bus, he took a final bus to Toronto with $70 in his pocket. There he took a room above a jeweler's for a couple of months before renting a room further west on Delaware Avenue.

Christy laid low in a steady job for five months, not wanting to attract any attention that would send him back to the USA. Ellen also moved to Toronto after some months, and although the pair lived together for a while in a rented room on Boswell Avenue, Christy acknowledges that their lives by that time were set on different paths. It was around this time also that Christy met up with other fugitives of the Vietnam War who had made a new home in Canada. Many of these would tell their own stories in Christy's first published work, *The New Refugees: American Voices in Canada* (1972), comprising seventeen stories edited by Christy and of which his own story is the final chapter. These fellow exiles included the writer Joe Nickell, known today as a senior research fellow for the Committee for Skeptical Inquiry and for his skeptical paranormal investigations. Christy first met Nickell in 1969 when they were both working for Simpson-Sears on their catalogs, Christy in downtown Toronto and Nickell out in one of the suburbs. The pair met on a business trip to the Toronto headquarters of Simpson-Sears and were immediately drawn to each other, having both investigated the Kennedy assassination (story related in previous chapter). Nickell provides the following description of their early times together:

> Christy and I were part of a loose group of literati, artists,
> expatriates, and occasional folksingers like Blues guitarist Jim
> Byrnes. The center of the circle was the apartment of Elizabeth
> Woods, who was something of a Gertrude Stein of Toronto. Also
> living there were artist Bill Kimber and writer George Fetherling,
> who once brought Margaret 'Peggy' Atwood to the place. The
> group was known affectionately as The Church Street Gang and
> there was always something going on.

Christy denies he was ever part of the Church Street Gang or that he frequented Elizabeth Woods' apartment, but he was closely associated with both Nickell and George Fetherling, of whom more later. Nickell goes on to describe Christy as:

> ...a handsome, well-built fellow [who] looked like he could accomplish anything he wanted to. Mostly I think he wanted to write, and everyone I knew thought he was excellent at it. ... Jim knew something about pugilism, himself being what is known as a two-fisted kind of guy—literally. He and I were both (of occasional necessity) barroom brawlers, and once we were drinking together at some out-of-the-way dive when a fellow took some dislike to my friend. In a flash Jim was out of his chair pummelling the fellow—wiping his sneer and then his look of horror right off his face. The man's buddy started to get up to help him, but I sent a distinct, sign-language message that he should sit back down, and he instinctively saw the wisdom of that. I'm glad Jim and I never got in a set-to with each other: We'd have beaten ourselves to smithereens and vanished into nothingness."[2]

But more of Nickell later. Early in January of 1970, up until which time Christy had continued his relationship with Ellen on and off, he embarked on what he described as "a bumming and hitchhiking trip in Europe," of which he described Liechtenstein as his favorite destination. Other countries Christy visited on that trip were the UK, France, Spain, Belgium, Germany, Switzerland, Italy, the Netherlands, Luxembourg, and Morocco. It was on this trip, on a boat from Spain to Morocco, that Christy met up with the widow of the Irish tramp-writer Jim Phelan. Kathleen Phelan had been on the road with her husband for twenty-two years prior to his death four years earlier. The occasion of Christy's meeting with Kathleen Phelan was by no means her first tramp to North Africa. Sometime after her husband's death, Kathleen decided to tramp and hitchhike alone from Britain, through France and Spain to Morocco, then onwards through Algeria, Tunisia, Libya, Egypt, by boat to Turkey, and onwards again to Iran, Afghanistan, Pakistan, India, and Tibet. By the time Kathleen met Christy she was a fluent Arabic speaker.[3] One cannot imagine how it would be possible for a single, white woman to make such a trip today. For Christy, this meeting with Kathleen Phelan and tramping in her company for three and a half weeks was the most memorable event of that trip. Their meeting is described as follows:

Most of the other passengers on that boat appeared to be Arab, many in Western clothing. The rest, Christy says, were young Western men and women in hippie attire. After walking the deck for half an hour Christy saw a white woman, "older than the rest, and certainly no hippie." The woman had grey hair, a lined face, and appeared to be in her fifties.

> She must have seen me look her way because a minute or so later a voice at my side said, 'You look different from the rest of them.'
>
> 'I could say the same about you!'
>
> She smiled and told me her name was Kathleen and we began talking as if we were old friends who were continuing a conversation we'd been having just the other day.
>
> After a few minutes, she asked me what I did. I shrugged, told her I worked various jobs.
>
> She nodded, and said, 'Yes, but what do you *want* to do?'
>
> 'Well I guess I want to be a writer.'
>
> She nodded, as if she'd known it all along.
>
> 'My husband was a writer. He died a few years ago.'
>
> 'A real published writer?'
>
> Writers were an exotic species to me.
>
> 'Yes, widely published.'
>
> 'What was his name?'
>
> 'You've probably never heard of him, coming from North America. Jim Phelan.'
>
> '*Bell Wethers*? [short story by Phelan]'
>
> Her eyebrows shot up in surprise, rearranging the deep lines in her face. Her eyes which I remember as grey-blue seemed to sparkle.
>
> 'Yes, that's Jim's.'[4]

The pair talked of books and traveling and by the time the boat docked, they could have been the closest of friends. Kathleen suggested they set out tramping the roads of Morocco together, and Christy readily agreed. They avoided Tangiers, calling at small towns along the way. Christy describes how everyone they met seemed drawn to her. Men who would ignore other foreigners approached Kathleen smiling, "it was as if they wanted just to be in her presence." Children too approached Kathleen but the women regarded her from a polite distance. They were offered rides on camels and in donkey carts and sat drinking tea in the fields with shepherds. One day a man stopped Kathleen along the road and engaged her in conversation, then she turned to Christy and said, "This man's son has gone to Casablanca and he is worried about the boy." While Kathleen was translating to Christy, the man looked at him and nodded solemnly as if acknowledging the sound advice she had given him. Christy nodded back and all three pondered the problem. When the man had gone on his way, Christy asked Kathleen if he was an old friend, being sure that she probably did have friends in the Kalahari. "Just met him," she laughed back.

Kathleen told Christy about how she had met Jim Phelan and of their life together. She had been working in the office at a factory in England and the boss had been making advances to her, brushing against her, touching her, and pretending it was all innocent. One day she decided she'd had enough and walked out of the factory and down to the road. She stuck out her thumb and started hitchhiking until she saw a man walking toward her in the opposite direction on the other side of the road. Jim Phelan told Kathleen that he didn't encounter many women on the road, and after talking back and forth for a while, he said, "Why don't you come over here?" She did, and continued tramping with Phelan until his death twenty-two years later. The following version of how Kathleen met her husband is told in her own words from a handwritten pamphlet she wrote titled *Hiking a Hitch*:

> It was late afternoon and for a long while the road was very quiet. I began to regret not having gone to Blackpool [the destination of her lift].

> Then I saw a man sauntering towards me on the opposite side of the road. Occasionally he turned back to flag a vehicle southbound. Cars were few and far between in those days, but so were hitch-hikers, so we eyed one another plenty. When he was directly opposite, he stopped and stared across. About six feet tall, he wore a leather jacket and corduroy trousers. A large black hat was pushed to the back of his head and around his neck was knotted a red silk scarf.

He strolled across the road and stood in front of me and grinned. He looked as though he hadn't a care in the world. High, wide, and handsome. I had never seen anyone more colorful or alive-looking.

He stood and looked at me a while, I stared back. Then in a deep, lilting, Irish voice, he said, 'And where might *you* be going?'

Me—I said nothing, just kept looking.

Then he spoke again. 'You didn't answer me. Where might you be going?'

'Nowhere,' I replied.

'I'm going there myself," he said, 'Do you mind if I come along a bit of the way with you?'

We turned and headed out of Garstang together.

I'm fond of saying that the road is like one great supermarket. Whatever you want is there for the asking.

Even a husband.[5]

Christy and Kathleen continued tramping together for several weeks, staying in unadvertised lodging houses in small towns along the way, "beautiful rooms behind unmarked doorways, rooms arranged around mosaic courtyards with fountains," until eventually Christy decided to set off on his own once more, a decision he says he has often regretted. Christy recalls a very tender scene in his book *Jackpots*[6] where one night after retiring for the night, Kathleen came to Christy's room and asked if she could lie beside him. In response to his look of alarm, she reassured him saying, "I don't want to seduce you. I just want to be close. I haven't been held since Jim died, and that's nearly five years ago." Before they parted, Kathleen gave Christy one of the pamphlets of Jim Phelan's writing that she sold along the way to support her travels, inscribing it on the cover to recall a meeting on the road in Morocco.

Regarding this same tour, David Duplain, a fellow Canadian Christy met in Europe, noted that "At that time the value of our dollar was so good that it allowed the travel from one city and country to another without problem."[7] The only other events described by Christy from that trip included a lift from Paris to Madrid in a Mercedes limousine owned by a Sikh, with another Canadian and a Pakistani guy who argued with the Sikh all the way to Perpignan, where they finally dumped him. Then there was a particular hitchhiking trip in the Jura Mountains that Christy had decided to make because of centuries of anarchist watchmakers. There he got a ride from a guy who took him to the house where he lived with his parents and grandparents, "a blood red A-frame." The grown-ups argued all day long, cursing "Communists and dusky people." The grandfather had been a friend of the Russian anarchist philosopher Prince Pyotr Alexeyevich Kropotkin. He later led Christy to a particular chair in the house, invited him to sit in it, and then told him, "he'd sit right there where you're sitting now."[8]

Having already been involved in but disillusioned with left-wing politics during the sixties in the States, on returning to Canada from his European trip in March, 1970, Christy started looking for an outlet for his own brand of agitation. Organizing rallies and petitions were not his thing, and having developed a love of writing, Christy turned his hand to producing an "underground" newspaper. The difficulty Christy encountered from the outset was that his own personality and artistic style clashed with those of his earnest, middle-class, student co-founders, whose own contributions were limited to political rhetoric and regurgitating tired slogans. This difference was particularly acute when it came to his colleagues' lack of a sense of humor; when Christy suggested introducing some satirical irony to the magazine by naming the first publication "Gorilla" instead of Guerrilla, he was told that humor could wait until after the revolution. The first issue of *Guerrilla* was launched in June, 1970. It was initially a success, thanks to Christy's work and the newspaper's artist giving it a professional feel. First the student editors got rid of the artist because his work was too accomplished to convey the revolutionary message, and then Christy left after being given the cold shoulder because his work was getting too much media attention.

Christy's early brush with politics is revealing about the nature of the man. Individualism is an essential characteristic of tramps and cynics who, like Christy, are hostage to no political cause or tribe. Christy's politics is to say it like it is, and to hell with sentimentality and popular dogma. But Christy's primary attribute, the one lacking in his co-conspirators and which ultimately resulted in his disillusionment with political journalism, was his gift at the art of irony and ridicule; not only his ability to see the absurd side of revolutionary zeal, but more importantly, his ability to laugh at himself. As the German philosopher Peter Sloterdijk commented about those who take themselves and the world too seriously, "Those who do not want to admit that they produce refuse ... risk suffocating one day in their own shit."[9]

Early in 1971 Christy jumped a freight and headed west. The story of this first trip through the prairies and the Rockies is told in Chapter 17 of the aforementioned *The New Refugees*. Christy had mainly hung around Toronto for the first two years of his exile, keeping his head down to avoid being returned to America and an inevitable prison sentence. Before attempting to explore the remoter parts of that vast country, Canada, Christy says he spent his time developing "insights into the mysteries and machinations of what had been in every sense of the word, a foreign country."

> ...after 22 months in Canada my reflexes were still American. My cognisance of the Canadian experience was solely on an intellectual level. I could not repudiate my past—my American heritage—nor would I wish to, yet I sought to penetrate to the core of the Canadian experience. I wanted to grasp intuitively the force and dynamics of this experience.[10]

Here we have further confirmation of Christy's Cynical philosophy; he will never feel Canadian simply by filling his head with "information" about his adopted country, he must experience Canada by total immersion of all his senses into the very guts of the place. This is, after all, how he became an American: "...this knowledge was a part of me, it was in my blood," not least by embracing the lifestyle of a hobo which as a child tramp had more thrills than spills:

> I overlooked all the hardships, the dreariness, the loneliness of America and went out there again and again to look. I learned, even—especially—when it seemed the most lonely, the most desolate. Take a bus across Ohio in the evening and you'll see

America in its most hideous guise. The barren junk-littered neon
stillness, the drive in wilderness approaches to Columbus or
Dayton, the irrevocable horror of it all.[11]

But if such was Christy's induction into becoming and feeling American, in
contrast he found Canada an altogether more welcoming nation. Loneliness
there was "less frequent and of a different texture." When one is moving forward
on one's travels and spies the lights of the next city ahead, there is that "innate
assurance that you will find friendliness, you can expect the loneliness to fade
away." Not so in America. Below Christy describes a country and its people
who have an innate suspicion of difference, who take any sign of rejecting
their narrow codes of acceptability, even in dress, as a personal threat to their
own way of life. And all this in a country built out of diversity and pioneering:

In America the hitchhiker, the drifter, is not regarded as a seeker of
freedom or knowledge, as an explorer of his land and the ways and
doings of his fellows, but, rather as a breed of criminal, a jobless,
shiftless no-count, out to rob and rape and worse. A man on the
road meets all the narrow paranoia, the fear and ignorance of that
'pettiness that plays so rough.' I appreciate Canada because I can
go to a truck stop, lay down my pack, relax, and eat a meal even
though my hair touches my collar—and, my God, someone may
even engage me in a friendly bit of conversation![12]

And so to the trip itself. Anxious to be on his way, and knowing that hitchhiking the first leg of the journey was tough, Christy bought a train ticket to
Winnipeg where, on doing the rounds of the city's hostels, his decision to
travel by rail was justified by fellow travelers telling him they taken up to ten
days to cover that leg of the journey. From there on, Christy took time to walk
through towns whose names alone intrigued him. And now the kindliness of
Canada became evident: "Morse and Mortlach, Walpella, Bassano, and Indian
Head, Golden, Grenfell and Gull Lake; especially Piapot where an old farmer
told me the story of the Indian chief and the mounties, and, of course, Moose
Jaw and Medicine Hat."
Christy slept in the hostels and armories provided along the way and talked
to the travelers he encountered in such places. These included "old-type
drifters, a few hoboes and Indians looking for work." One night, when Christy

got stuck outside Varden in Manitoba, he was allowed to sleep at a service station in an old school bus. Another night he stayed with a fellow traveler in a ghost town in Saskatchewan. They found the weather-beaten old general store and spread their sleeping bags on the floor "amongst the shoots of grass growing through the boards." Christy talks about the generosity of the folk who gave him rides and also bought him meals and beer. One was a suave distillery vice president from Montréal who picked up Christy and two other hitchhikers. He bought them drinks and a full-course meal at the Portage la Prairie. Then there was the old farmer in Manitoba who owned "all this here land as far as the eye can see," a Mr. Bowden, who gave them breakfast and offered the promise of a job. Other rides Christy recalls from that trip provided cheese sandwiches and pop from kids driving a decrepit old truck filled with hitchhikers, three joints from a young couple from the state of Maryland, and a wild four-hundred-mile ride through the mountains with a tugboat captain from New Westminster that included a seafood dinner.[13]

In *New Refugees*, Christy reflects on the experiences of this trip and in what way it had started to shape his understanding of his adopted country: "A bombardment of impressions, a flurry of ideas, a host of answers. All of it added up later and hopefully produced insight into the nature of this country." Christy would later come to internalize and recognize these experiences, rooted in the very texture of the land he was now passing through, as "the feel of Canada."

> But it didn't happen that way, my cognition wasn't the summation,
> the totalling, of these experiences. An event, nurtured perhaps
> by these people, places, and things but existing nevertheless,
> in isolation and coming at a time when my mind was still and
> attuned to the countryside, was the catalyst to what I realize is my
> knowledge of Canada.[14]

The experience that followed was the defining moment for Christy in feeling and becoming Canadian. He describes the ease with which he beat a train out of Calgary. After a cop had told him to have a good trip, he just waited for the right car to come along, "ran alongside it, tossed the bag in, then swung up, and I had a ride." And now, approaching the Canadian Rockies for the first time, the real magic of the landscape overwhelmed Christy as evidenced from the poetic prose in the extract that follows, a voice he often lapses into when awestruck by the natural wonders of the world. When connecting with nature in this way, Christy is able to paint for the reader an exacting image of just what might have been before his eyes. Add to this sounds, smells, temperature, and train vibrations, and the reader will find themselves experiencing powerful reminiscences of similar encounters with nature:

> Somewhere after Banff it happened. I was sitting by the open door
> and staring with wonder at the dusky green-grey carpet of trees.
> I could not see the shapes of the mountains because they were
> so close. The train seemed to be slithering among them, meeting
> them unaware in their most wild and virginal countenance. My
> mind put aside all thoughts and flowed with what was before me.
> Somehow the insane crashing of the boxcar dimmed and faded.
> The clear smell of earth and nature filled my nostrils and I just
> watched. Everything was hushed and silent, the woods were like
> a great still cathedral. Then, suddenly, without warning, they
> fell away and before me lay a vast panorama which revealed
> the immensity of the land, mountains going on and on into the
> distance, the rivers, the tributaries of the Columbia, snaking in
> crystal-blue through the brown and green and grey. Then down
> again into the woods, the silence, and out beside a clear fast river.
> Then right by the shore, racing along with it, a finger of sand
> beach visible on the other side met by a fringe of fir trees. Then
> we swing behind a patch of woods and the river flicks by blue and
> white foam in a staccato rhythm punctuated by the line of trees.
> It was a barrage of wonders, awesome, fantastic, and continuous.
> As the pageant unfolded I watched with reverence and as I sat
> there before that door tears came to my eyes. I was astonished.
> Everything was stopped except for the passage of nature.[15]

The piece continues for a paragraph or two in a similar vein, before finding Christy in the middle of the Rockies on a crisp mountain morning where he breakfasted in the town of Revelstoke, took a stroll, chatted to a local Indian, and clearly felt that he was, at last, a Canadian:

> The sense of belonging remains and it is to this consciousness that
> my fate is committed. Our words and reasons are but futile grasps

at the essence of this experience. It is what Canada means. I feel it. Now I am not a stranger, I can empathise, I can fight, I can build, I can understand. It is in my blood.[16]

After eventually being dropped off by the tugboat captain in New Westminster, Christy took a bus on into Vancouver, but not before being accosted in the bus station washroom by two hoodlums whose carnal intent he only escaped by facing them down with the metal lid he hurriedly ripped from a trash container and brandished like a machete.[17]

This trip west marked the first of many, and by 1973 Christy had started making annual trips to the Yukon Territory, fifteen in all, between that year and December, 1981 when he moved his home to Vancouver. A well-researched history of how the Alaska Highway, or Alcan, came to be built, together with an introduction to the many colorful characters who made the project happen, can be found in Christy's fourth book *Rough Road to the North* (1980). The book includes some of Christy's own Yukon adventures and is the subject of the next chapter. Not that Christy confined his travels to exploring Canada. Throughout this same ten-year period, and on top of the aforementioned European trip he made in 1970, Christy also visited the Amazon five times, France three more times, made five trips to various Caribbean islands, four African nations, and visited Colombia twice, Peru, Austria, and Yugoslavia. But let us stay in Canada for the time being.

On his return to Toronto from this first trip out west, Christy had another go at underground journalism, this time on the paper *Dreadnaught* in collaboration with the artist Robert MacDonald. Cultural conflicts and different views of the world collided and Christy moved on again. His co-publisher insisted on featuring the superficial "truths" of self-styled gurus like John Lennon and George Gurdjieff, whereas the more anarchic and cynical Christy spoke on behalf of no one but himself and his own conscience. Following *Dreadnaught*, there was a more successful collaboration with the writer George (then Doug) Fetherling and Joe Nickell on the magazine *Tabloid*. Christy joined them for the premier number of the magazine in June, 1971. The magazine was printed on yellow paper, a wink, Joe Nickell wrote, to yellow journalism:

A *Globe and Mail* columnist wrote that we were probably the best-written newspaper in Canada, and that was no doubt largely

due to Jim Christy. ... [Christy] produced two big reviews—one of
the Country music scene with the likes of Waylon Jennings at the
Horseshoe Tavern. (Country was never written about like this:
brilliant, provocatively insightful, almost lapsing into stream of
consciousness.) The other, 'Ellis the boxer v. Chuvalo the slugger,'
took the reader to a bruising punchfest in 'the old and battered
ring at Maple Leaf Gardens.' Jim's opening sentence ran for half a
newspaper column.[18]

Joe Nickell tells how Christy was forever going and coming, even though
Nickell himself was doing pretty much the same. Nickell had been, among
other things, a stage magician and a Pinkerton undercover detective, but around
the time he met Christy he had decided that he wanted to become a blackjack
dealer. Now the problem was, so far as Nickell understood it, legal gambling did
not exist in Canada at the time. But Christy had just returned from the Yukon
Territory with news that gambling was legal in the frontier town Dawson City,
explained by Dawson's historical importance as the center of the Klondike
gold rush. And so Nickell left for Dawson soon after and did indeed become a
blackjack dealer, living a couple of the best years of his life in that town. Christy
describes meeting up with Nickell in Dawson City in the next chapter.

Back in his room at 54 Howland Avenue, Toronto, Christy continued
his writing and hanging out with a loosely knit group of artists, musicians,
and writers. And then there was Marlyn. After Christy returned from his
European tour in March, 1970, the relationship with Ellen fizzled out and by
the autumn of that year he had started a wild romance with Marlyn Rennie,
a twenty-year-old he met in a cafeteria. It was a relationship that, in spite of
Marlyn's hot temper, would continue off and on for the next three years. Joe
Nickell describes Marlyn as follows:

>...a particular girlfriend of his—a young cocktail waitress who was
>apparently as volatile as she was beautiful. I don't think it was
>the content of the writing she objected to, but, being angry over
>something (probably his spending too much time writing), in a fit
>of pique she sailed his typewriter out a window![19]

In 1971, Christy had a serious relapse of wanderlust. First he made another
trip to Europe, this time accompanied by Marlyn, involving some high times,

a whirlwind tour of France, Italy, Germany, and Switzerland, and including their shared passion for attending live jazz gigs. After their return to Canada, Marlyn returned to France alone after enrolling in a university program in Nice, including a class taken with the French philosopher Michel Butor. Back in Toronto, and Christy's next trip was to make it to the Yukon in a rental van, this time accompanied by Doug Fetherling. On their arrival in Vancouver, Fetherling, obsessed at the time with becoming a poet of note, was irritated that Christy did not know any literary types in that city. When Christy casually dropped into the conversation that he had been corresponding with George Woodcock, the anarchist Canadian writer and literary critic, Fetherling insisted Christy call up Woodcock on the phone. The call produced an invitation for the pair to meet Woodcock at the University of British Columbia Faculty Club. So impressed was Fetherling at meeting the man of letters that he immediately bought a train ticket back to Toronto to resume his literary ambitions, leaving Christy to continue the expedition alone.[20]

Arriving broke in Vancouver, and now without his traveling companion, Christy worked for a few weeks in a metal workshop to replenish his funds before heading back east to the Russian Doukhobor community at Gilpin, near Grand Forks. Here Christy had arranged to meet up with one of his closest friends, the fire-breathing, knife-throwing, and mystic carnival performer Marcel Horne. Horne was in Gilpin with his girlfriend Katherine because a small community of carny types had been drawn there by a veteran sideshow owner.

Christy had first met Horne backstage when he was managing a band at a large auditorium in Toronto where Horne was sharing the same bill. The two immediately hit it off. Joe Nickell remembers being introduced to Horne by Christy at another gig, and after watching the performance. Nickell wrote a poem for Horne, "The Fire Breather," which appears in Nickell's book, *Secrets of the Sideshows*, 2005. In that book Nickell refers to Horne as follows:

> Long ago in Toronto I knew Marcel Horne, who sported on each upper arm a tattoo of a fire-breathing god. He performed in the carnivals as 'Diablo the Human Volcano.' ... Marcel was a fire-breather, that is, one who sips the fuel, then spits it at a torch, thus throwing a great ball of fire across the stage. It is a dramatic effect. It is also a dangerous one. Performers now avoid gasoline and use only less volatile fuels such as kerosene or lamp oil, but the stunt is

still dangerous. Failure to spew the liquid as a fine, atomised mist can mean fuel on the performer's face.[21]

With Christy's support and encouragement, Marcel Horne published his own book, *Annals of a Fire Breather*, which was reviewed by the aforementioned Doug Fetherling in the *Toronto Star* on September 1, 1973 under the title, "Poverty, mistrust dog the footsteps of an ex-convict."

> Horne, an ex-convict and carnival performer who is something of a legend in Canadian alternate culture, is amazingly skilled at evoking the depressing places and circumstances in which most of his 30-odd years have been spent. ... In his preface, Jim Christy likens Horne's story of personal adventure to Henri Charrière's autobiography, *Papillon*. ... While not so dramatic as all that, Horne admittedly has had one hell of a time of it in the U.S., Canada and North Africa.
>
> He first ran afoul of the law in 1959, when he was 17, by stealing a car with a friend. Since then there have been many arrests for this and that including one for bootlegging. Prison life is just one of the things Horne, who once did 9 months in solitary confinement, describes in force and the loud ring of authenticity."

After elaborating on Horne's hobo life, carnival existence, and narrow escapes, from knife thrower to being shot by a crazed guy on a bus in Waco, Texas, Fetherling concludes with the following anecdote:

> But perhaps the most incredible adventure is the one at the book's end—being jailed in Casablanca with a homosexual leper and making good his escape to Canada, via Paris, after the frontiers had been closed.[22]

The following entries selected by Joe Nickell from his journal provide some independent notes of Christy's work and movements between 1971 and 1972, with and without Marlyn:

> *Dec. 9, 1971*: Issue #4 (of *Tabloid*) is now out and looks good. We had to leave out some things ... due to lack of space, but what is in

is good—notably Jim Christy's piece on Arthur Craven. We'll have to send him a copy since he and Marlyn are traveling in Europe.

Jan. 6, 1972: (pasted-in clipping of Kenneth Bagnell's column in *The Globe and Mail*, headed "Underground Paper," about *Tabloid*. He writes in part:) 'There are a number of good pieces in recent issues, one being an article by Jim Christy, a prominent, promising writer in the underground press. It's on Fredericton, NB and Christy's report on a summer visit is both evocative and indignant: "Fredericton is as American as apple pie...."' (his ellipsis).

Feb. 3, 1972: Already late to meet Doug, I hurried over to *Tabloid* and found him gone. Erling (Friis-Baastad) soon showed up though to tell me he'd waited with Doug & then Doug had to leave. There also, Erling said, had been Jim Christy, back from his travels. Hope to see him again soon.

Feb. 5, 1972: Robert Fulford's column in the *Star*...(on American exiles in Canadian culture, appeared with) a list of several people—Rbt. Bowers, Christy, &c.

March 29, 1972: Picked up the new *Amex* (American exiles magazine) with 4 of my cartoons and an ad for *The New Refugees*, ed. by Jim Christy, in which I appear.

April 3, 1972: Erling came by and we went to my bank, later running into Jim Christy and going to the Pilot (Tavern).

October 3, 1972: After supper (my girlfriend and I) went to Erling's (and Patty's). *The New Refugees* was just out with my piece—an interview—in it, and Peter Martin had sent me a copy, so Erling broke out a bottle of tequila and salt and limes.

Nov. 14, 1972: (To birthday party for Patty Friis-Baastad) I took Yago wine, someone brought sake and another person vodka, and Jim Christy brought another case of beer to add to that Erling already had. By midnight there was just enough left to toast

Patty, who had just that moment turned 25. Marlyn—Jim's lovely girlfriend—was there. First time I'd seen her for about a year. She'd spent a short time in Paris.

Dec. 8, 1972: ...stopped in the Arcade magic store.... Also ran into Jim Christy who said he & Marlyn are separating.[23]

More of Marcel Horne later, but on his arrival at Gilpin, Christy found the place overrun with hippies and so took off again, getting a job on a local ranch to restock his wallet. There he hung out for a while at a roadhouse run by an old cowboy truck driver from Montana, but he was already starting to miss Marlyn and determined to get back to France by all means possible.

Returning to Toronto, with no means of purchasing a flight to France, fate was to lend a hand. As Christy was leaving Toronto's Pilot Tavern on Cumberland Street, he was jumped by a mugger who, when Christy refused to hand over his wallet, attacked him with a brick. There was a tussle in which Christy got the upper hand and relieved the mugger of his own wallet. Christy is at pains to point out that at no time in his life has he ever been a thief. He justified his actions on this occasion, firstly because the mugger had attacked him with a brick and tried to take his money, and secondly, because it was unlikely to have been the mugger's own money anyway. But now Christy had his plane fare to Nice, and there he met up again with Marlyn and they continued their adventures. This trip included the pair riding to Monaco on rented motorcycles and later meeting up in a bar in the old port of Nice with writer and gypsy scholar from the University of British Columbia, Werner Cohn. Cohn took Christy along to an annual Romani pilgrimage at an encampment on a nearby beach. Apart from Cohn and some tame bears, Christy was the only non-gypsy at the festival, packed out with tents, campers, horses, and wagons. Cohn was clearly a regular visitor to the event and was known by many of the festival-goers. When their energy and funds were finally exhausted, Christy and Marlyn returned to Toronto via a stopover in Paris.

Like many with the hobo in their blood, Christy was continually pulled between the attractions of big-city life and the solitude of the wilderness and the open road. In the summer of 1972, he disembarked from a train in the small rural town of Estevan, just north of the U.S. border in eastern Saskatchewan. He was accompanied by a woman he'd met on the journey whose looks he summed up as those of "a corn-fed prairie girl," wholesome and smooth-skinned. The girl invited Christy to stop over at her mother's farm where he got some work and was allowed to sleep in the barn. But instead of being joined at night by the girl as he had hoped, it was the mother who visited Christy for several nights in a row. Not being able to bear the tension that followed, compounded by hostility from a farm hand who clearly had his own designs on the two women, Christy took off walking westward.

After turning down lifts from the first two cars that pulled over, Christy was overcome by an urge to traverse the province on foot and crossed to the opposite side of the road to avoid the generosity of passing motorists. He spent his first night in a small ghost town by the side of the road, and after that, in the crevices and riverbanks of the Big Muddy Badlands that marked the northern end of Butch and Sundance's Outlaw Trail. When he needed sustenance or some cash, he would stop by or get work at the farms he passed on his way. "The troubles at the farm were all but forgotten, hassles of the city a hundred miles away. I had some money in my pocket and a farmer's tan. I was happy."[24]

In the end, Christy walked the 350 miles from Estevan to Maple Creek in two and a half weeks. There he met up with a contact he'd been given in Toronto and was introduced to an old timer who claimed to be a hundred years old. As a boy, the old man claimed to have spent time with Sitting Bull, driving him to church in a buckboard. The chief had headed north to escape the aftermath of Little Big Horn, being permitted to stay in Canada by the authorities from 1877 to 1881 before returning to the USA where he and his remaining 186 family members and followers were forced to surrender. When Christy asked the obvious question, "Sitting Bull went to church?" he got the reply, "No, we stayed outside in the wagon. He used to like to see the young girls ... dressed in their Sunday finery." After hanging around town for another day, Christy renewed his trans-Saskatchewan tramp as far as the border with Alberta, at which point he stuck out his thumb and continued his journey with lifts.

But back again to the metropolis of Toronto. A report from another of Christy's acquaintances, Barry Dickie, provides an independent description of the eccentric lifestyle Christy was living on Howland Avenue with Marcel Horne and "a mix of crazies and misfits." Dickie described himself in 1973 as "a cab driver of no great distinction with limited social skills and no girlfriend." Dickie had spotted an ad stating "furnished room, cheap rent, artistically inclined person preferred." That is how he ended up at the door of the house on Howland Avenue and was invited in by Marcel Horne who showed him the room. When Dickie queried the "artistically inclined" part of the deal, he was asked, "Do you smoke dope?" Dickie replied yes and Horne replied, "That's artistic enough."

54 and 56 Howland Avenue were a duplex and Horne lived at 56. Horne had the job of keeping the rooms occupied and collecting the rent for the landlord. Christy had the same role in number 54, but as Dickie observes, "our half wasn't as nuts as Jim's side—he had the heavies over there—one tenant kept five or six Dobermans in her room, huge bloody things, plus she was a Jehovah's Witness." Dickie tells how he was sitting in the kitchen with Horne drinking coffee when in strolled Christy. They were all laughing together at the story of how Dickie, not particularly "artistically inclined," came to rent the room, when Dickie heard a woman shrieking and moaning somewhere in the house:

> She was crying out the name HANS...HANS...HANS.... her voice
> blasting through the ventilation grill on the floor. It sounded like
> she was being murdered or something, but nobody seemed too
> worried. Then Marcel told me it was just Hans the caveman down
> in the furnace room making love to his girlfriend Maria. It still
> sounded a little scary, their passion pulsating so loudly through the
> heating ducts. I guess Hans should've moved his mattress further
> from the furnace, but nobody had the heart to tell him.[25]

Hans was an old acquaintance of Horne's from his carnival days and was living in the basement of the rooming house rent-free, sleeping on a mattress by the furnace. "Marcel got to choose, more or less, who lived in the house because he collected the rent for the landlord, and he chose some doozies." Dickie goes on to describe another of his co-tenants:

> We had a mystical Korean poet on the top floor who'd start
> chanting at three in the morning, this loud mournful wail of a
> chant echoing through the house, intruding into your dreams.
> Once he came to my door—Bong his name was—and he handed me
> this poem he'd written—in Korean of course because he spoke no
> English. And he stood in the doorway waiting while I looked at the
> piece of paper, trying to make sense of the Korean symbols and not

having a clue. So I just smiled and nodded and Bong seemed happy that I liked his poem.[26]

Here Dickie sums up his overall impressions of Christy and Horne, and his own fond memories of living on Howland Avenue:

But life was still a pleasure, and meeting Marcel and Jim added another dimension to my world. They were both appealing souls, travellers and adventurers full of wit and stories. Jim also had a love for literature and encouraged me in my own writing. But it was more his celebration of the everyday parade, the cast of local characters, the oddballs and weirdos and just plain people he was so good at knowing and talking about that I most appreciated. The ordinary would take on a new glow when Jim got talking. It was a grand time to be alive. Anyway, that's how it was in that old house on Howland Avenue.[27]

Another of Christy's acquaintances from his Howland Avenue days, who still maintains contact with Christy today, is fellow writer and vagabond Len Gasparini:

I first met Jim Christy in Toronto, in 1974. I was newly divorced, at loose ends, driving [a] truck part time, and reviewing books on a freelance basis. I ran into Jim at a party—one of those literary, BYOB get-togethers—and discovered that we had a lot in common: wanderlust, favorite authors, rhythm and blues, rock and roll, baseball, a variety of jobs, and a disdain for academia. Somehow, despite our nomadic wanderings, Jim and I managed to stay in touch. He is the only person I know who embodies the true spirit of the troubadour, in the tradition of Rimbaud, Crane, and Kerouac. It amazes me how he has found the time to publish more than thirty books of poetry, fiction, and non-fiction throughout his travels in five continents. In this dark age, he is definitely a beacon.[28]

Christy recalls one of the parties that he and Marlyn threw at 54 Howland Avenue prior to his rooming-house superintendent days. Doug (George) Fetherling was going through his Welsh bard phase. Born in West Virginia,

Fetherling was fond of claiming whatever ancestry suited his literary obsession of the time, later claiming to be from London which better fitted his cultivated persona of that period.[29] But back to the Dylan Thomas characterization. Marlyn headed for the washroom but the door wasn't closed completely. She summoned Christy to where she was standing in the hallway, the party continuing around them, and through a crack in the door watched a sober Fetherling running water into the bathtub. He had grabbed a bottle from the other room and proceeded to throw some of its contents around the bathroom. When the bath was full, Fetherling methodically removed his shoes, got into the tub completely dressed, settled back, and began singing a noisy "drunken" ballad à la Dylan Thomas. The desired effect was achieved and the assembled partygoers witnessed the wild Welsh bard in all his glory.

Another comical episode from the Howland Avenue era involves a Jamaican guy named Leroy. Leroy shared with Christy his torment that the women who frequented the bars on Yonge Street went for the cooler black guys who came up from the States, treating the Jamaicans like country cousins. He asked Christy's advice on how he could pass for a black American.

So I, honest to God, tutored him on the ways of American blacks.
I had actually to give him diction lessons, walking lessons, and
advise him on fashion matters. If an American, black or white,
would have walked in and seen us, me heeling and toeing and
dipping my shoulder one after the other and him a step behind and
to the side imitating me, well, it would have been a wondrous and
ridiculous thing to behold.[30]

Christy recalls a similar incident on one of his nighttime walks through the streets of Toronto, one of many such memories as a nocturnal flâneur in all weathers. He was approaching one of those half-a-block-square parks that dot the city when he spotted a figure in the distance who appeared to walk in a curious jerky manner, continually falling to the ground then getting up again. As he got closer he came across an African guy attempting to skate in a shallow pool of ice. Turns out he wanted to learn to skate because he liked a girl who was big on ice skating, and practicing at two o'clock in the morning would minimize the embarrassment of his bungling attempts as a skater being observed. Ever willing to assist in such situations, Christy allowed the guy to hang onto his coattails while he walked around on the ice with his pupil in tow.

It was during this time also that Christy published his third full-length piece of writing, and his first attempt at fiction. "Bo" appears in Erling Friis-Baasted's anthology *Outlaws*.[31] Christy's contribution to the book was reviewed in the Toronto *Globe and Mail* as follows:

> Jim Christy, a writer familiar to readers of this page, occupies more than a third of the volume with its sole fictional piece, "Bo." The story is a kid-on-the-road-finding-out-what-life-is-all-about one, the kind of thing Hemingway did in some of the Nick Adams stories, an achievement surpassed by no one since. Christy's story is in the Kerouac manner—loosely written, awash in explicitly stated sentiment, its ironies muted into sadness—and it isn't a bad example of that kind of thing. Still, the vein has been thoroughly worked. When a solid box office smash movie like *The Last Detail* can pick up on the inconsistencies and self-delusions of an ain't-gonna-take-no-crap pose that produces more rhetoric than action, then the observant writer ought to be pushing further, out to where the real outlaws live.[32]

A footnote here on Marcel Horne. In January, 1980, fifteen minutes after Christy received a phone call from Horne to meet up in Florida and help him drive his act to a carnival in Cuernavaca, Mexico, Horne was knocked down by a hit-and-run driver and killed. Gibtown, near Tampa in Florida, was a winter quarters for carnival people, and Christy recalls how it was one place that carnival freaks could hang out without being hassled or stared at. Horne was in the habit of walking from the camp to a nearby roadhouse from where he would regularly phone Christy in Toronto. Christy bought the ticket to Tampa as planned, but now to organize and attend Horne's cremation and funeral accompanied by Barry Dickie. An ignominious affair, with the crematorium attendant—"this ditsy bottle-blond in pedal pushers, heels, six inches of makeup, fake fingernails dagger-like and sort of fuchsia colored"—thrusting a cardboard box at Christy with the explanation, "Here he is!" Christy had already had news of Charlie Leeds' death just before Christmas, and so had lost two of his closest friends within two weeks of each other.[33]

It was not until 1974 that Christy acquired his Canadian citizenship and passport and his globetrotting would start in earnest. His first trip back to the States, though, would not be until the autumn of 1976: "I was curious. I needed that Canadian passport before I could even think of going back. It felt alien to me. I was a goddamned Canadian by then and proud of it. Also, I had refused Amnesty so I was still wanted by them."[34] Naturally, this first trip to the U.S. in eight years took in Philadelphia, and then all points west to California, stopping off at Cincinnati, St. Louis, Kansas City, Denver, and other former hangouts along the way. It was a trip down memory lane taking in old haunts such as a greasy spoon by the stockyards in Kansas City where Christy had once worked the grill. Even on this trip, Christy admits he was still able to find and hang out with "old Wobblies, hobos, drifters, tramps and other ne'er do wells." Val Santee was still in prison but Christy stayed a couple of nights with his folks, then wound up in San Francisco where he stayed for a while earning a few bucks at a variety of jobs including ringing a bell for the Salvation Army to collect donations.

As with most itinerant vagabonds, it would be impractical, nigh on impossible, to recall all of the jobs Christy has taken throughout his lifetime to make ends meet. Some of those he repeatedly engaged in far and wide included delivery boy, landscape gardener, painter and decorator, truck, van, and tractor driver, factory and construction worker, farmworker, warehouseman, and gas station attendant. There was also the inevitable restaurant work: short order cook, grill man, dishwasher, busboy; not to mention less run-of-the-mill jobs such as film actor and extra, carnival roughie, boxer, Wells Fargo messenger, line rider, car hop, private eye, journalist, explorer, assembling bleachers around a football field, and of course his nefarious activities with the Mob.

But to return to Valentine's Day of 1975. Christy's relationship with Marlyn had pretty much fizzled out the previous year, and according to the photographer and artist Myfanwy Phillips, the woman who would become Christy's next on-off partner, "he appeared to be pretty much free-wheeling, traveling, and at the beginning of his writing career." In the intervening years, as well as the tramp across Saskatchewan and the crazy times on Howland Avenue there had been an interlude with a young First Nation woman up in the Moose Factory 2 Reserve in northeastern Ontario, and Christy's first trip to the Amazon, including a sojourn with Indians in which—untypically for Christy—he got high on hallucinogens. Christy had also spent January of that year locked up in a dungeon beneath the castle walls of Cartagena, Columbia, but that story can wait for Chapter 7. Myfanwy Phillips kept a journal and so, at least for the time they were together, certain events can be dated with some accuracy. Here Myfanwy recollects her first meeting with Jim Christy with the aid of her journal entry of February 14, 1975:

> I went round to Kay's for supper, we ate dates and drank a whole bottle of Szegedi Hungarian and I teetered off to this party. It was given by the woman who runs A Space, a sort of dancing, drink party full of people I didn't know—'artists' as they saw themselves. I was being something of a success with various men, none of whom I particularly admired, but there was a man there who was very attractive, wonderful shoulders, Jim Christy. He was a great dancer. I went back home with him. It was a nice thing to do, he was really friendly. Talked about being writer. ... A few days later: I called up Alive Press to get Jim Christy's number. They said he moves around a lot.

Christy's recollection of their first date is that he'd spent most of the previous night in jail for traffic violations and had then gone to the party at the house of the artist friend, Marian Lewis. Christy was with his friend Jason Rooke, who had scrounged the traffic fine money for his release from George Fetherling. At any rate, Myfanwy invited Christy back to her boyfriend's house on Sumach Street—he being out of town at the time. Myfanwy recalls her immediate attraction to Christy, "I first saw a most good-looking man—then I met a grand character, a serious talent, a person willing to take risks." But Myfanwy also acknowledges that the relationship had its flaws. Her career in painting, writing, and photography was just beginning to take off. She had just had a solo show in a relatively prestigious gallery and, if it was to continue, needed the stability, if not of a studio, at least of a room, table, and chair. In contrast, Christy was a free spirit with the wanderlust in his sails and the next adventure never far from his mind. Trying to get Myfanwy to share his passion for jazz, she being more of a soul and R&B fan at the time, was another challenge for Christy. One of their first dates was a Mose Allison concert, which Myfanwy recalls enjoying, and Christy encouraged her to listen to his favorite artist, Lester Young. But Myfanwy maintains, "Jim never convinced me about jazz." She acknowledges that the attraction between them was electrically charged but coming from very different backgrounds they both remained fiercely independent. Myfanwy acknowledges never really liking Canada, considering it a place both "betwixt and between" England and America, neither one or the other. In contrast, she says, Canada had had a huge impact on Christy who embraced it with enthusiasm. Myfanwy continues as follows:

> Looking back, I can't imagine how we managed to stay together as long as we did, or even why we tried so hard to do so. We may have seen the possibilities of the combination of our talents. We thought we were in love, but I'm not sure about that. We were young, that is for sure. ... We were never going towards each other, we were always going away. I don't think that we wanted it to be like that, but so it was.[35]

Then there was that thing that had clearly not worked for Christy during high school when, away from his natural environment on the streets of South Philadelphia, he was ignored for the most part, ridiculed at worst. But during his twenties, in another country and an altogether contrasting zeitgeist, things were very different. Christy's physical demeanor, his multiple talents, and the unconscious aura of cool he exuded, was something of a curse as the following remarks from Myfanwy suggest:

> I remember Jim was always surrounded by 'wannabes' standing in the wings. He conjured much admiration and sometimes envy amongst, mostly, male writers. How the women felt about him was a whole different kettle of fish! Jim was very attractive. It was sometimes hard to go out with him in public, he was such an attraction, but he seemed to manage it pretty well.[36]

Myfanwy also refers to Christy's "fling with Janis Joplin" as she describes it. But Christy did not willingly invite such attention (unless the attraction was mutual and desired), preferring to lay low away from the public eye. Marlyn and Myfanwy met on three occasions and here Myfanwy provides a first-hand description of Marlyn:

She was something. Tall, gorgeous. I have no idea what kind of a woman she was other than to recall that Jim used to joke she was convinced the old Charlie Rich song, "The Most Beautiful Girl in the World," was all about her.[37]

Myfanwy acknowledges the different backgrounds and circumstances she feels may have caused some degree of strife between her and Christy, even though she was clearly something of a rebel herself. His background is by now familiar, so what of Myfanwy? She was born in 1945 in Dehra Dun, India, the last of several generations of British Army expatriates to be born in that country over a two-hundred-year period, the only exception being her grandmother who was born in Bermuda. Myfanwy's mother was born in Poona in 1920, and her father in Srinigar in 1912. Following the death of her mother in London in April, 2017, Myfanwy shared an amusing story concerning her mother and grandmother:

> My mother inherited quite a lot of money from her mother, way back. Her mother owned the Butterfield Bank in Bermuda. ... When she died, she left her three children quite some cash. My mother went shopping. She spent everything. Every penny. No joke. I remember being in London to help her with her apartment (i.e., clean it up) and she took me to the ATM machine and said to me, 'Isn't it just magical how all this money just comes out?' She had dementia, at that point![38]

But back in India, Myfanwy's parents spent a fortune on her "incarceration," as she described it, at The Royal School for Daughters of Officers of the Army in Bath, England, a miserable time in which she ran away from school several times before, at the age of seventeen, absconding permanently for the bright lights of London at the height of the "swinging sixties." At the age of twenty-one, Myfanwy left London and headed out for Canada.

In Toronto, Myfanwy met and lived with a man for nine years in an apartment they owned downtown, during which time she made a career for herself as a photographer and fine artist. At the time Myfanwy met Christy she says she was not looking for another relationship but acknowledges being unhappy with the one she had, describing herself as being "in transition." For a while after they got together, Christy and Myfanwy both worked for Doug Marshall, editor of *Books in Canada* and journalist on the *Toronto Star*. Christy had already been writing reviews for *Books in Canada* under two previous editors. Myfanwy describes Marshall as a very supportive editor if "difficult." Marshall, she says, was very fond of Christy and regarded him as a very talented writer. Given Christy's recurrent wanderlust, the pair were not destined to remain in Toronto, and this is when the early tensions started to emerge between Myfanwy's need to maintain her career as an artist and Christy's need for travel and adventure. Myfanwy recalls that a lot of the friction in their relationship at the time was about being broke:

> Most of the problems between Jim and I at the time had to do with lack of cash. Not just lack of cash—no cash. And then we would insist on going places and doing things where cash was really a necessity! We both needed/wanted to work. And the peripatetic journeys we made, took us both away from that. Jim was writing of course. I couldn't paint and be on the road.[39]

The following notes from Myfanwy's journal[40] are reproduced below to provide a chronology of the pair's ongoing adventures and changes of fortune from the month following their meeting to the final breakup of their relationship in March, 1980. The journal entries are interspersed with longer discussions of certain memorable events.

April 26, 1975. George Foreman Fights Five at Maple Leaf Gardens.

May 6, 1975. Jim flies to Whitehorse.

June, 1975. We meet up in St. Louis.

Christy had been spending some time in Atlantic City, but at the end of that month he arranged to meet up with Myfanwy at the St. Louis airport. First they flew over the state line in "a tiny airplane with propellers and only 12 seats" to Carbondale, Illinois, to visit Val Santee, who by then had been released from prison. Santee came roaring down the road in a pick-up truck to meet them. He had remarried and settled down with a woman named Carole and they were living in student housing on the top floor of a two-story building.

Myfanwy recalls how she took an immediate liking to Santee and his wife and that they seemed very happy together. She describes Santee as gentle and thoughtful. After supper they all drove out to Santee's parents' place where they were entertained with stories and ice cream made in a yellow electric churn—some respite from the oppressive heat. The next day they drove out to the banks of the Mississippi River where they sat surrounded by other folks sitting around in chairs behind their trailers parked on the riverbank. From there they went on to Santee's brother's place for a supper laid out on picnic tables and continued to defy the heat with gallons of sweet iced tea.

Back to a deserted St. Louis, July 1, 1975, where the couple booked into a Holiday Inn. The reason for the empty streets: most of the population were watching Muhammad Ali and Joe Bugner's second fight beamed live through closed circuit TV from the Merdeka Stadium in Kuala Lumpur. Myfanwy describes how they joined the populace of St. Louis to watch the fight, "in a fantastic 1920s-style building, kind of like those big old post offices, only two of a handful of white faces in a crowd of a thousand or so Afro-Americans":

> ...the audience were looking fantastic; dressed to the nines in suits, two toned shoes, satins and boas—extravagant hats. The whole nine yards. What a sight to see. I seem to remember us discussing how we might proceed out of there if Bugner won. Fortunately, he lost![41]

There would be many more such trips together over the next five years but Myfanwy was already spending more of her time working back in Toronto while Christy continued with his tramping and writing.

> *March, 1976.* We seem to be in Toronto leading somewhat separate lives.

> *May 13, 1976.* We go to Ottawa. Jim stays with his friend Vernon McKelvie.

> *July, 1976.* We fly to Edmonton for the first leg of the Alaska Highway trip. I appear to have given up my apartment and cat. We go from Edmonton to Dawson Creek. Then we do the Alaska Highway thing.

The trip up the Alaska Highway is the subject of the following chapter, with an extended discussion of Christy's B.C., Yukon, and Alaskan adventures. Myfanwy was the photographer on a major leg of this trip and in spite of her note below, many of her illustrations do appear in *Rough Road to the North* even though the original project was more of an illustrated affair supported by text than the other way around.

> *Sept 13, 1976.* I'm back in Toronto. I go and print the photographs, very few of which got printed.

> *November 28, 1976.* I'm on a plane to San Francisco. I have friends in Berkeley to stay with. Jim is there but I'm not sure where. Not with me.

> *December 15, 1976.* We went to Palo Alto to talk with John Montgomery of the Dharma Bums. I found a place to live in town but it was short-lived and I went back to Toronto.

> *January, 1977.* We sat the New Year's out in the Sportsman's Bar in Santa Barbara, CA.

> *January, 1977.* We were in L.A. and then went up to Santa Barbara. We completely ran out of $$$. Jim went to stay at the Neal Hotel and was working for $2.50 an hour. I went out to house sit a ranch in Santa Inez. Jim goes to stay at the Salvation Army. He has a book of poems coming out.

When Christy read Myfanwy's journal entry about sleeping in the Salvation Army hostel, he commented, "I recall too well sleeping on that cot in the big warehouse on the floor with fifty or a hundred other guys, many of them Vietnam vets who started screaming in their dreams." And while Christy was staying at the missions, Myfanwy was house-sitting the ranch of a woman who kept cougars and other animals she rented out for movies and television. A parallel strand of Christy's life as an actor and movie extra is discussed at the end of the following chapter, but California being California, even the regular jobs Christy got to make ends meet were movie-related, including gardening for Duncan Reynaldo who played *The Cisco Kid* in the television series of that name, and the movie actor Jack Donovan. Christy lived in and worked as Donovan's chauffeur for a while, "posing as somebody else, often a journalist from *Esquire* Magazine, with fake letters of introduction."

> *March, 1977.* We spent a night in Joplin, Missouri and two in Illinois with [Val Santee] and his wife Cathy in their trailer outside Carbondale. [Val] is working in a coal mine to put his wife through nursing school.

> *March 5 & 6, 1977.* We drove to L.A. Drove around Venice Beach. Sat on the beach in Beverly Hills and shook hands with Sylvester Stallone. This is the era of my painting with the white dog. Breakfast at Barney's Beanery. Drove up Coldwater Canyon. Back to Toronto. *The Alaska Highway* was turned down by the Toronto publisher Mel Hurtig.

> *March, 1977.* We go back to Toronto via L.A. and Philadelphia. Stay with Jim's parents.

> *End of July, 1977.* Jim and I take a bus to Nashville. There's a whole lot of drinking going on.

The following description is the full journal entry followed by recent reflections of that trip. It shows that in spite of their vagabond credentials, Christy and Myfanwy were yet able to enjoy doing the tourist thing, even if in their own vagrant style:

> Jim and I went to Nashville, Tennessee. Of course, it sounds better in the re-telling. Mostly it was eighteen hours each way on a bus, with a bunch of boring people. When we got there, we stayed in a motel 12 miles from town—a place called Goodlettsville. We went on a tour of the country music stars' homes. Loretta Lynn, Tammy Wynette, etc., and we drove down Music Row, past the fake Parthenon! Didn't have much in the way of money, and in fact, on the way back, sold some Toronto streetcar tickets to a lady for $2 in order to get a meal! There were two young girls on the bus who took a great fancy to Jim! On Saturday we sat for hours in Tootsie's

Orchid Lounge, a famous country bar downtown. A lot of drinks
were bought for us by an attractive man called Tommy Reggurio.
We missed the last bus back to the Rivergate Plaza and hitched a
ride with a black guy who took us approximately 12 miles out of
his way. We bought a bottle of Almaden wine and sat on the porch
drinking it. All the people seemed really friendly—lovely southern
accents. We saw a great country singer in a little bar, dressed in a
pink jumpsuit! Very professional. Came back on the bus talking
to this crazy guy from Etobicoke who talked to himself a lot and
giggled at the same time! Tired. Late back.

Myfanwy's retrospective on her journal entry:

Aside. I liked Tootsie's Orchid Lounge a lot. Waylon Jennings and
all the greats had played there. I liked the fake Parthenon too. It was
a small building but perfect in its proportions and right there on
the main drag. I think that the country singer in the pink jumpsuit
was playing in a place behind our motel, so a bit out of town. It was
a kind of 'open mike' deal. I was struck by how good everyone was,
and how strange it is that some become famous and some do not. ...
I think I liked Nashville back then. It was a small town. Now it looks
big and busy and hustling. I think we had quite a good time in the
day or two that we were there. Hard to recall now.[42]

Return to journal notes:

August 16, 1977. Elvis Presley dies!

September 1977. Jim is going to London and Brussels. He visits my
brother in London.

Nov 8, 1977. We are in Tampa Florida. We had a drive-away car to
W. Palm Beach. Went first to Philadelphia and spent a night with
Jim's parents. Erling Friis Baastad was coming with us. Then down
to Petersburg, Virginia, where Jim's aunt Louise lived, and his
grandmother, who was 90 years old. Bought the 1961 blue Chrysler (in
my painting) from a garage near Daytona Beach. The muffler went.

December 23 1977. St. Augustine, Florida. Rented 15 Rhode Ave. Jim is investigating the murder with a machete of the mayor's wife on her front porch that happened in 1974. Erling was there for a while.

After setting up home in St. Augustine, Myfanwy recalls them driving out to an old, deserted school for the deaf where Ray Charles had been a former student. There they acquired some abandoned tables and chairs to furnish their new home. But as Myfanwy admits, although they did have some high old times together, there were also the inevitable tensions caused by one partner wanting to put down roots and the other, as she describes it, having a "peripatetic nature." Given what we already know of Christy's character, it is no surprise then that he was not entirely enthusiastic about committing to a life of domesticity. As Myfanwy further reports:

> ...we both became nervous and it seemed to me that neither of us were able to stay true to ourselves when we were together. There was just no way either of us was about to change much and I don't believe it was even necessary that we should have.[43]

But in spite of these difficulties, the relationship would continue on and off for two more years during which time Christy continued with his travels and adventures, some with Myfanwy, others solo or with other friends:

> *Jan 29 1978.* Jim goes to South America to write some articles. I go to New York. Then we seem to be in Jacksonville.

> *March 22 1978.* We are still in St. Augustine. Go to baseball's Spring Training in Daytona Beach where Jim interviews Rod Carew and Gary Carter for some articles he's writing.

> *June 23 1978.* Jim is in Africa. We seem to have spent a month in Philadelphia.

> *Nov 26 1978.* We spent 5 weeks with Jim's parents. We thought we might live in Philly, but we went back to St. Augustine. Then we went back to Toronto it seems. I didn't want to be there and drove

back to St. Augustine and rented an apartment at 33 Grove Avenue, overlooking the softball park.

March 27 1979. We seem to be still in St. Augustine. I go to London.

July 1979. I leave St. Augustine and go to live in Boston. Jim stays in Florida.

Dec 21 1979. Jim had a letter saying that his friend Charlie Leeds died.

Jan 4 1980. Jim's friend Marcel Horne is murdered in Florida. Jim goes to Florida with Barry Dickie for the funeral.

March 4 1980. First copy of *Rough Road* arrives.

March 7 1980. Jim moves in with Jack Kapica. We have split up.

May 26 1980. Jim goes to Vancouver to look at a volcano [Meagre Point Mountain]. He then seems to be back in Whitehorse. It's a year since he was in Fairbanks.

Prompted by Myfanwy's notes, Christy recalls some further adventures that followed this trip, a madcap series of events that are only possible for the lone tramp adventurer who sets off for the horizon with no particular itinerary in mind. First he found himself a free trip on a small airline from a military base near Ottawa to Frobisher Bay and then onward to Greenland, landing in the capital Nuuk. "My first weird sight after checking in was three or four Inuit men dragging parts of a whale up a street of low and medium rise apartment buildings like ones in Denmark." After meeting a group of Eskimo musicians in a pub, Christy was invited by them to play a part in a rock video. The setting of the video was on an iceberg where Christy played the role of an uptight Danish businessman typing away at his typewriter, getting angry and tossing the crumpled papers away while the band jumped all around him with their electric guitar leads plugged into the iceberg. The rest of the trip was spent in more conventional style, first in the company of an Inuit woman Christy met during the gig and then a five-hour boat ride into a fjord with the rocks glowing orange and yellow in the sunlight from the lichen. He still thinks fondly of both.[44]

From Greenland Christy flew to Jacksonville, Florida where he was met at the airport by the woman who would later become his second wife, Mary Anne Silva, and from there to St. Augustine, the place he had first sighted Mary Anne in 1965 (see Chapter 7). Christy was taken with how "un-American" St. Augustine seemed with its almost subtropical feel and colonial architecture. Ten years of harsh Toronto winters later, Christy started wintering in St. Augustine. As well as meeting up with Mary Anne, Christy also became friends with Chris, black owner of the Gator Club. Chris had a day job at the local alligator farm wrestling the creatures for the entertainment of the local Afro-American community who, in spite of segregation being long over, continued to live very separate lives from the whites, something Christy was acutely aware of from the hostility he attracted when visiting that part of town. The story continues as follows:

> One afternoon I was driving around St. Augustine Beach ... when I spied parked by the side of a service station, a three toned (green, white and gold) 1958 Cadillac four-door hardtop with a For Sale sign on the windshield. It was love at first sight.
> I stopped to enquire, and the old redneck owner was asking about a quarter of what I figured it was worth. I told him I wanted it, and he ran his big hands lovingly along the front fender.
>
> [...]
>
> He said, 'Boy, I will sell you this car but you got to promise me one thing.'
> 'What's that?'
> 'Should you ever want to sell her, you won't sell her to no nigger.'
> 'Okay.'
> 'No, you got to promise.'
> 'I promise.'
> 'Well, okay, then.'[45]

This was 1977; the car was bought and Christy enjoyed many thousands of miles behind the wheel of the '58 Cadillac, including driving it up to Toronto and back. But back to 1981 where this tale started, and Christy, knowing he would be moving to Vancouver and severing his winter sojourns in St. Augustine, decided to part company with the car. Chris, the alligator wrestler, had been asking Christy about the car for the past three years. Now he said to Christy, "Mary Anne tells me you're not coming back to town and you have to get rid of the Cadillac. Well man, you got a buyer, you know that." So Christy had to explain to Chris why he could not sell him the car.

'Well, you see, I made a promise to the peckerwood that sold
me ... if I ever sold the car I wouldn't sell it to a "nigger," and
I'm quoting.'
    He gave me the flat look.
    'I didn't think you were like the rest of them.'
    'I'm not. But I'm a man of my word.'
    'Shit.'
    'So I'm not going to sell it you, Chris. I'm going to give it to you.'[46]

And so Christy handed over the keys and left for his new home in Vancouver. But before relating the adventures that follow, it is now necessary to backtrack to 1976 and devote the next chapter to discovering how and why Christy decided to relocate to Vancouver in the first place.

---

1   *Jackpots*, op cit., p. 127

2   Joe Nickell, correspondence with the author, May 1, 2015

3   Kathleen Phelan, "I am a Vagabond," photocopy of undated magazine article sent to author by acquaintance of Kathleen Phelan.

4   Jim Christy, "The Name's Phelan," unpublished short story

5   Kathleen Phelan, *Hiking a Hitch*, unpublished, handwritten pamphlet. Copy provided to the author by Liz Shaw who was given the pamphlet by Kathleen.

6   *Jackpots*, op cit., pp. 33-36

7   David Duplain, letter to the author, January 21, 2017

8   Jim Christy, *This Cockeyed World* (Toronto: Guernica Editions, 2013), pp. 41-42

9   Peter Sloterdijk, *Critique of Cynical Reason* (London: Verso, 1988), p. 151

10   Jim Christy, *The New Refugees: American Voices in Canada* (Toronto: Peter Martin Associates, 1972), p. 143

11   Ibid., p. 145

12   Ibid., pp. 145-146

13   Ibid., pp. 147-148

14   Ibid, p. 149

15   Ibid., p. 151

16   Ibid.

17   Jim Christy, email to the author, November 17, 2016

18   Joe Nickell, letter to the author, May 1, 2015

19   Ibid.

20   Jim Christy, email to the author, November 15, 2016

21   Joe Nickell, *Secrets of the Sideshows*, University of Kentucky Press, 2005, pp. 219–220

22   Doug Fetherling, "Poverty, mistrust dog the footsteps of an ex-convict," *Toronto Star*, September 1, 1973

23   Joe Nickell, report to the author, January 24, 2017

24   *Jackpots*, op cit., p. 41

25   Barry Dickie, email to the author, August 1, 2015

26   Ibid.

27   Ibid., July 27, 2015

28   Len Gasparini, email to the author, May 13, 2015

29   Wikipedia describes Fetherling as: "One of the most prolific figures in Canadian letters." en.wikipedia.org/wiki/George_Fetherling Accessed on November 16, 2016

30   Jim Christy, email to the author, April 17, 2017

31   "Bo," in Erling Friis-Baasted, *Outlaw*, Alive Press, 1974

32   *Toronto Globe and Mail*, December 28, 1974

33   Jim Christy, email to the author, May 3, 2015

34   Ibid., February 4, 2015

35   Myfanwy Phillips, email to the author, December 2, 2015

36   Ibid.

37   Ibid., October 22, 2015

38   Ibid., June 21, 2017

39   Ibid., January 24, 2017

40   Ibid., February 4 & 5, 2017

41   Ibid., August 11, 2015

42   Ibid., February 8, 2017

43 Ibid., August 24, 2015

44 Jim Christy, email to the author, January 21, 2017

45 Jim Christy, *Sweet Assorted* (Vancouver: Anvil Press, 2012), p. 14

46 Ibid., p. 16

6

ROUGH ROAD TO THE NORTH AND A NOTE ON THE MOVIES

I have made numerous trips up this Alaska Highway ... Formerly
called the 'Road to Tokyo.' I have even labored on the road,
maintaining it around Whitehorse in the Yukon. So I have lived
and worked up here and truly know it well, yet when I am away
and begin to think of the land, it stirs in me a wanderlust that
some might describe—and some do!–as youthful or naïve, but I
am a youth no longer. Naïve, yes, in the sense of a wonder one
cannot help but feel in the presence of nature.... And I think
of that Far North road just snaking through the tall trees and
bending around the vast cold lakes. And I know I will have to
pack up and take off, have to find some excuse to get there; it
being maybe tomorrow or two months from the first time the
feeling hits me but I will get there....

(Jim Christy, *Rough Road to the North*)[1]

Such is the seduction of the natural character of the far northwest of
the American continent. To illustrate the incongruity of the human
character of that region a full reading of *Rough Road* is recommended,
but the following immortal line uttered to Christy by a native of that land

sums up better than anything else the unexpected awaiting the traveler of this strange territory: "The first white man I ever saw was black."

Christy's fourth book, *Rough Road to the North: Travels Along the Alaska Highway*, is loosely based around his fifth trip to the Yukon, this time in the company of Myfanwy Phillips. The original plan had been to produce a small book of photographs supported by text. In the event, Christy secured $750 from the Ontario Arts Council for a print version of the project which was subsequently accepted by Doubleday. The first seventy pages of *Rough Road* became a comprehensive social and political history of how the 1,523-mile-long "Alcan" highway (abbreviation of Alaska-Canadian Highway, which following road improvements is now some sixty miles shorter) came into being; an "umbilical cord as long as the eastern seaboard from Maine to the tip of Florida" linking Alaska with the lower forty-eight. The remainder of the book, interspersed with further historical and cultural references, describes Christy's personal adventures in the Yukon and Alaska, as well as the stories of the characters he meets on the way. Myfanwy was Christy's traveling companion for a large part of the 1976-77 trip, but the latter part of the book also recounts various adventures Christy made solo or in the company of others.

To return to the wanderlust expressed in the opening passage, below Christy describes, in the writing style he is wont to lapse into when his vagabond spirit is stirred, just what it was that prompted this particular journey:

> My excuse this time was snow, the cold and the snow. I had never made the entire trip along the Alaska Highway, done the 1,523 miles, when the land, every bit of it, was covered with snow.
> There would be no tourists, no recreational vehicles raising dust and throwing rocks, the fireplace would be roaring in the 98 Saloon in Whitehorse, the old timers would be gathered around their barrel stoves spinning yarns and telling lies. It was all the excuse I needed.[2]

As the sleeve of the book describes: "Alaska: the last great North American wilderness, a landmass approximately the size of England, France, Germany, and Spain combined, a repository of natural resources and pioneer romance." And yet in spite of the considerable intrusions upon the region as a result of the fur trade, logging, the discovery of huge gold and other mineral deposits, not to mention the military paranoia that created the Alcan in the first place, the combined mountainous wilderness of northern British Columbia, the Yukon, and Alaska adds up to the largest unexplored region of the world, here captured by Christy's description of just one single group of mountains:

> The range stretches far into the distance, hundreds of peaks
> disappear truly as if into eternity. No one has named the peaks,
> no one has even seen them in their entirety; there are unimagined
> worlds beyond the first mountain walls and hidden tarns where
> mountain sheep have come to drink for thousands of years.[3]

The existence of unnamed mountains in the backyard of two of the most technologically advanced nations on the planet is testimony to the region's scorn of civilization. The naming of peaks that existed millions of years before humans arrived on Earth is a symbol, in any case, of human arrogance in thinking we can domesticate the natural world.

Christy is not the first vagabond writer to have been captivated by this part of the world. Other tramp-writers who have explored and described the region include: William Henry Davies, Leon Ray Livingston, Bart Kennedy, Jack Everson, Morley Roberts, and Jack London, not to mention Jim Tully, tramp and scriptwriter for *The Gold Rush* (Hollywood's Little Tramp's seventy-fourth movie) in which hundreds of extras, including real hobos brought in by train complete with their own blanket rolls, were used for the march up the Chilkoot Pass scene, filmed on location in the Sierra Nevada. Christy's own fascination with the Yukon is evidenced by the fifteen trips he made to the region between 1973 and 1981 from the urbanity of southeastern Ontario, before finally moving west in 1981. Christy's move out west was facilitated not by the publication of *Rough Road* the previous year, but by a book tour he made to Vancouver to publicize his fifth book *Streethearts*. He simply decided not to return to Toronto and stayed on in the apartments of various friends between Vancouver and Seattle until eventually moving to Saltspring Island, B.C. to take up landscape gardening. In 1983 he moved back to Vancouver, interrupted only by a year in Peachland and Kelowna, and didn't return back east to Ontario until 2005.

This is the story of one of those inveterate vagabonds for whom the lure of wanderlust ensures that he never settles in the same place for any length of time. Although Christy based himself in various locations in British Columbia for the twenty-four years between 1981 and 2005, during this period he also spent time in twenty-eight other countries, many of them more than once.

But for now, let us confine ourselves to Christy's adventures along the Alaskan Highway. In an anecdote about Christy's first trip to the Yukon, he admits that it was not only the wilderness and the pioneering spirit that aroused his fascination for the region, but his childhood memories of the 1950s radio and then television show *Sergeant Preston of the Yukon*, with its images of the legendary mountie chasing down wrongdoers with his trusty dog King. On his first trip to the Yukon, Christy had arranged to meet up with a friend, Erling Friis-Baastad, another old *Sergeant Preston* fan, at the Taku Lounge in Whitehorse. Both planned to find work on their arrival and Erling arrived first. Christy's first impressions of the region, following a six-hour stop at mile zero of the Alcan, Dawson Creek, were not favorable. During the first leg of his journey by bus through the monotonous, flat, snow-covered terrain around Taylor and the Peace River, he recalls writing in his journal, "what indomitable purpose it must take to live here winter after desolate winter." But after Fort Nelson the scenery suddenly changed:

> The mountains began looming beyond the woods in endless ranges white and shadowy in the twilight. Here finally was my dream of the North and I stayed awake long into the night wanting to see the sign that announced YUKON but I fell asleep and missed it, woke as the bus stopped at Rancheria.[4]

After the first seventy pages of *Rough Road*, devoted to a history of the Alcan, Christy starts recounting his fifth trip to the Yukon in the winter of 1976-77, once again setting out from Dawson Creek and this time accompanied by Myfanwy. Because Christy does not write chronologically, the stories that include Myfanwy get somewhat mixed up with those where Christy is traveling solo or with others, but we pick up the tale as Christy and Myfanwy approach the town of Taylor. Of course, by this time Christy knows folk, and folk know him, and as he crosses the Peace River he chuckles to himself at his first impressions of the place. He had since met Jesse Starnes who lived in a trailer and epitomized that indomitable Northwestern spirit that had foxed Christy some years earlier.

He is in his mid-eighties, but to him decades are meaningless notations, for he has the energy of active men a third of his age. His interests are boundless, his horizons limitless. He gets up every day full of enthusiasm and with a thousand things that must be done. There is his trapping, his gold-panning, his lapidary concerns, his study of astronomy; he has to tune his pick-up truck and take some geologists out into the bush and, hopefully, he can arrange an hour in the evening to read the old books about the pioneers. ... He was born in Texas and spent his earliest days there and in Oklahoma, which was then still Indian Territory. When he was still a boy his folks moved to a farm in Saskatchewan, but working a patch of prairie earth wasn't for Jessie. He took off for the West at the age of fourteen, just drifting. Stopping now and again to work as a logger, camp cook, or on the river boats. The work was just an excuse to allow him to wander around in the wilderness he so loved. He came to the Peace when he was seventeen and has been there ever since.[5]

Christy recalls hiking along the river with Jessie one time, learning about the type of crops grown there, how to trail deer, the different types of animal spoors, types of leaves and berries to eat or make tea with, how to catch fish with your bare hands by driving them into the rocks along the riverside or a beaver dam, and how to cook grouse by packing them un-plucked in clay, baking them in an open fire, and then removing the shell of clay, feathers and all, to get at the succulent flesh beneath. At a sandbar on the river he then gave Christy a gold-panning demonstration, casually mentioning, without a hint of boasting, that he had recently returned from Berlin where he had given a gold-panning exhibition and that he was shortly due in Atlanta to give another. "Somehow folks heard about me and started writing me letters to come and teach 'em. Particularly in Europe. So I got me a new career now that I'm pushing ninety."

On their return to Jessie's place, Christy spent an hour in Jessie's lapidary workshop from where he operated a mail-order business in cut and polished stones, and fossils that included insects, birds, dinosaur teeth, not to mention a dinosaur egg cut in half, and corresponded with museums and other lapidarists from around the world. While continuing his journey northwards, Christy reminisces about all the other characters he'd met and scenes he'd witnessed along the Alcan:

...little tableaux of which I'd been a part. Other bus rides, car trips, truck trips, plane rides, walks, camping trips, hunting trips, and side trips. Some wonderful people and a few not so very nice ones. Everything occurring in the midst of this great land and with the road running through and connecting everything.[6]

Next stop Fort St. John, and after a drink in the Condill Hotel with Myfanwy, Christy follows a crowd, solo, to the Frontier Hotel. The spectacle he describes is typical of many other such venues he has visited in frontier towns:

> It is a masculine scene and any white woman venturing to the washroom is sent along her way accompanied by hoots, whistles, jeers, catcalls, and a stray grope or two should she venture too close to certain tables.
> Soon the music stops and everyone quiets down for the main attraction. She enters the room from a door behind the bar and she is nothing if not statuesque ... Now, despite all the beer-heavy, dirty clothes, rough talking, ready-fist activity, all that masculinity waiting to break loose, when she appears the men are models of decorum and respectability. When a minute before they were ready to cop a feel from anyone's normally dressed wife they are silent and shy in the presence of painted fantasy.[7]

Christy's description of the stripper and her show continues for a further two pages, and the scene well illustrates the rather strange behavior of a certain type of man in particular social situations, and in the company of other such men. Christy was there too, of course, but there is an altogether different relationship between male and female "tramps" than there is between "working girls" and certain working men. Christy had been initiated into the company of chorus girls and hookers from the age of twelve and shared a bond of fellowship that can only be understood by vagabonds of both genders.

Then on to Wonowon, an Indian name for blueberry but also mile 101 of the Alaska Highway, during which leg of the journey Christy muses on conversations of all the bus passengers he has previously shared a seat with on this monotonous three-hundred-mile stretch of road from Dawson Creek to Fort Nelson—the reason being, Christy says, is that they "didn't have anything else to do but shoot the breeze and sleep." But twenty-five miles past Fort Nelson, the road forks off to the left (the right fork goes north up into the Northwest Territories) and the first "grand country" begins:

> The highway meanders through dense forests and then opens
> to incredible far-flung vistas, mountain ranges visible beyond
> wide river basins or vast plateaus of snow, all white plains save
> for strings of dark red water, birch trees indicating the course
> of streams. ... We passed Steamboat Mountain ... and ten miles
> farther, Indian Head Mountain. ... Then far down I see two
> wolves emerge from the woods to walk across the wide flood
> channel of the iced-over Tetsa River. Big white beautiful animals
> with thin almost delicate looking legs and heavily muscled
> shoulders. Their eyes are visible as pieces of pale blue glass in
> the all-white world.[8]

When the bus arrived at the Toad River Lodge, a woman was greeted by one of the locals who exclaimed, "You been to the Big Smoke, eh?"—referring to Fort St. John. The journey on to Muncho Lake prompts Christy to recall his first trip up the highway when he decided to leave the bus at Summit Lake, midway between Steamboat and Toad River, and tramp the sixty miles from there to Muncho Lake, "for no particular reason other than all the flat land was left behind and this was the most rugged stretch of the northern Rockies." The area was home to moose and grizzly; mountain sheep and goats could be seen crossing the road. Christy planned to camp out at Muncho, "Big Deep Lake," and do some fishing. As he was pitching his tent and lighting his fire by the lake, he noticed a rowboat coming to the shore. A Dogrib Indian father and son were taking a huge catch of fish back to their lodge but invited themselves to join Christy for a coffee.

> 'I made the coffee open-pot style with a little salt.'
>   The man said, 'You know a good way to cut the grease off the top?'
> 'Eggshell?'
>   He laughed, 'Yeah, that's right!' He looked at his son and
> grinned.
>   From a pocket of his red and black checked mackinaw the
> father took a paper bag wrapped in plastic which he unraveled and
> came up with a piece of dried moose meat. From another pocket

he took a folding buck knife and cut off, first a piece for me, and then for his son and himself.

He dipped his chunk into the coffee and bit at it. Then he asked me, in a roundabout way, what I was doing up in this country. I told him I had come up to do just what I was doing now and I told him I liked talking to people who lived here and especially liked listening to their stories.[9]

And Christy was told a story by the Indian that day on the shore of Lake Muncho, but a copy of *Rough Road* will need to be acquired to read it. Back on the road and just past Contact Creek at mile 588 is the first Yukon marker, but for the next forty miles the road crosses backwards and forwards across the border between B.C. and Yukon before finally heading north for the last time into that territory. Next the Indian village of Lower Post at mile 620, set up as a fur-trading post in the late 1860s by a Robert Sylvester, one of the Yukon's first white settlers, who later sold the post to the Hudson's Bay Company.

Here Christy describes the fabled land of Yukon Territory, which at the time was home to twenty thousand people in an area two and a half times the size of Texas. First stop Watson Lake, "with its rustic, wilderness village ambience lacking in the highway towns to the south." The highway runs parallel to the lake which is used as a base for a float plane. At this point in the book Christy takes some time to identify what he believes to be the unique character of those who live in the Yukon, a different breed of person, he says, from those one encounters elsewhere, even in Alaska. He acknowledges that although the inhabitants of the Yukon arrived from all over the U.S., Canada, Europe, and farther afield, they all remain very much individuals, "stamped not only by the land but also by the spirit that has brought them here." As Christy explains it, the folk who inhabit the Yukon do not come for the usual reasons that North Americans relocate; one would not simply move here for a job transfer, or even to see something new. The Yukon is one of the "ends of the earth," bordered to the north by the Arctic Ocean. Whitehorse, though located in the south of the Yukon, is still three thousand miles north of San Francisco; one doesn't have to travel that far just to see something new. Whatever reason folk have for living and working in the region, "they share that Yukon thing."

There is a romance involved and if people don't go around talking about it and examining it out loud that is no reason to think it doesn't exist. Some lined and wrinkled old fellow with his prospector's slouch hat pulled low over his eyes is not about to wax eloquent over the lure of the frozen North or the spell of the Midnight Sun, at least not until he's had a couple of drinks.[10]

But talk they eventually will, of an awe and comfort that comes from knowing that one lives in magnificent surroundings and that "just beyond most any mountain is land that no one has ever seen." But even more powerful is the exhilaration those folks Christy met during the 1970s felt from knowing that they were part of history, part of a small and dying breed of pioneers who had conquered one of the last frontiers on Earth. Over four decades later, it would be interesting to ask the grandchildren of these same pioneers about their relationship to the Yukon, and the legacy that their grandparents and great-grandparents left behind. Christy, who has also spent time in the Amazon and been alarmed at the encroachments of the modern world on that former wilderness, acknowledges that in comparison, the Amazon has seen many more years of civilization than the Yukon: "The white city of Manaus had flourished and died before the first white man ever saw the Yukon."

Next stop along the Alcan, just before it dips again into B.C. for the last time on its journey north, is the settlement of Rancheria, so called because a couple of gold prospectors from the Mexican border area around San Diego stopped at the small Indian village there in 1873 and renamed the settlement and the river. Then on to the village of Teslin at mile 803, situated on the seventy-eight-mile-long, two-mile-wide Teslin Lake at the point where Nisutlin Bay juts out at right angles from the main lake necessitating the 584-meter, seven-span bridge to carry the highway across the bay. The highway follows the east side of the lake up to its northerly point at Johnston's Crossing where it passes over the Teslin River and continues westward to mile 865 at Jake's Corner. The junction at Jake's Corner has a road going southwest down to Carcross at the north end of Bennett Lake. It was from Skagway at the top of the Chilkoot Inlet (accessed from the Gulf of Alaska) north to Carcross, that the White Pass & Yukon Route Railroad was built in 1898 following the gold rush stampede. A reconstructed railroad still carries passengers from Skagway to Carcross today, but the original route north to the goldfields follows the Klondike Highway which runs due north from Carcross, joining the Alaska Highway again just south of Whitehorse, then splitting off from it again a few miles north of Whitehorse and continuing to Dawson City.

Here we take a break from the geography lesson to recount one of Christy's previous Alcan adventures. McCrae's Truck Stop was situated at mile 909 just south of Whitehorse, where the rail extension from Carcross to Whitehorse and beyond, built in 1900, crosses the Alcan. For Christy, mile 909 was the jumping-off point for one of those incongruous tales that beset most travelers; no matter how much one tries to avoid getting involved in other tourists' lives, some have a habit of creeping up on you when you least expect it. Stan was from Tennessee, a gravelly-voiced, drunkard, sometime country singer, who claimed to be a friend of Johnny Cash, and who together with Bobby (a B-52 pilot), the singer's embarrassed son, had stopped off at McCrae's on a trip up to Fairbanks, and were camping at McCrae's in their Airstream trailer.

> Stan proceeded to tell me about his wife and Bobby's mother and how they had split up a long time ago and she hadn't let him see Bobby for years and now they were taking this great trip together to Fairbanks to meet up with the eldest son Lloyd who worked on the pipeline.[11]

As it is with such unintended soirées, Stan's persistent buying of beers for Christy helped to relieve the latter's reluctance to befriend his persistent host. Stan's effort was not helped by his insistence, in spite of Christy's protests, that Christy himself would make a pretty decent country singer. Stan wanted to make the rounds of the bars of Fairbanks and take that city by storm—all the time accompanied by grimaces and shakes of the head from Bobby to indicate "that Daddy wasn't as successful and well known as he made out."

To cut a long story short (it's a nine-pager) Bobby was keen to get on with the journey but Stan, returning to the bar with his guitar, insisted on doing a set at McCrae's. Bobby and Christy excused themselves and drove down to the Copper King to catch a set there, all the while Bobby cursing his father and regaling Christy with stories of his screwed-up life. On their return, by now the worse for drink, they were surprised to see Stan all packed up and waiting in the pick-up truck, having revived himself with a thermos of coffee. By this time Christy was up for the trip, and after depositing a semi-conscious Bobby in the truck, the trio set off for the 588-mile trip to Fairbanks, Alaska.

> So we took off down the Alaska Highway, guzzling beer and singing whatever we could remember of C&W hits of yesterday. An hour

into the trip I had begun to consider that this little venture was
entirely feasible, that somehow upon landing in Fairbanks I would
find myself transformed into a bona-fide country troubadour. Two
hours into the trip I was asleep.[12]

The next thing Christy knew, he was being shaken awake—"My eyes felt
as if they were covered in battery acid"—by a grinning, foul-breath-smelling
Stan, who announced, "Wake up, we're in Alaska!" The seasoned traveler
Christy muttered, "Huh, what? Already?" Stan had missed the turning at
Haines Junction. Yes, he had driven all the way to Alaska, but to the town of
Haines, 147 miles south on the coast: "She-et. Don't wake Bobby. We'll just
get back in the truck and go back there to the turn-off."

> We started walking back to the truck and Stan stopped cold in
> his tracks, stared back the way we'd just come, and closed his
> eyes.
> 'Oh, good holy Jesus!'
> 'What's the matter?'
> 'Oh, sweet mumbling baby Jesus. Bobby's gonna kick my ass
> good. Oh, what am I gonna do?'
> 'What happened?'
> 'Forgot the trailer.'[13]

Bobby woke after half an hour and made up for all the wrongs his father had
ever done him by cursing him for the remaining two-and-a-half hours it took
to return to Whitehorse. Stan never uttered a word, and both ignored Christy
who concludes this tale with the observation—"My hopes of country-singing
stardom dashed."

But to return to the 1976 trip with Myfanwy, as Christy arrives in Main
Street, Whitehorse, on that particular occasion, he bemoans the fact that they
have closed down and boarded up the iconic Whitehorse Inn, to be replaced
by a modern bank:

> What will the city be without the tall prancing white stallion
> hanging over the sidewalk? It was the hottest scene in town during
> the war and the roughest afterward. It became the main Indian

drinking and brawling spot, earning the nickname Moccasin
Square Garden.[14]

Christy suggested that the Whitehorse Inn sign should be preserved as a
historical monument. Eventually the illuminated neon sign *was* preserved, and
can still be seen today at the MacBride Museum on First Avenue. Picking up
his mail from the Edgewater Hotel and strolling over to a coffee shop to open
and read, he is pleased to see that one envelope contains his Yukon driver's
license. "The other, nearly two years old, informs me that my application for
a job on the Arctic Circle as a weather technician ... has been turned down."
Armed with his Yukon driving license (special conditions were required to
drive in the Yukon due to the cost of rescuing broken-down motorists from the
wilderness) Christy and Myfanwy find and buy a '67 Chevy from the back of a
garage on Fourth Avenue to take them on the rest of their trip up to Fairbanks.

> On to Haines Junction, nestling below the towering peaks of the St.
> Elias range. They stand in iron-grey majesty above the little town
> and the icy trails through the passes mark the path of moist Pacific
> air like fingers of white candle wax.[15]

There, in the shadow of the mountains, they stop at Mother's Cozy Corner
for pie and coffee, where the sign reads "Small in Size but Big in Hospitality,"
then on to Burwash Lodge at mile 1103 where Christy and Myfanwy spend
their first night out of Whitehorse.

> ...a veritable cliché of a mountain hostelry set right on Kluane Lake
> and at night from your window you can hear the thumping of the
> water as it hits the shore and washes the gravel with a shoosh like
> brushes on a cymbal. At dawn and dusk the mountains on the other
> side of the lake are black cut-out forms against a dark pink-tinged
> sky. The cool lake air carries a hint of early fall wood-smoke.[16]

Over a few drinks in the lodge they are invited to sit at a table with a lone
Indian, who after a long silence then proceeds to tell them the story of his
cousin, an honest trapper, who was in debt to the trading post thereabout, and
no matter how hard he tried to settle his debts just kept on running up more
credit. To add to his misfortunes, that winter his wife died, but the ground

being too frozen to bury her, he hauled her body up into a tree. When he did this it made all the animals come around to prowl and sniff at the body. So the guy's cousin sets his traps by the tree in which they had hauled up the dead woman, as a result of which he had his best trapping season ever and made a small fortune.

The story prompts Christy to reflect on the absurdity of Alaska in general, and about those (starting with the Russian fur trade in the 1700s) who have lost and made their fortunes since. In 1867, the Americans bought Alaska from the Russians for $7,200,000 in gold (having earlier that century already bought Louisiana from the French and Florida from Spain). Initially criticized for the stupidity of paying that sum for a piece of wilderness, the fur trade having already declined, it was simply left as Indian territory until someone discovered gold. At the time of writing *Rough Road*, Alaska was still booming, this time with oil. It has since, in the summer months at least, become overrun with tourists, a trade that was only just emerging at the time of Christy's trip. But here Christy describes the boom years of Alaska during the 1970s:

> No sooner do they finish building one pipeline than they start on
> another one. Land of the six-thousand-dollar-a-month welding job.
> Waitresses who dabble in real estate. Gold nugget watches on the
> arms of boys a year off the farm. Fairbanks! One of the few places
> on God's earth where you will find Eskimo men wearing mascara.[17]

And so over the Alaska border go Christy and Myfanwy, where Christy recalls the absurd spectacle of U.S. citizens actually going down on all fours to kiss the asphalt. On to Tetlin Junction at mile 1311, cutoff for the Top of the World Highway to Eagle, Alaska, and Dawson City, Yukon. At the time, Tetlin Junction consisted of a lodge, truck stop, and four log cabins. By way of emphasizing the random individuality of the Yukon/Alaskan character, here in Tetlin Christy encounters "the world's coolest gas station attendant. A forty-something, gaunt Inuit with a pencil-thin mustache, who glides around the pumps, snapping his fingers, scat singing, and uttering a string of hip cant, "Wow. Say, man, where you headed? . . . Fairbanks, hmmmm . . . well, groovy." Christy doesn't have time to hang around and hear the hip Eskimo's story, so he makes one up that is probably as crazy as the real thing.

Next, mile 1314 at Tok, Alaska. It's Saturday night and the pair head for Young's Husky Lounge roadhouse where the band is wailing out rockabilly and raucous behavior is going on inside. The dance floor is crowded with construction workers, oil men, dog mushers, and breeders, all wedged in four-deep at the bar. The only way of getting a drink is to pass money hand over hand through the crowd and have your drinks handed back in the same fashion. The only conversation is about dogs or nostalgia.[18]

At Johnson Rivera, mile 1330, after driving the Chevy for three hundred miles over rocky and rutted terrain with nothing untoward happening to the car, it then takes a dislike to the smooth asphalt of "civilization" and blows a tire. The jack is rusted and useless and so Christy and Myfanwy settle down next to the river and wait for someone to come along. Eventually they manage to flag down a car, borrow a jack, and get mobile again. Then twenty miles farther on Christy spied a wrecker's yard down a muddy lane off the highway and managed to get a serviceable tire from one of the wrecks. His observations on the wrecks themselves and how their license plates hail from all states south, tells its own story:

> They had penetrated far enough into the land of the future that
> when they expired their owners could not be too angry, just gave
> them a final push into the woods, or else, broke, their drivers
> pulled in here and sold them for the bus fare into Fairbanks.[19]

Delta Junction, mile 1422, and officially (according to the good aldermen of Delta Junction) the end of the Alaska highway. This is where the Alaska and Richardson highways merge for the remaining hundred miles to Fairbanks. But as Christy points out, because a good portion of the Alcan was built on existing trails anyway (as was the Richardson), and its destination was also Fairbanks, it is not unreasonable to assume that Fairbanks be considered the terminus of the Alcan. Whatever the relative merits of these arguments, Christy and Myfanwy made the most of Delta Junction's hospitality:

> Rainier and Olympia beer signs are glowing in the window of the
> Club Evergreen. ...what better way to meet the people and get
> the true feel of these little communities than by visiting the local
> watering holes? ... Drinking is a big part of the life of the North,
> some would say the biggest part, and a teetotaler knows not the
> land of the midnight sun.[20]

We do not know if the pair continued imbibing at other establishments along the way, or whether here Christy is just simply offering us a social history of the Alcan; in any event, twenty miles farther on he points out the Richardson Roadhouse, "one of the original log-cabin inns that were built every twenty miles along the old trail." Farther on again, twenty miles from Harding Lake, and just past the Boondox Bar, Christy and Myfanwy came across another one of those northern absurdities, a curious two-story building covered in a forest mural with bear cubs climbing trees and fish leaping out of streams. The blinds were all drawn and so they both stopped to explore. They were invited in for coffee by a strange lady, "with a severely lined face, eyelids like walnuts, and her iron-grey hair is arranged in a disconcerting Veronica Lake peek-a-boo style." A small, active woman in her middle fifties who spoke out of the corner of her mouth tells them the place is a social center for the elderly. "So where are they then?" asks Christy:

> That's the problem, sweetie. I run it for the old people but the city
> has stuck it way out here twenty-five miles from town where the
> rent is cheaper but where the old people can't get to it. ... I haven't
> gotten paid for two months. But if I don't do it, who the hell will?[21]

They stay for coffee and the woman tells them, slitting her eyes to exhale the smoke from her Camel cigarettes, that she came up from St. Louis with her husband who was a navy pilot. He had the choice of posting to either Hawaii or Alaska and chose Alaska because of his fascination with Jack London's writing. She had wanted Hawaii. But within three months of arriving in Alaska he died in a plane crash. "The poor bastard. I just stayed on."

Then onward to North Pole, the last community before Fairbanks. So called because the developer who bought it hoped to coax a toy manufacturing company to take advantage of the name and location. Didn't quite turn out that way, but a fur buyer named Con Miller, who had arrived in Fairbanks in 1949 with his wife Nellie and only $1.49 in his pocket, eventually saved up enough cash to open a trading post in North Pole. Because Con dressed up in a Santa suit each Christmas, he soon became known as Santa by the local kids which prompted him to name his store Santa Claus House. He gave gifts to poor kids in remote Alaskan settlements, and when Con's wife Nellie became postmistress, the store also served as a post office, receiving mail from kids around the world who address letters to Santa Claus, North Pole.

Con and Nellie's family continue the tradition to this day and, as Christy points out, many other businesses in North Pole have cashed in on the Santa theme in one way or another, resulting in much of the town being dressed up with Christmas kitsch all the year round.

And so finally to Fairbanks, of which town Christy gives a fascinating history, before recounting the views of locals and writers about how the city had changed from pre- to post-pipeline only a few years previously. The town used to be acclaimed as an "all-American city." "There was a spirit of friend-liness uniting the people that helped ... hardships to be endured." Fairbanks had a touch of the French Foreign Legion about it inasmuch as: "the people came from everywhere. No one cared about whatever deeds lurked in their neighbor's past. ...it was all good natured back in the old days.... Used to be an Alaskan whore had a heart of gold."

By contrast, as many of the old-time pioneers lamented, now it was all hustle, making a quick buck, and getting out again. "Ah, these people, what do they care for this country? They'll make their twenty-four dollars an hour for as long as they can take it, and get out. Good riddance, but they leave mementos of their presence all about; each one of them destroys a little bit of Alaska before they leave." But the greatest regret of the old-timers was the legacy that the surge of "progress" had on the Indians. There was a time when they co-existed with the white man, when they became interdependent, the one on the other. "Now they lie on the floor in the washroom of the white man's bars." And as for the whores, "the white man turned the Indian woman into a whore and then they couldn't even earn money that way because the black women came up from Detroit and Seattle and drove the Indian woman off the street." A fact that was borne out by the first sight that greeted Myfanwy and Christy as they drove into downtown Fairbanks along Second Avenue, the rest of the following passage being a fair description of downtown during the late 1970s:

> ...black hookers in blond Afro wigs parade, shaking the shakable, showing the stuff, licking frosted lips with pink tongues, and offering fake lascivious leers to short-haired, fresh-faced soldier boys. ... The big parking lot is filled with dented Jeeps, mud-splattered campers, hillbilly Fords, old Volvos owned by geologists, and long cream-colored Coup de Villes. Kids lie around in sleeping bags, their heads propped against tyres. Over in a corner of the lot

behind a van a couple of people are completing a deal of some kind while Eskimos pass around a bottle of California port a few feet away. Three pipeliners with beards and long hair and ample bellies commandeer the middle of the sidewalk, drinking beer and smoking cigarettes, tossing each dead Oly can into the street, vying with one another in exclaiming what they'd like to do with their section foreman. Down the street, tourists take photos of gold nugget watches in a jewellery store window and Indians in tattered clothes sprawl on the curb in front of them.[22]

Christy and Myfanwy confronted the other side of the human face of Fairbanks as they walked to their motel room that night and passed a door open on the following vista, accompanied by country songs coming from a radio: "a man was sitting on the edge of the bed with his elbows on his knees and he was staring at a spot on the rug between his feet. Beside him the desk with the peeling veneer top; in front of the mirror were gilt-framed photos of a woman and some children."[23] Later they were woken at four in the morning by a truck door slamming, heels clicking, and a screaming female voice, "If you think I'm going to give you a blowjob you're crazy!" An intrusion that provokes from Christy the following assessment: "Fairbanks! More pollution than Los Angeles! Home of the world's busiest McDonald's!" Also, a terminus of six highways and a railroad, not to mention a flight a day from New York and Tokyo. And this last description of Fairbanks must be included simply to further showcase Christy's observational powers of the absurd, and his poetic prose:

> A young Eskimo boy with teased hair, painted eyes swishing down the midnight avenue. The North Carolina couple picking each other apart in the fantastic Mexican restaurant. The hordes of dirty-clothes working men. ... Okies pumping gas. The Jewish man running the Viennese delicatessen with Aleut waiters. A crowd of Eskimos gesticulating under a street lamp outside a Bingo parlour. Men in Fairbanks formal attire—leisure suits—plotting big deals with Arabs and Japanese in the basement restaurant of the Chena View Hotel. ... And always the whores: young ones working the streets and lobbies; old ones turned to waitressing in the greasy luncheonettes.

[...]

Fairbanks, the terminus to the Alcan. The All-American town smack dab in the middle of the tawdry future.... The beginning of the dream and the end of the road.[24]

And so to the return trip, departing from the Alcan at Tetlin Junction to take the Top of the World Highway northwards to Dawson City (not to be confused with Dawson Creek). The drive was made all the harder due to heavy rain turning the already potholed and rutted road to mud. To add to the dangers, the Chevy was skidding dangerously around bends that were unbanked and close to the unguarded edges of mountain passes. At the top of Fairplay Mountain, 5,700 feet up, the view, when it appeared through the rain and clouds, was straight down. It took seven and a half hours to make the last 150 miles into Dawson City.

> The town bursts into life on August 17 each year. The streets
> are jammed with tourist campers and every pick-up truck from
> 500 miles around. Indians, miners, families from Colorado, as
> well as the entire city of Whitehorse throng the dirt streets and
> elbow their way through Diamond Hall Gertie's, home of the only
> legalized gambling in Canada.[25]

Here Christy met up with the aforementioned Joe Nickell, who had traveled to work in the casinos after hearing from Christy that there was legalized gambling in Dawson, at that time the only legal gambling anywhere in Canada. Christy describes the three days of action before "bills are paid, tents are taken down, camps are broken, and the line of cars and trailers begins making its way out of town." The following notes from Nickell's journal describe the meeting:

> *August 11, 1976* (At the Eldorado Hotel bar in Dawson City,
> Yukon): Erling came in and was accompanied by Jim Christy &
> his girlfriend Myfanwy, so I jumped up from the table to greet
> them and afterward had a talk with them over drinks before going
> to Gertie's (Diamond Tooth Gertie's Gambling Hall, where I was
> operating a Crown & Anchor).

Sept. 7, 1976: "I . . . went out for an evening's drinking (and) joined Erling, Jim Christy and another local writer (in Dawson City).[26]

At this point of the trip, Myfanwy had had enough of the "inclement weather" and the "bleakness" of the small towns along the way and was getting homesick for the bright lights of Toronto. Christy drove her back to Whitehorse from where she flew home. Christy stayed on and worked in Dawson for two months, unloading the twice-weekly supply truck that came up from Whitehorse and delivering mail and supplies to the stores around town, until, that is, the days started to grow shorter and colder, and ice started to form at the edges of the river. Christy describes how only about three hundred people inhabited Dawson in the winter of that decade, about the same number as did before the gold rush. He compares this to the 30,000 who inhabited the city during the boom years. The city itself, he says, looked the same during his stay as it did in 1898, only without the people:

> ...there are all these houses, enough for thousands of people, and
> they all stand empty, collapsing, buckling on their foundations
> of permafrost. They are being reclaimed by the bush. There is an
> eerie sense of time to Dawson in the fall and winter as you look up
> the street at the decrepit buildings.... Your footsteps really do echo
> on the board sidewalks in the night. Ghosts lurk in the abandoned
> buildings.[27]

A reading of *Rough Road* is recommended to fully appreciate Christy's fascinating accounts of some of the old gold rush characters—and not only those who made their fortunes directly from pay dirt. Christy also debunks some of the Jack London myths. In London's case, his Yukon pay dirt was the books and articles he wrote as a result of the year he spent in the region. But as Christy observes, London was no different from the thousands of others who just "drifted into the Yukon and drifted out again at the earliest opportunity." He credits London with a rich memory of the things he saw and heard on his Yukon travels, and a vivid imagination when it came to exploiting those experiences later. That London's great Yukon adventures were in large part fictional has been pretty much accepted, but this of course should not diminish his earlier audacious adventures as an oyster pirate and teenage hobo. Though only twenty-one when he traveled to the Yukon, London had already determined to give up the harsh life of a drifter and become a writer. He had enrolled in university to further this goal but quickly realized that college was not going to provide him with the skills he needed to write. It was during his second term that he decided to quit university and seek his fortune, as so many others were doing, in the gold rush. The trip was financed by his sister, and his brother-in-law accompanied him on the venture. While they never made any money from the trip at the time—in fact returning broke—in terms of London's writing, the Yukon became his real university and gave him some of his best material: "I never realized a cent from any properties I had an interest in up there.... Still I have been managing to pan out a living ever since on the strength of the trip." London would never overcome his battle with alcohol, which eventually killed him at the age of forty.

The true laureate of the Yukon, Christy maintains, was Robert William Service (1874–1958). Born in Lancashire, England, and brought up in Scotland from the age of five, Service followed his father's footsteps into banking when he left school. At the age of twenty-one he tramped across America to Vancouver Island, from where he drifted up and down the West Coast between Mexico and British Columbia. Christy tells us how Service, drawn to the Yukon by London's recently published works, settled down to work at a bank in Whitehorse. After coming to the attention of the Yukon journalist Stroller White, who had heard Service reciting poetry at gatherings around Whitehorse, White persuaded him that writing could be profitable. Late that night, after everyone else had left the bank, and to the sounds of merriment coming from the nearby Malamute Saloon, Service paced about his office wracking his brains for something to pen. Mistaken for an intruder, the night watchman fired a shot at Service—an event that spawned his narrative poem "The Shooting of Dan McGrew," a melodrama that subsequently generated two movies by the same name. After reciting the poem at a church social, an aged miner approached Service and told him the strange tale of a prospector who cremated his own partner. Thus was born Service's second acclaimed work, "The Cremation of Sam McGee," with its famous opening lines: "There are strange things done in the midnight sun—By the men who moil for gold." And if Service's crude rhyming ballads are frowned upon by poetry snobs today, Christy warns them not to indicate such prejudices in the bars around Whitehorse and Dawson—not if they value their hides, that is!

But to return to the adventures of our more contemporary vagabond: During his two-month stay in Dawson, Christy made a five-day trip up the Dempster Highway with two brothers on a moose hunt. Today the Dempster runs all the way from ten miles outside Dawson City, straight north for the remaining 470 miles to Inuvik. From there, the coastal settlement of Tuktoyaktuk (Tuk) on the Arctic Ocean can be reached via the Mackenzie River Delta or by plane. At the time of Christy's trip, the Dempster was no more than a rough road as far as the Arctic Circle boundary at Eagle River. Below Christy describes the ever-changing landscape up the Dempster Highway:

> Forests to plains to rolling dun-colored hills. Then Alpine forests, which gave way to the strangest Max Ernst landscapes: flat tableland with eerie mesas rising like mysterious growths bubbled up from underground cauldrons. There was a stretch of strange peaks, white sulphur cliffs, brilliant white and dark red hoodoos thrusting out of their granite ramparts, solitary grey chimney peaks like the towers of medieval cathedrals far off in the distance, and one night we camped in sleeping bags and I woke at dawn to see the tumble of peaks black and silhouetted in the dim light like piles of rubble and ragged pieces of wall left standing after a bombing raid on a German city.[28]

The trio took their time, stopping to hike through woods, shooting grouse to clay-bake for dinner, hunching around campfires at night sipping brandy and swapping yarns. When they finally reached the Arctic Circle boundary, they got their moose (well, one of Christy's companions did; Christy himself has little appetite for killing) and headed back for Dawson.

By the time the worst of the winter started, Christy had saved up enough money to fix the battered Chevy and head south for Whitehorse, a route that he had tramped and hitch-hiked many times before. Just a few miles past Stewart Crossing, Christy saw a man walking north along the Dempster. Obviously not a local, lean, in his mid-forties and wearing a denim jacket with the collar turned up and greased-back hair. Christy's curiosity, and some concern, made him turn the car around to enquire where the stranger was headed. Turns out that the guy was tramping to Alaska, and some mean-spirited lift from Whitehorse had dropped him on the Dempster telling him it was the Alcan. Had the hobo continued on his way to Dawson, he would have been stranded as the road back south to the Alcan would have been closed for the winter and there was no work to be had in Dawson. Christy drove the man back to a lodge up the road where, over a coffee, he heard the man's story—a tale not uncommon to many who find it hard to conform to society's norms, and a tale that was to take Christy back to his early teens:

> He told me about how the world was going crazy. So crazy, in fact, that people thought he was crazy for noticing it. And when things got to that point, he figured it was best to be moving on. 'Why, I walk alongside the road and kids in cars throw stones at me or try to run me down. The po-lease run me in just to be ornery. I've spent my life drifting and it's getting harder to do. Man ain't free down South. You hardly meet anybody worth talking to. I'm just an old hobo.'[29]

As the tale continued, Christy started recognizing places and people the hobo knew. "He had ridden the rails and shipped out all around the world." When Christy asked if he knew Floyd Wallace, the man answered, "Floyd Wallace and me was good friends and I'm proud to have known him." To which Christy retorted, "Have known him? What's he dead now?" It seemed that Floyd Wallace had just disappeared, not been seen for some time, and not turned up at his usual haunts. Another old friend of Christy's, Frisco Jack, had suggested to Christy's new acquaintance that life might suit them better in Alaska, and so the rockabilly hobo was on his way to meet up with Frisco Jack in Anchorage when he got diverted up the Dempster Highway.

> I waved goodbye and drove on south. As I travelled I thought about him chasing that fading dream. As the forests and the mountains whooshed by outside the windows of my snug car I dwelled on some of the memories he had uncovered, and I thought back on old Floyd. Hadn't Bashō written about 'all the ancients who died on the road'? The Arkansas traveler was right, of course. If that old-fashioned honky-tonk, free-wheeling life existed anywhere, it was in Alaska. But I have a feeling it doesn't really exist there either and that is more than a little bit sad.[30]

The theme of the disappearing hobo was acknowledged by tramp-writer Jim Phelan in his book *Tramping the Toby* (1958), when he observed that "it is much harder to live the life of a vagabond in modern times than it was in antiquity." A theme picked up by Jack Kerouac a couple of years later in "The Vanishing American Hobo" from *Lonesome Traveler* (1960) when he wrote:

> In America camping is considered a healthy sport for Boy Scouts but a crime for mature men who have made it their vocation.
> — Poverty is considered a virtue among the monks of civilized nations — in America you spend a night in the calaboose if youre [sic] caught short without your vagrancy change. ... They pick on lovers on the beach even. They just dont [sic] know what to do with themselves in those five thousand dollar police cars with the two-way Dick Tracy radios except pick on anything that moves in the night and in the daytime on anything that seems to be moving independently of gasoline....[31]

Humans have adapted more than any other animal to survive as a species; it's what makes us human. But our explosion in numbers means that, for most of us at least, we have had to abandon our genetically programmed role as hunter-gatherers to live in vast metroplexes, governed by increasingly complex systems of laws and conventions in an attempt to impose order and control out of what should be a natural state of chaos and caprice. In the urban landscapes of North America, the domestication of human life has reached such a state of evolution that walking in the suburban sprawl, much of it too scattered and dispersed to make public transport viable, has long since given way to the exclusive use of the automobile as the only acceptable means of travel. Christy found this out to his own cost when he got jailed just for hitchhiking on the highway.

Rebecca Solnit in *Wanderlust: A History of Walking* (2001) describes how more than one thousand pedestrian crossings were removed in California, quoting an announcement from L.A. planners in the 1960s that "The pedestrian remains the largest single obstacle to free traffic movement." And in New York, Solnit describes the scenario where the then-mayor, Rudolph Giuliani, ordered police to start citing jaywalkers and fenced off sidewalks in some of the busiest areas of the city.[32] And so in spite of the current hysteria over carbon emissions and damage to the environment, there is a much deeper panic about tramping, which explains the continued paranoia about the pedestrian in America today. The ubiquitous closed circuit television and electronic database analyze even our shopping habits. To remain under the radar today requires no little skill: not just the absence of a registered address but also foregoing welfare payments, health care, and brushes with the law—and all this in a nation built by tramps. If tramping was tough for Kerouac's hobos, in the introduction to Christy's latest book, *Rogues, Rascals, and Scalawags Too* (2015), he updates Kerouac's observations for the contemporary reader when he comments:

> 'The woods are full of wardens,' said Mr. Kerouac in antediluvian times (the mid-fifties). How quaint that comment seems in light of the present homogenized era—nothing less than a security state— we live in. Instead of wardens who were actual human beings, there are now video cameras in the crotches of trees, microphone buds in the very buds, and drones above the forest canopy.[33]

Homelessness, joblessness, poverty, illness, persecution, isolation, et cetera; if it's tough these days for those who choose poverty as a lifestyle, how much tougher for those who have poverty thrust upon them. Bearing Christy's warnings in mind, for the millions of people today facing personal catastrophe (intensified correspondingly by the personal greed of those who already have more than is dignified), the option of becoming a hobo requires more energy and tenacity than does finding and keeping a job. End of vanishing hobo digression.

Back in Whitehorse and, in contrast to Dawson, Christy feels as though he is back in a metropolis, even though in the seventies the population of Whitehorse was only 14,000 (half its current figure). Here Christy gives us a seven-page history of flying in the Yukon, prompted by a winter trip he made with bush pilot Mike Fritz on his return to Whitehorse. On this occasion Christy joins Mike Fritz and a nurse for a childbirth emergency in the small community of Mayo, 210 miles away. They return just in time to transfer the mother—now in the final stages of labor and having screamed throughout the trip—to the waiting ambulance where they hear the baby cry before the ambulance has time to pull off from the runway.

Christy's next trip was more conventionally hobo, tracing the railway route of the early gold prospectors between Skagway and Whitehorse, even if he made the return trip in reverse order and from the relative luxury of the cupola atop the train's caboose. This trip prompts Christy to give us a potted history of the gold rush, from the pre-railway days when gold-hungry adventurers climbed through the Chilkoot Pass on their way to the goldfields, to the building of the White Pass & Yukon Route Railway at the turn of the last century. On the return run out of Skagway, Christy was the only passenger:

> I sat in the caboose next to the kerosene-burning stove. It was cozy during the slow climb up the hill. My feet, which were near the stove, were warm but the rest of me wasn't. I huddled in my parka. … The caboose must date back decades. The insides are wooden like an old cottage and there is a porch out the back and a lantern over the door. … It took three hours to negotiate the twisting nineteen-mile uphill route to Dead Horse Gulch, named after the three thousand pack animals that died during the summer of '98. At White Horse summit, the British Columbia Boundary, I looked out across the mountains to where the old trail is covered with snow and I thought of Robert Service making this same train ride in 1904 and glancing down from this same point and writing in his journal, 'I was glad I had not been one of those grim stalwarts of the Great Stampede.'[34]

One of Christy's last adventures of that particular year was, in exchange for a ride, helping a young Yukon-born trucker with his deliveries to all the remote settlements and work camps along the three-hundred-mile stretch of the Alcan between Whitehorse and Beaver Creek on the Alaska Border. Perhaps when Christy had made the trip previously, he was too busy watching the road from a lower vantage point than the cab of a semi-trailer to notice and indulge in the sheer poetry of the scenery—poetry both in terms of Christy's writing and the spectacle that prompted the writing on catching sight of the Auriol Mountain Range not far from Haines Junction:

> If a Cinerama camera topped the same rise it would be with Wagnerian accompaniment, but in real life silence is appropriate because before the panorama of mountains folding in on themselves—dissolving into one another in a ragged series of ridges working upward from the vast glaciers, the far-flung ice fields, a great grey granite world played upon by icy fingers

and volcanoes gushing snow and candle wax—one can only
feel the hush of awe. The range stretches far into the distance,
hundreds of peaks disappear truly as if into eternity. No one has
named the peaks, no one has even seen them in their entirety;
there are unimagined worlds beyond the first mountain walls
and hidden tarns where mountain sheep have come to drink for
thousands of years.[35]

The end of this trip, and the end of *Rough Road*, is Christy being dropped
off at the Canada-Alaska border from Wayne's big Mack truck after fulfilling
the last of his deliveries in and around Beaver Creek. And so this section of
the chapter ends as it was started, with "the sense of a wonder one cannot
help but feel in the presence of nature." In the passages above and below,
Christy sums up perfectly two of those contradictory, and at the same time
complementary, aspects of being on the road. Firstly, the awe of the natural world that reveals the human world as the ephemeral and relatively
insignificant phenomenon it is, and secondly, when we have had our fill of
the wonderment and desolation of nature, the irresistible and compelling
allure of a glassful of beer in the warm and convivial ambience of a neon-lit
tavern. The lure of both mountains and beer can be equally strong, and of
course there are times when one can satisfy both simultaneously—such is
the adaptability of humans:

It is pitch black at eight in the morning and cold, which is the way
it should be on the Alcan. I pull my parka close around me, grab
my duffle, and feel the fresh snow under my boots. I've covered
the wildest part now, in a couple of miles the pavement and Alaska
begin. Down the road the lights of Far West Texaco are glowing
in the dark and America is just over that ridge. Maybe one of the
Alaska trucks will give me a ride and I'll have my next beer, make
it a Bud, tonight in a club on Second Avenue and a fitting reward
it will be too, after all these miles. So I set off walking toward the
lights, feeling crazily elated despite the dark, the snow, the cold,
right down the middle of that deserted road.[36]

A DIGRESSION ON CHRISTY AND THE MOVIES

One should not be misled into believing that Christy's sojourn in British Columbia was entirely taken up with exploring the wilderness and jetting off overseas. He was as equally at home in urban surroundings as he was on the open road, as much the flâneur as the rover. During his twenty-four years based in and around Vancouver he spent a lot of time in that city writing, gardening, producing artworks, and hanging around in bars, jazz joints, fight clubs, and movie sets. Little has been said so far about Christy's strange, parallel life as an actor and movie extra, and this chapter will conclude with a brief mention of some of these exploits, starting with an anecdote from an old friend of both Christy and Marcel Horne, Joe Ferone. Sailor, docker, logger, wrangler, carnival performer, writer, authority on outlaw history, and all-round vagabond in his own right, Ferone describes Christy as "a true scholar of the arcane, the offbeat and the Beat, an illuminator of the criminally obscure, which he is himself." Coincidentally, the set of the Walt Disney production where the pair first met concerns a Depression-era tale about a female road kid, starring Meredith Salenger, who tramps two thousand miles, partly in the company of another young hobo, played by John Cusack, in search of her father who has gone in search of work.

> I first met Jim Christy in Vancouver on the set of a Hollywood movie, *The Journey of Natty Gann*. We were lined up at Wardrobe to be fitted in hobo garb, and when he gave his name, I asked him if he was the Jim Christy who knew Marcel Horne. Marcel had run a sideshow, the Circus of Wonders, in a traveling carnival and had hired me as a knife-thrower and bed of nails man. Winters he lived in our house on Hamilton Street and did his fire-breathing act in dives like the Kit Kat Klub. Later in Toronto, he befriended Jim, who arranged the publication of Horne's book, *Annals of the Fire-breather*.
>
> A day or so after the movie shoot I bumped into Jim in Grant's Café on Commercial Drive and over four or five coffees we discovered several mutual obscure passions. A detail I remember, is surprise the other guy knew the real names of Blaise Cendrars (Frederic-Louis Sauser) and the boxing champion Tommy Burns (Noah Brusso). This led to years of similar discussions over

hundreds of beers, arguments over ring records, who wrote which song, or discovered which ruin. We hit many roads, chronicling strange houses, petroglyphs, and counter-terrorist camps for the slicks and underground papers.[37]

Christy was in more movies and television shows than he is able to recall, and those that he can are presented here in no particular order. He remembers that he and Ferone were together in another movie filmed in Vancouver, *Year of the Dragon* (1985), filmed in the docks and starring Mickey Rourke. In another dock filming, directed by Mario van Peebles, Christy had to perform a stunt riding a crane hook from one dock to another across the water. He was paid extra as the stunt man didn't show up and he had to break union rules by taking it on. In another movie, *If I Had Wings*, filmed at Langley Airport a hundred miles from Vancouver, Christy recalls a lot of shooting and flying around in old-style biplanes. Then there was *The Christmas Star* (1986), a Santa Claus prison movie starring Ed Asner, in which Christy had to sing "O Come, All Ye Faithful" with a guy who had actually served time in that prison, the New Westminster Penitentiary where the tramp-writer Jack Black had been incarcerated. Then there was *Rocky IV* (1985) in which Christy had a line in Russian—but only in the Mexican version of the movie. Given Christy's knowledge of boxing and his acquaintance with many in the game, not least his friendship with the trainer Richie Giachetti who had choreographed some of the fight scenes for the movie, it was not long before he was sitting alongside Sylvester Stallone on set, embroiled in a discussion about boxing movies. Stallone had the idea of making a documentary about a real-life Rocky character and talked to Christy about featuring the Vancouver fighter Gordy Racette for the part—he didn't. Reflecting back, Christy comments, "I met a hell of a lot more interesting characters in the boxing world than I ever did in literature or the movies." Then there was a Mexican movie, *La Desconocida* (1983), where Christy was auditioned for his horse-riding skills, and a German film *Gold* (2013) shot in northern B.C. in the role of "man in saloon wearing a big hat, looking surly, and giving dirty looks to the movie's leading man."

There were also television series, a couple of episodes of *21 Jump Street* starring Johnny Depp, and several episodes of *Wiseguy* and *MacGyver*. In *Wiseguy*, Christy remembers having to deliver a line to the former Andy Warhol superstar Joe Dallesandro, and in *MacGyver* he played the part of a hitman faking a hospital emergency, then getting up from the gurney when the doctor turned his back and strangling him with the intravenous catheter tube. In more than half of his acting roles Christy was an SOC (Silent on Camera), meaning that he took individual direction but had no lines. Christy's mother gave him a hard time about always being cast as the bad guy, the hitman, the mercenary, the terrorist, "why never the good guy?" Christy's first acting part was as a KGB agent, and a dubious talent gained from his roles as a villain was that, although having no particular need for guns, he became adept at disassembling and assembling Kalashnikovs and M-16s.

As a result of his biography on the millionaire adventurer Charles Eugène Bedaux, *The Price of Power* (1983), Christy was also involved with two documentary films about the eccentric industrialist, *Champagne Safari* and *Looking for Bedaux*. Then there was the television show *Secret Lives* that ran from 1995 to 1997. The show involved exposing the secret double lives of folks who had deceived partners and friends. The format was to divulge the deceptions and wash one's dirty linen on screen in the presence of a so-called counselor. The show was a charade and the guy Christy worked with had quit his former role as a psychologist to become an actor. Christy was surprised—as was the other guy—to be auditioned alongside an older Afro-American man in the role of his son. Neither had any clue what was going on until they discovered they were being tested out for their skills at improvisation. When Christy did appear on screen, it was alongside a woman presented as his "wife." They were having non-specific relationship difficulties and told to improvise while the off-screen crew held up prompt signs such as "talk about sex." Christy says that when the fictional wife tried to upstage him he forgot he was acting and threw himself into the ensuing argument in earnest. Following the show, everyone from little old ladies to young guys would stop Christy in the street and offer advice on how to rid himself of his troublesome spouse. Then there were the inevitable commercials, including an eyeglass commercial in Vancouver and a foot massage commercial in Vietnam.

Although Christy is a huge movie devotee—his friend Warren Fraser describes his amazing recall of movie stars and lines from old films—he regards the whole acting business with disdain, simply regarding many of his forays into acting as necessities: "A guy's gotta eat." Christy particularly struggled having to audition alongside wannabe male actors who took the business far more seriously than he did, including investing in plastic surgery to give them an edge. Apart from the odd vagabond like Ferone who drifted into auditions for the same reason as Christy, these guys were the male equivalents of their airhead, actress counterparts. "The people trying to rise in the business were obnoxious, those at the top weren't so bad."

One of Christy's more recent flirtations with the movie business arose from a chance encounter with a Romanian artist while Christy was running an art gallery in Toronto in 2005. The Romanian guy asked Christy if he had ever been in the movies. Some days later Christy overhears the guy chatting to someone in Romanian on his cell phone, looking over at him, nodding, and then continuing the conversation with the person at the other end of the line. It turned out that the other Romanian guy shot crime movies and dubbed them into a string of Eastern European languages. So it was that Christy ended up involved in fifteen days straight shooting in a variety of locations alongside other "tough guys," where all he had to do was say anything that came into his head—so long as his lips moved—and into which was spliced a whole variety of Eastern European tongues from which, the painter told Christy later, the guy made at least ten movies.

---

1   Jim Christy, *Rough Road to the North: Travels Along the Alaska Highway* (New York: Doubleday, 1980), p. 2

2   Ibid., p. 3

3   Ibid., p. 189

4   Ibid., p. 7

5   Ibid., p. 78

6   Ibid., p. 83

7   Ibid., pp. 85-86

8   Ibid., pp. 93-94

9   Ibid., p. 96

10   Ibid., p. 104

11   Ibid., p. 109

12   Ibid., p. 112

13   Ibid., p. 113

14   Ibid., p. 115

15   Ibid., p. 117

16   Ibid., p. 189

17   Ibid., p. 120

18   Ibid., pp. 124-125

19   Ibid., p. 128

20   Ibid., p. 129

21   Ibid.

22   Ibid., p. 133

23   Ibid., p. 139

24   Ibid., p. 141

25   Ibid., p. 144

26   Joe Nickell, report to the author, January 24, 2017

27   *Rough Road to the North*, op cit., p. 146

28   Ibid., p. 156

29   Ibid., p. 160

30   Ibid., pp. 160-161

31   Jack Kerouac, *Lonesome Traveler* (London: Penguin Books, 2000), p. 149

32   Rebecca Solnit, *Wanderlust: A History of Walking* (London: Verso, 2001), p. 254

33   Jim Christy, *Rogues, Rascals, and Scalawags Too* (Vancouver: Anvil Press, 2015), p. 16

34   *Rough Road to the North*, op cit., p. 179

35   Ibid., p. 189

36   Ibid., p. 197

37   Joe Ferone, email to the author, January 28, 2017

7

THE VAGABOND ADVENTURER AT HOME AND ABROAD

I've never burdened me memory with dates. A brain's given you for thoughts, not dates.

Dates? ... Excuse me sounding impatient, but I'd say my books are built on facts, not dates. ... When you're here there and everywhere for seventy years you can't be as neat as a lawyer's ledger. A man's got to choose between being a bit o' nature and being chained to the office calendar.[1]

—Alfred Aloysius Smith (alias Trader Horn)

We have now reached the limit of where any strict chronology of Christy's life is possible. As with Trader Horn, having notched up his own seventy years of vagabondage, Christy expressed his own irritation with dates in an email dated January 1, 2015 following a request to get his early foreign adventures into some kind of sequential progression: "a Seventies chronology is impossible! Who needs linear thinking, anyway?"

Given that Christy has covered half the globe and back several times over since he commenced his Canadian exile, it is entirely reasonable that his brain should be kept free for memories rather than straitjacketed by dates. A cursory glance at the list of Christy's peregrinations below demonstrates why holding a clear chronology of his adventures in his head would not only be impossible, but painful. However, with patience and persistence, no doubt aided by reference to old passport visas, Christy has recalled pretty much the entire extent of his global ramblings. In addition to the countless destinations that Christy has tramped and hitchhiked to across the USA, Canada, Mexico, and Guatemala, and continues to do so—albeit by more convenient modes of transport—here is a list of destinations farther afield:

Argentina (2007)

Australia (1989, 2003–04, 2008)

Austria (1971)

Bahamas (1997)

Bali (2001)

Barbados (1982)

Belgium (1970, 1980, 1982)

Belize (1999)

Bermuda (2012)

Bolivia (1976)

Brazil (5 trips between 1974 and 1981)

Cambodia (2001, 2004, 2005, 2007, 2010)

Colombia (1973, 1975, 1979, 2005, 2007)

Cuba (2010, 2012, 2013, 2014)

Curaçao (1979)

Dominica (1993)

Ecuador (1976)

Ethiopia (1978)

Germany (1970, 2009, 2010, 2012)

Fiji (1985)

Finland (2011)

France (1970, 1972, 1973, 1974, 1983 [twice], 1990, 1996, 1997, 2001, 2010, 2012)

Germany (1970, 2009, 2010)

Greenland (1981)

Honduras (1987)

Hong Kong (1990)

India (2010, 2012)

Italy (1970, 1997, 2012)

Laos (2006)

Liechtenstein (1970)

Luxembourg (1970)

Macao (1990)

Malaysia (2000)

Morocco (1970)

Namibia (1978)

Netherlands (1970, 1996, 2011, 2013)

Netherlands Antilles (1976)

New Zealand (1989, 1996, 2003–04, 2008)

Norway (2012)

Panama (the islands, 1977)

Peru (1975)

Philippines (1990)

Portugal (1983)

Rhodesia (1978)

Russia (2012)

South Africa (1978)

Spain (1970, 2013)

St. Maartens (1983)

Surinam (1979)

Swaziland (1978)

Switzerland (1970, 1980, 1983, 2007)

Thailand (2001)

Trinidad (1978, 1990)

United Kingdom (1970, 1983, 1987)

Venezuela (1979, 1981, 1990)

Vietnam (5 trips between 2000 and 2008)

Yugoslavia (1972)

It is a hallmark of the true adventurer that they must go farther than even the most intrepid sightseer and, furthermore, by way of the remote and the undistinguished. Not for them the grand locations described in the tourist brochures, even though this sense of wanting to be part of the everyday rather than the celebrated when in foreign places results in standing out even more vividly as a tourist. That is the paradox of being Caucasian in exotic locations; however much you might want to blend in, you remain conspicuously conspicuous. It is, in any case, a fantasy in modern times to believe that any unspoiled places still exist on this planet easily accessible by humans. We corrupt by virtue of being there at all. Perhaps the new and the novel today is to be found in the corruption itself, the "undiscovered" treasures in our own backyards; and it is from just this kind of habitat that in his later years Christy would procure the raw material for his sculptures and construct them for others to stumble upon.

But to return to Christy's wanderlust: when taken to the kind of extremes enjoyed and suffered by Christy, the curse is that the world grows smaller the more one mines its secrets. Our ability to appreciate the rare and the exotic is diminished by our constant exposure to it. Yet Christy tramped in the dying decades in which novelty still did exist. He has taken his wanderlust to bizarre extremes, risking life and limb in the process. Not the kind of risks that mountaineers or extreme sports fanatics expose themselves to, although Christy has faced such dangers of nature too. Christy's perils came in human form, as is shown in some of the stories that follow. But before recounting some of these adventures, let Christy describe his particular brand of wanderlust in his own words from two of his poems:

THE HEART OF THE WORLD

I'm on my way, happy
to be going again. Coming back
maybe never. My passport pages
are filled with all these
pretty stamps and visas.
I've got no baggage
to check nor am I carrying on
any preconceptions.
I do have, however, more dreams
than can be stowed in the overhead
compartment or under
the seat in front of me. Oh, I
can go to Tiflis or, maybe,
Toronto; Hudson's Bay,
or Havana will do but what
I really want to find
is the place that's not
in the seat pocket by my knees
or on the map at the back
of the airline magazine.
Maybe the flight attendant
can be of assistance.
I press the button and the light
goes on: "Sir/madame
help me, please. I am
looking for the Heart
of the World."
(*This Cockeyed World*²)

In response to Christy being asked if there was anywhere in particular he never made it to but still wanted to, he responded, "That's easy, first: the Island of Pohnpei, Federated States of Micronesia, to see the mysterious half-submerged civilization of Nan Madol. Second: I'd like to make the Trans-Siberian railroad trip. I was on my way in 2013 but in Russia my plastic all failed. Otherwise, I just want to walk out the door and keep going."

Maybe Pohnpei is the heart of the world, for Christy at least, and he will make it there and add a hotel receipt to all the others that have been tossed over the years into a battered old leather suitcase that serves as a repository for memories of random rooms where he has laid his head for a night:

NOMAD NUMEROLOGY

Last night, December 22, 2013, King
Edward Hotel, Toronto. Add receipt to
others in a leather suitcase, older
even than the very first trip. Here're
some: Room 12, Lee Garden Guest House,
Hong Kong, 3-12-90; Room 1, Eagle's
Nest Motel, Concrete, Washington; #16,
GST Guesthouse, sometime, somewhere in
India; #32, Venus Hotel, San Ignacio,
Belize, C.A, 16/03/98; #749, Imperial
Palace, Las Vegas, 1983; #109, Lucky
Pacific – 28 Inn, New Hazleton, B.C.;
#272, Yukon Inn, Whitehorse, 1975;
#123 Koski's Motel, Glasgow, Montana. #
26, Dewagga Hotel, Ubud, Bali, and so
on. Most forgotten but I turned 45 in
room 35, 23 years ago at the 4 Pines in
Lillooet, B.C. and paid $52.92 for "2
in party" but the other gone these past
11 years. And here's a key attached
to yellow plastic, number 106. Where
was that? When? Do these rooms
and dates in an old suitcase add up
to anything? Maybe if I divide them
by years? What will be the number of the final
hotel, motel, guest house room? Will all the
numbers of all the rooms come back to me,
and I'll recite them each and every
one from Manaus to Malacca? My

last words just some nomad's
numerology.
(*The Big Thirst and Other Doggone Poems*[3])

The pages that follow chronicle in date order just some of Christy's most notable adventures, though the original texts of those in print are recommended to fully appreciate both the writing and the tale. The following narratives also serve to highlight the various guises that Christy has employed over the years: tramp, journalist, private eye, explorer, carnival roughie, or just plain old vagabond doing what vagabonds do best—all the while maintaining a faithfulness to whatever persona he adopts. The fact that Christy defies being pigeonholed into convenient stereotypes, being able to hold his own in whatever company or tribe he finds himself, is also the reason why Christy has been able to survive the kind of hostile social environments that most people would not. Joe Nickell observed these many faces of Christy when he commented, "Shakespeare's 'one man in his time plays many parts' is true in spades for Jim Christy, who has had many, many roles." Here then, is an example of Renaissance historian Jacob Burckhardt's "all sided man," but more than that, a character who, though entirely comfortable in the modern world, at the same time seems to evoke a more innocent, romantic, and authentic older world that sadly no longer exists. One can imagine that Christy would have found a place and felt at ease in any historical epoch.

"In Search of the Golden Madonna," "On the Caddy Trail," and three of the other Latin American tales below involve the kind of high drama normally identified with the movies—indeed part of "A Month in a Cartagena Dungeon" reads like an Edgar Allan Poe horror, only more abject. Hence the "Indiana Jones" tag linked to Christy that he finds so irritating. But unlike the whip-cracking hero of the big screen, while Christy is certainly motivated by adventure, he regards many of the scrapes he gets into as tragicomic and absurd. He does not seek danger for the sake of it; it just has a way of finding him. If anything, Christy plays down his adventures and is embarrassed about mentioning them, precisely because those with mundane lives insist on questioning the validity of those whose lives are extraordinary, unless, of course, those lives are recorded in the "history books," which is where one finds the biggest lies of all. I have no doubt at all about the veracity of Christy's stories, even if his memory for dates and chronology gets mixed up. The more one digs, the more one gets from Christy, even if getting at those nuggets about his life is as painful as pulling teeth—both for the dentist and the patient. The frustration is that there is so much more to report than Christy is willing to tell. But as he is now a septuagenarian, perhaps he is entitled to enjoy his memories unmolested.

Considering all of Christy's close encounters from his early days as a junior mobster and child hobo onwards, it is a wonder that he ever survived to tell so many fantastic tales at all. Not surprising then that Christy suffers no small amount of anxiety that ghosts from his past will come back to haunt him—maybe in his dreams they do. And even though he lives in the relative safety of Canada, Christy insists on obscuring certain facts about his past, either to protect others or protect himself.

The first six tales below introduce some of Christy's globetrotting adventures between the ten-year period from 1975 to 1985, in the middle of which, in December, 1981, Christy moved his home from Toronto to Vancouver. There he divided his time between friends in Vancouver and Seattle, Washington. At the beginning of 1983 Christy went to live for a year on Salt Spring Island, B.C., a year broken only by trips to France, Belgium, Britain, Portugal, Switzerland, and St. Maartens. Of course, throughout this same ten-year period Christy was still making annual trips to the remote wilderness of northwestern Canada. But Christy would continue putting himself in harm's way for a further twenty years or more. Our last story finds Christy, at the time approaching his sixtieth year, still doing what he loves doing best: traveling to remote and exotic locations, flirting with danger—no doubt women too—and immersing himself in the local habitat and culture, all the time chronicling his thoughts and escapades in artworks and writing commissions.

A MONTH IN A CARTAGENA DUNGEON

There is a part-fictionalized version of the Cartagena story in *Travelin Light* titled "La Mordida," meaning both "bite" and "bribe," both of which feature in this tale. Fictionalized because, as Christy says, the publisher "thought the drug stuff would have trendy sales appeal. I did not smuggle cocaine in frozen chickens though it would have been a good idea."

Given the success of the hit television series *Breaking Bad*, the publisher may have been on to something, though sadly cannot claim the credit for the idea even if she had come up with it first. But the cocaine was the only fabrication; the rest of the story relates the facts of that trip, which were every bit as catastrophic for Christy as the fictionalized version. If the cocaine bit was added by the publisher to this story for effect, an actual cocaine deal was very much at the center of another story in this chapter, "Drug Deal in Bogotá."

But back to Cartagena, and having enjoyed a convivial New Year's Eve in that city with friends, his second visit there, Christy was spending the morning of New Year's Day, 1975 sleeping off his hangover on the beach only to be relieved of his cash by a passing mugger. As a result of giving chase and retrieving his money, Christy was arrested by armed police, beaten up, and thrown into a dungeon in the fortress walls of Cartagena where he languished for about a month before his eventual release. Christy suspected that the whole affair might have been a ploy to extract a hefty bribe from their prisoner for his release. He was told that he could expect to serve several years in that cell, accompanied only by rats and biting bugs, and so who would not have been willing to hand over any amount of money to get out of that place. Ignoring the unnecessary additions made by the publisher, the factual arrest and prison sequences are graphically described in the "La Mordida" version, only small sections of which will be reproduced here:

> The van slowed and entered the gateway of the great fort. The men around me began muttering among themselves. I watched their black boots as they stirred in anticipation. I looked at their olive fatigue uniforms and the sten guns or bolt action rifles cradled in their arms. None of them looked more than twenty-two. ... The Spanish had used Indian labour to build this fort that protected the gold of the new world. They made the cement from coral and they built the walls sixty feet high and fifty feet wide. ... The van came to a halt and the back door was opened. The soldiers pushed me to the edge and the big shot who had taken charge when they got me, reached up, grabbed my belt and pulled me forward. I fell to the ground and before I could raise my head from the hard dirt, a steel-toed boot slammed into my ribs. The Captain was grinning with sincere pleasure. ... The second-in-charge was the driver, his teeth yellow, laughing, imitating his boss. ... I tensed, waiting for

it, and when it came this time it caught me higher up, on the skull, and my knees began to buckle.

[...]

They took me to a windowless stone room where the captain was waiting along with his superior. ... They didn't interrogate me, they didn't lay any charges, asked no questions, all they did was form a circle and put me in the middle. Then they proceeded to beat me nearly senseless. Rifle butts, fists, knees, boots. ... When they were done I was dragged out and down a steep flight of steps. I was only vaguely aware of what was happening. It was damp. ... They stopped before a thick green door, opened it and shoved me inside. ... The stone floor was slimy under my hands. I saw black and red bugs coming for me like something spilled on a sloping floor. Then, I stumbled into a corner and was sick.[4]

I leaned with one hand against the wall and threw up into a hole, the ragged gash that had been worn out of the stone.... When I was finished, I saw that my hand was covered with small red insect bites. I collapsed onto a bench. It was four feet long and two and a half feet off the ground and the only furnishing in the cell. For the first time I became aware of the pain and soreness from the beating. I was reaching down, tenderly feeling my shins when I saw the first rat come out of the opening, move toward the vomit and begin to poke around. Soon it was joined by another. They darted back and forth until they'd had their fill. ... There had been no concession made to the functions of the body. Not even a bucket or hole. The floor and the lower parts of the walls were encrusted with a scum of indescribable colour and odour. Four hundred years earlier the first pirate had been beaten and thrown into this cave and it seemed no one had hosed it down since. ... I sat on the wooden bench and waited. I leaned against the wall and felt the biting on the back of my neck but I didn't move. They crawled across my boots and under my pant legs and more welts the size of quarters appeared all over my body but I didn't care. I accepted it.[5]

One night passed. Another. Sleep was very unlikely on that 48 inch long bench. It came only after I had exhausted myself with frustration. I lay on my back and drew my feet up, but my knees would stiffen. The hard wood offered no comfort to vertebrae they had bruised with their rifle butts. I turned on my side and it was agony to my ribs. ...my arms were nearly covered with bites ... and now there were fresh bites on top of the welts. ...the trap door in the middle of the door opened and a tin plate of beans was slid into the cell. I was sick all over again. I dumped the beans into the rat hole and put the plate in the corner but still I was sick. ... On the third day, El Jefe came and told me that the situation was grave indeed ... they were obliged to put me in prison for 20 years. Unless, of course, I gave them ten thousand dollars.[6]

To cut a very long story short, Christy did not have this kind of money, something his captors found very hard to believe, assuming that all gringos had access to large sums of money. Eventually they accepted that all they were going to get from Christy—that had not already been stolen—was three fifty-dollar travelers' checks and eighty dollars cash that he had stashed away in his clothing. But after taking the money as a bribe for his release, they left him languishing in prison with no word of when he would be released. Later, after walking out of the jail, Christy checked out the pensión where he had been staying but his suitcase had long since disappeared. Avoiding the disgusted looks of fellow passengers on the bus to the beach, "I walked into the Caribbean in my underwear and washed. Then I scrubbed my clothes, spread them out on the sand and lay down and slept." Christy managed to find enough money to fly to Miami around the fourth of February, where an old gangster buddy of his father helped him out with a large wad of bills. After splashing out three hundred dollars on new clothes, bored with the Miami scene and not to wanting to expose his bitten, bruised, and sore body on the beach, Christy flew back to Toronto shortly before meeting up with Myfanwy on Valentine's Day of that year.

UMTALI MASSACRE, RHODESIA

An example of Christy's journalistic independence can be evidenced by a report he wrote on the Elim Mission massacre by ZANU-PF fighters that took place on the night of June 23, 1978 in Rhodesia's Eastern Highlands. Eight British missionaries (five women and three men), together with four children aged between three months and six years, had been beaten, bayoneted, or axed to death. Even the baby had been beaten before being killed. Four of the women were raped and the fifth managed to hide but died a week later in the hospital. The day following the massacre, Christy was the first Westerner to arrive at the Mission, nine miles southeast of Umtali (today's city of Mutare) and only four miles from the Mozambique border:

> I was there all day but never saw any other Westerners, except
> dead teachers and their families. The massacre was the work
> of Mugabe's forces, who before hacking those people to death,
> delivered a political speech to the young black students. The
> kids were told that education just played into the hands of the
> whites. The students watched their teachers and their families die.
> Children first.[7]

The precise timing of Christy's trip to the Rhodesian capital had been a coincidence. He had been in South Africa on an assignment for Canada's *Weekend Magazine* to report on the general troubles of the region, Soweto, Namibia, and Mozambique included. Following his arrival in Salisbury and booking into the Meikles Hotel, Christy avoided the hotel bar where all the other journalists reporting on that country's revolution were congregated and headed straight for local pubs. The only time the press left the hotel, he says, was to troop over to the Ministry of Information to receive the handouts on the war. These were then ridiculed and twisted to suit editorial needs and often enhanced, Christy says, with reports from "a source close to Robert Mugabe." These turned out to be the black waiters of the Meikles Hotel in their starched white uniforms who, when not serving drinks to the journalists, spoke to someone who knew someone who knew someone.

After spending a night with a white Rhodesian army soldier he met in a pub, Christy returned to the hotel at dawn where news of the massacre had started to trickle through. After taking a taxi to a train station on the outskirts of Salisbury, he took a train to Umtali through what he describes as incredibly beautiful hills and mountains. "It really felt like the Africa of your imagination. All those thorn trees. Rhodesian red earth." He then took a local bus from Umtali to the mission, to find the scene described at the beginning of this piece.

Christy had taken a risk traveling alone into such hostile territory and very nearly lost his life on the return journey. He left the school simply hitchhiking down the dirt road to Umtali until picked up by a soldier in an army truck who asked him what the hell he was doing: "There's a war going on out there, sport." Then, after spending a night in a lodge near the train station, he picked up a lift to Salisbury the following morning with Philemon, a young black Rhodesian army soldier in his Ford Anglia. After they passed the town of Odzi and were climbing a long hill in the Mtanda mountains, they were ambushed by rebel forces:

> Several shots hit our car like a line of period marks. They came
> from the right, the driver's side, and Philemon swerved the Anglia
> the other way. A bullet shattered his window and went through the
> roof a few inches behind my head. Before we bumped to a stop on
> the dirt shoulder, I had gotten the door open and tumbled out on
> the ground. Philemon, grabbing for his pistol, came out on top of
> me, rolled off, and began firing blindly into the bush on the other
> side of the road.[8]

More shots hit the car before the army trucks arrived that they'd seen way in the distance prior to the ambush, but from his hiding place behind the front tire of the Anglia, Christy could clearly make out one of the resistance fighters in a red beret, black T-shirt, and holding a Sten gun before he disappeared into the bush. The rebel fighters fled before the approach of the Rhodesian soldiers, but not before one of them was killed in the ensuing skirmish. Philemon concluded that the army was the intended target for the attack as they had to slow their trucks coming down the steep incline, and that the Ford Anglia and its occupants had just passed by at the wrong time.

It would be a further two days before television crews and other journalists were flown to the site from the Meikles Hotel, but as Ian Smith's government represented a pariah state, most press editors were unwilling to openly criticize what they regarded as Rhodesia's liberating forces. When Christy returned to his paper's Toronto office, the chief editor, Peter Sympnowich, had rewritten Christy's copy to remove any suggestion that Mugabe's forces were implicated, and furthermore, had maliciously illustrated the piece with photographs of South African police holding back Alsatian dogs from small black children, in order to highlight white-on-black brutality. They had not used any of the film footage taken by Christy, nor did he ever receive his film back. After trying to confront Sympnowich in the office, the latter fled into his room to be pounded by Christy's roaring from the other side of a locked door. Christy threatened his boss with a lawsuit and the piece was modified, but not as hard-hitting as Christy had intended. Even so, the result of the report was that the editor still received letters denouncing Christy as a racist and "right-wing fanatic." Letters to the editor in the same issue also criticized a piece Christy wrote on Soweto published the week before, this time denouncing him as "a Commie dupe."[9] The issue here is the way in which political correctness serves to mask the truths that moralistic liberal-minded folk do not want to hear. It takes the truly independent-minded like Christy to lift the veneer and expose hypocrisy for what it is. While on the subject of the tyranny of language in today's self-conscious times, it is worth emphasizing the pointlessness of imposing the values of today on those who survived a very different age, culture, and circumstances. As that other vagabond writer Louis L'Amour says in his autobiography, *Education of a Wandering Man*: "A mistake constantly made by those who should know better is to judge people of the past by our standards rather than their own. The only way men or women can be judged is against the canvas of their own time."[10]

Another rare example of a journalist who defied the language police was Auberon Waugh (son of the British writer Evelyn Waugh), also branded as a right-wing reactionary simply for saying it how it was and to hell with liberal sensibilities. Waugh was in fact allied to no political interest group; he was fiercely independent and chose his friends from across the political divide. This can be verified by him being the only person outside of the Irish Republican Army to publicly voice the opinion that he wished Margaret Thatcher had died in the Brighton bombing.[11] Hardly the sentiments of a right-wing bigot, unless that is of course the remark was read as misogynistic, of which Waugh was also accused. Waugh's death in January, 2001 prompted the left-wing columnist Polly Toynbee to write a scathing obituary on Waugh. The following comment by writer Charlotte Raven was just one of the many responses to Toynbee's idiotic criticism of Waugh. Importantly here, Raven's words cut straight to the whole business of "politically correct" journalists—and also, how to expose them:

> There are many left-wing people who take things at face value and many liberals who congratulate themselves on their moral superiority when all they are doing is restating the bleeding obvious. The earnestness of each of these groups is a signal that they don't really grasp what's going on. People who live on this level and never travel anywhere else are unlikely to make jokes about plane crashes.... Their humourlessness is a symptom of their lack of judgment.... They are people whose souls are cold and whose bullet-point priorities close the window on imagination and genuine freedom of thought while increasing their own claims to ethical superiority.[12]

Like Waugh, Christy spoke his own mind and was political hostage to no one, a troublemaker par excellence. But there is a price to pay for being a vagabond writer, and that price is to be ostracized by the establishment press, those who, anxious to protect their own narrow interests, banish to the margins dissenters like Christy who choose delinquency over obedience.

DRUG DEAL IN BOGOTÁ

One wonders what possessed Christy to return to Colombia after the punishment he took on his previous visit, but in 1979 Christy was given a journalistic assignment to report on the plight of a former *gamino* (street urchin) who had lived out of garbage cans from the age of four until thirteen. Now around thirty, the wealthy businessman was making it big in the cocaine industry. Arturo Amundez, as he is named in "Staying Alive in Bogotá" (*Between the Meridians*), meets Christy in the bar of Bogotá's largest hotel, the Tequendama, where pyramids of cocaine and girls, "Playboy bunny types only harder," are part of the hospitality on offer. But Christy has no interest in either. Amundez tells Christy his life story and acknowledges being worried that organized, corporate crime, unofficially supported by government officials looking after their own interests, could put him out of business, or worse:

He has survived because he is oh so cool, very smart and well armed. But he is an independent operator in a country where eventually an independent operator meets, not his match, but forces beyond his control.[13]

Later, Amundez meets Christy in Christy's hotel room with an airline flight bag containing, among other things, two bakery boxes. He has planned with Christy to meet an American who is desperate to make some big money in order to pay unpaid taxes to the Colombian government. One of the bakery boxes contains a cake which the dealer proceeds to slice up with a switchblade, the other contains 6.6 pounds of cocaine. Thirty minutes before the American is due to show up there is a knock at the door:

> Amundez's face freezes. ... Hockley [the American] is not due until eight. Amundez reaches under his coat and brings out a .25 caliber Browning automatic. He hands it to me and then takes out a clumsy old police special from the small of his back. 'If it's not an American,' he says, 'start firing.'[14]

This is the scene that confronts the frightened American when Christy calls "Come in." He has arrived thirty minutes early. As a relieved Christy later observes, "Participatory journalism has its limits."

DEPORTED FROM CURAÇAO ... AND ON TO CARACAS

Someone was obviously keeping tabs on Christy as a likely operative because when in 1979 he was hired by *Weekend Magazine* to travel down to the island of Curaçao to report on rumors that it was becoming an organized crime center, he met up with a guy involved in intelligence who produced a twelve-year-old file on Christy. The file was on Christy's 1967 assignment to New Orleans when he had been hired as an investigator to interview New Orleans District Attorney Big Jim Garrison. Garrison had been challenging the Warren Commission findings on the Kennedy assassination (see Chapter 4).

There are many reasons, not necessarily connected, why Christy might have been selected for the kind of assignment that follows: he had "mobster" credentials from his early days in Philadelphia, not least having Angelo Bruno as his godfather, had proven himself as a competent writer and investigative journalist, spoke Spanish, was an intrepid and resourceful traveler, was cool under pressure, and being afflicted by wanderlust, he was probably persuasive when it came to getting himself paid work that involved both travel and writing. One can only wonder what Christy might have listed on his résumé.

After a week in Curaçao, Christy was visited in his hotel and given a note from the intelligence guy telling him that he must leave the country immediately, that it was dangerous to stay. Christy was taken to a freight hangar at the airport and hidden amongst some boxes. From there he was given free plane passage to Toronto.

> While doing my rounds in Curaçao I discovered that Caracas had taken over from Marseilles as the world's major 'Mob' city and not only that, it was controlled by Canadian organized crime. The magazine gave me more money to fly to Caracas. The new reform-minded Justice Minister of Venezuela had been murdered a couple of days earlier, supposedly by a deranged gunman who fled to Naples. In reality, he was killed by two Canadian organized crime figures who were still in town, staying at the penthouse of the Sheraton, I think it was. Anyway, my Curaçao contact came over and took me to see them. They were straight-up and we got along fine. They laughed at the whole thing. There were fancy women and dope there. Neither of which did I see or partake of. Both of these guys were known to me by name. One told me that if I had any sense I would leave Toronto and move to his city [Vancouver.][15]

Two years later while in a coffee shop in the Italian district of Vancouver, a guy came up behind Christy and placed his hand on his shoulder. "The old moustaches in there go quiet with respect. It was that guy. He says, 'See, it's better out here. I'm glad you took my advice.'" When Christy wrote the original piece up (not the meeting in the coffee shop which hadn't happened at the time) the publisher refused to print the story considering it too far-fetched, particularly a story about an upcoming mob heist of a shipload of coffee sent by Castro to Europe.

Anyway, a month or so after I submitted my piece and had it rejected, the coffee heist occurred. I delivered a news clipping to the magazine but, naturally, they did not have the grace to say they were sorry.[16]

GUNFIGHT AT THE OK CORRAL

Yes, he was some guy, Wyatt Earp. Some guy who killed my poor, defenceless 19-year-old Great-uncle Billy. And he would have killed my other great-uncle, Ike, who was unarmed at the time, there in Tombstone, Arizona more than 100 years ago, if he could have shot better.

Jim Christy, *Between the Meridians*[17]

Christy was completely unaware of his connection to one of the most notorious events in American history until 1981, by now already aged thirty-six. He was drifting through Virginia on his way up-country from Florida with his friend Erling Friis-Baastad, when he stopped off at the house of his aunt:

There, drinking coffee at the kitchen table with my aunt Louise, was my mother. After the surprise, we took to reminiscing about my grandmother who had passed on two months earlier at the age of 95. 'She left plenty of papers about the family history, all sorts of stuff about the Clantons,' my mother announced.

'Who are they?'

'I declare! You know who I mean. The "Clantons."'

'We're related to the Clantons?' I thought she meant Jimmy Clanton, the guy who sung "Venus in Blue Jeans."

She leaned across the table and whispered conspiratorially, 'The outlaws. The OK Corral?'[18]

And so, after poring through pages of documents—including evidence of intermarriage and numerous wills signed with an X—confirming that Billy Clanton's father, Newman Haynes Clanton, was indeed his great-great-grandfather (not to mention other defamatory information concerning slavery that he will not expand on), Christy made the pilgrimage to Tombstone via Phoenix and Tucson, a journey he describes as "retreating through the past hundred or so years of American history."

> I stroll into an old Wild West hotel with polished tile floor,
> marble-topped registration desk, and wide, dark wooden stairs
> that swoop away in a sweeping curve. I half expect to see Katy
> Jurado slinking down the stairs, fingernails like weapons trailing
> along the banisters. It could be 1947.[19]

After climbing the rise to Tombstone's Boot Hill, Christy stood by the graves of Newman and Billy Clanton, before returning to the Crystal Palace saloon in town for a well-earned drink. As an aside, it was around this time that Christy had started cataloguing his fascination with strange destinations, and not just those like the Crystal Palace that he had a personal connection with. This led to the publication of his book *Strange Sites* (1995), and in turn spawned the show *Weird Homes* on Canadian TV's Life Network that was launched in 1998 and broadcast in both Canada and the U.S. The television producer contacted Christy after hearing him on radio discussing his obsession for eccentric personal spaces and the characters who inhabited them, such as old barges down by the lake, fishing shacks, lean-tos, the old hobo who lived in the Nash sedan, and Pop Stewart in the Kansas City rail yards. Christy was given the job of locations manager and clocked up huge mileage around the U.S. and Canada over a three-year period identifying suitable new locations for the show.

But back to Tombstone. In *Between the Meridians*, there follows thoroughly researched particulars about the "Cowboys" and the Earps. The Cowboys were the band led by Christy's great-great-grandfather, Newman Haynes Clanton, so called because of their principal trade of stealing cattle and horses in Mexico and selling them to American ranchers back over the border. The Cowboys numbered around two hundred at any one time and included members of several different outlaw gangs including a branch of the band centered around the McLaury brothers' ranch, John Ringold (Johnny Ringo), a cousin of the Younger Brothers, and "Curly Bill" Brocius. Christy takes on the OK Corral legend, dispelling the lies that have been handed down as historical facts. Not least, Christy points out, because the author (via his proxies) of the events of

October 6, 1881 (and perpetuated in twenty-three film and television versions) was none other than Earp himself—mightily edited to present himself as a hero, or "Brave, courageous and bold" as the opening line of Christy's "It Ain't O.K." (and a line from the television theme song) ironically suggests. Christy's characterization of Earp, ably assisted by recent forensic evidence of the real facts (including a handwritten transcript of the Earps' trial for murder following the shootings), presents a very different picture. His essay on the Earps and Cowboys allows Christy to combine his personal history with his passion for cinema, providing a summary critique both of the productions and the actors who have played Wyatt Earp and Doc Holliday across the decades since the first movie in 1932, *Law and Order*, starring Walter Huston.

Christy relates that, having previously been in trouble with the law in several other towns, the Earps and their cronies were latecomers to Tombstone, and ready to take advantage of, rather than eliminate, the lawlessness of the town, in particular, to control the town's gambling and levy taxes of which they would be the main beneficiaries. Christy portrays the gang as scheming political opportunists. Wyatt was soon fired from his job as deputy sheriff and took up a job as a saloon bouncer, where he continued to organize the gambling. Virgil Earp was defeated in his bid for the marshal's job, and a long feud commenced with those who had displaced the Earps. Events leading up to the infamous gunfight at the OK Corral can be determined from recent research, but below is Christy's description of Wyatt Earp:

> ...the thing with Wyatt was, he had to be real close to kill you. It is a fact that Wyatt liked to sidle right up, usually accompanied by two or more brothers, and preferably when you had your back turned. Wyatt let off seven or eight shots at Ike, who was about ten feet from him, and missed.[20]

Of Doc Holliday, Christy describes him as Earp's "alcoholic, tubercular, lying, cutthroat, Georgia peckerwood, dentistry-college-graduate sidekick," so no punches pulled there. One might think, well, as a descendent of the Clantons, Christy would say that, wouldn't he? But Christy has a track record of saying it like it is, regardless of personal interests. Indeed, as a journalist, there is much evidence that he goes against editorial bias and political partisanship, even to his own disadvantage. This is particularly evident in his report from the Rhodesian Highlands on the Elim Mission massacre described earlier.

As a cynic of the Diogenes school, Christy would not let anything so arbitrary as family affect his compulsion to expose the truth, and Christy's essay "It Ain't O.K." should be required reading for students of that historical event.

HOUSE ARREST IN MANAUS

C hristy's fifth trip to Brazil in 1981 was again funded by *Weekend Magazine* whom he had convinced to send him to investigate the Trans-Amazonia Highway backed by the billionaire shipping magnate Daniel Ludwig. When Christy started asking questions around Manaus, center of the construction operations, he was later braced in his hotel by cops, taken for questioning, and returned to the hotel where he was put under house arrest.

> During my grilling, I discovered that some Indian workers had been gunned down by their foremen. They had been promised some days off for Carnival but when the time came around the holiday was denied them. They assembled—peacefully—at the foreman's office/trailer and he opened the door firing; killed about seven.[21]

Christy had not known about the incident at the time he was questioned but found out later from his interrogators. This particular incarceration was a different experience altogether from the grim time he'd had in the Cartagena dungeon. The hotel didn't have a dining room but the cops brought Christy dinner each day on a silver tray with a cover over the hot dishes. After six days he was permitted to stand in the hotel doorway and every now and then step out onto the pavement. At such times he would pay kids pennies to fetch him street food. Otherwise he was confined to the premises. "It was quite enjoyable. I caught up on my reading and got friendly with lots of passers-by." Eventually Christy was released into the custody of a "huge native gun-toting guard" who took him to the airport and on to the first plane out of Brazil. Christy was excited by the thought that he might get sent to Portugal, but the first plane was bound for Caracas and so Christy landed up back in Venezuela.

A HALLOWEEN DINNER IN FIJI

C hapter 6, concerning Christy's Yukon and Alaskan adventures, discusses the way the natural world has of defying attempts by human animals to tame and control it. If we die out as a species because we have screwed up the natural environment needed to sustain life, that would be the ultimate revenge of nature on this arrogant and selfish parasite of its resources. There is something totally alien to the mindset of the tramp about humans "owning" land and creating borders to keep people in and out; the tramp is more akin to birds and wild animals in their need to be free to go anywhere on the planet they choose. Wanderlust represents an addiction to continually seek out the remotest corners of the world and to get as far away from the human herd and their manufactured paraphernalia as is possible. Christy's next adventure illustrates an extreme example of the repugnant side of this human greed and selfishness.

In 1985, Christy made a trip to seven of the outer Fijian Islands and spent some of the time with a woman companion he had met on the trip. They had been staying as guests of a Californian couple who had made their home on one of the neighboring islands:

> They had built a boat, sailed it across the Pacific, bought a piece
> of an island and built four or five bures—native huts—slightly
> modernised inside for tourists. They employed the locals but
> behaved as gracious guests, careful to be as noninvasive as possible.
> They kept a low profile, bleeding into the existing culture, and as
> a result were adopted by the natives as their own. The following
> tale of a neighbouring island describes everything that this island
> paradise was not.[22]

Wall Street Journal editor Christopher Winans' book *Malcolm Forbes: The Man Who Had Everything* was published the same year that Forbes, multimillionaire entrepreneur and publisher, died of a heart attack in 1990. In his book, Winans discusses Christy's visit on Halloween night to Forbes' private island paradise, Laucala, bought by Forbes in 1972 to establish a playground for the rich and famous. Most accounts of Forbes describe him as some kind of generous benefactor who cared for and improved the lives of the local people, offering them work, free education, and improved housing. Winans' and Christy's observations of Laucala in 1985 contradict those impressions.

While staying with the couple from California, Christy and his companion had been invited to Forbes' island by one of his vassals, a Jim Donohue, described as "a very blond guy probably two years out of college." As property tycoons go—and Forbes' real estate included a palace in Morocco, a château in France, and a mansion in London (recently on the market for twelve million pounds)—it seems he had appallingly poor taste in architecture which Christy describes as "a little part of New Jersey."

> Forbes had moved the Fijians inland a few hundred yards away from the beaches, razed their bures ... and replaced them with parodies of suburban bungalows. A modest canteen that sold mostly canned goods had been erected, though the Fijians had little use for canned goods, living in a lush tropical paradise brimming with fresh produce. Among the new housing were concrete patios and a nautilus gym in a sort of community centre. ... The crowning insult to what otherwise was a beautiful island paradise was the New Jersey-style suburban ranch house Forbes built on the topmost point of the island along with an Olympic-size pool whose sole decoration was a statue of a nude Greek boy. While this was no castle, the house had a commanding view of the entire island, like a fortress from which a king might be able to look down at the little people below.[23]

Given the money that Forbes was able to throw around, Christy and his companion, now also in the company of the only other guest at the ranch, an oil company executive, might have expected something more exotic for their Halloween dinner. After their host had proudly shown off the ranch house's high-tech kitchen and boasted about the wine cellar, they were served up the usual bland American fare of meat loaf, mashed potatoes, "lousy warm white wine" and a Jell-O dessert.

There are hints that Forbes might have been a pedophile, although in Winans' book the charge is not made directly: "...visitors would notice a somber attitude among the residents [of Laucala] compared to that of their laid-back, neighboring islanders. And residents on those other islands would hear of vague misgivings among Laucalan parents about the influence of the rich, hedonistic Forbes on their children."[24] When Donohue was asked why he thought Forbes had given him the Laucala job, he replied that, "Malcolm liked to be near young people. It was one of Forbes' traits that some of the island's parents found worrisome." Yet another commentator has a rather distasteful recollection of Forbes, "driving a small four-wheel-drive vehicle past hordes of children and tossing them handfuls of hard candy."

In any case, this was never an allegation made by Christy, who got into enough trouble just describing Laucala in a story he wrote about his visit in the *Toronto Globe and Mail* on January 7, 1986. After phoning Forbes Inc. offices in New York as part of his research for the story, a company official became suspicious:

> 'He might have glimpsed that I may have had a few negative
> impressions,' Christy says. 'Immediately after talking to him
> I started getting strange anonymous phone calls. In one
> conversation a guy tells me, 'You know, nothing bad has ever been
> written about Forbes.' 'Why?' I ask. The guy says, 'Well, anybody
> who did want to write anything bad about him is dead.'[25]

But Christy did write the story. In it he challenges the popular myth put about by Forbes' cronies that the native Fijians were grateful to their lord and master for relocating them from their thatched homes at the water's edge to "new homes ill-suited to their culture. ... cheap symbols of an old way of life." Forbes needed the seaside location to build luxury chalets for his paying guests. Christy described Forbes' project as "a little bad part of New Jersey stuck out there in the middle of Laucala." And as for Forbes' vassals, "The people who are free in Fiji were free everywhere but there."

SECOND MARRIAGE, MORE COINCIDENCES, AND PRELUDE TO THE STORY THAT FOLLOWS

As with many of Christy's ramblings, his trip to Honduras in 1987 was impromptu, with no planning involved. Here we also have evidence of Christy the romantic, with regard to both his love of women and his wanderlust—the two being often mutually exclusive, at least so far as long-term relationships are concerned. Being an incurable romantic is certainly not incompatible with being either a tramp or a Cynic; it goes with the territory, and for this part of our story we must first return to 1965. Christy and Val Santee were on their aforementioned road trip through Florida in the company of the hillbillies Pete and Marie in their beat-up old Studebaker. As they were passing the old slave market in the center of St. Augustine, their attention was drawn to a dark-skinned young girl of around sixteen years of age. Santee asked of Christy whether or not this was the most beautiful woman he had ever seen. Christy agreed that indeed she was—with the possible exception of Jean Simmons whom he had met the previous year.

It was more than ten years before Christy would have occasion to visit St. Augustine again, being in the habit by then of wintering in the South to escape the harsh Toronto winters. There he saw and recognized the same woman whose appearance he had commented on all those years earlier, and who was no less arresting than the first day he set eyes on her. They nodded to each other in acknowledgement on a few occasions before being introduced by mutual friends and then going out together. It was a holiday romance that lasted for a couple of winters or so before Christy moved from Toronto to Vancouver in 1981, at which point Mary Anne decided to move nearer to Christy, first by moving to Seattle where he would take the bus down from Vancouver to spend time with her, then following this they set up home together in Vancouver and eventually married in 1987. This whole period of time with Mary Anne was also a time of prolific travel and writing for Christy. Initially solo trips, but following their wedding Christy and Mary Anne went to Zihuatanejo in Mexico for their honeymoon and stayed on for eight months from where they made other trips including Antigua and Guatemala. Mary Anne's looks would continually draw comments, particularly from old ladies who would stop her in the street to pass comment on her appearance. But Christy's own fascination with Mary Anne was beginning to wane. He says that it was impossible to read her feelings or emotions. She came, Christy says, "with batteries not included," never giving anything of herself away. Christy says that he could never take anything Mary Anne told him at face value, even which supermarket she had just returned from with shopping.

The extended honeymoon was also the prelude to a permanent separation. Shortly following the honeymoon, the pair ended up going their separate ways: Christy to Honduras on his quest for the Golden Madonna of San Jorge de Olancho, subject of the tale that follows, and Mary Anne returned to St. Augustine. The last occasion they met was in 1988 but they remained married until a formal divorce in 2004.

There is a literary digression to the liaison between Christy and Mary Anne. Mary Anne told Christy that she was half Portuguese and that her father was a seaman who sailed away and never returned. Later she announced that her real father was a Mexican bail bondsman living in East Los Angeles. Mary Anne went down to visit him but later when Christy asked about him he got no response. Some years later, Mary Anne's mother, Patricia, married an Italian from Brooklyn named Mel Longo who made a living repairing appliances before setting up business in his own shop. Christy spent time with both Mel Longo and Patricia, from whom he learned more about Mary Anne's family history. Both Mary Anne and her mother spoke fluent Spanish. Patricia was born in Sonora, Mexico, and had been schooled in France and Spain, constantly moving homes because her father, formerly in mining, was at the time in the diplomatic service, and herein lies the literary connection. It has been impossible to establish how, but Patricia insisted to Christy that she and consequently Mary Anne were directly related to Phyllis Playter, who in 1921, at the age of twenty-six, met and started a forty-two-year relationship with the British writer and philosopher John Cowper Powys up until his death in 1963. Phyllis Playter continued to live in the remote mining and slate quarrying town of Blaenau Ffestiniog in North Wales, UK, until her own death in 1982. Mary Anne's mother, Patricia, died in 2014 aged 102.

But this is not the end of the Phyllis Playter connection. On Christy's first trip to New Zealand in 1989, the year after he parted company with Mary Anne, he met up with the scholar Donald Kerr, special collections librarian at the University of Otago in Dunedin, due to their mutual interest in Blaise Cendrars and Henry Miller. Kerr is something of a rambler himself and met up with Henry Miller's associate, the writer Alfred Perlès, on a trip to the UK shortly before Perlès' death. Kerr also turned out to be a John Cowper Powys reader, and on the same trip had actually met Phyllis Playter at her home in Wales two years before she died. He had tried to persuade Richard Perceval Graves (of Robert Graves' family) to visit Phyllis with him but he had been previously frightened off by Phyllis' minders. Kerr remembers from his own visit being confronted by a coal miner with a patch over one eye coming out of the miner's hut near Phyllis' home, and that the old lady was smoking Woodbine cigarettes, a strong unfiltered brand popular at the time. Here Kerr recalls his first meeting with Christy:

It was about 1989 when I first met Jim Christy. I was working
in the rare book collection at Auckland Public Library (now Sir
George Grey Special Collections), starting there on the auspicious
date of 8 August 1988 (a fire at the library that day prevented me
from actually starting work). My surrounds included a plush blue
carpet, a number of exhibition cabinets, three reading tables, and
an office, enclosed with sliding glass windows. It was heavenly,
and visitors calling had to have persistence to battle through the
public floors and take the stairs or lift to the rare books collection,
the only public area on the second floor. I cannot remember what
time of the day it was, but Christy walked in and peering through
the glass windows said – in his distinctive drawl – 'Donald Kerr.' I
replied in the affirmative. I have no distinct recall on what was said
after that, but we did end up discussing Blaise Cendrars. Indeed,
that was how we connected. Christy had seen my name in Feuille
de Routes, the bulletin of the Blaise Cendrars Society, and although
only my home address was listed (see issue No. 17, November
1987), he had somehow tracked me down in New Zealand. Christy
is good like that! And we would have talked about Henry Miller,
the American writer whom I had corresponded with briefly, and
who had introduced me to Cendrars, John Cowper Powys, Knut
Hamsun, and a whole host of other writers through his *Books in
My Life* (1952), a passionate appreciation about all those writers,
stories and narratives that had influenced Miller (Miller dedicates
a chapter to Cendrars in *Books in My Life*, pp. 58-80). I probably
took Christy to tea in the staffroom and continued our discussion.
However, on this first fleeting meeting there is one thing I do
remember. At one stage, Christy asked me if he could borrow $100.
He was not 'skint'; it was for tyre repairs on a rental car that he
had. He promised to pay it back. Librarians are not rich, and I was
pretty typical; first real job, mortgage, and the usual expenses. I did
not hesitate. 'Of course,' I said. And so ended this rather vague first
meeting. One thing, however, was certain. I liked Jim Christy. This
vagabond fellow was my kind of guy, and I was sure our bookish
relationship would continue.[26]

The relationship did continue. Kerr would next meet Christy in Vancouver in 1991 and 1997 when visiting his wife Jude's relatives, and again in New Zealand in 1996, 2003-04, and 2008. But more of those other visits later—we are still in 1987.

IN SEARCH OF THE GOLDEN MADONNA

One premise of this book is that Christy, like other tramp-philosophers, places freedom of thought and movement above the acquisition of wealth (over and above, that is, what is necessary to sustain life on a day-to-day basis), some even following an aesthetic lifestyle. It would seem a contradiction, then, that these same tramp-philosophers would be smitten by gold fever, unless, that is, it sparked their sense of adventure rather than a desire to acquire a fortune. But there is no doubt that many of them *were* drawn to inhospitable places in search of gold. William Henry Davies lost a foot jumping a train on his way to the Klondike, Leon Ray Livingston nearly died of starvation and illness traveling to the Klondike by dog sled, as also did Jack London. Bart Kennedy and a friend narrowly escaped with their lives after an attack by hostile Indians on their way to try their luck on the Fraser River after a strike in the Similakameen Valley. We know that Trader Horn panned unsuccessfully for gold on more than one continent—even after he made his fortune from writing and movies, and, although Jack Everson earned himself six hundred dollars when he proved his theory that dry gulch pickings were richer the farther one panned from the river, he continued tramping anyway.

Christy follows an honorable tramping tradition, nearly losing his own life on an adventure in 1987 prompted by a search for gold. In Christy's case, it was his search for the location of the legendary Golden Madonna of San Jorge de Olancho. Christy seemed impervious to the dangers of traveling alone into the inhospitable rainforest region of eastern Honduras, patrolled as it was by local bandits. To put these dangers into context, according to a *New York Times* article dated June 24, 2012, Olancho was one of the most violent parts of Central America at the time, with its narcotic smuggling and other criminal activities.

And so to the legend itself. In 1525 Spanish explorers, under the orders of Hernán Cortés, established the port town of Trujillo on the north coast of

Honduras as a staging post to explore and colonize the interior of the Olancho region, thought to be rich in gold deposits. By 1530, the Spaniards had established the town of San Jorge de Olancho at the foot of a mountain, El Boquerón, and, as some reports have it, on the right bank of the river Aguán. Other versions of the story say there was already an ancient city in the same location, and that gold and silver were so plentiful that the indigenous inhabitants fashioned it into tools and utensils, being the only available metals in the region. At any rate, the area was so rich in gold that the Spanish soon set to work mining it and hauling it to the port of Trujillo for its onward passage to Spain.

As elsewhere in Latin America, the invaders abused and cheated the Indians, and when local priests demanded taxes from the conquistadors for all the gold they were removing, the latter responded by melting down gold which they fashioned into a nine-hundred-pound golden madonna. The legend goes that not having enough gold to finish the statue, the conquistadors fashioned a coronet of cow hide, following which insult the side of the mountain fell away, burying the town and many of those in it. The surviving inhabitants relocated to other locations, including Olanchito (Little Olancho). The latter certainly exists in northern Honduras today, but in the Yoro rather than Olancho department. The site of Olancho Viejo (Old Olancho) remains the subject of controversy, not made any easier by the fact that there are two mountains named El Boquerón in Olancho, one in the north and one in the south. The illustration in William Wells' 1857 account shows the more northern El Boquerón.

Christy's interpretation of the legend, that Olancho Viejo was located on the river Guayape, and not the river Aguán in the north (site of Olanchito), seems more credible. Particularly as the Guayape river has a long history and reputation for placer mining that continues to this day. Furthermore, Christy's own research is backed up by several historical records. Below is the relevant passage from just one such historical account:

> The infamous desecration of the Holy Mother was speedily avenged.
> While the population were collected in the church, the mountain
> broke forth with terrific violence, and in an hour the whole town
> was destroyed with showers of rocks, stones, and ashes. Many were
> killed, and the remainder fled afrighted out of the place. ... Those
> who escaped set their faces to the north, and journeyed to the coast
> in search of another site, carrying with them the crown of hide,

which alone had been preserved from the general wreck. They pitched upon what is known as Olanchito (little or new Olancho), now the chief town of the department of Yoro after Truxillo. ... How Olancho Antigua was destroyed is a matter of conjecture; but that a thriving and well-located town once existed there is beyond dispute. It is generally believed that much gold lies buried beneath the ruins, but no one is valorous enough to seek it. Oblivion has thrown her mantle over the place, and only exaggerated monkish legends remain to tell of its former existence.[27]

But back to Christy's own adventure, undertaken following his separation from Mary Anne. "In Search of the Golden Madonna," from *Between the Meridians* (1999), opens with the following line describing his guide to the mythical home of the Golden Madonna: "If Geraldo was just a little bit smarter, I would be three months dead."[28] Not that Olancho's reputation had dissuaded Christy from setting out alone and unarmed on his own perilous quest for gold:

Thievery is a national pastime and the roads are the special workplaces of the ladrones. But in a country where everybody is armed it is difficult to pick out the hold-up men. ... Twice on the trip to Mt. Boqueron, I came upon clusters of people stopping traffic with ropes stretched across the road, revolvers dangling from their hands, shotguns across their shoulders ... two masked figures wearing animal skins around their shoulders and dirty bedspreads that hung down below their knees emerged from the crowd. They held rusty paint cans. ... After I tossed some coins into the cans, the ropes were dropped, the crowd backed away, and I drove off.[29]

When the road eventually ran out, Christy parked and continued down a cattle trail to the edge of the forest from which El Boquerón could soon be seen emerging. There he encountered a group of fourteen-year-old boys, the leader of whom agreed to take Christy to his uncle's shack a mile into the forest, while the other boys were sent back to guard the jeep. Some distance farther on, the pair encountered a man Christy describes as "short, stocky, with thick wrists and arms." The man, Geraldo, happened to be going in the direction of El Boquerón, and the boy suggested Christy let him act as his guide. A string of questions from Geraldo soon led Christy to suspect that he might be in some danger from the machete-toting guide: Where were his companions? Was he alone? On an impulse, Christy took a photograph of Geraldo at the start of their hike, which he still has today; although had Christy been murdered, it is unlikely that the film, never mind Christy, would ever have been found.

After some strenuous climbing Christy realized that Geraldo was trying to exhaust him and get him lost, but the guide-*cum*-bandit had not reckoned on the fact that Christy was no ordinary gringo but a seasoned hobo and some-time street-fighter. At one point Geraldo stopped by the river and bent down to take a drink, then urged Christy to do likewise. But Christy had already spotted what looked like the remains of buildings and the site of some kind of avalanche that had torn away from the mountain and covered the spot where stone structures had formerly stood. When Geraldo confirmed that this was the site of Olancho Viejo, Christy tried to pay him off and dismiss him so that he could explore the site at his leisure. The guide complained that it was not enough money for him to buy the pair of new boots that he desperately needed, but Christy refused to pay more:

> I looked at his boots and was actually thinking that they were no
> worse than my own, probably better, when he went for the blade.
> His hand moved in a blur, but I was close enough to leap and grab
> his forearm before the machete was halfway out of the scabbard.[30]

The rest of this battle is described in the book but concludes with Christy relieving Geraldo of his machete and throwing it into the river, whereupon the angry Geraldo, with his pride sorely wounded, runs off to get the aid of companions from a nearby settlement while Christy, frustrated from arriving at his destination with no opportunity of searching for treasure, makes a run for it back down the trail he has just climbed, and with a gang of angry *campesinos* in hot pursuit:

> I had not gone very far before I heard the call and answer of the
> whistles behind me. ... That must be Geraldo giving instructions to
> his pals. I had been crashing along trying to outdistance the noise,
> but I stopped to listen, to try and place them. The whistling ceased.
> It started again when I began to move.[31]

We know—because we are reading this tale—that Christy did make it back to his jeep and out of Honduras. Not that it was his last time to be staring down the wrong end of a barrel before his final departure. Christy may not have found any buried treasure, but he may still be the only person outside of the locality who knows the location of the burial site of the legendary Golden Madonna. As some historians have testified, the locals are too terrified to disturb the site due to the superstition that surrounds it and, so far as we know, no serious search for or excavation of the site has ever been commissioned. Others who told Christy of their own claims to have found the site described a different location altogether. Even historians can't agree on the location of Olancho Viejo, nor which El Boquerón it is associated with. If Christy's description of the location of San Jorge de Olancho, or Olancho Viejo, is deliberately misleading, then he has his own reasons for maintaining the myth surrounding this legend. Such is the privilege of the vagabond storyteller.

But having discovered the whereabouts of Olancho Viejo, and in spite of the obvious dangers involved, the vagabond romantic was not about to abandon his quest. Back in Mexico a year later, with the intention of returning to Honduras, Fortuna would again intervene. By now, separated from his second wife, happenstance in the form of the offer to play a part in a Mexican movie (a continuation of Christy's on/off acting career) resulted—instead of finding buried treasure—in the equally quixotic adventure of riding around on a horse for some days before getting beaten up by the hero as one of the movie's highlights. To date, Christy has not made a return visit to Honduras.

WEST OF KEREMEOS

A lurk is a place to which the vagabond returns often, for no particular reason. Every tramp has a favourite spot in each district, a centre to which he goes at times, when he is at ease or wants to be so. ... It is not home-love, or anything like that. Nor is it a return to some district where pleasant things happened in the past. It seems to be merely the adoption of some piece of road.... My own lurks are all very ordinary places.... A signpost outside Stockholm ... in southern France, at Arles, there is a small bridge where ... I have sat, for days on end doing nothing and being very

happy.... A cross-roads near Faringdon in England, a patch of
green grass with a road-sign, where I can relax and go blank-eyed
and feel that the world is a good place.
(Jim Phelan, *Tramping the Toby*[32])

So wrote the Irish tramp-writer Jim Phelan in 1955. One of Christy's "lurks"
is at the base of a cliff in the Upper Similkameen River Valley, adjacent to and
about three hundred yards from the two-lane road that runs east and west
between Hedley and Keremeos. A trail leads near to the rock paintings from
the road, now long overgrown. Christy has returned to the spot many times
since his first visit there in 1988, has driven past the site innumerable times
("a hundred is no exaggeration), and hiked back to it maybe ten times. The
opening paragraph of Christy's piece on his first trip to discover the cave
paintings near Hedley mirrors the older tramp-writer's description of a lurk—
before Christy was ever aware there was such a term for the phenomenon:

> I've always had secret places in the outdoors, spots with special
> private significance, and I feel kind of sorry for people who don't
> have them. I don't mean recreational or commercial sites or tourist
> attractions. A secret place may be a waterfall that you can only get
> to after hiking a day and a half from the end of a logging road but
> it could also be a neighbourhood garden or a hidden shady spot
> at the back of a field. Whatever it is, it probably serves as a refuge,
> a place that, perhaps, calls to mind the hideaways of childhood
> and summons forth an almost atavistic sense of adventure and
> mystery.[33]

As a "dormant anarchist," Christy frequently debunks orthodox interpre-
tations of history offering alternative historical heroes to conventional role
models, for example, Blaise Cendrars and the British explorer Sir Richard
Francis Burton. Inviting controversy in his book *Between the Meridians*, Christy
debunks received scholarship. "According to the history books," Christy writes,
"the first white man to penetrate the southern interior of what is now called
British Columbia was the fur trader David Thompson in 1811." In his tale "West
of Keremeos," Christy summons his strengths as a maverick researcher and
adventurer to argue that Spanish explorers reached the Similkameen long
before David Thomson.

Back to the start of his quest in 1988 and Christy meets up with Ernie Joseph, a seventy-eight-year-old Indian, in a bar. According to Similkameen oral history, members of Ernie Joseph's tribe massacred Spaniards near their village of Keremeos and buried them in the fabled "Spanish Mound." Hundreds of these Spaniards had traveled along the river from the coast in search of gold before setting up their camp near the Indian village of Keremeos. Following a quarrel between an Indian and a white man, in which the Indian came off best, the Spaniards sought revenge and took the Indian village by surprise in an attack in which they killed many and took others prisoner. The Spaniards followed an old Indian trail north and around the east side of Okanagan Lake (see tale that follows) until they came to the future site of Kelowna where they erected substantial quarters and stayed over winter. On finding no gold in the area, having suffered illness, and tired of sniper attacks, they returned by the same route to Keremeos Creek. The Spaniards were in turn attacked by warriors of the Similkameen tribe in revenge for the earlier massacre and slaughtered to a man. The place where the Indians buried the whites between their latest campsite and Keremeos village is the site of the legendary Spanish Mound.[34]

Ernie Joseph tells Christy there are rock carvings, petroglyphs, that prove this story but that Christy must find the petroglyphs himself. When Christy asked Ernie when these events took place, the old Indian started counting the generations of his forebears on his fingers before replying, "Early seventeenth century." Christy countered that, according to the history books, the first white explorer to enter the interior of British Columbia was the fur trader David Thomson in 1811. The history books also confirm that there were no horses, even on the coast, until the 1750s, to which the Indian replied, "History books are written by white men. Even if I could read good, I wouldn't believe the half of it." In response to further protests from Christy, the old man continues:

> You say the history books say our people didn't have horses until the 1750s, and also the books tell there were no white men here until 18—whatever it is. So tell me how did the white men who wrote the history books know when there were horses and other white men if they hadn't got there yet?[35]

Christy then recounts his roundabout route to find the rock carvings near Hedley. We learn that the Spanish launched more than 150 coastal expeditions from Mexico in search of gold and the "Strait of Anian," a mythical passage that supposedly split the North American continent. "It seems preposterous to insist that no European reached the southern interior of British Columbia until the 1800s," he writes. "By the latter part of the 16th century, Cabeza de Vaca had already traveled overland from Florida to the Pacific Northwest." Christy also cites the travels of a Greek mariner named Apostolos Valerianos. While Valerianos was using various pseudonyms—including Juan de Fuca, after which the Strait of Juan de Fuca is named—Valerianos apparently sailed north three times to the Pacific Northwest for the Viceroy of Mexico in the late 1500s. According to Michael Lok, an Englishman who financed Martin Frobisher's three trips to Baffin Island, Valerianos claimed he made a journey across the North American continent from west to east.

This leads Christy to his hard "evidence" of Spanish inland infiltration: 1/ Historian Bill Barlee has observed that the appearance of the Similkameen band is different from neighboring tribes (they're taller), 2/ The Similkameen are the only interior band to pronounce a pure "r," a predominant letter in Spanish, 3/ Armor made from heavy copper has been found in a native burial ground identical to Spanish mail (and neither the Spanish or anyone else wore armor in the nineteenth century), and 4/ The only piece of turquoise ever discovered in an Indian grave in B.C. was found near Okanagan Falls (now displayed at the Penticton museum). After finding and examining the picto-graphs, Christy provides the following analysis: 1/ There are men on horseback with peaked hats (like the helmets worn by the Spanish), 2/ There are four standing figures attached by a line drawn through their necks (like prisoners chained together in the Spanish fashion), 3/ The prisoners are guarded by dogs with open mouths (like the vicious guard dogs the Spanish were known to have used). Dismissed out of hand or regarded as a troublesome crank by academics, Christy has persisted:

> Over the years I have returned to the spot, studied it, and, consequently, gathered more pieces of information. For instance, the iron neck-collar the Spanish placed around their prisoners was called a cerebance.
>
> On each visit, I had been particularly intrigued by the care with which the helmets were drawn. Not only was the brim, or lip, of the helmet distinct, the peak, as mentioned, was rendered just-so. I often thought of it. I learned the helmet worn by conquistadors, and shaped exactly the same way, was a morion.

But my primary discovery occurred in Mexico, near
Cuernavaca, on a cliff wall in country not unlike the dry land above
the Similkameen River. I located an ancient pictograph that shows
a soldier on horseback wearing a morion, and in front of him are
five Indian prisoners guarded by dogs and chained at the waist.[36]

Glenn Douglas, a native researcher and librarian in Keremeos, is also
convinced that the legend of the "Spanish Mound" is for real. "If the story
wasn't true," says Douglas, "it wouldn't have been handed down as truth from
generation to generation." The cover illustration of *Between the Meridians* is
a photograph taken by Christy of the Hedley pictographs.

History, you know, is really a lie and changes its mind every day.
Blood red lines drawn on protected cliff walls will last through
millennia. In the end, the only historical truth is in the blood of the
people. That's the secret of my own special place.[37]

THE EDDY HAYMOUR STORY

The version that follows of another British Columbian tale is based
mainly on Christy's unpublished work *The Castle*. The original
story—one Christy now regrets—was published in *Canadian Business*
in 1990. At the time, Christy was living in the West End district of Vancouver
and got a call from the magazine's managing editor, Jim Cormier, asking him
if he would cover a story in the Okanagan Valley.

There's a Lebanese guy out there who was recently awarded a
quarter of a million dollars by the B.C. government because, it
seems, his rights were violated years ago when he tried to build
some sort of theme park on an island in Lake Okanagan. Evidently
he was unjustly imprisoned and even put in a mental hospital. The
story sounds weird and I can't decide what's legitimate and what's
not. You want to look into it? If there's any substance to it, we'd like
you to do a story.[38]

So began Christy's curious adventure with Mohammed (Eddy) Haymour, notable for the fact that it was the first occasion that Christy was hoodwinked into writing a story that did not present the naked truth. Christy's initial impression of Eddy Haymour was that he was the victim of malevolent state persecution and corruption. Christy now describes Haymour as "Probably the lowest human being I've ever met. He was like badness spilled on the floor and seeping everywhere. ... I had always thought I could spot a phony but I failed miserably with him.[39]

But back to Christy's first meeting with Haymour in Peachland where, with the proceeds of his court settlement, Haymour was in the process of building a luxury hotel on a hillside overlooking Lake Okanagan. "He was a stocky, dark man about five feet nine inches tall with a thick black mustache. His dark eyes seemed to look inside your mind. He served sweet black coffee on a silver tray and told me his story."

Haymour had come to Edmonton in the mid-1950s from the Bekaa Valley in Lebanon with very little money, no English, and bearing a piece of cardboard with two words written on it, "Me Barber." He got a place in a barbershop, worked hard and saved his money by sharing rooms with other Lebanese immigrants. Within three years Haymour was able to buy his own shop.

> He prospered, expanded his business, bought and sold properties, even had a television show where he gave instructions on cutting men's and women's hair. In other words, he was an immigrant success story.[40]

In the early seventies, Haymour and his first wife, Loreen Janzen, with whom he had four children, made a trip to the Okanagan and, after being captivated by the scenery that reminded him of his home in the Bekaa Valley, decided to sell up and resettle in Kelowna. Sometime after re-establishing his businesses around that town, Haymour spotted Rattlesnake Island, the only island of any size in Lake Okanagan, and his great vision was born. He would turn Rattlesnake Island into an Arab theme park. Haymour purchased the island but when the local community and provincial government realized what Haymour had planned, they conspired to put every obstacle in his way. "It must have struck horror in the minds and souls of the local people, ninety percent of them white and Protestant, to think that there was going to be a mini-Marrakesh, a tawdry casbah, a cut-rate Cairo, in the middle of their pristine WASP paradise."

At the time, there were no legitimate means to prevent Haymour from constructing his island paradise, as unzoned property could be developed outside of formal planning regulations. But all kinds of skullduggery was employed to stop him. After two years of legal wrangling in which permits were granted and then rescinded, of being passed from one department to another, but still not being able to thwart Haymour's plans, the authorities had him arrested by the Royal Canadian Mounted Police on a trumped-up charge, thrown in jail, released, and then arrested again, following which he served ten months in Okalla Prison. Only four weeks after his release, Haymour was giving the authorities grief once more, following which he was arrested, tried, and sentenced to the Riverview Mental Hospital in New Westminster where he served a further eight months. The deal for his release from Riverview was that he signed over the deeds of Rattlesnake Island to the local government; by now the island was already the proud beneficiary of a concrete pyramid.

And now the story takes an even more bizarre twist. For on his release from the hospital, Haymour traveled to Lebanon where, with the aid of six cousins armed with AK-47 assault rifles, they seized the Canadian Embassy in Beirut and took thirty-three embassy staff hostage. His sole demand was that the Canadian government grant him the opportunity to present his grievances in court. The outcome of the siege was that the Lebanese government fined Haymour a few hundred dollars and the Canadian government bought him a plane ticket home, bizarrely agreeing to his demands. He arrived in Canada a free man but the government refused to hear his case. Eventually, in 1986, he got a hearing in the B.C. supreme court. The outcome was that the trial judge, Justice Gordon MacKinnon, acknowledged that the British Columbia government had indeed conspired to deprive Haymour both of his island and his liberty, adding: "To subject the plaintiff to that charade was, in my view, highly improper if not consciously cruel." The British Columbia government was ordered to pay Haymour damages amounting to $250,000.

After hearing Haymour's story, Christy and Haymour rented a boat at the marina and crossed over to Rattlesnake Island where Haymour showed Christy the remnants of his theme park dream. Then back to the house, and the entrepreneur regaled Christy of his times in prison with tears in his eyes, urging Christy to write the truth about his story.

Christy returned to Vancouver believing Eddy Haymour to be a courageous champion of justice, a hero figure who had retained his warmth and dignity in the face of the worst kind of cruelty at the hands of the authorities. Phoning around people who knew Haymour, Christy encountered those who praised him thoroughly but an equal number who called him a liar, a thief and a charlatan. The latter Christy dismissed as small-minded and not in possession of the facts. On contacting Haymour's first wife, at first she refused to speak to Christy saying she was afraid of what Haymour might do to her if she spoke up. But a couple of weeks later she phoned Christy to say that she would tell him "the truth about Eddy Haymour." He replied that it was too late, he had already submitted the story.

A few days after the article appeared in the magazine, there was a knock on the door of Christy's apartment in Vancouver and there stood Eddy Haymour, "holding a bushel of apples." Over a coffee in Christy's kitchen, Haymour said how much he had appreciated what Christy had written about him and that Christy would always have a place in his heart. On leaving, he grasped Christy's right hand in both of his, looked him in the eye and said, "Jeem, I wish when I went into that Embassy, I would have had you with me." At that moment Christy believed that he had made a notable new friendship. And so when Haymour telephoned Christy some time later and made him an offer to be his partner in the new hotel venture, telling him to come over and stay for a weekend with his lady friend, relax and get to know each other before making a decision, Christy needed little encouragement.

Christy and his then-girlfriend, a sometime English actress going by the name of Nicola Lake, traveled to Peachland where they stayed at the recently completed hotel, Castle Haymour. There they met Eddy's second Canadian wife, Pat Hay, and their eight-year-old daughter. The dining room and two most expensive suites were on the top floor. "The rest of the rooms were down below and designed around themes; there was a Taj Mahal Room, the Egyptian and Persian rooms, and the room of the Thousand and One Nights."

> It was a sunny late Okanagan autumn. From the balcony of the Taj
> Mahal room, we could see the sun glittering on the waters of the
> lake. Two evenings Nicola and I watched the stars from our same
> perch. Eddy and his wife entertained us, or rather, Pat cooked Arab
> meals and he, dressed in Bedouin garb, told stories about himself,
> not only to us but to customers in the dining room which was also

open to non-guests. Eddy would approach a table and sit down without being invited.[41]

Christy's girlfriend was clearly less enamored with Haymour than Christy was; when she suggested that perhaps the guests wanted to have a romantic dinner alone, Christy replied that perhaps Haymour regarded his presence as one of the hotel's attractions, to which Nicola replied, "Yes, well, it certainly isn't the food."

The next morning at breakfast, Christy asked Haymour what his role would be at the hotel. "We will be partners," came the reply. But when Christy looked across at Haymour's wife Pat he noticed her expression was blank.

> 'But what will you expect me to do.'
> 'Whatever you want to do.'
> 'Could you give me a few details?'
> 'Your dream will be my dream. My dream will be your dream.'

> Later, talking this over with Nicola, I said, 'Well it must be a cultural difference. Me, the westerner wanting facts; he, the easterner from the bazaar taking a more encompassing view.'
> 'Maybe, but he's been out of the casbah since, what did you say, 1954?'[42]

In any event, Haymour told Christy that he was willing to pay what sounded like a very good deal to his new partner. Not only that, but Haymour promised that when they had been together for a year, he would give Christy the down payment on a piece of land. Christy must have thought he'd really struck it big. "That's what I most wanted in this world, a piece of B.C. land."

Back in Vancouver and the world seemed good. Christy could get out of a city that no longer held any charms for him. He had started drawing his own castles in the air when Nicola cut in: "Pat took me aside when Eddy wasn't around and said, 'Tell Jim to think very, very carefully before coming out here to stay.' " But this is not what Christy wanted to hear, and he waved Nicola off telling her what a great guy Eddy was, "a guy with real soul." He gave notice on his apartment, put most of his things in storage, and was back in Peachland in two weeks. But it only took Christy two days to conclude that Eddy Haymour was deranged.

During those two days I was able to see beyond the façade, the act that he put on as easily as he donned the Bedouin garb. Gradually, day by day, or hour by hour, he ceased to be the warm-hearted victim of injustice and began to emerge as a deluded solipsist who saw himself as standing alone against a bitter world that was out to get him.[43]

Haymour's duping of Christy must be viewed in the context that few were as street-wise and cynical as the hero of this book. Christy would learn the full extent of Eddy Haymour's psychopathy the hard way. Firstly, the receptionists, department heads, even presidents of companies he approached to advertise the hotel showed him the door when he announced whom he was representing, even when offering coupons for discounts on rooms and meals. Some felt sorry for Christy, warning him, "Look, you're new in the Valley. You don't know the whole story ... how he acts when he doesn't get his way." But when raising these concerns with Haymour, he was told first he was using the wrong approach, and then that he did not look trustworthy. The former terrorist even insulted Christy by telling him he looked like a gangster.

Then there were incidents in the hotel. Christy had volunteered to act as sommelier because the young inexperienced waitresses Eddy hired could not tell one drink from another. Even Eddy himself did not have a clue about the alcohol trade, but he forbade Christy from working the tables, saying, "You scare the customers." But when customers started sending wine back, again Christy confronted Haymour:

'Eddy," I said. 'The wine is the worst possible plonk.'
    'What?'
    'It's terrible. Cheap. You can't charge these prices and serve this stuff, especially the red wine.'
    He didn't say anything just gave me what I came to realize was supposed to be his bad look, he was looking inside me and he could see my faults and he'd use what he saw to get even.[44]

Sure enough, one morning, Haymour announced that they were going on a little drive. He was amiable and chatty but would not tell Christy where they were headed or why.

We drove up into the hills through the pine trees, the morning light glittering on the lake below, and when he saw me notice the winery sign at the entrance to the parking lot, he smirked and nodded his head, as if to say, 'Here's where you get your comeuppance.'

Inside, the boss of the winery and a few underlings were waiting. There was a table covered in white linen holding glasses and six bottles of wine, three each of red and white. It had all been arranged. A wine tasting, a blind one, and I was to be the only taster. Eddy tossed around the compliments and played the big shot.

What I was supposed to do was to sample each wine and rank them in terms of quality. Well I love wine but I'm far from an expert, certainly not a wine snob. Even so this was not much of a challenge. ... The vintner and owner were pleased, especially since I recommended to Eddy that he buy the best wine which also turned out to be the most expensive.[45]

Eddy was livid, but because he was in company simply flashed Christy a glare denoting that he would get even with him later. There was then a similar incident following a power-cut when meat had to be thrown out and the beer went flat. Haymour was furious at having the throw out the meat but refused to throw out the beer.

'Don't move that beer!'
'They'll send it back.'

Friday evening, the first customer orders a beer and starts drinking it and doesn't complain. After the guy's first swallow, Eddy looks at me and smirks.

But the second person to order and taste a beer sends it back, and so does the next and the one after that. Again, Eddy was incensed. At the end of the night, I saw him take a beer out of the fridge and study it carefully, watched him rub his thumb along the edge of the cap, as if trying to discover how I'd gotten it back on after doctoring the contents of the bottle.[46]

But Haymour's behavior did not daunt Christy and, in any case, the former could be as charming as he was obnoxious. Being the naturally curious investigator that he was, Christy was not ready to quit until he had fathomed the full extent of the Eddy Haymour mystery. Then one day, Haymour's wife Pat took Christy to one side and said, "You know the real reason he got you out here is to write his story." Christy thought that he had dealt with that one, having already made it clear to Haymour that he could not undertake such a project. But he played along with the idea to see where it might lead, and Haymour did tell some interesting stories.

> He said that I could write something and he'd publish it himself,
> sort of like a pamphlet. Finally, after a month or so of his lobbying,
> I allowed as how I'd be willing to look through the material and
> see what I might make of it, reasoning that what I'd turn out
> wouldn't be any more than ten or twelve thousand words. And,
> while writing it, I'd be relieved of hustling clients.[47]

At first Haymour treated Christy with some respect. "He reverted to sincere, kindly Eddy." There were piles of papers in no particular order and it soon became clear that Haymour did not have a clue what his boxes of files contained, and "what he had was not exactly the raw material of a flattering biography." On reading through all the material, it became clear to Christy that Haymour had already approached at least four other writers to tell his story. Even more surprising was that the details of each version of the same story built on the others, adding more details with each telling. For instance, in an account of being in a particular jail, he was there three days, was lonely and depressed and spoke with no one. In another version he was there for three weeks and saved the life of a cellmate who was suicidal. Then there was another version in which he not only saved the life of the suicidal cellmate but won over a mean guard and later gave a job to the guard's son. In another version again, he was there for six weeks, cleaned out all the cells, played doctor to some of the other inmates, and taught the guard's son how to cut hair.

When Christy came across the names of certain individuals in Haymour's archives, he would ask for more information about them. One of these was a supreme court judge named Davy Fulton, leader of the British Columbia Progressive Conservative Party. Haymour clearly had a grudge against the judge who was included on a revenge list he had compiled. When Christy asked what the list was for, Haymour said it was to get people for what they had done to him.

> 'What are you going to do to him?'
> 'You can help me. The bastard. I am going to kill his two daughters.'
> 'His daughters. Why would you do that?'
> 'Revenge.'
> 'But why don't you kill him, if he's the one who done you wrong?'
> He looked at me like I was a hopeless case and shook his head.
> 'If I kill him he cannot suffer. But if I kill his daughters....'[48]

Haymour also told Christy, with tears in his eyes, how his father had begged to let him come to the Okanagan and kill a certain official who had not issued a permit when Haymour was trying to build on Rattlesnake Island. Haymour told his father not to worry as he would have the official killed himself. But Haymour's vengeance even included his own family. He had told Christy that he was going to divorce Pat and go back to Lebanon for a new wife, that women needed to be hit frequently, but being a Canadian, his wife would not put up with it and would go to the law. His reasoning was that he could beat a Lebanese woman with impunity, that they deserved to be beaten and would be too scared to call the police. Concluding that Haymour was clearly some kind of maniac, Christy resolved not to end up on the list himself. Haymour was clearly capable of carrying out his crazy plans, as the armed raid on the Beirut embassy testifies. This is also the reason why Christy has made no attempt until now to see his version of the "truth" about Eddy Haymour in print.

> I finally came up with a manuscript and handed it over. A day later, Eddy angrily told me that it was a terrible job and didn't present him the way he wished to be presented. He also accused me of changing the "facts" of his story. I replied that no one would take the thing seriously if he was made out to be some comic book hero and, furthermore, as to facts, I'd not written anything that he hadn't told me or one of his earlier writers. He denied ever saying certain things but didn't want me to show him where I'd gotten the quotes. On more than a dozen occasions he counselled me to

change legal facts and the wording of documents. When I wouldn't
do it, he stomped away.

He stopped talking to me. It was time to leave.[49]

Christy confronted Haymour in the dining room soon afterwards and told
him he was leaving. He also asked for back wages as Haymour had stopped
paying him weeks before. The conclusion to the tale is told in Christy's own
words:

> Pat and their daughter Laila were in the dining room. I didn't even
> waste my breath repeating all his promises. I did, however, remind
> Eddy that, besides seven weeks' wages, he owed me half of what I
> had paid for the car I'd bought to use to sell ads and do errands. He
> claimed never to have agreed to such a thing. We'd made the deal in
> front of Pat back when I first got to the Castle. I didn't expect her to
> back me up but when I glanced over at her, and Eddy glanced at her,
> she lowered her head and stared at the dark red carpet.
>
> Eddy told me he wasn't going to pay me a cent. I didn't holler
> at him but I didn't back down. Finally, he left the room. When he
> came back he had a long length of two-by-four that was studded
> like a medieval weapon, with spikes and thick nails. I stared at it in
> awe, it was so strange-looking; I caught myself even trying to count
> the spikes. He took a few measuring swings at me, gripping the
> weapon in both hands. He was angry and his colour deepened, he
> looked at me with fury. I figured if I evaded a couple more swings,
> he'd get even angrier and swing wildly which would allow me time
> to get at him before he started the back swing.
>
> But the daughter was screaming and Pat was hollering. Eddy
> stopped, breathed deeply. I felt sorry for him. I thought he was
> going to have a heart attack.
>
> 'You bastard,' he managed to gasp.
>
> 'Yeah, and you're really cool Eddy. That's a nice memory you
> just gave your daughter.'
>
> That hurt him and he wanted to lift the weapon for another try
> but was too exhausted. He was at my mercy and he hated that.
>
> He told me to put my keys on the counter. I tossed them at his
> feet. He started to raise the club.

'If you even start to take another swing at me, I'll ruin your life.'

I left the Castle Haymour.[50]

There are several versions of the Eddy Haymour story, including two books: *From Nuthouse to Castle* (1992), written by Haymour himself, and *Married to a Terrorist* (2008), by Haymour's first wife, Loreen Janzen. Needless to say, these provide contradictory accounts, both of Haymour's story and character. The story related above is, of course, Christy's version, informed both by his close relationship with Haymour over a three-month period and extensive research of Haymour's own archives.

There are three third-party anecdotes concerning the Eddy Haymour story that illustrate a bizarre link between Christy, Haymour, and strange coincidences, something that many of Christy's friends have noted during the research for this book.

The first concerns Kevin Brown, who in the 1990s was working in the then-booming Vancouver television and film industry. Brown, sometime film technicians' union rep, also spent time in Los Angeles promoting his union membership's services at outfits like the American Film Market. One of Brown's contacts in L.A. was Gloria Morrison of Unistar International Pictures who at the time was collecting "true life" stories. There is a divergence of recollections about how Brown met Christy for the first time, but the idea of using Haymour's story as the subject of a film came up and when Brown pitched the idea to Gloria Morrison, she casually mentioned that Kevin Kline would make a great Eddy Haymour.

When Brown met up with Haymour he mentioned the conversation with Gloria Morrison, only to discover days later that the *Kelowna Daily Courier* had run a story that Kevin Kline was to play Eddy Haymour in a movie about the local entrepreneur. Fortunately for Brown, in Haymour's enthusiasm to have Kevin Kline be shortly starring in a movie about his life, he had neglected to name Brown as the source of the newspaper story. The idea was not picked up by Unistar but Brown continued to pitch the idea with little success and dropped it altogether after being told by the Hollywood agent Mike Wise that "Hollywood is not in the business of making films with sympathetic lead characters who are Arab."[51] The coincidence in this case is that Christy continued a friendship with Brown only to discover that the Browns' family home in Edwardsville, Illinois, was on his route while working briefly for New Era Dairy in 1968. Christy had been the family's milkman.

The second set of coincidences concerns the University of Otago librarian Donald Kerr, introduced above in the story concerning Christy's second marriage because of the coincidence of both Mary Anne and Dr. Kerr's links to the British writer and philosopher John Cowper Powys. After Christy's first meeting with Donald Kerr in New Zealand in 1989, there was a second meeting with Kerr in Vancouver in 1991. Kerr was visiting his wife's relatives in Vancouver but also, through his work at the Grey Collection at Auckland Public Library, had come to know the private book collector Sir John Galvin, who had invited Kerr and his wife to call round and see his collection. On the day of their arrival in Vancouver, although thoroughly jet-lagged, they decided to take a bus to downtown Vancouver after leaving a voicemail for Christy that they were in town and would catch up "somewhere."

> The 10 Dunbar bus arrived, and we paid the fare to downtown Vancouver. We walked to the seats at the end of the bus, and ended up looking twice. There was Christy, sitting at the back, downing a beer. Jokes like 'you come here often' and 'I always catch this bus' followed. It had turned out that Christy was returning from working as a gardener for an Arab sheik.[52]

Kerr reports that over the six or seven times that he has met Christy, "there has always been some strange coincidence; some very strange happenstances." There was another trip to Canada in 1997 when Christy attended a barbecue at one of Kerr's sisters-in-law in Vancouver. The conversation turned to eccentric characters and their madcap schemes. Then later, on the same trip, in Montréal at another of Kerr's sisters-in-law they turned on the television to watch a story of a certain Captain François Élie Roudaire, who proposed the building of a 120-mile canal that would connect the Mediterranean Sea to a part of the Sahara Desert, a scheme estimated to cost twenty-five million francs. Who should appear on the screen as an expert witness to the bizarre escapade? Jim Christy. On a visit to Kingston, Ontario in 2012—Christy was at the time living on the farm in Belleville—Kerr arranged to meet Christy outside the apartment block of his wife's father's in Kingston.

I thought the instructions were clear, but obviously not. I sat on
the seat outside waiting for him to turn up. Nothing. A no-show
after two hours. Disappointed, I knew there were a few bookshops
in Kingston that deserved attention. So I headed towards the first
on the list. I remember walking into the shop, which was crowded
with shelves of books. A large double shelved bookstand stood in
the main area of the store, with the owner sitting behind a desk
in the corner. Rather than browse (something I enjoy) I asked
the owner: 'I am looking for books on Henry Miller and Knut
Hamsun.' And who popped his head up from behind the bookshelf:
Christy. 'I knew I would find you here!' he said. We laughed and
joked about the lack of communication and mis-directions, and
repaired to a local pub for fish and chips and a few drinks.[53]

The third coincidence concerning Eddy Haymour was triggered on a Friday
the thirteenth in 2012. Christy contacted an Amsterdam-based writer, David
MacKinnon, through his writer's website to discuss—as he had with Donald
Kerr—their mutual obsession with the vagabond writer Blaise Cendrars.
Although they shared the same Canadian publisher, the two had never previously met or even been aware of the other. The outcome of this contact was
that in 2016, *Blaise Cendrars Speaks ...* was published by Ekstasis Editions, B.C.,
comprising transcripts from a series of radio interviews by Cendrars, with
Christy providing the editing and introduction, and MacKinnon the translation
from the French. But to return to the initial contact between the two writers,
on receiving Christy's email in 2012, MacKinnon started researching Christy
to find out more about him:

While searching for his work on the net, I fell onto a video of a
reading of a poem called 'Forever Maria,' a 2008 performance
in Melbourne, Australia. The video was a fuzzy-toned sepia
production that was filmed about ten rows back from the stage.
Christy stood on a stage, dressed in a white linen, two-button suit,
straight out of Miami, and was rasping a poem while a four-piece
band led by a clarinetist screeched out a torpid New Orleans jazz
number—it was hard to tell whether the band was back-up or
there'd been a double-booking that day for rehearsal space. People
in the audience were shuffling in front of the cameraman blocking

the view of Christy. Christy however was oblivious to it all—he seemed to feed off the casual disorder of the reading to tell his poetic tale of Maria, a woman who was kicking the poet out of her apartment and her life. The tone of the reading seemed to imply that it wasn't the first time the performer had been kicked out of an apartment, and that quite possibly one of those 'I quit; you're fired' conversations had just taken place. I was witnessing that rarest of rare events—an artist actually enjoying himself onstage. An almost extinct species, to be treasured alongside the Java rhinoceros and the cross-river gorilla.

Christy was self-deprecating to the point of carelessness, but at the same time he looked like somebody who could throw a little deprecation your way if he felt like it. His delivery was flat and his voice raspy, and immediately you got the sense that Jim Christy had never really picked up the habit of taking orders from anybody.[54]

Some days later MacKinnon received an email from Christy telling him that he was making a trip to India, and was scheduled to speak at a festival in Amsterdam on the way back. Could he come around? MacKinnon recalls that Christy was involved at the time in a dozen or more projects simultaneously, including running his own private investigation agency, "Extreme Research." Sometime in February, Christy wrote MacKinnon an email from Pondicherry, India, where "twenty dramas were going on simultaneously ... swimming elephants, pygmies, naked people, the usual stuff!"

No, listen, this place is truly unique but ruined somewhat by the groups of young 'hip' tourists who all look exactly alike whether from Germany or Israel. Dressing like slobs they are totally unaware that they are insulting the locals who, although dirt poor, try to maintain the respectable appearance. I sincerely hate this smug self-righteous middle class 'hippie' bullshit.[55]

Their correspondence continued over the next month or so, latterly to plan Christy's upcoming visit to Amsterdam. He was coming to town for the Fiery Tongues festival but also meeting up with Brooklyn's "Gangster Poet" Eddie Woods and Amsterdam's mystic poet and writer Hans Plomp, both of whom, like Christy also, were making their own contributions to keeping the spirit of the Beat phenomenon alive.

> I hadn't had a visitor in about six months, but as luck had it, the morning Christy arrived, there was a group of stick-in-the mud anthropologists in my back yard droning on about Merleau-Ponty and Bourdieu. Christy showed up four hours late at my home—2:30 pm for a mid-morning meeting. He looked jet-lagged, and was skinnier than in his photos, as if he didn't care enough about eating to get around to it, but you could see the man still had plenty of resilience. I was reminded of the early twentieth-century gentleman super-tramp, W.H. Davies.
>
> 'I just want you to know that I'm late due to bad directions, and not from lack of concern. My landlady pointed me to the right bus, but the wrong direction. Doesn't anybody have road maps in this city?'[56]

There follows a lengthy description by MacKinnon of the garden party held at his house that day, of the wacky guests and the conversation that ensued, including numerous discussions on writers. He also recalls how Christy had just been taken on as an actor in a German gold rush western being filmed in British Columbia. But, as the reader will by now be wondering, what has any of this to do with Eddy Haymour? The relevant section of this digression continues as follows:

> 'Funny, your name being MacKinnon. I just lost out in an outdoor sculpture commission worth ten grand to a guy named MacKinnon.'
>
> 'Sorry to hear it.'
>
> 'Don't worry about it. I won't hold it against you. You any relation to that Judge MacKinnon?'
>
> 'Sure. He's my father.'
>
> 'Was he the Judge MacKinnon presiding over the Eddy Haymour trial?'
>
> 'One and the same.'
>
> 'Every single thing the government said about him was true. A complete psychopath!'

'Everybody seems to have an opinion on that case.'

'Look, I didn't just have an opinion on the case! I wrote an article for *Canadian Business*.'

'You're an Eddy Haymour expert?'

'Listen, buddy, I didn't just write about him. At one point I even took a job managing his hotel. Even though his wife tried to warn me off.'

'Why would you move in with Eddy Haymour?'

'I was at Castle Haymour "managing" his joint—which meant mollifying customers who complained about the beer and wine. This might sound trivial, but Eddy would turn off the beer-filled fridge at night to save electricity, and he wouldn't put the white wine in the fridge to save electricity, and then he got me to wash dishes to save electricity. Are you getting the picture? Then it was some landscaping and hustling customers.'

'How does that save electricity?'

Christy ignored me. He was somewhere else, washing dishes for Mad Dog Eddy Haymour.

'Three months of pure hell.'

'My old man wouldn't have changed his mind. He was no fool, and on the evidence, he thought Eddy deserved a million bucks for his troubles.'

Christy dismisses the next two years of his life as follows:

After that the *Kelowna Courier* said I could file my weekly column from Mexico, so I went down there. Had a show of my art at La Mano Magica gallery, hooked up again with Nicola Lake and we got an apartment above the Bambi Bakery in Oaxaca. Then she flew to Vancouver and I took the long bus ride from Tampico near Vera Cruz diagonally across the continent. Saw America as a third-world country. Saw my first wife's tombstone from the bus. There were no signs of civilization from the border to Idaho.[57]

The fact that Christy dismisses seeing Linda's grave from a bus in just eight words, is testimony to the distress of the memory of losing her in the first place, and later hearing the news and circumstances of her death.

A longer reference to this event is acknowledged in the following verse from his poem "Bus Ride," an assemblage of notable experiences from bus journeys taken by Christy.

> Off the grand, plush seat Mexican
> bus to cross the trickle of brown
> Rio Grande into a third world-like
> U.S.A. The tired Trailways and
> the tired driver's drug and gun warning.
> On past Brownsville graveyard, tombstones
> make a tenement skyline. That day, March 5
> marked her birth date, stars big
> and bright in the double layer cake night.
> She's sleeping eternity second
> from the left,
> third row back from the road.[58]

A DESCRIPTION OF JIM CHRISTY IN 1992

This account of Christy in 1992 is courtesy of another friend of his, Robert Markle Kinnard, whose first sighting of Christy was at the Langdale ferry landing on the Sunshine Coast in British Columbia where it crosses the strait to Horseshoe Bay and West Vancouver.

> It was my girlfriend at the time, Heidi, who pointed him out. He looked kind of weathered and tough in his old beaten leather jacket, like he'd just been paroled or something, but there was more to how he looked than that. I sensed that he was a person to reckon with, a real character, someone worth knowing.[59]

Kinnard had only been living in the area for a year or two, but soon after this initial sighting of Christy, encountered him again at the Sunshine Coast Arts Center in Sechelt where he'd been attending life-drawing classes and Christy had just torn down his exhibition. Immediately prior to this, Christy had been living above a woodshop owned by an exiled English earl in Roberts

Creek, B.C., midway between Gibsons Landing and Sechelt. It was above the woodshed that Christy wrote one of his most successful books, *The Redemption of Anna Dupree,* in a record seven weeks. Kinnard already had his own one-man show at the Center and was hanging out with a number of other artists where they were in the habit of attending opening receptions for artists that were showing there.

> At one of these events there was Jim standing in cowboy boots in his inimitable bold and confident posture, talking to the attendees. No one in my small group of associates knew him but he was recognized as the artist whose work was being shown in the gallery. Displaying one's creative efforts in public can be a nerve-racking experience at the best of times. He seemed to be on his own, so I suggested to my colleagues that we invite him to the local pub for a beer with us after the reception. The only response I got was 'he scares me' from one. I think my friends were intimidated by him.[60]
>
> A few weeks after Christy's exhibition had folded up, Kinnard got a phone call at home from the art center curator, asking if he could help "Mr. Christy" move his artwork to a storage shed in someone's yard. Kinnard was the proud owner of a 1969 Dodge van that he used for hauling stuff around for his artist friends, so he readily agreed. The move went well, at the conclusion of which Christy gave Kinnard one of his ready-made sculptures, a small leather-clad figure assembled from among other things, old bathroom-sink stopper chains and wheels off a toy truck.
>
> On the way back to town we stopped off for a beer at the cottage I rented across from the marina in lower Gibsons. We had lots to talk about and I soon found out there was a great depth to Jim's experience and interests and a keen artistic sensibility that belied his tough-guy persona.
>
> Jim's inclusive nature and generosity of spirit is rare. Once when I stayed with him for a week in Mexico, I offered to pay him my share of the rent. He declined my offer and said I had already paid, referring to a small watercolour I had painted there and given to him.[61]

In Gibsons, Christy introduced Kinnard to the writer Al MacLachlan, and Kinnard started to look forward to the Sunday afternoon socials with writers and artists at Al's place. Later in Toronto, Christy was accompanying Kinnard, padding around commercial art galleries in the Yorkville district trying, unsuccessfully, to find a dealer for Kinnard's work. After a few exhausting hours of getting nowhere, Christy suggested they get a drink and the pair headed off to an Italian café, bought a mickey of gin, one of rum, and spent the rest of the evening talking about art and literature and listening to Christy's tales of adventure. Kinnard remembers Christy's generosity and being helped out more than once when he was in trouble. This culminated in a trip to Toronto in 2005 when Christy put Kinnard up in his apartment for a week and organized a party where Kinnard met the writer Julia McKinnell to whom he is now married.

ON THE CADDY TRAIL IN BELIZE AND FURTHER ADVENTURES

The Caddy Trail refers to the 1839–1840 expedition by the Canadian artist and explorer John Herbert Caddy. Christy followed Caddy's original route from Belize City, through Guatemala's northern region of Petén, and across through Mexico's southern states to the ruins of the ancient city of Palenque, inhabited by the Maya from around 200 BCE to 800 CE. Christy made his "vagabond trip," as he describes it, in 1999. The journey was made by various transportation including tramping and freighter canoe, and Christy claims he was the first gringo to ride "an ancient creaking and squealing bus" across the Petén region in twenty years. But, typically for Christy, much of his essay concerns exploding myths. He presents evidence that it was the 1839 chronicle of Caddy, rather than John Lloyd Stevens and Frederick Catherwood, that provides the most remarkable account of the region (following the earlier discoveries of the Spanish conquistadors). Furthermore, Christy celebrates the fact that Caddy injected humor into his adventures, rather than the pompous self-interest sought by many of his peers, hence the reason they are better known than him:

> Caddy was just the sort of person I've always been drawn to: a creative adventurer, an original who wouldn't buckle under. ...

Caddy never got his due. Had he been a careerist and played by the rules, the fellow would have made something of himself.[62]

And so Christy embarked on his own trip, following Caddy's route and fortified by Caddy's sense of humor. The modern-day rambler's adventures are remarkable in themselves, but as there is not the scope here to recount all of Christy's escapades and the fascinating characters he encounters on the way, a full reading of "The Caddy Trail" is recommended. The trip describes many of the places Christy stops at on the way: the towns of San Ignacio, San Jose Succotz and the Xunantunich ruins in Belize; the Tikal ruins, the town of Flores in the middle of the caiman alligator-infested lake Petén Itzá, Santa Elena, Sacpuy, and Narnjo in Guatemala; then onwards to the Mexican state of Tabasco and his eventual destination of Palenque.

Twice on the trip Christy would be held up by bandits. On the first occasion, having taken a ramshackle bus in Guatemala, rather than the "express" version, precisely to reduce his chances of being robbed, the bus was stopped by a gang wielding machine pistols and Sten guns. Passengers on the bus made Christy lie on the floor under a blanket on top of which were seated two small girls. After briefly scanning the inside of the bus for anyone who looked like they might be carrying money, the bandits let the bus move on.[63] The second occasion was in Mexico after Christy got a lift across the state line from Tabasco into Chiapas. The car was stopped and the driver badly beaten. The assailants on that occasion were youthful political revolutionaries, considered by Christy as more dangerous than simple robbers. They relieved Christy of the seventy-four dollars he had made available precisely for such an eventuality (carefully hiding his main stash), but not being impressed with the amount, Christy then offered up an out-of-date bank card and PIN, having to repeat the PIN number again a while later to make sure he hadn't lied.[64]

One further story of the many adventures Christy encounters on this trip will be repeated here. It relates to a deadly poisonous fer-de-lance snake. Christy encountered the snake while walking alone down a dirt road near the Mayan ruins of Xunantunich. On later reporting his encounter with the snake to a park ranger, the man became alarmed and asked Christy, "Did you apologise to the snake for looking its way?" When Christy replied that he had not, the ranger shook his head in concern and said, "Well, you will see Señor fer-de-lance again." Not encountering the snake on his way back, Christy put the superstition out of his mind. Sometime later, after Christy had survived the bus holdup and arrived safely in the town of Naranjo, he was bought a drink by a man sitting at another table in the bar:

> He looked like a well-bred killer from somewhere in Latin America. He nodded and came over to the table. Turned out he was a well-bred killer from somewhere in Latin America by way of Luxembourg. ... I'll call him Astorias Baumann. He had spoken only to Indians for the last couple of months so he was eager to talk to me. I was eager to listen, and I did for two days. The man never said anything trivial.[65]

It turns out that Astorias had served in both the French and the Spanish Foreign Legions, before being hired by the Guatemalan government to train its elite troops in jungle survival. Anyway, when Astorias took Christy with him on horseback to visit his camp in the jungle, a short distance from the camp he suddenly stopped, took his rifle out of its saddle sheath, fired twice at a dark shape up ahead on the trail, then sat still in the saddle for a full minute watching.

> 'What's that?'
> 'You'd know it as fer de lance.'
> He climbed down and approached the seven-foot-long snake cautiously, carrying a canvas tarp. Only after standing over the thing for another full minute, then prodding it with a stick, did he wrap up the fer de lance and sling it over his saddle.
> So the Indian at Xunantunich was right. I would see the Señor again.[66]

It was from Astorias also that Christy first heard about the huge trade already developing in looting Mayan antiquities from the numerous archeological sites in the region. Astorias told him that the looters were practically falling over antiquities as they penetrated the last of the forests, also being plundered by loggers. And so it was that Christy learned of Astorias' new venture. It turns out he was buying antiquities from the *huecheros* (looters) for a few dollars, who in turn paid local *campesinos* and loggers a few *cruzeiros* for their finds, only to sell them on to his network of international collectors for thousands, if not hundreds of thousands, of dollars:

He had a few pieces around his shack. ... For this, he said he'd
get four hundred thousand dollars from a man in Berlin. He was
going to deliver it to a man in Antigua in a week or so, once the
go-between, an archeology professor, had the piece, he'd fax the
collector in Berlin who would have the money transferred to one
of Baumann's accounts.[67]

There was an unspoken agreement between Baumann and Christy that the
latter would not rat on the former, Christy being fully aware that:

...this is a man who could walk blithely through a barroom of angry
hockey enforcers without spilling his drink. I've changed the
details just enough to protect myself....

Christy was relieved to wake up the next morning and travel back safely
to Naranjo with his host, from where he departed for the Mexican border in a
homemade freighter canoe together with the captain, his son, and three other
passengers. After a brief stop at the customs shed to have his papers checked,
the canoe continued on its journey, this time including the customs official
as a passenger. On arrival at the river settlement of La Palma, Christy was
coerced into joining a party and robbed the following morning while sleeping
off the effects of the night before. Christy traveled on to his destination where,
after describing the ruins, he relates the manner in which Caddy had already
arrived back in Belize and into obscurity, just as Catherwood and his party
were arriving nearby at Palenque.

From Belize City Christy flew to Paris via Miami where he met up with
two of his publishers, Richard Olafson and his wife, author, jazz vocalist, and
songwriter Carol Ann Sokoloff. Christy did three readings in Paris, one at the
Canadian Embassy where the ambassador provided a keyboard, the second
at a monastery, and another reading at the Paris Book Fair. There was also a
reading as an entr'acte at the Shakespeare and Company bookstore on rue de
la Bûcherie, but that was a separate trip.

Later that year, back in Gibsons on B.C.'s Sunshine Coast, Christy was
already planning his next trip to Mexico to escape the Canadian winter, this
time in the company of his friend, Paul Murphy. Murphy was several years
older than Christy and had been a paratrooper in the Korean War. He had

also been an organizer and front man for B.C.'s New Democratic Party and close friend of B.C. Premier Dave Barrett, at whose Vancouver Island home Christy once spent a pleasant afternoon over a few beers. At the time, though, Murphy was no longer active in politics but involved with the theater, acting and directing. "He was a handsome devil though short. In Mexico many of the locals would call him Fidel. He could walk into a room full of strangers and approach anyone and talk to them." Another guy Christy used to see around Gibsons but had never spoken to, Brad Benson, fell into conversation with him one day on the street. When Christy told him about his planned trip to Mexico with Murphy, Benson said that he'd like to join them and Christy agreed. On telling Murphy that Benson was joining them, Murphy was none too pleased, saying Brad was boring and always going on about "the environment." But the invitation had been issued and Christy was a man of his word; regardless of which Murphy would eventually become close friends with Benson. In the event, Benson drove on ahead to Puerto Escondido on Mexico's southern coast and Murphy and Christy flew out later. They landed late at night having been delayed in Mexico City, and had just bought local bus tickets, when Christy heard his name shouted across the airport lobby. There was Benson waiting for them. The rest of the trip is related by Christy:

> We got a beautiful, first-floor apartment with tile and a private courtyard and all had a great time for four months—including trips to Guatemala. Brad and Paul became real close.
>
> Brad had been a bank vice president in Chicago and quit to follow a woman to B.C.. When that didn't work out, he opened a couple of businesses and finally became a successful carpenter. He had a volatile temper and a strong sense of "justice." I might have saved his life (and my own) on more than one occasion. Once trying to cross the border from Guatemala to Mexico by car, we arrived late and the guard, a muscle-bound Indian with a Kalashnikov, wouldn't let us cross. Brad got angry and the guard got even more angry and pointed the gun at him. I told Paul to get Brad out of there. Brad is six-four; Paul was five-six—I still have that image of Paul pushing him. I did the deal with the guard—paid him the "fine" (*la mordida*).
>
> Another time, Brad and I were waiting for a flight at Ho Chi Minh Airport, Saigon. We passed the counter for the First Class Lounge and wanted to grab a piece of fruit from a big crystal bowl.

The young woman told him it was for first-class passengers only and he flipped out. She was going to call security, and he was about to bust a blood vessel at the "injustice" of it until I reminded him that we paid a thousand bucks for our ticket and First Class paid $7,000—so they were entitled to a banana! (I'd been in a cell at that airport for five hours once, and it was no fun.)

I got a job building a mosaic tower at our apartment building and Brad made the form. We threw him a great 60th birthday bash. He is the scariest driver, though a great one, that I have ever met. I finally knew what Jack Kerouac felt like riding with Neal Cassady. Murphy would be curled up on the floor calling on the saints.

Brad left for Canada via the States before we flew back. He wanted to take along with him a sculpture I'd made from scraps of wood; when I asked why, he replied that it would allow him to use the HOV lanes (restricted for cars with more than one passenger). So he drove away with Señor Peligroso in a seat belt by his side, tall enough that any cops giving a quick look would think he was a passenger. He's an Iowa farm boy and always open to whatever experience, situation, or adventure presented itself. Never got grumpy except when his beer ran out. I guess he's four years older than me.[68]

Attempts to get versions of events from Christy's friends and acquaintances often produces mixed results, or no results at all. But in Benson's case, what was presented as a sorry attempt to respond to the request produced some real nuggets. Some of the best writers are those who apologize that they cannot write at all, and in Benson's case, the following apology resulted in a simple list that says as much as polished prose ever could:

> If you are talking about writing memories of Jim and our travels, I have tried 3-4 times, but it all turns to shit and I go to bed and try to get some sleep. Seriously, not being able to string thoughts together in any meaningful way is why I have exited from all my activist activities, including letters to the editor, though I still try. Sorry to be a disappointment on this because I would like to be able to tell what I can. I have very good feelings about our travels together, i.e.:
>> —we never, ever ever fought
>> —he never ragged on me (or anybody) about anything

—he was a very good driver

—there were never boring moments with him, because he would pull out one of his thousands of interesting "stories" and let rip

—Jim (and what's his name in Guatemala, Peter something) had some great ideas of places to visit that I would never have seen

—he was always square with money

—I was always in awe of Jim's work ethic; every morning, if we were not traveling or eating, Jim was writing

—on the negative side, the ladies were always more interested in Jim than me

I have great memories of:

—the car ferry in Guatemala

—and that knoll in Guatemala with the big spreading tree on top and the ceremonies of the locals, burning cigars like logs in honour of their gods or family

—drinking beer on the beach anywhere

—great conversations from Jim and Paul

and on and on.

Jim and I shared a lot of good traveling times together. Two winters in Mexico, including a week or so in Guatemala, and a month in Vietnam. But it was here on the Sunshine Coast where we spent the most time together and where another good friend, Paul Murphy, also lived. It was Pablo, Jimbo and Myself, Bradski, (as we occasionally referred to each other) that traveled together for two winters in Mexico and Guatemala. Fond memories.[69]

Back in Gibsons, Murphy introduced Christy to Peter Trower, the logger poet already a legend on Canada's west coast having spent twenty years working in the woods and writing lyrical old-fashioned verse in a style combining the modes of Robert Service and Gerald Manley Hopkins. To most people, Trower was the two-fisted, boozer logger-bard, oscillating between the woods and Vancouver's skid row bars, but Christy tells of his upper-middle-class English background before arriving in Port Melon, B.C. (after his RAF pilot father died in a plane crash) and graduating from an exclusive private school in West Vancouver.

VIETNAM'S KILLER ELEPHANTS

> I was in Saigon in December [2003] when a story appeared in the
> *Viet Nam News,* the country's English-language daily, about some
> rampaging elephants that had killed a number of people in the
> Central Highlands. The herd was incensed, the article suggested, by
> human encroachment on its territory. I was astounded, first to realize
> that Vietnam had wild elephants—I had thought they were found
> only in Africa and India—and second by the fact that the attacks were
> a group effort. Most elephant attacks are the work of rogues cut off
> from their herd and driven mad by loneliness or pain. There are very
> few recorded incidents where the animals conspired to kill humans.
> (Jim Christy[70])

Rapid development in the area had meant that these animals, desperate
at the loss of their habitat, started killing random humans who crossed their
paths, but later, as Christy suggests, "had gone looking." An Agence France
Presse report in June, 2001, reports that after the elephants trampled to death
their latest victim, marking over twenty in the previous three years, attempts
were made to relocate them with the help of Malaysian mahouts. The plan
was to tranquilize the elephants and relocate them to the Yok Don National
Park in the central highland province of Dak Lak near the Cambodian border.
But early attempts were suspended when the first two tranquilized elephants
died. After the animals were eventually moved and released in the jungle of
Yok Don, they had gone on the rampage again, trampling people and destroying
homes in the village of Ban Don. In *The Walrus* article Christy reflects on the
phenomenon as follows:

> We've always feared the predator beast—the man-eating lions,
> tigers, jaguars, crocodiles. But if one of them kills you, it's probably
> because it wants to eat you. What other animal kills you and walks
> away? The bear? Perhaps, but the biggest grizzly is a tenth the
> weight of an Asian elephant, and it doesn't come looking.[71]

By the time Christy had arrived in Vietnam two years after the elephants
had been relocated, Ban Don had been taken over by elephant trainers as a

center for domesticating those of the wild elephants who were considered trainable. Many of the more dangerous animals were still at large nearby. Not surprisingly, Christy decided to take a trip up to visit the scene of the crime and write his own report. He took a plane from Saigon to Nha Trang on the coast, and then a small bus to Buon Ma Thuot, the largest city in the Central Highlands. It took five hours, Christy all the while sitting in the back on rice bags, for the bus to twist and climb through the banana-covered hills to Buon Ma Thuot. The following day Christy completed the remaining fifty-five kilometers to Ban Don village on the back of a motorbike.

> Walking around the village you can hardly help bumping, literally, into elephants that, just months before, had roamed free. I saw Vietnamese tourists climbing up on a work elephant to have their photos taken. The ranger in charge of the herd of killer elephants was a tall, lean, fierce-looking man who spat when I mentioned the tourists. When I asked him to lead me to the wild elephants, he told me, through the translator, that he thought I was a crazy old guy, but he eventually agreed.[72]

Christy's first night in Ban Don was spent on the floor of a wooden shack on stilts over the backwash of the river, musing on the ranger's comment and trying to console himself with the fact that "old" in Vietnam "comes around sooner than back home." But the next day the ranger cried off with the excuse he had to stay in bed to nurse a cold, leaving Christy to set off for the jungle on his own. After two fishermen took Christy across the Ea Krong river in a dugout canoe he followed the trail he had been advised to take through the jungle. After about eight kilometers he came across the clearing where the ranger had told him he would find the bamboo stake enclosure of his camp. Outside the enclosure a young male elephant was chained to an iron stake by a shackle around his leg. After observing the animal and turning to proceed on his way, "the animal let out a bellow that shook the trees." Christy concludes his tale as follows:

> After walking another four kilometres, I came to a second clearing and was about to start back when I saw a full-grown elephant about a quarter of a mile away in a patch of second-growth forest that had probably been defoliated by the Americans during the

war. I knew this had to be one of the killers, otherwise it wouldn't be here. I stood still, watching him, remembering what a mahout in the village had told me: 'We don't want to share our terrain with that which we fear, with something other than ourselves that can "think" and is dangerous.' I watched the elephant until the picture of him in his wild state, the picture of him the way he is supposed to be, was burned into my brain to stay. Then I went back.

Still on the subject of Vietnam; frustratingly, there being so many other stories that Christy refers to in emails that will probably remain no more than notes:

> As for 'the Vietnam trip' you suggested yesterday that I write up, went to those areas at different times. Once with my Vietnamese pal Thieu, and once by myself on rickety buses from the beach town of Nah Trang. I went on a nice little trip once from Saigon to Cambodia and Laos, on to Indonesia, Singapore, Malaysia. Spent several hours in custody at Saigon airport over a visa mix-up. Another trip was from the mouth of the Mekong River to Phnom Penh and back to Saigon. Virginia Dixon and I once traveled by boat from India to the Andaman Islands, truly the end of the world.[73]

LAND MINES AND LOOTERS

I n this article,[74] Christy discusses the illegal trade in Cambodian antiquities in the wake of twenty years of unexploded ordnance dropped or planted in that country: half a million tons of bombs dropped by the USA between 1969 and 1973; followed by the Vietnamese with Chinese-manufactured land mines; the mines planted by the Khmer Rouge between 1975 and 1979; and the fourteen-year civil war that followed the overthrow of the Khmer Rouge in 1979. Christy reminds us, "Khmer Rouge veterans were still laying mines in the late 1990s. Cambodia has more amputees per capita than any other country in the world."

Christy reports the plunder of Cambodia's heritage, for example, the discovery of two ornate temple bells dating back to around 200 BCE and a half-meter-tall head of Vishnu stolen from the stone banks of the Kbal Spean River:

> ...sophisticated thieves ... are part of complex international
> operations. Because there are thousands of temples and pagodas,
> towers, steles, and pyramids throughout the county, and there
> is not enough money to guard more than a fraction of them, the
> art is there for the picking. ...the entire stretch of the Kbal Spean
> from its source above a waterfall to the plains below is guarded
> not by automatic-weapon-toting guards but by one unarmed kid in
> overalls and flip flops who says he's twenty but looks fifteen.[75]

A UNESCO observer points out that "the shipment of these big pieces out of the country can only be accomplished with the collusion of the military. The collectors claim they are helping to preserve Cambodia's heritage." But, adds Christy, "the usual way is still to invade a site after it has been de-mined, and spirit your treasure over the border."

---

1   Trader Horn, *Trader Horn in Madagascar* (London: Jonathan Cape, 1932), p. 204

2   *This Cockeyed World*, op cit., p. 17

3   Jim Christy, *The Big Thirst and Other Doggone Poems* (Victoria, B.C.: Ekstasis Editions, 2015), p. 55

4   *Travelin Light*, op cit., pp. 93-95

5   Ibid., p. 106

6   Ibid., pp. 108-110

7   *Sweet Assorted*, op cit., p. 167

8   *Between the Meridians*, op cit., pp. 130-131

9   *Sweet Assorted*, op cit., p. 168

10 Louis L'Amour, *Education of a Wandering Man* (New York: Bantam Books, 1990), p. 24

11   Charles Moore, "Moore pays tribute to Waugh," *The Guardian* (UK), January 17, 2001

12   Charlotte Raven, "Love across the divide," *The Guardian* (UK), January 23, 2001

13   *Between the Meridians*, op cit., p. 167

14   Ibid., p. 168

15   Jim Christy, email to the author, April 8, 2015

16   Ibid.

17   *Between the Meridians*, op cit., p. 215

18   Ibid., p. 218

19   Ibid., p. 219

20   Ibid., p. 215

21   Jim Christy, email to the author, May 11, 2015

22   Christopher Winans, *Malcolm Forbes: The Man Who Had Everything* (New York: St. Martin's Press, 1990), p. 85

23   Ibid., p. 86

24   Ibid., p. 85

25   Ibid., p. 87

26   Donald Kerr, report to the author, December 29, 2016

27   William Vincent Wells, *Explorations and Adventures in Honduras* (New York: Harper & Brothers, 1857), p. 381. William Wells was an author, explorer and sailor (who survived four shipwrecks) born in Boston, Massachusetts, in 1826. He later became U.S. consul-general of Honduras.

28   *Between the Meridians*, op cit., p. 138

29   Ibid., pp. 144-145

30   Ibid., p. 150

31   Ibid., p. 151

32   Jim Phelan, *Tramping the Toby*, (London: Burke Publishing Co. Ltd., 1955), pp. 118-119

33   *Between the Meridians*, op cit., p. 33

34   Ibid., pp. 34-35

35   Ibid., p. 35

36   Ibid., p. 44

37   Ibid., p. 45

38   Jim Christy, *The Castle*, unpublished manuscript

39   Jim Christy, email to the author, July 28, 1915

40   *The Castle*, op cit.

41   Ibid.

42   Ibid.

43   Ibid.

44   Ibid.

45   Ibid.

46   Ibid.

47   Ibid.

48   Ibid.

49   Ibid.

50   Ibid.

51   Kevin Brown, email to the author, January 11, 2017

52   Donald Kerr, email to the author, December 29, 2016

53   Ibid.

54   David MacKinnon, report to the author, October 16, 2015

55   Ibid.

56   Ibid.

57   Jim Christy, email to the author, January 21, 2016

58   *This Cockeyed World*, op cit., p. 70

59   Robert Markle Kinnard, report to the author, February 1, 2016

60   Ibid.

61   Ibid.

62   *Between the Meridians*, op cit., p. 177

63   Ibid., pp. 187-188

64   Ibid., pp. 175-176

65   Ibid., p. 189

66   Ibid., p. 190

67   Ibid., p. 191

68   Jim Christy, email to the author, April 4, 2016

69   Brad Benson, email to the author, November 2, 2015

70   Jim Christy, *The Walrus*, April/May 2004

71   Ibid.

72   Ibid.

73   Jim Christy, email to the author, February 5, 2017

74   Jim Christy, "Land Mines and Looters," *The Walrus*, September 12, 2004

75   Ibid.

NARROWING HORIZONS AND WORK AS AN ARTIST

C hristy's tramping at home and abroad continued right through to 2014, only forestalled by a series of events that would leave the (almost septuagenarian) vagabond down but not out. But to bring Christy's adventures up to date, it is first necessary to backtrack to the early 1990s, during which time, and between his globetrotting escapades, Christy was living and working as an artist on British Columbia's Sunshine Coast. Robert Kinnard, who describes above his first sighting of Christy on the Langdale ferry between the Sunshine Coast and West Vancouver, was not the only person to have taken an interest in the ferry passenger. Cher Lynne Monroe was working on the ferry at the time and recalls her initial observations of Christy as follows: "Thought he was good-looking. Loved his walk. Very straight, casual, sauntery. Didn't speak for the first few times. Saw him very occasionally. Out of town, I presumed."

Out of town was something of an understatement, but Cher was not to know the extent of Christy's ramblings from these first few brief encounters. One day, Cher says, they just started chatting, she thought he was a "nice guy, loved the voice," and the attraction was clearly mutual. But these things don't always pan out the way it is hoped and, not anticipating that Christy had any romantic attentions in her direction, in July, 1995, Cher got engaged to be married. The flip side being that, as Cher was wearing an engagement ring, it did not occur to Christy that she would be responsive to overtures of a romantic nature. Given Christy's previous impulses when it came to dating women, this episode of his life feels quaint and old-fashioned by comparison. There is also something of the romantic tragedy about these two nomadic souls finding and losing each other in spite of the mutual recognition of the "difference" in each other—Christy being the vagabond he was and Cher's dark complexion which had always drawn comments about her heritage. Then again, Christy was still married at the time to Mary Anne Silva, even though they had been separated for some time.

As time and years rolled by, Cher's marriage began to unravel at the same time that her relationship with Christy strengthened. "We would stop and chat whenever we saw each other on the ferry or in town ... I think we developed a pretty good friendship." Christy had often told Cher that she looked different, "other." Not Native American or Italian or anything like that, rather "gypsy-other." Her grandmother had told her as a child that they had gypsies in the family, which is where she got her gypsy blood. The family had always been on the move and couldn't settle down for long.

It was not something Cher had given much thought to before the comments from others and talking about it openly with Christy. The ignorance and prejudice she encountered in provincial Canada had always been a source of irritation and upset; not that the unenlightened identified her as Romani, she was more often taken as First Nation, East Indian, mixed-race Afro-American, anything but white Anglo-Saxon. What does one say in the face of such stupidity—"No actually, I'm a gypsy," with all of the added stigma and ignorance that designation attracts? Other more enlightened and worldly folk, including complete strangers, did see the Romani in Cher and commented on it to both her and Christy.

> The first time someone referred to me as a gypsy was when Jim was talking to a woman, Dvora Levin, when we were in Victoria B.C.. She referred to me as his 'gypsy girlfriend with the big red lips.' She and I did not know each other. Then again, when Jim did his lecture at the Fraser Valley University in Abbotsford B.C., Sept., 2016, his friend, Brenda Frederick, the art professor at the university, asked Jim if I was gypsy. ...Jim never said anything

to her to provoke that remark. Since I've been here in Belleville, when they've seen me, people have asked Jim, 'What is she?' Then one of the instructors in Jim's cardiac rehab asked Jim, straight out, 'Is she a gypsy?' Then there's a Russian lady here who apparently is quite familiar with gypsies, thought I was one.[1]

With encouragement from Christy, Cher was happy to explore her heritage further. She also started using the name Reyna. Firstly, because she was reviving her singing career and was tired of being asked if she did "Cher" impersonations, but also Reyna is a traditional gypsy name derived from the Spanish *reina* (queen) and held a particular appeal. "I was comfortable talking about it with Jim. I was comfortable with being different." And it was the "difference" in each of them that forged a bond of friendship between them. Both understood and experienced wanderlust even if the condition had different ancestral roots. Reyna's maternal grandmother frequently traveled with her as a child. Both Reyna's maternal grandfather and great-grandfather had been blacksmiths. Reyna and Christy's research revealed that metalwork and horses were key occupations of the Lowara Romani people. The indications of a familial connection to that tribe were there:

> I know that whenever she'd say her gypsy blood was starting to boil, she [grandmother] was gone.... Couldn't stay in one place for a long time. ... As a child we moved around a lot. I went to about 7 different elementary schools. Only one high school but quit half grade 9, half grade 10. Worked, took off when my gypsy blood started to boil, came back, got another job, took off again. I found it difficult to settle for long periods of time.[2]

Tramps have always had a particular fascination and respect for gypsies and Christy is no different in this respect. For "gadjo" vagabonds, the Romani people represent the tribe or race who managed to defy Western "civilization" that they, the tramp, struggle to exile themselves from with some difficulty. For them, the gypsy represents the natural, wandering lifestyle that was the norm before the civilizing process domesticated humans into settled communities and forced them into work to make money—which became, and still remains, the standard currency for survival. All of the tramp-writers listed in the prologue have expressed their admiration for gypsies. "Children of a glorious far, far away past when men wandered about taking life as it should be taken!" This is how Bart Kennedy describes the positive attributes of the gypsy in his book *A Tramp's Philosophy* (1908):

> The gipsies are honest and intelligent and healthy. And, moreover, they are a picturesque feature in a rushing, drab, unintelligent and unpicturesque age. Let 'em alone, you policemen and lawyers and landlords. Let 'em alone, you rogues. There is more honour and honesty in one gipsy's finger than in the whole pack of you. ... How I revere this intellectual, clear eyed, ragged race. These people who wander along, carrying their houses with them. ... Do you really belong to us, the foolish people of this earth?[3]

Reyna had a lot of gigs around this time as a lounge singer all over the coast, and actually wrote and performed with Christy including background vocals on one of his jazz poetry CDs. When Reyna was going through particularly bad times and needed to cry or rant about life, Christy would just sit quietly and listen. One day she sounded off about the fact that, even though she had a full-time job, she was the only person in the house who knew which buttons to press on the washing machine and consequently the only one qualified to wash everyone else's clothes. After Reyna had exhausted her frustration and Christy started to walk away, he turned, looked straight at her and said, "I do my own laundry." "My heart jumped!" she recalled.

In 2005 Christy decided to move back to Ontario from B.C., Reyna had separated from her husband and was bringing up her ten-year-old son on her own. Christy still made occasional trips back west and kept in touch with Reyna. Then there was "Extreme Research," Christy's venture into private investigating. Christy "interviewed someone who was part of an anti-communist submarine spy situation; the man who brokered the deal for Errol Flynn's yacht; a couple of others." The problem, as Christy saw it, was that the nature of the business made promoting it difficult: you can hardly give a potential client a testimonial because all previous clients have been promised anonymity! Christy explains that in his detective novel *Shanghai Alley*, "the protagonist finds the identity of a man who is sending obituary notices to another man; no signature, just clippings." The idea came from a real test case Christy was given for an assignment in Toronto. He found the guy's identity in just three hours:

All recipients were Jewish, all mail arrived on Thursday or
Friday morning. The newspaper type-faces were not from the
local dailies; they all arrived, like I said, on the same day or days.
I searched weeklies for a Jewish one and saw that it was a fit;
the postmarks in those days had different little knob-like lines
around the circle. From these one could ascertain the location of
the post office from which they were mailed. The one in question
was mailed from the Dovercourt Post Office. There I asked after
anyone who appeared on Wednesday once a month to hand over
letters. One clerk knew the guy. I asked the client if he knew the
man. Yes, he was a former partner. Case closed.[4]

And so, when he advertised Extreme Research, Christy guaranteed privacy.
For instance, Christy went to Cambodia in 2010 on behalf of a client who was
writing a doctoral thesis on Khmer Rouge fighters and wanted them interviewed. The old officers were living in a certain town where they were still
tolerated, and Christy went there and talked with those who were prepared to
talk. On his return he handed over the notes of the interviews to his client who
made it clear that *they* would take the credit for having traveled to Cambodia
to conduct the interviews, not Christy. In 2007 he also acted as a "delivery
boy" to Bogotá, Buenos Aires, and various other exotic destinations, handing
over messages in person to clients who did not want to be identified.

By 2007 also, Christy had started spending time back east with the artist
Virginia Dixon. He had first met Virginia through the Pteros Gallery she
opened in September, 2001, and where Christy would have his own exhibition
the following year. At the time, Virginia had been separated from her husband
for two years, her two boys were in university, and her daughter was living
with her father. She describes the gallery as follows:

It was situated near arguably the ugliest intersection in Toronto
but it was a 4-storey commercial-residential-mix building on a
main artery with streetcar in front, a laneway at the rear. The
gallery was on the first level and my residence on level 2 and 3,
with a 20' x 40' warehouse addition at the rear. My new studio.
Its roof served as a walkout patio from the second-floor kitchen.
There was also a sub-level where other things happened.[5]

Aside from having art and literature in common with Christy, Virginia had also been something of a traveler before they met. She describes trekking on a camel through the Moroccan desert, hiking in China's Szechuan province, and sleeping in a fly-infested barn in Austria. Virginia first started taking notice of Christy at the launch and reading of one of his detective novels, *Terminal Avenue*, at the Mockingbird Tavern in Toronto.

The exhibition, held in March, 2003, was a three-man show titled "3 Beats to the Wind," with Christy featured as a solo artist in the main gallery. He stayed and slept at the gallery for a few nights before the show and Virginia helped him with sourcing last-minute found objects and materials for his exhibition pieces. Virginia comments, "I didn't know then it was the first of hundreds of our trips together junk and treasure hunting."

Christy returned to B.C. following the show, returning to Toronto again in early November, 2004. He had a second solo exhibition at the gallery from February to March, 2005, but was in Cambodia at the time. Now living permanently in Toronto, Christy only met up occasionally with Virginia for the next couple of years. She describes him as:

> ...living below the radar in an apartment near Shaw Street where
> he had 'an arrangement' with the property manager, living rent-
> free in exchange for managing the property, not to mention
> allowing others to live there rent-free [the same arrangement he'd
> had on Howland Avenue in the '70s.] The apartment was sparsely
> outfitted with a mattress on the floor, books, and a TV. The halls
> were a crazy patchwork of black and white tiles on an uneven
> floor that made the interior feel like an Alice in Wonderland set.
> One dark rainy evening when I was driving along Bloor Street, I
> spotted him ... under a black umbrella artfully dodging the puddles
> to keep his shoes dry. I felt happy knowing he was still in Toronto,
> still well. ... When we did see each other in those days it was for
> afternoons of wine and relaxation, no strings attached.[6]

By 2007, Christy had started living informally at the gallery, now simply a residence and studio space, with his own set of keys. After closing the gallery in 2005, Virginia had been painting and writing exhibition reviews and also caring for her father up until his death in 2006. As Virginia reports on Christy: "Our relationship was still more of an arrangement since he maintained his own schedule and life without informing me of much and I also felt I needed to be unattached, despite my ardor for him." During this time Christy continued with his private investigator and journalistic missions abroad, including that year in Cambodia, Argentina, and Colombia. But later that year Christy and Virginia took the first of several trips abroad together, on this occasion traveling around France. The following year it was Mexico but Christy flew out ahead on his own, something Virginia observed he did often in those early days of their relationship. "I don't know whether this was to make a point that he was travelling solo, to do some research prior to 'holiday,' or visit with friends. I didn't ask." It was the same on the return journey too, with Virginia flying home alone while Christy stayed on for a week on his own.

Here Virginia describes the same degree of compromise required for her relationship with Christy as Myfanwy Phillips described decades earlier. "There is a fair amount of tact involved in being Jim's friend. At one end he needed total independence, at the other he needed a guardian angel." But clearly the upsides of the relationship outweighed the down. As Virginia further observes, "I so admired his intelligence, his convictions, his sweetness and toughness, his humour and his Cynicism." There were several further trips abroad with Christy. Virginia met him in New Zealand following a reading tour Christy made of Australia in 2008, a trip to Cuba in 2010, and the same year a month at a friend's apartment in Paris with a side trip to Hamburg in Germany to watch the Vitali Klitschko versus Shannon Briggs fight, Virginia's birthday present to Christy.

> It had been a dream of mine since I was a child to attend a heavy-weight boxing match, dressed in a gown and furs and tux, etc., the way I must have seen them on TV as a child. We did have VIP tickets and attended a very posh reception and it was one of the highlights of my life.[7]

In 2012 it was India and then back to Germany, this time to watch the Wladimir Klitschko versus Jean-Marc Mormeck fight in Düsseldorf in March, 2012. Christy had been talking to Virginia about wanting to ride the Trans-Siberian railroad across Russia to write a poem to coincide with the hundredth anniversary of Blaise Cendrar's prose-poem about the Trans-Siberian written in 1913. She encouraged him knowing it was something he had to do on his own. The plan was to start off attending the fight in Düsseldorf, then fly on to

Helsinki and from there take a train into St. Petersburg and then on to Moscow. Virginia would then fly home and Christy would take the Trans-Siberian across Russia and into Mongolia and come home from there or China. The fight was postponed due to an injury in training but they went to Hannover anyway. From there they went on to Helsinki and then the train into St. Petersburg and on to Moscow.

> It was a fabulous experience and another dream come true and we were both genuinely happy. I know Jim would love to return to Moscow, he felt very 'at home' there. I loved it too, at least in December with the romantic snow and Christmas lights and no crowds of tourists. I had my plane ticket home with my visa expiry date stamped in my passport so I had to depart on a certain day. Because Jim had an extended visa he could stay on longer according to whatever plans he made. But a mishap occurred.[8]

The pair were in an internet place catching up on correspondence and Christy was trying to book a train ticket on the Trans-Siberian. But when they went to pay the hotel bill the evening before Virginia's early morning departure, the card failed. Fortunately, Virginia had enough emergency travelers' checks and a bit of cash to pay the bill. At the same time, Jim got an email notice indicating his train ticket purchase had gone through. Virginia was left with only enough cash to get them to the airport the next morning and no other credit card. Christy could have stayed on, having an extended visa and his rail ticket, but had no money to fund the trip; his back-up card for emergency funds was also locked. The next morning they hopped into a taxi to head for the airport, praying that the credit card would miraculously work and finance a ticket for Christy to join Virginia on the plane out.

> It was a stunningly beautiful snowy morning in Moscow and the driver was so warm and friendly. We were nervous wrecks, not even sure if we could afford to pay him! We arrived at the airport and, without knowing our situation, the driver wouldn't accept the fare! We ran inside and to the airline counter to beg a second ticket for Jim. There was a seat available but my card failed. The last ditch hope was that there was enough credit on Jim's personal CC to pay for it—very expensive as you can imagine at that last minute

purchase. Miraculously again, his worked and we were going home together. We had just enough money to buy one coffee between us while waiting for the flight.[9]

On their return they learned from Visa that the card had been locked because, unbeknownst to Christy, when he was purchasing his train ticket online in Moscow for the Trans-Siberian he was on a British website which triggered the lockdown on the card. The following year they traveled to Spain and Italy.

Here, Virginia confirms observations made earlier about the complex side of Christy's character, for instance, Christy giving off an air of supreme confidence she describes as narcissism, but in positive terms (in reality he was anything but confident) and adding how extremely unpretentious, even apologetic, Christy was, particularly about his writing. "In these moments one sees how modest and even self-deprecating he can be about his own work and accomplishments." But there is no conflict between these two aspects of Christy's character. Narcissism is another one of those terms like cynicism that are too often used as an insult when in reality they should be taken as a compliment. As the writer Raymond Federman observed when he acknowledged that, to truly sacrifice oneself for one's art, "One must have the courage of one's own narcissism."[10]

Sometime later Christy noted to Virginia that he was not happy living in Toronto and planted the idea in her head of finding a place outside of the city:

> Eventually I realized if we went far enough east, not only was it much cheaper but accessible by train rather than driving the 401. ... On the long May 24 weekend we drove out to look at an 1840s stone farm house on a 100-acre property. We were already smitten by the realtor photos but when we arrived and cruised up the long gravel lilac-scented driveway, we were transported into a wonderland that was our inevitable destiny. Nothing could have stopped us and I put an offer on the property immediately, knowing nothing about the complexities and potential pitfalls of a rural property purchase. Our impetuous side served us well in this instance![11]

This was in May, 2008, and the sale was not to close until September. That summer, Virginia went out to Qualicum Beach on Vancouver Island to put a holiday home she owned out there up for sale to finance the farm. But once at the farmhouse, for the first time Christy experienced a settled period, throwing himself into country life with a vengeance. Here Virginia describes what was for some time an idyllic lifestyle, an opportunity for Christy to return to some imagined childhood existence. We also learn more intimate details such as how Christy likes his coffee and toast.

Jim and I were immediately humbled by the place, its power entering our psyches. Here we would be the labourers of our art without the interruptions and annoyances of contemporary living. We had no intention of working the land, growing our food or raising chickens—it was never that romantic dream of stepping back in time. We simply wanted to have our feet on the ground, the air in our lungs, the sun in our hearts, and grow. We felt like children only this childhood was Edenic. It was situated on 100 acres of land and we had an arrangement with a neighbor farmer. He worked several fields growing the hay he needed to feed his cattle over winter. Part of the acreage was wetland, a beautiful marsh with birds and grasses, that divided the land from its northern, forested parts. We had access to all of it once we made ourselves familiar to the bull. The marsh was the bigger obstacle, as there was no dry path to cross into the forest.

The milking barn was in sight of the house, still magnificent despite needing some boards replaced. It had been left as is by the previous owner, unkempt with the soiled hay from when he had briefly kept cows, with dozens of sweet smelling wax infused bee boxes stored in the loft. ... It quickly became the primary residence. ...

Jim enjoyed getting up in the cold and lighting the morning fire in the wood-stove. We did this for the first several years. Generally we would start the day with the morning coffee and steel-cut oats. Jim would move on to tea in his oversized plastic travellers' mug, taken in the studio where he sat quietly to plot out his day. Depending on where I was with my work I'd either say yes or no but these were always fun excursions, especially after Jim acquired his red Ford Ranger pick-up truck. In high spirits we'd head off.

There were several different directions to head depending on which kitchen prepared the most palatable eggs and sausages and coffee and toast without botching his specifications: fill his black coffee to the rim and be sure it's very hot. Various eggs with a substitute of tomato slices for the bacon, extra DRY toast, and no butter—hold the potatoes.[12]

Trips to the city became less frequent, but when they did stray outside of their rural retreat, Virginia and Christy were always glad to get back to the farm, "hear the lowing of cows and the scolding squirrels…. Wolves howled in the moonlight, deer and bears wandered the yard." Even the stars were more vivid in the isolation of the farmhouse and each night Christy waved at what he believed to be the last flight bound for Paris. Christy would retire to bed early each night with a book and read before turning off the light.

After a couple of years Virginia sold her home and gallery in Toronto to pay for an economical, low-maintenance bolthole in the city. This building would take three years to complete but by the third year, cracks were starting to appear in the magic of the farm and the relationship itself. There was a clash of work spaces and habits. Virginia decided she needed more time on her own, not to mention planning for the arrival of grandchildren. Twin granddaughters did arrive in September of 2013 and so Virginia's focus shifted in the direction of Toronto. The farm was no longer the practical option it had once seemed and Virginia sold it in October that year and bought a bungalow closer to Belleville while she was waiting for the condominium to be completed. She also purchased and started converting an industrial property near Belleville railway station with a view to this eventually providing a permanent home and workplace for both her and Christy, but the ingredients for separation were already emerging. Virginia had new family commitments and Christy was planning a solo trip to Cuba in the New Year. There was the possibility of a film deal on one of his books.

But on March 8, 2014, soon after arriving home from his trip to Cuba, an unexpected event would change Christy's world and put a stop, for some time at least, to any further travel plans, including driving, which, given his love affair with the automobile and relentless push toward hidden horizons, was catastrophic. The event is recounted in Christy's unpublished work *Wandering Heart*:

I was taken to emergency at Belleville General, immediately slotted into an ambulance and rushed an hour down the 401 to Kingston. It was very exciting with lights flashing, the siren screaming, and pleasant too, after several injections of morphine stilled the beast that was inside my chest trying to hammer and claw its way out. Curiously, I had no fear or any thought really that my time might be up. I accepted what was happening. I keep thinking it must have been the drugs but I don't remember any panic in the hour or so before that. I was curled on the living room floor when my partner came home to the announcement that I was having a heart attack. I recall watching the passing scene as I huddled in the passenger seat. My only thought was that she might go at least a few kilometres faster.[13]

Virginia's version is that Christy had his coat on, and was clutching his chest while waiting for her at the door; that it was several weeks later when he had his stroke that she found him curled up on the floor. Either way, Christy was kept for six days in Kingston General Hospital, then readmitted a week following his discharge because of difficulty breathing. He drove himself to the hospital in his pick-up truck and just left it in the emergency entrance. On this occasion he spent three weeks in the hospital recovering from pneumonia and congestive cardiac failure. A further ten days after his second discharge came the stroke. Christy remembers collapsing to the floor, having no feeling in his hands, and being carried to the ambulance on a stretcher. This time he was thirty-eight days in the hospital, the first few in intensive care before being transferred to the stroke ward. He was unable to get out of bed unaided and could not touch his head with his left hand. As the days passed he started gaining more use of his arms and legs and being able to move his fingers, even if he couldn't do much with them. After the first eighteen days Christy was allowed outside into the warm May sunshine.

The cars were all colours in the parking and put me in mind of May flowers. Then I caught a whiff of the Lake and was brought to tears. The cliché about the connectedness of all things, the Oneness of the universe, which I would have acknowledged, grudgingly, it seeming so hackneyed, was a truism after all. But it is a feeling or insight that has to be experienced to be understood and appreciated. There really are no words.[14]

Christy continued to make a steady, if not complete, recovery. He threw himself into walking, hand and finger exercises, then graduated from a wheel-chair to a walker. Most of the other patients on the ward seemed to be in worse condition and a doctor confirmed to Christy that if he had not kept himself in such good physical shape he might not have survived the stroke at all. Christy had been working out at the YMCA gym in Belleville only a couple of hours before his first heart attack and was soon back there again to try and recover his former strength and dexterity.

Virginia notes that the first seven months following Christy's hospitaliza-tion were very focused on his heart and rehab, but as Christy grew stronger Virginia sensed that he became more distant. She later acknowledged that when people are given a second chance at life and have survived the odds, there is often a "sense of urgency for what time is left," prompting a need for change and moving on. Such a change of perspective would naturally be enhanced in someone already disposed to wanderlust, and having to face his mortality did prompt Christy to reevaluate his life. But life would not be the same. The lasting effects of the stroke affected both Christy's peripheral and frontal vision seriously enough to stop him from driving. Certain light condi-tions also caused Christy to become disoriented and working at the computer had become a strain on his eyes. Reading and typing would require frequent breaks that impacted Christy's writing and journalistic activities. But it is worth noting here that one does not need to hit the road to experience the thrill of wanderlust. Some of the characters in the books of Samuel Beckett tramp in their imagination, even from a bed or other confined space. Christy noted this same possibility of tramping in the pages of books, in a newspaper article in 1992:

> ...one can view like a movie in the privacy of one's mind,
> particularly during those housebound months of winter.... Ah, yes,
> there was the strange encounter with the Obeah witch doctor on
> the island of Dominica; a long day under house arrest in Manaus,
> Brazil for suspicion of being a spy; a wonderful couple of days in a
> village on one of the remoter Fijian islands; climbing in the hills of
> the Coromandel peninsula in New Zealand....[15]

Not long after his recovery from the stroke, Virginia responded to these changes of circumstances. Christy would not return to Toronto but she wanted to spend increasing time near her grandchildren. He could not stay at the bungalow or the industrial property alone without the ability to drive, neither was Virginia happy that he should live in a rented room in Belleville with the possibility of being evicted should he have another stroke. So she sold both the bungalow and the industrial property and purchased a condominium on Belleville's main drag where Christy was living at the time. If the relationship had had its ups and downs before Christy's stroke, things got more strained following it. Contact between Christy and Virginia diminished as she was spending more time with her family and Christy was starting to re-engage with former pursuits, including getting new commissions for art installations.

It is worth digressing briefly about the fact that Christy himself has never had any children, at least as far as he's aware, and yet kids have always had a particular trusting fascination for him. This is not necessarily a helpful attribute to have these days with all the heightened anxiety about kids being spirited away by bogeymen. Three recent incidents, described below, illustrate this aspect of Christy's persona. The first is recalled by Christy about an incident when, just before Christmas 2016, he was walking through a shopping mall. He noticed that a baby being carried by a young mother just in front of him was staring at him intently. The baby reached out its arms toward Christy and starting calling out "Daddy, Daddy." The girl-mother turned and shot Christy a dirty look when she realized he was old enough to have been the kid's grandfather. The other two incidents are recalled by people who were with Christy at the time:

> We were in Victoria, B.C. Jim & I were walking through a park.
> There was a little boy about 4-5 years old with an older man,
> maybe grandfather. No one else in the park. The boy was racing
> around the playground area when all of a sudden he came running
> over to Jim, took his hand and pulled him to a large pipe wheel.
> The boy was pointing to something in the wheel maybe trying
> to show Jim how it worked. Not sure. But the grandfather didn't
> seem alarmed. Jim made eye contact with him and gestured a
> shrug. The grandfather smiled. All was well.[16]

The following anecdote is from Warren Fraser, a recent acquaintance and friend who was visiting Christy in 2016:

> One day last year, as we moseyed down Front Street in Belleville, we encountered a black child of about 5 years old who was with two adult women. As we were passing by, the youngster came up to us, smiled, looked up at Jim, then took hold of his hand and continued walking with us. It was as though there was an instantaneous bond betwixt them. Jim was taken aback thinking that the kid's mother would get angry with him. Jim just shrugged at the mother when she looked around but she just smiled and nodded. So sweet and memorable.[17]

But to return to Christy's artwork: incredibly the stroke had not affected his ability to mix cement or hoist heavy objects. With reading and writing having become something of a strain, Christy embraced his work as an artist with a new vigor. As mentioned in Chapter 1, although principally acknowledged as a writer, Christy had nurtured artistic inclinations from the age of six, ever since he wanted to attend the free art classes in the Fleischer Art Academy across from the family home on Catherine Street, South Philadelphia. When in Vancouver with Mary Anne, Christy had kept on about wanting to start painting so much that Mary Anne went out and bought him a cheap set of acrylics for beginners. Earlier, Christy had revived his interest in art during his time observing Myfanwy painting, but searching for a medium that better suited his personal style and interest, he first started with collages and then moved on to assemblages and strange little figures made from found objects.

During a stay in Mexico with Mary Anne in 1987, Christy had hung some of his sculptures on a wall and noticed that passers-by started crossing themselves when they passed his artworks. From this he concluded that he must be on to something. After returning to B.C., Christy continued with his sculptures and some years later had his first show at the Pitt International Gallery at 36 Powell Street in Vancouver. The curator, the artist Ken Gerberick, who owned the KRAK studio gallery on 311 W. Hastings, recalls his first meeting with Christy:

> I think we got to know one another because of our Art Cars, he had the little Acadian covered in toys, etc., on the Sunshine coast and I had a 1957 Pontiac covered in vehicle emblems (about 6,000 of

them) in Vancouver. I had never heard of an Art Car before that, creating one was something I just had to do starting in late 1989. He was the one who, in about 1994, first told me about the big Art Car event in Houston, Texas. That changed my life. ... Jim was very intrigued by the fact that my sister and I picked up Jack Kerouac hitch-hiking from St. Louis north toward Chicago (he got out at a turn-off heading east) as we were running away from our high school graduation. We knew who he was and had read a couple of his books. That was in 1961, and Jim figured out which of Jack's trips across country that was.[18]

From his sculptures of found objects, Christy's artworks became more ambitious, including permanent installations that involved Christy's already developed skills as a landscape gardener. Numerous such installations of Christy's still exist, not only from the west to east coast of Canada but around the globe. The following description from Reyna concerns a particular tropical garden with bananas, palm trees, and gunnera, that Christy cultivated for a house in Gibsons Landing on the Sunshine Coast:

He then created magnificent mosaic sculptures within and around the garden. These included what I call a Greek fireplace, walkways, towers, planters. The house was sold and not knowing what was going to happen to the sculptures, I asked the new owner if I could have the ones I could move so they could be put into a park. The owner wanted to keep some of them but let me have the rest. Unfortunately the Greek fireplace could not be moved as it was far too big nor could it be saved and the owner didn't want it so it was destroyed. Heartbreaking! I called a fellow who owned a crane & had the rest moved to the parks yard where they were to be distributed. ... He saw art in the simplest of items. Driftwood, plastic toys, things he finds here & there, he can put them together, creating the most wonderful pieces. ... Although most people know him as a writer, I think of him as an artist and someone who is musically oriented.[19]

Photographs of the "Greek fireplace" still exist, as do images of other of Christy's mosaics and his sculptures. Many of the smaller, intimate pieces that were not sold are still retained by Christy and his friends, the rewards of the ever vigilant scavenger with an eye for the alluring in what others regard as trash. Below is an extended description of the work Christy was engaged with at the time he met Virginia from a piece she was prompted to write in response to the vagabond art that started to inhabit her gallery space. In order to accommodate the passage below, detailed descriptions of individual artworks in the essay have been omitted to focus more on the essential nature and character of the work itself:

> Both as figure and metaphor, it is very difficult to isolate matter from spirit in a Jim Christy work. Debris is easily recognised as such but cannot remain superficial when read for its own histories. Wood has been uprooted, waterlogged, hard-knocked, dried out, split up, and often burned. Found doll parts—limbs, eyes, hair—feel as innocent and dirty as a dead child in a dump. That is the matter of these sculptures, with occasional adornment of seeds, fabric scrap, or chipped tile, but they are not "just" that any more than we are "just" water, flesh, and bone. Paradoxically, these wooden characters are not wooden at all. They are highly animated, inciting a strong desire to get up close to gaze into their glassy eyes. They want to be seen, to be read with the eyes. They remind us of how to look and of how much we enjoy looking, especially at our fellow human beings. They wake us up to the grand spectacle of life, engage us and relieve us of our personal burdens. The twisty sticks on *The True Cross* bear the weariness of a pilgrim's legs; the dental gloss on the smile of *Unrequited Love* flashes his availability; the bow-tie noose on *Lonely Guy* flags a mama's boy. This kind of familiarity is delightful and makes you laugh. Other details point to deeper troubles. Who is the character in the beret and moustache determinedly throwing his arms wide and shouting *No Pasaran*? He is an unarmed rebel of the Spanish Civil War. What will become of the charred farmer of *Burnt Harvest*? This cast of hustlers, dweebs and heroes has no pretensions and the creator clearly loves them for who they are.
>
> [...]
>
> Assemblage, collage, mosaic, writing are additive processes that have a practical aspect; Jim Christy is always travelling.

Installed pieces are found world-wide in the mosaic floors and façades and gardens commissioned during his longer stays. His artworks are mementoes of the voyage, but they are also 'invitations to the voyage' prodding you to stay awake and alive to your own experience. There is an ingrained patience in his work, an attention to detail and a writer's pacing of such details to build narrative. The more you return to Jim Christy's works the more you see the assimilation of material, form and content. ... Jim Christy's got a part in every scene (just like the bit-parts he plays in movies—that's him standing behind Sylvester Stallone in *Rocky IV* when the champion delivers his K.O. speech). Jim Christy abandoned popcorn for the real life a long time ago.[20]

Another anecdote, involving both Christy's assemblages and his continuing influence on other artists, comes from Brenda Fredrick, former director and curator of the Art Gallery of the South Okanagan in Penticton, B.C. Brenda recalls how in 1990 she had spent the day at the *Artropolis* exhibition in Vancouver:

I took some time to wander down Robson Street to clear my mind of the overload. Browsing in store windows I came upon an optical store that had the most intriguing sculptures in the windows: crazy smallish figurative assemblages—some standing alone and others with eye glasses strategically placed onto their limbs. ... The works snared my curiosity and I went inside. The staff didn't have much information about the artist, so I asked if I could leave my card. ... About six months later the gallery education coordinator called up to my office, indicating that some guy named Jim Christy was on the phone and that he had the most incredible voice. I won't repeat what she *actually* said about Jim's voice, but on hearing Jim's voice for myself, I must admit to the thought of recruiting it for a spoken word project.

Following our conversation and a few back and forth letters and visits, we scheduled the solo exhibition "Sunny Side of The Death House" which opened April 2, 1993. I asked Jim if he would consider a reading as well and, recalling all the reviews I had read, was astounded to learn that this would be his first public reading.

Jim is remarkably self-deprecating. We have kept in touch and in 2016 as a visiting artist/author, Jim shared his personal insights into the importance of risk taking with my class in the Department of Visual Arts at the University of the Fraser Valley, Abbotsford, B.C.. His influence was significant and the students' subsequent work showed the kind of fearlessness and challenge Jim had inspired in them; politically correct they were not—Jim would be pleased.[21]

End of art digression and back to the long overdue relationship with Reyna. They had talked a lot about Reyna relocating to Ontario which finally—her son now living independently—she did in 2015. Christy flew out to Abbotsford, B.C. from Toronto and Reyna picked him up from the airport. After making a stop at her son's place to pick up some stuff on the way, they embarked on the road trip east. No longer able to drive himself, Christy made the most of the opportunity of having four wheels and the company of a fellow gypsy spirit to revisit some of his old haunts along the way, including retracing the tramp he made through Saskatchewan. In Manitoba, before arriving back in Ontario, Christy proposed marriage to Reyna. They wed on September 1, 2015 and after living for some time in Belleville, Ontario, eventually returned to Gibsons where Christy still writes and assembles artworks.

One would imagine by now that Christy would be living in some degree of comfort and security on the proceeds of his lifetime endeavors, as several of the Victorian tramp-writers listed in the prologue of this book managed to achieve—those who survived into later life at least. Not so Christy. He continues to lead a Diogenean lifestyle on minimal royalty checks and whatever resources he and Reyna can scrape together, but managed enough in the spring of 2017 to get themselves to Cuba.

As this book was being written in July, 2017, Christy headed west again to B.C. for what will be the last recorded trip of this biography. While Reyna visited family and friends, Christy took off on what he had planned to be a road trip up the Alaska Highway with his aforementioned traveling companion Brad Benson to revisit old haunts in the Yukon Territory (the pair's earlier adventures in Mexico, Guatemala, and southeast Asia are referred to in the previous chapter). At least, that was the plan. But the forest fires raging at the time around B.C. put a stop to making a trip to the Arctic Circle by automobile and so Christy and Benson took a flight from Vancouver to Fort St. John in B.C. to commence their trip by whatever means presented itself.

The next day, with no buses running up the Alaska Highway, the two septuagenarians stuck out their thumbs and began hitchhiking. They got their first ride in seven minutes from a young couple returning from church and out for their Sunday drive, and were dropped off at Wonowon (mile 101 of the Alcan). The next ride took five hours to acquire but a middle-aged woman drove them as far as Pink Mountain where she met up with her son to join him on his road-working crew. Christy and Benson got bunks in an oil drillers' work camp for the night and the trip continued by whatever transport was available, until finally making Dawson City, 1,157 miles from Fort St. John.

Christy's disappointment after arriving at Whitehorse at four in the morning and finding only one of the old-time saloons, the '98,' still standing (the rest having been replaced by characterless affairs catering to the burgeoning tourist industry), was consoled on his eventual arrival in Dawson City to find the place pretty much as it had been the last time he was in town twenty years earlier. "In fact, it probably isn't much changed from the days of the Klondike Gold Rush at the tail end of the 19th century."[22] Christy reports meeting many of those fascinating old-timers like the ones he had encountered on previous trips and listening to their stories, not to mention the stunning scenery and wildlife he remembered from earlier trips. Sadly, Benson's hopes of reaching the Arctic Circle were dashed because the terrain was too rough to hire a rental car and chartering a mini-bus and driver would have cost the pair $2,500 they didn't have. But if this is the last adventure for the reader of this book, be sure it won't be the last adventure for Christy who, funds permitting, is already planning his next trip to who knows where.

That Christy's writing has not been more widely acknowledged, or come to that the literature and philosophy of the tramp-writers who preceded him, raises questions about the current state of literature. It must also be acknowledged that Christy's disdain of the book industry should not be taken as a signal that he has no interest in recognition for his literary endeavors, even if he refuses to solicit or crave it. Len Gasparini has referred to his and Christy's mutual disdain for the Canadian pseudo-intellectual literati, acknowledging that Christy is simply a victim of the fact that the self-styled, scholarly guardians of literature look down their noses at those outside of their own narrow circle of influence. They are suspicious of hard-boiled writers like Christy, whose writing style (and lifestyle) they consider too crude to fit their narrow commercial or scholarly interests.

In an article titled "A true original, well worth framing" by James Eke, published in the (Toronto) *Globe and Mail*, December 13, 2000, we are provided with further commentary on Christy's relationship to Canadian literature. Eke quotes one of Christy's publishers, Ekstasis Editions' Richard Olafson, who builds on Len Gasparini's sentiments when he says that:

> Canadian literature is drying out for not drawing from the well
> that writers like Jim Christy draw from. Jim is the other side of the
> coin to the mainstream literary establishment, an establishment
> which doesn't represent current writing or the average person's
> real tastes.

From the same article, a comment from *The Globe and Mail's* cultural editor of the time, Jack Kapica:

> Jim Christy is what Jim Christy is. The literary mafia in Toronto
> 30 years ago was moving away from writing because they had
> something to say, into writing because they wanted to be in the
> club. Christy writes because he has to. You have to understand
> where the urge to write comes from to understand Jim Christy.

From the actress Jackie Burroughs (*Anne of Green Gables* and *Road to Avonlea*):

> Canadians aren't hungry for persons. Personalities are seen as
> almost scary here. Canadians like things that are subtle. But Jim
> Christy is brilliant, visceral and the words he writes ring true. He's
> a person who is very much physically in this world and it can't
> help but come through in everything he does. He has a great way of
> telling it like it is in a way that the literary establishment might not
> be used to.

And in the same article Christy describes his own writing style:

> This is a market no one is going after yet except the smaller
> literary presses like Ekstasis Editions. Readers will continue to
> pick up these books by writers whose work is like a light shining

brightly in the corner of a room, showing the warts of a person, yes, but the beauty as well—things the average person can relate to. ...good writing should never be dull—it's about life and life can be wild. ... Everything I've ever written came to the page with rhythms and beats in my head. A lot of writers work so hard at the metaphor, seeming to spend all their efforts on it. The hell with feeling or the meaning of the poem as long as they get that metaphor. For me, what really matters is the actual sound of the words and how they all flow together—it's music to me. I can hear it. It's jazz.[23]

James Eke later contributed his own thoughts to the commentary about Christy and literature:

It wasn't until Jim had an art show in Toronto in around 2000 that I realized just how big he actually was. Sure, there had been the readings in Vancouver with girls and guys coming up to him to say how much his writing meant to them. But the art show—it was packed. I spent the night hearing different people talk about this mythic guy.... The one constant from them all was they couldn't understand how he wasn't a household name in Canada. Truth is, knowing what I know now, neither do I.[24]

One explanation offered by Eke builds on this notion of Christy as a mythic character, a quality enhanced by avoiding the kind of publicity some artists and writers deliberately seek. "Jim has always walked a lonely and shaded road that you have to find on purpose." Eke notes that whereas at times Christy's unplanned roads lead to places where the masses *do* notice him, more often than not "this road goes off on tangents." Tangents that make Christy's life appear more like something one reads in books from another world and another time, full of "characters who simply couldn't have been real." The truth is that most of Christy's characters *are* real; even his so-called fictions are to a large extent autobiographical. But because Christy, as the vagabond he is, operates outside of the contemporary literary establishment's rules and codes, refusing to be managed as a "product," it is safer to ignore him.

As was acknowledged in the prologue, the tramp-writer's disregard of literary genre and convention poses a challenge for publishers and booksellers alike who are at a loss how to market vagabond literature or where to display it on the shelves. The sadness for Christy is that this is a relatively recent phenomenon since finance and marketing folk have supplanted good "old-fashioned" patrons of the arts who had an eye for the inimitable. Imagine for a moment if an unknown Jack Kerouac, Samuel Beckett, or even Homer, the father of Western literature, were to submit a manuscript to a mainstream trade publisher in the twenty-first century. They would be dismissed as "experimental," not commercially viable. There are further hints of Christy's frustration with Canadian literature in his unpublished work *Wandering Heart*, composed during his hospital confinement following his stroke. After singing the praises of great Russian and American railway literature, Christy provides his own reasons for the lack of authentic tramp literature in Canada:

> Many have noted the lack of train-oriented literature in this
> country and advance different reasons for why this is the case. To
> me the reason, one that others do not seem to have mentioned,
> is simple: We have never really had a popular literature. The
> Canadian poetry that has come down to us has been almost
> invariably written by academics, most of whom wouldn't know
> the sound of the Eastbound 411 from the dinner bell on the
> quadrangle.[25]

And in a response to reading this section of the book, Christy further notes:

> The lack of a popular literature displays itself much more than in a
> dearth of train or vagabond writing. It is at the root of the vacuity
> of Canadian writing. There were never, and could never have
> been, any Londons or Steinbecks or such as the great overlooked
> John Dos Passos. The notion of a Dickens is totally inconceivable,
> unthinkable.[26]

A final footnote on the perversity of the Canadian literary establishment is that this biography was not able to be published by any of the smaller Canadian independent presses who publish Christy's work because the Canadian Council for the Arts does not provide any support for books not written by Canadian writers—never mind that the subject of the book *is* a Canadian writer. Such are the vagaries of the literary world. This book, and Christy's writing also, freed from the will of their vagabond creators, will now embark on their own life and adventures.

1   Reyna Lynne, email to the author, January 25, 2017

2   Reyna Lynne, report to the author, January 15, 2017

3   Bart Kennedy, *A Tramp's Philosophy* (London: John Long, 1908), pp. 59-60

4   Jim Christy, email to the author, February 1, 2016

5   Virginia Dixon, report to the author, March 9, 2017

6   Ibid.

7   Virginia Dixon, report to the author, March 25, 2017

8   Ibid.

9   Ibid.

10   Raymond Federman, in Eckhard Gerdes (ed.), *The Laugh that Laughs at the Laugh: Writing from and about the Pen Man, Raymond Federman: Journal of Experimental Fiction 23* (Bloomington, IN: iUniverse, 2002), p. 327

11   Virginia Dixon, report to the author, March 9, 2017

12   Ibid.

13   *Wandering Heart*, op cit.

14   Ibid.

15   Jim Christy, "Just what is this elusive thing called adventure?" *The Daily Courier*, April 12, 1992

16   Reyna Lynne, email to the author, January 25, 2017

17   Warren Fraser, letter to the author, January 20, 2017

18   Ken Gerberick, email to the author, February 2, 2017

19   Reyna Lynne, email to the author, October 23, 2015

20   Virginia Dixon, essay to the author, March 9, 2017

21   Brenda Fredrick, email to the author, June 5, 2017

22   Jim Christy, email to the author, February 14, 2017

23   James Eke, "A true original, well worth framing," in (Toronto) *Globe and Mail*, December 13, 2000

24   James Eke, email to the author, May 25, 2017

25   Jim Christy, *Wandering Heart*, unpublished manuscript

26   Jim Christy, email to the author, May 25, 2017

PHOTO GALLERY

ABOVE Christy's first literary endeavour at two hours old—radiogram announcing his arrival into the world.

ABOVE Christy aged five, Disputanta, Virginia.

BELOW Christy aged nine, South Philadelphia.

TOP Christy aged eleven at his brother David's third birthday.

MIDDLE Christy's father, Angelo Christinzio.

BOTTOM Christy with his mother Kathleen.

TOP August, 1968, at Townsend Inlet, New Jersey: "I'd just seen Charlie Leeds that day; he was to report the next day to begin serving his prison sentence for the drugstore caper."

BOTTOM Christy in Toronto with his brother David c. 1974. The shades are being worn to cover a cut eye received the previous night after getting into a fight with two off-duty cops who had insulted Christy's girlfriend.

ABOVE Christy with Ed Vogel's Plymouth Fury in Pecos County, Texas, August 1968 (it was Vogel who advertised for a female companion for the San Francisco trip of 1967).

RIGHT Pamphlet given to Christy by Kathleen Phelan in Morocco.

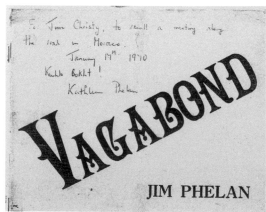

TOP, CLOCKWISE FROM TOP LEFT Val Santee, Cher Lynne Monroe (Reyna Lynne), Charlie Leeds and Marcel Horne.

BOTTOM Christy (right) with Frisco Jack at the annual Britt, Iowa hobo convention in 1977. Photo by Myfanwy Phillips.

ABOVE "Rough Road to the North," Christy by the Yukon River. Photo by Myfanwy Phillips, winter of 1976/77.

OPPOSITE TOP "Rough Road to the North," Alaska Highway. Photo by Myfanwy Phillips, winter of 1976/77.

OPPOSITE BOTTOM 1958 Cadillac Eldorado Christy bought from the redneck in St. Augustine, Florida in 1977 and 'given' to Chris the alligator wrestler in 1981 after thousands of miles' use.

ABOVE Christy with his half-Rappahannock maternal grandmother Reatha (Bailey) Dolby. Reatha Dolby's great-grandmother, Rebecca (Clanton) Bailey, was an aunt of Newman Haynes Clanton, leader of the loosely formed 200-strong outlaw gang known as the "Cowboys." Photo by Myfanwy Phillips, 1979.

RIGHT Driftwood sculpture by Christy who, though a poet himself, ridicules the narcissistic pose of the ubiquitous Canadian poet.

TOP "A Halloween Dinner in Fiji," Christy's island home in 1985.

MIDDLE "In Search of the Golden Madonna," Geraldo, Christy's would-be assassin taken at the start of the trip through the rainforest in 1987.

BOTTOM "West of the Keremeos," rock pictographs taken by Christy in 1988.

fool along the yukon

FOOL IN A SILVER BIRD
OVER LAKE LABERGE
30,000 FEET AND
DESCENDING

SO I REALLY HAVE DONE IT
LEFT YOU 4,000
MILES AWAY
TO THE RIGHT
OVER GREY MOUNTAIN
WISPY CLOUDS TAUNT
ASK ME WHY

TO THE LEFT THE RIVER
EMERALD
FEATHERED BY
BANKS OF SNOW
AND NOW THE ROOFS OF
WHITEHORSE

Within the suitcase assemblage, the following typed text appears on paper labels:

THOSE OLD AUTUMN HILLS NEAR DAWSON
TELL THE STORY
OF THIS FELLOW'S LIFE
THE BRILLIANT LEAVES HAVE FALLEN

AND THREE DAYS RAIN

STICKS THEM TO THE EARTH

ALL ASKEW
LIKE SO MANY EXOTIC STAMPS
ON A LETTER THAT NEVER

CATCHES UP

YUKON HOTEL

ABOVE Suitcase assemblage based on Christy's poem "First of October Dawson."

LEFT Christy during time on the farm in rural Ontario working on one of his many mosaic sculptures that still exist at locations across the globe. Photo by Virginia Dixon circa 2010.

RIGHT AND BELOW Christy's "art car," the 1978 Pontiac Acadian festooned with memorabilia from around the globe.

OPPOSITE Reyna seated on Christy's "Greek Fireplace" circa 2001.

ABOVE "Land Mines and Looters," Christy with the Cambodian Mine Action Committee, 2004.

LEFT Getting directions from bikers in Saigon. Photo Brad Benson, 2003.

LEFT Christy at the 2015 launch of his book *Bad Day for Ralphie*. Photo by John Hamley.

BELOW Christy in one of his many bit part acting roles, here in the German 'western' *Gold* (2013) in the role of 'man in saloon wearing a big hat, looking surly and giving dirty looks to the movie's leading man.'

ABOVE 72-year-old Christy hitchhiking at Wonowon (mile 101) on the Alaska Highway, August 2017. Photo by Brad Benson.

EPILOGUE: ANATOMY OF THE VAGABOND-PHILOSOPHER

At one time nearly all the world was nomadic; the people who
lived in houses were the few and the strange, the folks who were
different.
(Jim Phelan, *Tramping the Toby*)[1]

He [the tramp] knows that trouble will come to this civilisation,
but not from men like him. It will come from the idiot slaves whose
ideal is to be as well off as their masters. ... He is the only honest
shirker of work in the world. He is the pioneer of a finer and
calmer life. He wanders along, a real philosopher.
(Bart Kennedy, *A Tramp's Philosophy*)[2]

As Jim Phelan reminds us, long ago we were all tramps! It was those
who lived in settlements who were odd. Now we all live in settled
communities (whether transient or permanent) and regard with
suspicion the nomadic vagabond in our midst. And as Bart Kennedy further
observes, we should listen to, rather than ridicule, those who maintain the
tramping tradition today for it is they who truly understand how to live the

"finer and calmer life." Yet in recent times, right under our noses, there was a renaissance of vagabondage in the very heart of Western civilization that, as Jack Kerouac observed in 1960,[3] was already being outlawed and driven out of existence.

A chance combination of three major events heralded a golden age of tramping in America (and also in Canada, which is less reported): the end of the American Civil War in 1865, the development of the railways, and the financial crash of 1873. At the end of the Civil War, thousands of former soldiers, well used to an outdoor life and tramping, now found themselves homeless and certainly ill prepared for the domestic responsibilities of civilian life. With the first transcontinental railroad opening in 1869, followed by the first of a series of catastrophic international financial crashes and associated depressions (1873, 1893, and 1930), it is not surprising that, through choice or necessity, large numbers were thrown into and maintained a transient life, forced to roam the continent surviving on whatever resources came to hand.

Between 1870 and America's involvement in World War II at the end of 1941 (which provided a distraction and alternative occupation to many former hobos) tramping developed into a significant parallel culture, one that was about more than simply homelessness and joblessness. From the mainly white male hobos of the late 1800s, through the organized political tramp movements, black, Latino, and Chinese work gangs, and "Okie" migrant families of the Dust Bowl era, to the "skid row" bums between the two World Wars, what emerged for thousands of individuals caught up in the depressions (aside from simply meeting the basic need for food and shelter) was a philosophy and way of life for those alienated from, and dispossessed by, the rest of society drunk on the capitalist dream.

It is not surprising, then, that some of those who chose a tramping lifestyle did so from their own sense of moral purpose, a rejection of wider society's misguided morality that the tramp finds difficult to reconcile with. Like the ancient Cynic Crates, perhaps the tramp has a sense of a "republic," one not restricted to a geographical place, an ethnic group, religious or cultural traditions; a republic without boundaries or social distinctions. In this sense, the Cynics regarded themselves as "citizens of the world," free to roam wherever they felt the fancy, and adopting any customs and habits that suited their needs. Christy certainly seems to have embraced this lifestyle as a personal philosophy, and fully accepted the risks that such a lifestyle brings—as beatings and his many visits to jail testify—even if such risks were not motivated by any external, political "cause." So it is with most itinerant vagabonds; they live out their existential existence without the political sermonizing or sentimentality one associates with some others who choose "alternative" lifestyles, such as the hippie or new age traveler.

But is adopting the lifestyle of a tramp or Cynic a conscious choice at all? Perhaps the tramp is simply born a tramp through some endogenous but unexplainable sense of "not belonging," or belonging to the world in a different way to his or her fellows; some kind of autistic gene that does not identify with the superficial preoccupations the tramp regards as satisfying the "neurotypical" world. Certainly in Christy's case, and in true Cynic fashion, his attitude to his fellow human beings had been formed for as long as he can remember.

BEYOND THE SPECTACLE

Christy wrestled with these questions in his first published essay *Beyond the Spectacle* (1970). *Spectacle* is a plea for a return to the basic human instinct of filtering the world through our own senses rather than through the spectacle of our television screens and the rhetoric of those peddling salvation, whether of the political, commercial, religious, or mystic kind. The main objects of Christy's cynicism are on the one side the "Corporate Capitalist Ogre," and on the other impotent, left-wing, revolutionary ideologues parroting tired old slogans and promoting their own celebrity. It's an old, old story, where both sides of revolution and counter-revolution depend on the other for the rewards (power, money, prestige, et cetera) that accrue to those maintaining the confrontation—neither side able to deliver utopia.

If, as Christy maintained in 1970, our actions and language are woeful testaments to the slick packaging of the mass-media machine and the empty promises of self-styled experts and leaders, what greater suckers are we in our willingness to still trust in slick advertising and the sinister manipulation of our voting preferences, forty-seven years on from Christy's warnings, now with even more immediate brainwashing via our personal computers and cellphones. He poses the following questions that—if we substitute the current war against Islam for the Vietnam war—remain unchanged today: "What would radicals do if there was no Vietnam war? If the racial situation was not disastrous; if we weren't faced with an ecological crisis; if we weren't Policemen of the world; etc., etc., etc?"

> The basic problem confronting us, which we don't see, is the
> hollowness of our daily lives. How do you measure the depths
> of despair between demonstrations? Armed with outdated
> ideologies—any ideology—we press forward. Afraid to look to
> ourselves, we look to Marx, or Lenin, or Chairman Mao, or Jerry
> Rubin, or Abbie Hoffman—pick one, it doesn't matter, the game's
> the same. ... We can't even TALK to each other anymore. We spew
> rhetoric and respond to rhetoric.[4]

The answer to the question "What makes Jim Christy a vagabond philosopher?" can be answered by that other modern-day vagabond and cynic philosopher, Raymond Federman, when he stated, "true cynics are often the kindest people, for they see the hollowness of life, and from the realization of that hollowness is generated a kind of cosmic pity."[5] Both Christy and Federman agree that the hollowness of our daily lives is one of the principal reasons for human beings' desperate need to replace that vacuum with idealist rhetoric that in its turn creates its own hollowness. And in his eloquent, diatribal style, Federman makes no bones about just what we have replaced basic human instincts with:

> This fucking world is saturated with false hopes . . . we are
> drowning in a cesspool of theosophical emanations, cosmic
> influences, occult powers, spiritual visitations, stellar vibrations
> and divine farts, and yes yes it's all shit, de la merde molle et
> fumante, do you hear me, de la saloperie, de la crasse?[6]

Tramp-writer Jim Tully, in his autobiographical third-person narrative *Jarnegan* (1926), also regards cynicism as a positive response to the noise of those who offer truth and meaning, identifying himself as a "cynical realist" in the process:

> A man of no *isms*, he was tolerant of everything that did not touch
> his life. He knew nothing of nations or their rulers. He had never
> voted. Neither had he any theories about life. A cynical realist, he

fought against the sentimentality that was his Irish inheritance. At times, in his cups, he ended by being that most ironical of humans—a sentimental cynic.[7]

There is no contradiction here to being a sentimental cynic. The acerbic and forthright nature of cynicism is often interpreted as rudeness, and therefore misinterpreted as contemptuous and sneering, even nihilistic. This is to misunderstand the true nature of cynicism. To be positive, idealistic, even sentimental, reveals the true soul of the cynic, who simply mourns the fact that human beings have made a mess of the world they inhabit and act so foully toward one and other. Neither is there a contradiction when Tully says he hasn't "any theories about life." He is not referring here to his personal philosophy, but to the grand narratives that feed the march of progress but always fall short of delivering human happiness. The cynic knows that the human project is fundamentally flawed and so any theories are confined to maintaining one's integrity against what he or she views as a hostile world. The cynic's mission is to maximize their own life here on Earth rather than seek to change or control the world around them. And what Christy proposes in *Spectacle* is the same strategy for survival that the ancient Cynics identified over two thousand years ago: that in order to achieve happiness—or more accurately, reduce suffering—as well as minimizing our dependence on material possessions, one should rely on one's own natural instincts rather than listening to the daily babble of egotistical buffoons:

> Ideologies are merely obstacles to this liberation. They are based on domination and their pushers are moral gangsters. Can one imagine a more despicable enemy than the self-deluded demigod who would have you fight and die for his ideals?
> The methods of the left-wing ideologists are similar to those of their Capitalist counterparts. They are conspirators in the creation of Spectacles, the object being to "politicize." To make the masses aware. The success of this manipulation depends on averting one's responses from real-life situations, one loses touch, subjects events to "Interpretation."[8]

The ideas put forward here by the twenty-five-year-old vagabond philosopher at the end of the sixties uncannily echo those penned during the following decade by (so-called) postmodernist philosophers Jean-François Lyotard and Jean Baudrillard. They also warned us about the treachery of language and simulations of reality (now more real than the original) that daily assault our senses. As Christy himself puts it: "Embroiled in this verbal garbage, we display our disaffiliation from real life. We are losing our FEEL, our natural intuitive grasp of our surroundings."[9]

As is true also of earlier tramp-writers, what makes Christy a true inheritor of the Diogenes "school" is that, unlike university professors who build careers on their ideas, Christy rather lived his philosophy—the knowledge and wisdom that comes from hard living rather than books. This is the essence of Cynicism, a reconnection to our natural surroundings, trusting only the knowledge that we receive through our own senses, as opposed to academic, scientific knowledge and its belief in first principles and external absolutes—the mindset that has dominated Western thought for over two thousand years.

Cynicism was born out of the Socratic tradition and stood alone in its opposition to what Cynics regarded as the hijacking of Socrates' ideas by Plato and Aristotle, the dogmatic, scientific approach to knowledge discussed above. Plato frequently found himself on the receiving end of Diogenes' ridicule for selling out Socrates. Like the Cynics, Socrates conducted his discourse verbally (and non-verbally) rather than writing his ideas down as "truths." A later version of this tramp-philosophy was preached by Jesus of Nazareth (man or myth is irrelevant) whose own ideas were later corrupted by the Christian fathers to become, paradoxically, the banner of Western civilization and everything the tramp seeks to exile him or herself from. As the author of this book wrote in an earlier text:

> The image of fat bishops in their cathedral palaces clad in purple robes and gold chains, just does not sit comfortably with Jesus the ascetic sage entreating his followers to abandon money, possessions, and a roof over their head for a life of hardship and prayer. In some respects the asceticism of Jesus went even further than that of the Cynics, who at least were permitted to beg for food, wear sandals, and enjoy the comfort and security of a street corner or barrel.[10]

Unlike Plato, Aristotle, or the Christian fathers, the Cynics had no interest in converting others to their way of life. As with the philosophy expressed by other tramp-writers in these pages, Cynicism is no more than a personal philosophy, a strategy of survival in a world of lies and manipulations. Christy's response to the ideologies of the modern world—promising much but delivering little at best, catastrophe at worst—is what he describes as "the liberation of daily life":

> We must begin to live free, not postpone our lives until some
> mystical post-revolutionary era. Nor, one might add, waiting to die
> for the promise of a reward in heaven. We must struggle to live in
> a hostile environment. We must be our revolution. This involves
> wild-eyed experimentation and hungry exploration.[11]

In describing the urban revolutionary (Cynics, in spite of their use of nature and lower animals as a model for living, were nearly always encountered on city streets), Christy is clear about exactly the response required for genuine revolution—as distinct from those part-time, middle-class, lifestyle revolutionaries, who wanted to be "out on the street looking good":

> ...a real street person is at one with his environment; he is a
> natural born anarchist who creates situations and responds
> without preconceived notions. ...it is the struggle for the
> liberation of daily life.[12]

Here, of course, Christy is describing the modern-day cynic: the hobo, the vagabond, the tramp, all those who choose to exile themselves from the tyranny of mainstream society for the freedom of the road, or street, even though that freedom comes at the cost of being shunned at best, beaten—even killed—at worst. In terms of mass revolution as opposed to personal revolution, Christy is right. It is only when people take to the streets in sufficient numbers and with sufficient bravado that any change is brought about. Though, sadly, such change is always short-lived as those seeking the new order abuse power and in turn become corrupt. The only certain way to free oneself from oppressive forces would seem to be Christy's notion of liberating ourselves in our daily life.

Christy uses the term anarchy rather than cynicism, but to counter the idea that anarchy, like cynicism, stands for nothing at all, both positions are firmly rooted in a belief that the human project has become bankrupt, and that human beings could, and should, do better. Exactly what Christy feels has been lost from the world can be summed up in the following passage from *Rough Road to the North*:

> There is an ease to the people of the Far Northwest yet a toughness also that one does not find elsewhere. I sincerely believe that the wonderful thing about that country is that one can lead a life that is full and dignified, something that should be everyone's birthright but yet is becoming increasingly difficult if not impossible in the world today, a world that mitigates against such a thing at every turn and is forever devising new ways to crush the human spirit.[13]

If Christy's philosophy is anti-ideology, and deliberately so, it is because ideology has always promised much and delivered little. Again from *Beyond the Spectacle*, Christy's brand of anarchism sums up the philosophy of the vagabond. "Anarchism begins at home. ... It is not apathy but action. Action is synonymous with living free, incorporating anarchism into everything one does. The goal is liberation of daily life."

> I believed in anarchism because I thought anything less than total freedom was an insult to humanity. Ideologies offered only an exchange of rulers and all ideologies are based on domination. Their pushers I recognized as moral gangsters. ... This domination is dependent on deification. The human being functions as a commodity, no matter what the government, the philosophy, the religion.[14]

So far so good—this sounds like a personal philosophy of the individual, but here Christy is in danger of turning full circle to the object of his criticism when he continues that his brand of anarchy "must start out as individualism but seek to establish erotic networks of other adventurers who hold no truck with the social lie." This sounds as though it is getting dangerously close to starting a movement, which in turn leads to ideology, which leads us back to everything Christy has warned us against. But who does not have a trace of idealism in their twenties? Most of us embrace ideologies at some point in our lives, even if we get bored with them later. But it seems that Christy was always a rebel without a cause—"cause" in the sense of big ideas rather than living life to the full, which he has achieved in spades. Christy rescues his argument in *Spectacle* later, when he observes, "I believed all this in 1970 but rather than preaching it I tried to live it."[15]

PETER PAN PHENOMENON

Enter "Peter Pan Syndrome" in a search engine and up will come the following negative definitions: "male or female adult who is socially immature," "being unwilling to stay focused on becoming sufficiently expert at anything," "Blaming your failure on something your parents, spouse, or former employer did to you," "man of any age who shirks adult responsibilities," et cetera, et cetera. But what happens if we stand these definitions on their head? One of the fundamental questions to consider regarding the itinerant vagabond is whether it is *they* who should be regarded as the outcasts of society, or as Nietzsche suggested, the rest of us who have lost touch with what it is to be human. Before addressing this fundamental question, it is worth considering that philosopher's own contribution to an understanding of vagabondage. Regardless of the fact that Nietzsche chose to ridicule and attack academia from within its own hallowed walls, his personal philosophy and lifestyle embraced that of both the Cynic and the tramp-writer. Indeed, Nietzsche represents the philosophical link between vagabondage in its ancient and modern forms.

I described Christy in the prologue to this book as a Victorian vagabond adventurer born seventy years too late. In the introduction to H.L. Mencken's translation of Nietzsche's *The Antichrist*,[16] he described Nietzsche as "a Greek born two thousand years too late." And here Mencken was not referring to Plato's brand of philosophy which Nietzsche held in contempt; he meant Greek Cynicism. Nietzsche hated pretentiousness and narrow provincialism, and showed hostility towards political, academic, and other social institutions. He sought his own happiness in the Cynic sense of living an ascetic lifestyle on his meagre pension, embracing the minimum necessary to sustain life. As his sister Elizabeth[17] noted, the tiny room where he lived and worked, devoid of decoration or comfort, had parallels with Diogenes' own choice of dwelling: "There is no doubt that . . . my brother tried a little bit to imitate Diogenes in the tub; he wanted to find out with how little could a philosopher do."[18]

Nietzsche's typical day would start at five in the morning in his small rented room in the Swiss alpine village of Sils-Maria. He would write until midday and then take long walks up the surrounding peaks, eventually retiring early to bed after a snack of bread and ham or egg alone in his room.[19] An examination of Nietzsche's writing reveals many examples of his ascetic lifestyle as is evident from his comment: "Indeed, a minimum of life, an unchaining from all coarser desires, an independence in the middle of all kinds of outer nuisance; a bit of Cynicism, perhaps a bit of 'tub.' "[20]

But to return to the question of which philosophy truly represents what it is to be human, we should consider again Christy's poem "Ready or Not," presented in the prologue. Christy's scream of protest from the womb against being born is a useful starting point for an analysis of Nietzsche's observation that there is something that the child sees and hears that others do not, and that this "something" is the most important thing of all.[21] Could it be that when the tramp or vagabond turns their back on the tyranny of man-made rules and responsibilities and heads for the horizon, that they are engaged in no more than a desperate attempt to hang on to the innocence of childhood? Tramp-writer Jim Phelan takes the Peter Pan analogy to an extreme when he says that "a vagabond is really a lost child, who sometimes finds his mother— his mother being represented by a thousand women, in a thousand different towns."[22] Phelan could have added "and sometimes finds his father" or—in the case of the thirteen-year-old Christy's time spent in the company of Count Garbáge—grandfather. The "lost child" reference is a powerful one and there are certainly many references in tramp literature to individual tramps finding new families of fellow vagabonds on the road, maintaining contact with one another with the use of signs and monikers carved in wood alongside hobo "boarding points" at the side of rail tracks. Farther below, Phelan explodes the myth that tramping was necessarily a solitary profession.

A fundamental difference between the academic philosopher and the vagabond philosopher is that the former mines the world of all its meaning, but the latter is not interested in discovering why or how something is, because such knowledge would destroy the magic and exotic nature of the phenomenon or experience—rendering it mundane. For the purposes of this book, the term philosopher bears no relationship to the popular stereotypical university-educated boffin who gives formal lectures and publishes treatises on the meaning of life. Here we are concerned with those rare thinkers who live their philosophy rather than preaching it. Childish curiosity goes hand-in-hand with childish innocence but also wisdom. And there is no shortage of first-hand tramp-philosophy that "civilization" represents the downfall of humanity, not its triumph, starting here with Stephen Graham from his book *A Tramp's Sketches*, where he talks of maintaining youthful innocence at the same time as acquiring wisdom:

> Old age, old age; I was an old, bearded, heavy-going, wrinkled tramp, leaning on a stout stick; my grey hairs blew about my old red ears in wisps. I stopped all passers-by upon the road, and chuckled over old jokes or detained them with garrulity. But no, not old; nor will the tramp ever be old, for he has in his bosom that by virtue of which, even in old age, he remains a boy. There is in him, like the spring buds among the withered leaves of autumn, one never-dying fountain of youth. He is the boy who never grows old.[23]

Morley Roberts is another vagabond philosopher who admits to a desire for perpetual youth when he states in his work *A Tramp's Notebook* that "without illusion one cannot write," and that (and herein lies a perfectly expressed manifesto for the life of the professional tramp):

> When the Queen of Illusion illudes no more youth is over.' ... To do a little useful work (even though the useful may be a thousandth part of the useless) is the end of living. The only illusion worth keeping is that anything can be useful. So far my youth is not ended.[24]

Like Graham also, Roberts talks about the stupidity of adults absorbed through a process of maturation; not acquiring wisdom, but rather losing it through false learning. Compare for example Diogenes' response when asked why he was walking around in broad daylight with a lighted lamp, "I'm looking for an honest man," with Nietzsche's aphorism, "I looked for great human beings, but all I ever found were the apes of their ideals."[25] Essentially, humans are arrogant animals, oblivious to the fact that in their attempts to understand the world and shape it to their will, they instead create the very chaos and disorder that they seek to control. At the core of the tramp's determination not to participate in the conceit that afflicts so many of his fellow humans, is a search for a simpler, more meaningful life. But don't be fooled by the ragged appearance, something the modern vagabond philosopher shares with their historical forebears like Diogenes of Sinope and Jesus of Nazareth, for behind it lurks a superior intellect. This again raises the question of who the real outcasts from humanity are, a theme picked up by Bart Kennedy in his book *Sailor Tramp* (1918) and Stephen Graham in *A Tramp's Sketches* (1913). Both of these vagabond philosophers leave warnings for those who dismiss the tramp and hold him or her in contempt:

> Tramps and outcasts. Be easy with them. For it may come to pass that they will be held up to honour as the brave rebels and pioneers, who guided men up the tortuous path of intelligence and happiness.
> (Bart Kennedy, *Sailor Tramp*) [26]

> [The tramp] is necessarily a masked figure; he wears the disguise of one who has escaped, and also of one who is a conspirator. ... He is the walking hermit, the world-forsaker, but he is above all things a rebel and a prophet, and he stands in very distinct relation to the life of his time.
> (Stephen Graham, *A Tramp's Sketches*)[27]

Also from *A Tramp's Sketches*, Graham draws further from these same maxims when he describes the "irreconcilables," those who feel alien everywhere and search in vain for some corner of the world, or universe, that has not been plundered of its mystery.

> I sought them in towns and found them not, for the people ... slumbered and slept. ... We are many upon the world—we irreconcilables. We cry inconsolably like lost children.... For perhaps we are kidnapped persons. Perhaps thrones lie vacant on some stars because we are hidden away here upon the earth. ...we irreconcilable ones; we stand upon many shores and strain our eyes to see into the unknown. We are upon a deserted island and

have no boats to take us from star to star, not only upon a deserted
island but upon a deserted universe, for even the stars are familiar;
they are worlds not unlike our own. The whole universe is our
world and it is all explained by the scientists, or is explicable. But
beyond the universe, no scientist, not any of us, knows anything.
On all shores of the universe washes the ocean of ignorance,
the ocean of the inexplicable. We stand upon the confines of
an explored world and gaze at many blank horizons. We yearn
towards our natural home, the kingdom in which our spirits were
begotten. We have rifled the world, and tumbled it upside-down,
and run our fingers through all its treasures, yet have not come
upon the charter of our birth.[28]

The theme of Phelan's "lost children," whether searching for their home
or their mothers, is returned to yet again, and in the passage below from
Tramping the Toby (1958), Phelan also shares Graham's sense of loss of a bygone
age when old-fashioned wisdom prevailed, the loss of childhood innocence
clearly having parallels with the deprivation of earthly simplicity:

...people who live in the wild regions, shepherds and explorers and
vagabonds, those who travel the lonely roads and know the dark
silent places of the earth—those people have the old-fashioned
habits of thought, and they believe in many things which the
townspeople would call mere superstition ... and old-fashioned and
unscientific belief.[29]

There is no evidence that these three tramp-writers knew of each other
or had read each other's books, yet Roberts concurs with both Phelan and
Graham that the world is a poorer place for having abandoned "old-fashioned
habits of thought" and having allowed scientists to strip it of its magic. But the
thrust of Roberts' ridicule is reserved for "education" itself, which he claims
suppresses true knowledge. Rather than providing a true education, Roberts
describes his teachers as his jailers, whose only interest was the acquisition
of knowledge for its own sake and the passing of examinations. In the chapter
titled "A Graduate Beyond the Seas," Roberts' critique of education becomes
satirical when he presents the following parodic examination paper on tramping, a paper he is by now well qualified to formulate based on his experiences

as an American, as well as an Australian, tramp. Robert's satire highlights the absurdity of formal academia, at the same time forcing a reevaluation of the unique experiences and competencies of the American hobo.

...though I lack any learned degree earned by examinations, and may put no letters after my name, I maintain I passed creditably, if without honours, in the hardest schools of the world. ... My early work in New South Wales seemed to me then like sport. America was real life; it was forever putting the stiffest questions to me. I can imagine an examination paper which might appal many fat graduates.

1. Describe from experience the sensations of hunger when prolonged over three days.

2. Explain the differences in living in New York, Chicago, and San Francisco on a dollar a week. In such cases, how would you spend ten cents if you found it in the street at three o'clock in the morning?

3. How long would it be in your own case before want of food destroyed your sense of private property? Give examples from your own experience.

4. How far can you walk without food—(a) when you are trying to reach a definite point; (b) when you are walking with an insane view of getting to some place unknown where a good job awaits you?

5. If, after a period (say three weeks) of moderate starvation, and two days of absolute starvation, you are offered some work, which would be considered laborious by the most energetic coal-heaver, would you tackle it without food or risk the loss of the job by requesting your employer to advance you fifteen cents for breakfast?

6. Can you admire mountain scenery—(a) when you are very hungry; (b) when you are very thirsty? If you have any knowledge of the ascetic ecstasy, describe the symptoms.

7. You are in South-west Texas without money and without friends. How would you get to Chicago in a fortnight? What is the usual procedure when a town objects to impecunious tramps staying around more than twenty-four hours? Can you describe a "calaboose"?

8. Sketch an American policeman. Is he equally polite to a railroad magnate and a tramp? What do you understand by "fanning with a club"?

9. Which are the best as a whole diet—apples or watermelons?

10. Define "tramp," "bummer," "heeler," "hoodlum," and "politician."

This is a paper put together very casually, and just as the pen runs, but the man who can pass such an examination creditably must know many things not revealed to the babes and sucklings of civilisation. From my own point of view I think the questions fairly easy, a mere matriculation paper.[30]

Roberts' *A Tramp's Notebook* was published four years after Nietzsche's death, and so it is entirely likely that he was influenced by that philosopher's belief that real education is a far cry from the art of passing examinations, which as Nietzsche claimed "produce merely the savant or the official or the business man."[31] Opposed as they are to conforming to society's norms and expectations, the vagabond philosopher is fully aware of such perspectives on real education. Bart Kennedy also echoes Graham's, Roberts' and Nietzsche's views on education when he says that:

...the fact is that men get more stupid as they grow older. The human being starts with a good bright mind. As everyone knows, children are famous for their straight and apt and acute way of viewing things. But the child's mind is soon, alas! dulled by the process that is called education. Schools and colleges and other brain-benumbing institutions kill the mother-wit that the human began with.[32]

Aside from the treatise on education, the passages from the tramp-writers above go to great lengths to explode the negative popular stereotype of the tramp. Some further myths about tramping are challenged below, starting with the popular belief that the tramp is essentially lazy. Here from Jim Phelan's autobiography, *The Name's Phelan*:

> No wage-worker ever laboured as hard as a tramp will, on occasion. ... The glib explanation of laziness will not serve. ... Compare the degree of tenacity required to keep a job, by going to the office each morning at nine without fail, beside that called for by a walk from Calais to Vladivostok or from New York to San Francisco. Yet people have walked those distances. With no purpose known to anyone on earth, not for pleasure or profit or pride, people have walked them. Tenacity![33]

Linked to his notion that tramps are "lost children," Phelan challenges the myth that tramping is necessarily a solitary profession. Again from *Tramping the Toby*, Phelan stands on its head this conventional view of tramping, arguing that compared to city dwellers, the tramp has far more human contact, and of a far more intimate nature:

> The man and his wife will know one another's relatives, but not the neighbours of those relatives. Also, they will know a few friends from office or workplace, but will have little contact with those people's other acquaintances. ... Really the city folk know very few people as friends.... They sometimes group together in big crowds, at a football match or a political meeting.... But on these occasions each citizen is just a lost unit, in the middle of a thousand strangers. A city is a lonely place.
>
> Now consider the padman [slow-moving tramp]. He knows—it is his trade to know—all the people in every good-sized house along his next day's road. If his knowledge is deficient in any respect he will check up at the paddincan [tramp lodging-house], the night before he pads that toby [road].... He knows who is good-humoured, who is generous, who is mean. Also he knows who is away in London, or who has the 'flu and had better not be worried by tappers [beggars].[34]

Christy has provided his own evidence that vagabondage is not a lonely occupation throughout this book. It has already been acknowledged that Christy is not a member of any societal or political tribe, despising politically correct, left-wing liberals as much as he does right-wing bigots. What Christy does belong to is that tribe of misfits and oddballs who exist precisely *because* they do not fit comfortably within more conventional coteries. That is not to say that Christy is devoid of personal social skills. A feature he shares with many of the other tramp-writers featured here is that he is well able, chameleon-like, to morph into whatever character the situation demands and feel completely at ease in the process. Yet although Christy can feel comfortable in any company he chooses, he also maintains his personal integrity throughout. Even as a journalist, he speaks for no one but himself, attacking hypocrisy and lies wherever he finds them. But it is Christy's closest friends that testify as to his true family: Count Garbáge, Floyd Wallace, Val Santee, Charlie Leeds, Marcel Horne, not to mention all of the carnival freaks and other exiles from "civilized" society that Christy has been drawn to throughout his life. Such fugitives from the human herd have a way of finding each other, yet still remaining uniquely individual and fiercely independent. Such a description applies equally to some of Christy's long-term female companions, and may explain both the attraction and the conflict within some of those relationships. Many of these liaisons were with strongly independent-minded, professional women, and those who were not—like Marlyn who threw Christy's typewriter out of a window for not paying her attention—were feisty characters, not shrinking violets. At the heart of this conflict, as Myfanwy Phillips, Virginia Dixon, and others have testified, is Christy's unrelenting personal drive for self-achievement and fulfilment, and his inability, as the vagabond he is, to submit to domestication and remain rooted in one spot for any significant length of time. A more thorough examination of that condition described as wanderlust is now required.

WANDERLUST

Much has been documented on this subject by writers, poets, academics, and philosophers, not least Rebecca Solnit's excellent *Wanderlust: A History of Walking*[35] referred to earlier in Chapter 6. But I wish to devote this last section of the epilogue to accounts written by those directly burdened with the condition. And it is only right that the first attempt to interpret this slippery concept should be given to Christy himself. The following passages from his unpublished work *Wandering Heart* are particularly poignant as they were written from the confines of a hospital wheelchair where Christy, recovering from a stroke, was incapable of responding to those powerful forces calling him to hit the road. And in spite of the earlier discussion about tramping in one's imagination, Christy insists that the thrill of wanderlust itself can only be experienced when out "on the road"—"at home" the sensation is confined to one of longing. It becomes apparent, from the later passages cited below, that other tramp-writers have little to add to Christy's thesis on wanderlust, even though their writing style and mood vary considerably:

> What is this wanderlust? There's no way to define it, one just knows when one has it, or is afflicted by it. It is more than just wanting to go somewhere. Some might call it a form of neurosis, and maybe they're right. It may come upon you when you least expect it to. You don't need to have heard, as did Hank Williams, that lonesome whistle blow. You may be watching a police drama on television or buying your oat bran in the supermarket and all of a sudden you feel the need to change the view out the window or buy an airline ticket off the shelf. Some people, of course, never fall prey to such a feeling.
>
> I've had many a weary nay-sayer try to dissuade me from embarking on a journey. I'm thinking particularly of a Toronto magazine editor, Doug Marshall, sighing at my announced intention the next day to board the train to Vancouver. "You're wasting your time. What do you expect to prove?" I couldn't for the life of me make him understand that I didn't want to prove anything, that I just wanted to go. The notion was alien to him. It's not merely the decision to travel. Most people who take trips are not prompted by wanderlust. Nor is wanderlust what prompts people to complete their "bucket lists"—a horrible term—in order to say they visited seventy-five countries. It does not impel the tourism industry nor is it necessarily the *raison d'être* of bona fide world travellers. One meets these people, checking countries off their lists or filling the vacant three-week gap of the holidays. "My holidays are coming up. Maybe I'll go to Jamaica or visit my sister at the cottage."
>
> [...]

What I felt sitting in my wheelchair down at the end of that hospital hallway was the lust to wander, pure and simple. I've always wanted to carry my passport with me wherever I go whether to the supermarket or the next town on an errand. I fancy ducking out on my errand, giving up my serious pursuits to head for the airport and buy a ticket anywhere. With my horizons narrowed, I fancy walking out the door and just going with no preconceived notion, no plan, turn left or right it doesn't matter.

There is sometimes while traveling a powerful feeling of happiness without thinking of happiness, of expanded consciousness and being a part of everything around you. I once talked about this to George Woodcock, anarchist chronicler, man of letters, and world traveler. He smiled as I attempted to define this indefinable feeling; he knew exactly what I meant, and gave a couple of examples from his own wanderings. I distinctly remember him speaking of being in the hills of Tibet with a village in sight up ahead and another time approaching Proust's town in France.

My most intense memory of this state of being, perhaps it was what Colin Wilson called the St. Neot's Margin—a feeling of expanded consciousness that came over him while passing through that English town on a bus. For me it was the old bus station in Barcelona sometime in the early Seventies while I stood in the big hall waiting to leave for Morocco. I had never been happier or more at ease.

The feeling can come over you in the most unlikely of places; it is not necessary to be in Tibet or Barcelona. One time, I was sitting on the wooden steps of a general store in Effingham, Illinois, just come down from Chicago, waiting for the bus to St. Louis and bam, all of a sudden I felt as if I was hovering over the steps, floating above the rooftops, surveying the scene of shops and houses and cars; the small town bicycle world of kids. So many of my most vivid travel memories have to do with the smaller, less adventurous *sounding* trips. For instance I went looking for, and found, the supposedly legendary lost city of the Golden Madonna in the Honduran forests; a man tried to kill me and I was chased by machete-wielding *ladrones,* but that doesn't stand out as strongly (as) a five or six week trip in my old '54 Ford in 1964. I was living in

West Chester, Pennsylvania, a small city on the Mason and Dixon Line. I just threw some clothes and a book or two in the backseat and took off. The car had been parked pointing north so I went in that direction before heading west and driving through West Virginia and Ohio, then heading south. I spent a couple of those weeks in the relatively little known country of western Maryland. Had the car been pointed south, I would have done that first and continued on to Tennessee. I went wherever I chose, turned left or right, no matter.

A couple of decades later I was driving through western Canada looking for bizarre homes and gardens. In northern Alberta I picked up a strange old hitchhiker who'd been traipsing along the roadside toting a shovel over his shoulder. He was at least seventy, and when I asked, he told me he'd come from Weyburn and was looking for work. He'd brought the shovel just in case he found someone who wanted a bit of shovelling done but didn't have a shovel or a spade themselves. I took him to Grand Prairie where he hoped there was some shovelling to be done. I hope he found it.[36]

(Jim Christy, *Wandering Heart*)

It was acknowledged in the prologue to this book that part of Christy's wanderlust, and his alienation from conventional society, is that he was born several decades too late. It is a credit to the man that he continued to explore the world and marvel at its wonders long after most Westerners, smug in the knowledge that the world had already been mined of its secrets, sat back to glory in their cleverness in university campuses or simply be passive spectators on their now ubiquitous televisions and other devices. Perhaps many of those who experience wanderlust today are able to satisfy their curiosity by confining their adventures to the medium of virtual reality such as "open world" video games. But the purpose of this volume, through the life of a modern exponent of the art, concerns vagabonds compelled to travel beyond and outside of the screen. As with Christy's commentary above, earlier tramp-writers described different aspects of this phenomenon, and in their unique writing styles. The first, from Josiah Flynt, is concerned with the child tramp or road kid. A class of tramp of which he, together with Livingstone, Everson, Davies, Kennedy, London, Horn, Tully, Phelan, and Christy, was a representative:

...they [road kids] are possessed of the "railroad fever" ... the expression in its broader sense of wanderlust. They want to get out into the world, and at stated periods the desire is so strong and the road so handy that they simply cannot resist the temptation to explore it. A few weeks usually suffice to cool their ardor, and then they run home quite as summarily as they left, but they stay only until the next runaway mood seizes them.

(Josiah Flynt, *Tramping with Tramps*)[37]

This description of wanderlust, one in which the urge to hit the road comes in waves and for no particular reason, is commonly expressed, not least by Christy in his passage above. Below Christy's "powerful feeling of happiness" was also acknowledged by W.H. Davies who also emphasizes the health benefits of tramping:

What a glorious time of the year is this! With the warm sun travelling through serene skies, the air clear and fresh above you, which instils new blood in the body, making one defiantly tramp the earth, kicking the snows aside in the scorn of action. The cheeks glow with health, the lips smile, and there is no careworn face seen, save they come out of the house of sickness of death. And that lean spectre, called Hunger, has never been known to appear in these parts.

(William Henry Davies, *The Autobiography of a Super-Tramp*)[38]

The passage by Trader Horn below, emphasizes the flip side of Davies' exultation of tramping, the negative restraints one is trying to escape *from*. Horn makes the case that, given the world created for us, *not* to submit to wanderlust is an absurdity:

Doesn't the dawn come every day calling you to move on? No camp should last forever. And that's where civilization makes the mistake of its life, trying to cage the natural man. Trying to make a stationary object behind bars. Did the great Onlooker give us the world plus the ocean to entice the thoughts of the roamer if he meant us to stay in one spot? ... All the luxuries of the haut ton are neither more or less than neck-irons to a slave. And what's worse they make

heaven itself into the image of a cage. Why, the son of Mary Himself couldn't stand too much of the synagogue. ... Consider the lilies, he said. But the religioners've put no lilies in heaven.[39]
(Trader Horn, *Harold the Webbed*)

And below, Jack London reinforces the random and serendipitous nature of tramping described in Christy's opening passage:

Perhaps the greatest charm of tramp life is the absence of monotony. In Hobo Land the face of life is protean—an ever changing phantasmagoria, where the impossible happens and the unexpected jumps out of the bushes at every turn of the road. The hobo never knows what is going to happen the next moment; hence, he lives only in the present moment. He has learned the futility of telic endeavor, and knows the delight of drifting along with the whimsicalities of Chance.
(Jack London, *The Road*)[40]

But no one has captured the pure existential spirit of tramping better than Leon Ray Livingston when he describes his complete disregard for his own mortality in the thrill of hurtling at top speed through the night, hanging underneath a train, death only inches from his face as the tracks hurtle past beneath him:

I at last felt that I had given up everything but life itself, to please that bane of my existence. ... There, hanging on with only those weak, human hands, out of reach of any possible succour, speeding through the night, I felt at peace with all the world.
(Leon Ray Livingston, *The Curse of Tramp Life*)[41]

This passage reveals a fundamental element of tramp psychology, something Christy acknowledges at the end of the *Rough Road* episode where cold, exhausted, and hungry, even the desired beer in a neon-lit bar cannot quell the urge to be on the move once more. For it is the momentum of tramping itself and not the destination that pulls the tramp ever onward. Although the tramp is occasionally forced to stop and rest from sheer exhaustion, sometimes due to illness or disability, sometimes for the respite of a bite to eat, the destination of the journey is always deferred. This is tramping as a sheer life force, and something that fueled Christy's rapid recovery from his stroke. Without the constant onward movement the tramp is unable to breathe and loses the reason for their existence.

1   Jim Phelan, *Tramping the Toby* (London: Burke Publishing Co. Ltd., 1955), p. 37

2   Bart Kennedy, *A Tramp's Philosophy*, op cit., p. 16

3   See Jack Kerouac's "The Vanishing American Hobo" in *Lonesome Traveler*, op cit., p. 149

4   Jim Christy, *Beyond the Spectacle* (Montréal: Aline Press, 1973), pp. 15-16

5   Raymond Federman, *The Twofold Vibration* (Los Angeles: Green Integer, 2000), p. 126

6   Ibid., pp. 138-139

7   Jim Tully, *Jarnegan* (New York: Albert & Charles Boni, 1926), p. 131

8   *Beyond the Spectacle*, op cit., p. 17

9   Ibid., p. 16

10   Ian Cutler, "A Tale of Two Cynics: the philosophic duel between Jesus and the woman from Syrophoenicia," *The Philosophical Forum, Inc.*, Vol. XLI, No. 4, Winter 2010, p. 373

11   *Beyond the Spectacle*, op cit., p. 18

12   Ibid., p. 17

13   *Rough Road to the North*, op cit., p. 11

14   *Beyond the Spectacle*, op cit., pp. 201-202

15   Ibid., p. 202

16   H.L. Mencken, "Introduction" in *Friedrich Nietzsche, The Antichrist* (Tucson: See Sharp Press, 1999), p. 6

17   Although Nietzsche has been associated with National Socialism through his sister Elizabeth Förster-Nietzsche, the evidence is that he abhorred his sister's association with the Nazis as is apparent from the following extract of a letter from Nietzsche to his sister: "One of the greatest stupidities you have committed—for yourself and for me! Your association with an anti-Semitic chief express a foreignness to *my* whole life which fills me ever again with ire and melancholy . . . it is a matter of honor to me to be absolutely clean and unequivocal regarding anti-Semitism, namely opposed, as I am in my writings." (cited in Walter Kaufmann, *Nietzsche: Philosopher, Psychologist, Antichrist*, Princeton NJ: Princeton University Press, 1999, p. 45)

18   Heinrich Niehues-Probsting, 'The Modern Reception of Cynicism: Diogenes in the Enlightenment' in R. Bracht Branham & Marie-Odile Goulet Caze (eds.), *The Cynics: The Cynic Movement in Antiquity and its Legacy* (Berkeley: University of California Press, 1996), p. 359

19   Alain de Botton, *The Consolations of Philosophy* (London: Hamish Hamilton, 2000), p. 219

20   Heinrich Niehues-Probsting, op cit., p. 359

21   Luis Navia, *Diogenes of Sinope: the man in the tub* (New York: Greenwood Press, 1998), p. 75

22   Jim Phelan, *Tramping the Toby*, op cit., p. 90

23   Stephen Graham, *A Tramp's Sketches* (London: Macmillan and Co., Ltd., 1913), (Project Gutenberg eBook, no page numbers) www.mirrorservice.org/sites/gutenberg.org/1/1/9/8/11980/11980-8.txt Accessed on March 30, 2017

24   Morley Roberts, *A Tramp's Notebook* (London: F.V. White & Co. Ltd., 1904), p. 59

25   Luis Navia, *Diogenes of Sinope: the man in the tub*, op cit., p. 76

26   Bart Kennedy, *Sailor Tramp* (London: George Newnes Ltd., 1918), p. 107

27   Stephen Graham, *A Tramp's Sketches*, op cit. [Project Gutenberg eBook, no page numbers] www.mirrorservice.org/sites/gutenberg.org/1/1/9/8/11980/11980-8.txt Accessed on March 30, 2017

28   Ibid.

29   Jim Phelan, *Tramping the Toby*, op cit., p. 81

30   Morley Roberts, *A Tramp's Notebook*, op cit., pp. 57-59

31   Friedrich Nietzsche, "Thoughts out of Season, Part II" in *Complete Works*, London: George Allen & Unwin, 1909, pp. 173-174

32   Bart Kennedy, *A Tramp's Philosophy*, op cit., pp. 255-266

33   Jim Phelan, *The Name's Phelan* (Belfast: The Blackstaff Press, 1993), p. 65

34   Jim Phelan, *Tramping the Toby*, op cit., p. 185

35   Rebecca Solnit, 2001, op cit.

36   *Wandering Heart*, op cit.

37   Josiah Flynt, *Tramping with Tramps: Studies and Sketches of Vagabond Life* (New York: The Century Co., 1901), p. 53

38   William Henry Davies, *The Autobiography of a Super-Tramp* (Pwllheli, Wales: Cromen, 2013), p. 166

39   Trader Horn, *Harold the Webbed; or, The Young Vykings* (New York: The Literary Guild of America, inc., 1928), pp. 213-214

40   Jack London, *The Road* (New York: Macmillan, 1907), pp. 85-86

41   Leon Ray Livingston, *The Curse of Tramp Life* (Cambridge Springs, PA: A-No. 1 Publishing Co., 1912), p. 22

JIM CHRISTY PUBLISHED AND UNPUBLISHED WORKS

BOOKS BY JIM CHRISTY

The New Refugees: American Voices in Canada (anthology, editor, and final chapter), Toronto: Peter Martin Associates, 1972

Beyond the Spectacle (essays), Montréal: Aline Press, 1973

Palatine Cat (poetry), Four Humours Press, 1978

Rough Road to the North (history, travelogue, autobiography), New York: Doubleday, 1980

Streethearts (autobiography), Toronto: Simon & Pierre, 1981

Travelin Light (short stories), Toronto: Simon & Pierre, 1982

The Price of Power (biography), New York: Doubleday, 1983

Flesh and Blood (fight reportage, history and personal experience), Vancouver: Douglas & McIntyre, 1990

Letter from the Khyber Pass and other travel writing (editor and introduction of travel pieces by George Woodcock), Vancouver: Douglas & McIntyre, 1993

Strange Sites: Uncommon Homes & Gardens of the Pacific Northwest, Madeira Park, B.C.: Harbour, 1995

The Sunnyside of the Deathhouse (poetry), Victoria, B.C.: Ekstasis Editions, 1996

The BUK Book: Musings on Charles Bukowski (biography), with photos by Claude Powell, Toronto: ECW, 1997

Shanghai Alley (Gene Castle Detective Series), Victoria, B.C.: Ekstasis Editions, 1997

The Long Slow Death of Jack Kerouac (biography), Toronto: ECW, 1998

Junkman & Other Stories (Gene Castle Detective Series), Victoria, B.C.: Ekstasis Editions, 1998

Between the Meridians (short stories), Victoria, B.C.: Ekstasis Editions, 1999

Princess and Gore (Gene Castle Detective Series), Victoria, B.C.: Ekstasis Editions, 2000

Cavatinas for Long Nights (poetry), Victoria, B.C.: Ekstasis Editions, 2000

Terminal Avenue (Gene Castle Detective Series), Victoria, B.C.: Ekstasis Editions, 2002

Tight Like That (short stories), Vancouver: Anvil Press, 2003

The Redemption of Anna Dupree (fiction), Victoria, B.C.: Ekstasis Editions, 2005

In the Wee Small Hours (poetry), Toronto: Lyricalmiracle, 2005

Scalawags: Rogues, Roustabouts, Wags & Scamps, Vancouver: Anvil Press, 2008

Nine O'Clock Gun (Gene Castle Detective Series), Victoria, B.C.: Ekstasis Editions, 2008

Marimba Forever (poetry), Toronto: Guernica Editions, 2010

Real Gone (autobiography), Toronto: Quattro Books, 2010

Sweet Assorted: 118 Takes From a Tin Box (short stories), Vancouver: Anvil Press, 2012

Jackpots (short stories), Victoria, B.C.: Ekstasis Editions, 2012

This Cockeyed World (poetry), Toronto: Guernica Editions, 2013

The Big Thirst and other doggone poems, Victoria, B.C.: Ekstasis Editions, 2014

Rogues, Rascals, and Scalawags Too (biography), Vancouver: Anvil Press, 2015

Bad Day for Ralphie: Stories: New and Selected, Brighton, ON: Hidden Brook Press, 2015

ANTHOLOGIES INCLUDING WORK BY JIM CHRISTY

"Bo," in Friis-Baasted, Erling. *Outlaws*. Guelph, ON: Alive Press, 1974

"How I became champ," in Wolfe, Morris, and Douglas Daymond (eds.), *Toronto Short Stories*. Toronto: Doubleday Canada, 1977

"On the Bum in Toronto," in Peter Carver (ed.), *Earth*. Toronto: Peter Martin Associates, 1977

"Greenland," in Dobbs, Kildare (ed.), *Away from home: Canadian writers in exotic places*. Toronto: Deneau Publishers, 1985

"What Kerouac Did for Me," in John Montgomery (ed.), *Kerouac at the Wild Boar and Other Skirmishes*. San Anselmo, CA: Fels and Firn Press, 1986.

"Farewell to the Man Who Would Never Say Goodbye," in Laura Petersen (ed.), *A Man of Letters: Montgomery Remembered*. Pleasanton, CA: Fels and Firn Press, 1993.

"Visiting Carcross," in Martin, Carol (ed.), *Local Colour: Writers Discovering Canada*. Vancouver: Douglas & McIntyre, 1994

"Forever Maria" in Musgrave, Susan (ed.), *The Fed: Brand New Fiction and Poetry from the Federation of B.C. Writers*. Vancouver: Anvil Press, 2002

"Jim Christy On Álvaro Mutis," in Olafson, Richard (ed.), *Pacific Rim Review of Books*, Issue 1. Victoria, B.C.: Ekstasis Editions, 2005

"Crypto-zoology," "Callow Mariner," "Marimba Forever," and "Jazz One Day in the World," in Ron Riddell and Saray Torres (eds.), *Towards the Impossible*. Wellington, NZ: Casa Nueva Publishing, 2005

"Cape Fear," in Contento, Lily (ed.), *Garden Variety*. Thornhill, ON: Quattro Books, 2007

"Democratic Vistas," "Remembrance Day," "Saigon Joe," and "In the Desert,"
    in Briesmaster, Allan, and Steven Berzensky (eds.), *Crossing Lines: Poets
    Who Came to Canada in the Vietnam War Era*. Niagara Falls, ON: Seraphim
    Editions, 2009.

"The Wizard of What the Fuck," in Roorda, Julie, and Elana Wolff (eds.), *Poet to
    Poet*. Toronto: Guernica Editions, 2012.

MUSIC CDs

A Night in Grombalia, Trans-Siberian Records, Vancouver, 2002

God's Little Angle, She'll Be Right Records, Christchurch, NZ, 2010

"Show Me the Proof" on Jan Erik Lepsoe, *On the Countryside 2*,
Janke Music, Norway

"Crazy Kind of Romance" on Jan Erik Lepsoe, *On the Countryside
3*, Janke Music, Norway

UNPUBLISHED WORKS BY JIM CHRISTY CITED IN THIS BOOK

Shift and Glitter

Reet, Petite, and Gone

Brookdale

Rolling Hill Road

The Name's Phelan

The Castle

Wandering Heart

ACKNOWLEDGEMENTS

Firstly, I thank Jim Christy for being the vagabond he is, a character who came into my world and stayed there for several years, answering endless, prying questions about his life and his many, many friends and acquaintances. Next I want to thank my publisher, Jessica Parfrey, for believing in the book and in Jim, and helping to get these words out into the world. My appreciation also to the book's designer, Jacob Covey, for his editing and layout suggestions in bringing the book to life in a way that is beyond the capability of its author. A huge thanks to Luis Navia for writing the Foreword in his own vagabond style. Two of Jim's former partners, Myfanwy Phillips and Virginia Dixon, have provided significant contributions to this book for which I am extremely grateful, as has Jim's wife Reyna who, in spite of her initial reluctance to contribute, being more comfortable with singing than committing words to print, came through with some special insights and observations that were very much appreciated. You *can* write as well as sing, Reyna!

A special mention to all those others who contributed to this text and helped make it the three-dimensional chronicle that it is. Firstly the ones still living in the order they "appear": Daniel Zeleniouk, Joe Nickell, David Duplain, Barry Dickie, Len Gasparini, Joe Ferone, Donald Kerr, David MacKinnon, Robert Markle Kinnard, Ken Gerberick, Brenda Fredrick, James Eke, and lastly, my huge thanks to Val Santee for being the fascinating character that he is, even though I am not able to acknowledge him by his real name.

My thanks and appreciation also to those who have passed on but made this book an altogether more lively affair: Count Garbáge, Floyd Wallace, Frances (Frank) Marie, Charlie Leeds, Marcel Horne, Linda, Kathleen Phelan, and Brad Benson who sadly died the year following his tramp up north with Jim in 2017.

I wish to acknowledge the generosity of those publishers who still retain the rights to works by Jim Christy and provided permissions to use extensive passages from the original titles over and above what could be considered 'fair use':

Excerpted from *Rough Road to the North* by Jim Christy. Copyright © 1980 Jim Christy. Reprinted by permission of Doubleday Canada, a division of Penguin Random House Canada Limited.

The publisher Richard Olafson of Ekstasis Editions for passages from *Between the Meridians* © 1999 and *Jackpots* © 2012.

The publisher Michael Mirolla of Guernica Editions to reproduce from *Marimba Forever* © 2010 and *This Cockeyed World* © 2013, three of Jim Christy's poems.

The publisher Allan Briesmaster of Quattro Books for passages from *Real Gone* © 2010.

The publisher Brian Kaufman of Anvil Press for passages from *Sweet Assorted: 121 Takes from a Tin Box* © 2012.

Dundurn Press have deferred to the author for the passages from *Streethearts* © 1981 and *Travelin Light* © 1982.

Finally, not least, a big thank you to my family, Angela, Seth and Max, who shared Jim Christy in our life for the past three years and never complained.

A NOTE ON SPELLING:

The author has agreed for American spelling to replace his British spelling for the benefit of his American readers. Direct quotes throughout the text will remain in their original spelling and form. Although deliberate misspellings in quotations may occasionally be identified as such with the conventional identifier [sic], for the most part the author does not wish to draw attention to such misspellings and delinquent grammar in the spirit of what is variously identified in the book as "tramp" or "vagabond" literature.

Jim Christy: A Vagabond Life is part of the Tramp Lit
Series for Feral House. For further information about
these titles, see www.feralhouse.com

Feral House
1240 W Sims Way #124
Port Townsend WA 98368

Design by Jacob Covey / Unflown

ISBN: 9781627310741
Printed in the United States of America
10 9 8 7 6 5 4 3 2 1

ANNOUNCING FERAL HOUSE'S NEW TRAMP LIT SERIES

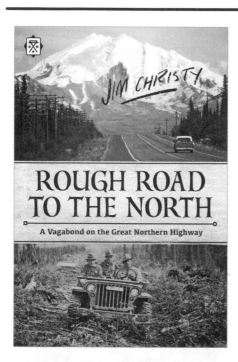

September 2019
***Rough Road to the North:
A Vagabond on the Great
Northern Highway***
By Jim Christy

Poet and Novelist Jim Christy explores the history of the building of the great ALCAN Highway through his personal experiences and the stories of residents and pioneers who came before him. This re-release includes new material and photographs.

FERAL
HOUSE

TRAMP
• LIT •
SERIES

February 2020
***The Lives and Extraordinary
Adventures of Fifteen Tramp
Writers from the Golden Age
of Vagabondage***
By Ian Cutler

Discover the stories of famous and infamous tramps who criss-crossed the globe in this riveting history of tramp literature and its authors.